Sweet Communion

Texts and Studies in Reformation and Post-Reformation Thought

General Editor

Prof. Richard A. Muller, Calvin Theological Seminary

Editorial Board

Prof. Irena Backus, University of Geneva
Prof. Susan M. Felch, Calvin College
Prof. A. N. S. Lane, London School of Theology
Prof. Susan E. Schreiner, University of Chicago
Prof. David C. Steinmetz, Duke University
Prof. John L. Thompson, Fuller Theological Seminary
Prof. Willem J. van Asselt, University of Utrecht
Prof. Timothy J. Wengert, The Lutheran Theological Seminary at Philadelphia
Prof. Henry Zwaanstra, Calvin Theological Seminary

Books in the Series

Caspar Olevianus, *A Firm Foundation: An Aid to Interpreting the Heidelberg Catechism*, translated and edited by Lyle D. Bierma

John Calvin, *The Bondage and Liberation of the Will: A Defence of the Orthodox Doctrine of Human Choice against Pighius*, edited by A. N. S. Lane, translated by G. I. Davies

Law and Gospel: Philip Melanchthon's Debate with John Agricola of Eisleben over Poenitentia, by Timothy J. Wengert

Martin Luther as Prophet, Teacher, and Hero: Images of the Reformer, 1520–1620, by Robert Kolb

Melanchthon in Europe: His Work and Influence beyond Wittenberg, edited by Karin Maag

Reformation and Scholasticism: An Ecumenical Enterprise, edited by Willem J. van Asselt and Eef Dekker

The Binding of God: Calvin's Role in the Development of Covenant Theology, by Peter A. Lillback

Divine Discourse: The Theological Methodology of John Owen, by Sebastian Rehnman

Heinrich Bullinger and the Doctrine of Predestination: Author of "the Other Reformed Tradition"? by Cornelis P. Venema

Architect of Reformation: An Introduction to Heinrich Bullinger, 1504–1575, edited by Bruce Gordon and Emidio Campi

An Introduction to the Heidelberg Catechism: Sources, History, and Theology, by Lyle D. Bierma with Charles D. Gunnoe Jr., Karin Y. Maag, and Paul W. Fields

Calvin's Theology of the Psalms, by Herman J. Selderhuis

Sweet Communion: Trajectories of Spirituality from the Middle Ages through the Further Reformation, by Arie de Reuver, translated by James A. De Jong

Sweet Communion

Trajectories of Spirituality from the Middle Ages through the Further Reformation

Arie de Reuver
Translated by James A. De Jong

Baker Academic
Grand Rapids, Michigan

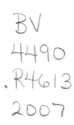

Published by Baker Academic
a division of Baker Publishing Group
P.O. Box 6287, Grand Rapids, MI 49516-6287
www.bakeracademic.com

Printed in the United States of America

Library of Congress Cataloging-in-Publication Data is on file at the Library of Congress, Washington, DC.

ISBN 10: 0-8010-3122-2
ISBN 978-0-8010-3122-9

Contents

Series Preface   7
Foreword   9
Author's Note   11
Translator's Note   11
Abbreviations   13

Introduction   15
1 Bernard of Clairvaux (1090-1153)   27
2 Thomas à Kempis (c. 1379-1471)   63
3 Willem Teellinck (1579-1629)   105
4 Theodorus à Brakel (1608-1669)   163
5 Guiljelmus Saldenus (1627-1694)   201
6 Wilhelmus à Brakel (1635-1711)   231
7 Herman Witsius (1636-1708)   261

Conclusion   281
Bibliography   285
Index of Personal Names   299
Board of the Dutch Reformed Translation Society   303

Series Preface

The heritage of the Reformation is of profound importance to our society, our culture, and the church in the present day. Yet there remain many significant gaps in our knowledge of the intellectual development of Protestantism both during and after the Reformation, and there are not a few myths about the theology of the orthodox or scholastic Protestant writers of the late sixteenth and seventeenth centuries. These gaps and myths—frequently caused by ignorance of the scope of a particular thinker's work, by negative theological judgments passed by later generations on the theology of the Reformers and their successors, or by an intellectual imperialism of the present that singles out some thinkers and ignores others regardless of their relative significance to their own times—stand in the way of a substantive encounter with this important period in our history. Understanding, assessment, and appropriation of that heritage can only occur through the publication of significant works (monographs, essays, and sound, scholarly translations) that present the breadth and detail of the thought of the Reformers and their successors.

Texts and Studies in Reformation and Post-Reformation Thought makes available (1) translations of important documents like Caspar Olevian's *A Firm Foundation* and John Calvin's *Bondage and Liberation of the Will*, (2) significant monographs on individual thinkers or on aspects of sixteenth- and seventeenth-century Protestant thought, and (3) multiauthored symposia that bring together groups of scholars in an effort to present the state of scholarship on a particular issue, all under the guidance of an editorial board of recognized scholars in the field.

The series, moreover, is intended to address two groups: an academic and a confessional or churchly audience. The series recognizes the need for careful, scholarly treatment of the Reformation and of the era of Protestant orthodoxy, given the continuing presence of misunderstandings, particularly of the latter era, in both the scholarly and the popular literature and also given the rise of a more recent scholarship devoted to reappraising both the Reformation and the era of orthodoxy. The series highlights revised understandings regarding the relationship of the Reformation and orthodoxy to their medieval background and of the thought of both eras to their historical, social, political, and cultural contexts. Such scholarship will not only advance the academic discussion, it will also provide a churchly audience with a clearer and broader access to its own traditions. In sum, the series intends to present the varied and current approaches to the rich heritage of Protestantism and to stimulate interest in the roots of the Protestant tradition.

Richard A. Muller

7

Foreword

This book could not have been written if I had not received support along the way. This help first took the form of inspiration. The source from which this emerged was, to begin with, Holy Scripture (words from on high); in the second place, the writings that enter into the discussion of this study (words from the past); and finally, the dialogue with students in Utrecht (words of today).

In addition to giving proper recognition to the staff of the Boekencentrum, who readied this book for publication, and to the foundation *Aanpakken* for the subsidy provided, I also want to thank a few people who have assisted me in various ways. Professor W. Otten, church historian on the theological faculty of the University of Utrecht, provided several hints in a collegial spirit that sharpened my thinking. Dr. W. J. op 't Hof, a church history specialist in the field of pietism, extended valuable information to me from his large reservoir of expertise. Mr. W. van Gent, who possesses a unique collection of material on pietism, generously and repeatedly loaned me valuable works from the treasures of his collection. My good friend, Dr. M. Verduin, took the trouble to work through the text with critical attention. Mrs. Maaike Bal-Plomp more than once sprang into action in reviewing the page proofs. Mr. Marco de Wilde, one of my students, prepared the index.

Fieke, my wife, put the entire, hand-written account into electronic form with admirable patience and accuracy. And it is with joy that I dedicate this book to her.

Author's Note

It gives me a great deal of joy and satisfaction that this study is now appearing in the English language. My sincere thanks goes to the Dutch Reformed Translation Society for taking the initiative to make this translation possible. My gratitude is expressed in a special way to Professor James De Jong, who was so generously willing to accept responsibility for the project. He tackled the demanding task with the greatest care. I could have asked for no more qualified translator: a competent theologian who is not only in command of the English and Dutch languages, but also of the pietistic tradition. Both for the work of translation and for the extensive email exchanges that he conducted with me, I give him my hearty thanks.

Arie de Reuver

Translator's Note

When Dr. Adriaan Neele proposed Professor de Reuver's superb study as a translation project for our society, several of us read it closely and with enormous admiration. The late Professor M. Eugene Osterhaven, Dr. Joel R. Beeke and I—all members of our subcommittee on texts from the so-called Further or Second Reformation in the Netherlands—endorsed the proposal with enthusiasm. The study is a wonderful, current introduction to our series "Classics of Reformed Spirituality." The board not only approved the project and underwrote its cost, but entrusted me with the work of translation, for which I am grateful. I also thank the three society members who generously provided the necessary funds and Professor Richard A. Muller for welcoming this title into his fine series "Texts and Studies in Reformation and Post-Reformation Thought." An unanticipated delight involved in the work has been my contact with the author, whose patience, encouragement and helpful suggestions and corrections are deeply appreciated. Unfortunately, recapturing much of the flavor and charm of the seventeenth-century quotations is beyond this translator's competence; settling for modern (American) English orthography, syntax and idioms will nonetheless, it is hoped, not impede a richer, deeper understanding of the Dutch Reformed spirituality profiled so masterfully by Professor de Reuver.

James A. De Jong

Abbreviations

SW	*Bernhard von Clairvaux. Sämtliche Werke, lateinisch/deutsch* (G. B. Winkler edition)
Opera	*Thomae Hemerken à Kempis. Opera omnia* (M. I. Pohl edition)
WA	*D. Martin Luthers Werke. Kritische Gesamtausgabe*
CO	*Ioannis Calvini Opera quae supersunt omnia*
OS	*Ioannis Calvini Opera Selecta*
TRE	*Theologische Realenzyklopädie*
TR	*Theologia Reformata*
DNR	*Documentatieblad Nadere Reformatie*
BLGNP	*Biografisch Lexicon voor de geschiedenis van het Nederlandse Protestantisme*
Schatkamer	J. van der Haar, *Schatkamer van de gereformeerde Theologie in Nederland (c. 1600-c. 1800). Bibliografisch onderzoek*

Introduction

Title

The expression "sweet communion" is based on an eighteenth-century Psalm versification.[1] Because this book describes forms of piety from a period preceding that century, the title is in a certain sense anachronistic. Moreover, it is hardly original. Under the same title, the young Miskotte published a series of reflections in his first congregation's newsletter already in 1924.[2] Nevertheless, I have opted for it. The reason is that it captures precisely what this study is all about: the interchange between God and humanity that is called "hidden" or "sweet" because it takes place in heart-to-heart intimacy. This fellowship is also called "hidden" because of its mysterious quality that never fully relinquishes its secrets. God allows his hidden self to be disclosed to some extent, but never to be fathomed. What the forms of spirituality reviewed here have in common is the recognition that they can only stammer what is fundamentally inexpressible.

The term "hidden fellowship" has assumed an identity apart from the Psalm versification, and as such has captured a unique place in the vocabulary of later pietism.[3] That is understandable. This combination of words characterizes the sweet communion that pietism understands to be at the heart of piety. The expression may be relatively young, but the reality which it identifies is as old as piety itself. The primary sources that are the foundation for this book are filled with it. Intimate fellowship with God is the heartbeat of the spiritual life examined in these texts.

Theme

The choice of the theme of this work reflects the course of my own life. I was born and was borne witness to in a pietistic environment, and I have carried the scent of that background with me ever since. In my student days and during my early years in the pastorate my interest in this tradition was certainly overshadowed by the strictly reformational and the Kohlbruggian legacies. But

---

1. Psalm 25:7 (1773 versification) in Dutch literally says "hidden fellowship," but is better captured in the English expression "sweet communion": "Souls find sweet communion with God wherever the fear of him is found." The Hebrew equivalent, *sod*, has the meaning—among others—of secret, reliable fellowship. See *Theologisches Handwörterbuch zum Alten Testament*, ed. E. Jenni and C. Westermann (Munich and Zurich, 1976), 144-48.

2. K. H. Miskotte, *Als een die dient: volledige uitgave van het "Gemeenteblaadje Cortgene"* (Baarn, 1976), 254-305. The explanation is also included in K. H. Miskotte, *In de gecroonde allemansgading: Keur uit het verspreide werk van prof. dr. K. H. Miskotte* (Nijkerk, 1946), 97-120.

3. Compare C. van de Ketterij, *De weg in woorden: Een systematische beschrijving van het piëtistische woordgebruik na 1900* (Assen, 1972), 172.

around the time that I was preparing my dissertation, the pietists came into focus in a new way. And over the last seven years this interest gradually intensified. Because the terrain of my academic research and teaching not only includes the history of the Reformation, but also that of the Further Reformation, the examination of the last-mentioned tradition and particularly its spirituality constitutes an essential part of my work.

Perhaps I might be permitted to add something else at this point. The choice of the theme for this work was not only motivated by the course of my own life, but also by my deep convictions about life in general. I believe that one of the most serious symptoms of the present crisis in church and culture is the increasing loss of sweet fellowship with God. I also believe that its renewed practice contains healing power. This in no way means that the piety of an earlier era should be imitated, let alone copied exactly. But it does mean that its vitality can inspire an authentic spirituality that is contemporary.

The Further Reformation

In this study attention is focused on dimensions of the spirituality of the Further Reformation, especially its mystical component. I need not provide an extensive discussion and characterization of the Further Reformation.[4] I am content to summarize a few of its main features.

As is generally understood, this seventeenth-century movement strove for a contemporary application of the sixteenth-century Reformation and pleaded for both an inner vitalization of Reformed doctrine and a radical sanctification of life. It is regarded as the Dutch version of an international and inter-confessional movement that along with Anglo-Saxon puritanism and German pietism is designated by the over-arching name "pietism." Willem Teellinck, who is properly regarded as the father of the Further Reformation, introduced the Puritan term "further reformation" from England to the Netherlands. In various writings he pleaded for "further reformation of the things entrusted to us." By so doing he was referring to the frustrating fact that a considerable part of the Dutch population was nominally Reformed, but in practice was not so in the least. The sad condition of Dutch popular culture indicated this.

From the very beginning, the concept of reformation had a dynamic significance, therefore. It functioned more like a verb than a noun, and in so doing it designated the activity of reforming. This process needed to advance further and to be taken more personally. These comparisons assumed a particular relation to the sixteenth-century Reformation. The intent was not to exaggerate it nor to minimize it, but to give it a more precise expression. Representatives of the Further Reformation like Gisbertus Voetius, Johannes Hoornbeeck and Jacobus Koelman were strongly supportive of the agenda: "The church must be continuously reforming because it is reformed" ("Ecclesia semper reformanda,

---

4. An orientation is provided in C. Graafland, W. J. op 't Hof and F. A. van Lieburg, "Nadere Reformatie: Opneiuw een poging tot begripsbepaling," in *DNR* 19 (1995): 105-84. The literature also refers to this movement as the Second Reformation, but I find the arguments in favor of calling it the Further Reformation more compelling.

quia reformata est").[5] Standing on the doctrinal foundations of the Reformation, these pietists wanted to realize its spiritual and ethical implications in a practical godliness (*praxis pietatis*) in which piety and scrupulousness (*pietatis* and *praecisitas*) were corollaries. The movement was temporally parallel with the cultural trend of individualization and was connected with the growing tendency to emphasize the inner life; therefore, it was historically comparable to movements like seventeenth-century Jansenism and quietism.

The Further Reformation developed a comprehensive pastoral psychology by which it intended to provide guidance on the manner in which the applied work of the Holy Spirit brought people to certainty of faith. It achieved its goal through an intense promotional effort and constant preaching. The sermons that it left us are characterized, therefore, not only by exegetical and dogmatic instruction, but especially by a pastoral dialogue designed descriptively as well as prescriptively to build spiritual life. However typical the theocratic spirit and as a result the social relevance of the bulk of the Further Reformation may have been—dimensions that went beyond a purely pietistic ideal—in my estimation, the Further Reformation was primarily a spirituality movement that was focused on the heart.[6]

On this crucial point, proponents of the Further Reformation certainly attached themselves to the spirituality of the Reformation, but they did not hesitate to combine this continuation with completion. In that regard, they did not hesitate to cross the boundaries of the Reformation and to appeal for assistance to the pre-Reformation's devotional literature. Just as Reformed scholasticism was driven to advance Reformed theology on an academic level, and in so doing made full use of patristic resources and medieval scholastic instruments,[7] the Further Reformation's movement in spirituality did not fail to consult pre-Reformation sources. To be specific, the spirituality reflected in the Modern Devotion by Thomas à Kempis was held in high regard. His spiritual authority was exceeded only by that of Bernard of Clairvaux, an outspokenly mystical author.

At present, the Reformation and the Further Reformation are repeatedly played off against one another. From the perspective of the Reformation, the Further Reformation would then represent a return to the so-called darkness of the Middle Ages. This perspective is to a great extent unnuanced. But it cannot be put that simply, since the Reformation itself was tied to the Middle Ages with so many threads, particularly its Augustinian theology and spirituality. The recent research of scholars like H. A. Oberman, D. Steinmetz and R. A. Muller has demonstrated this convincingly.[8] By not ignoring discontinuity with the

---

5. See "Reformation," in *Historisches Wörterbuch der Philosophie*, ed. J. Ritter and K. Gründer (Darmstadt, 1992), 8:[n.p.].

6. A. de Reuver, "Wat is het eigene van de Nadere Reformatie?" *DNR* 18 (1994): 145-54.

7. W. J. van Asselt et al., *Inleiding in de gereformeerde scholastiek* (Zoetermeer, 1998), especially 9-17; *Reformation and Scholasticism: An Ecumenical Enterprise*, ed. W. J. van Asselt and E. Dekker (Grand Rapids, 2001).

8. See, for example, Oberman, *Spätscholastik und Reformation*, vol. 1: *Der Herbst der mittelalterlischen Theologie*, trans. Martin Rumscheid and Henning Kampen (Zurich, 1965), originally published as *The Harvest of Medieval Theology: Gabriel Biel and Late Medieval*

Roman Catholic Middle Ages, particularly with respect to the doctrine of grace, one is less likely to misunderstand the continuity, particularly on the matter of spirituality. The transposition that spirituality experienced did not mean that it was replaced. Undoubtedly, its continuity depended on the common orientation of both the Reformation and medieval theology to the sources of the early church. Virtually all of the reformers had enjoyed an education in Christian humanism and shared the ideal of *ad fontes*. None of them represented the simplistic Anabaptist perspective that the unique authority of Scripture would render the retooling of the catholic tradition superfluous, let alone forbidden. Luther, Bucer and Calvin—to name only three reformers—certainly knew better than to accord tradition the highest authority, but they nevertheless eagerly emphasized the Reformation's agreement with the early church, and in so doing the catholicity of their own movement.[9] Their movement was no schism, but a legitimate, biblically purified advance.

This conviction was shared by the Further Reformation. This appears from the fact that the appeal of these later reformers to the spiritual legacy of Bernard and Thomas can be called both quantitative and qualitative. Apparently this understanding of catholicity was so powerful that its representatives drew appreciatively from pre-Reformation sources. The Reformation certainly functioned as a point of reference, but not as the final goal. This introduced an unmistakable ambivalence in its relationship to the Roman Catholic tradition. On the one hand, people emphatically rejected what they regarded as objectionable silt, especially with respect to the doctrines of grace and the sacraments; on the other hand, they adopted a large-hearted integration of pre-Reformation spirituality into their own. In this way, they incorporated such devotional nuggets as meditation, solitude, mysticism and contemplation into their own Reformed framework. In short, in the history of spirituality the Further Reformation was the lively experimentation of a movement that sought its spiritual identity in a synthesis of a reformational and a broadly catholic faith-experience.

Design

This study is not about the doctrinal side of the Further Reformation and even less about its theocratic ideals. What I am interested in is a spiritual-ethical

---

Nominalism (Cambridge, Massachusetts, 1963); idem, *Die Reformation: Von Wittenberg nach Genf* (Göttingen, 1986); D. Steinmetz, *Luther in Context* (Grand Rapids, 1995); idem, *Calvin in Context* (New York and Oxford, 1995); R. A. Muller, *Christ and the Decree: Christology and Predestination in Reformed Theology from Calvin to Perkins* (Grand Rapids, 1986); idem, *Post-Reformation Reformed Dogmatics*, vol. 1, *Prolegomena to Theology* (Grand Rapids, 1987); ibid., vol. 2, *Holy Scripture: The Cognitive Foundation of Theology* (Grand Rapids, 1993); idem, *The Unaccommodated Calvin: Studies in the Foundation of a Theological Tradition* (New York and Oxford, 2000). Also see *Protestant Scholasticism: Essays in Reassessment*, ed. Carl R. Trueman and R. Scott Clark (Carlisle, 1999). On Calvin's critical approach of the *patres*, see for example, D. C. Steinmetz, "The Judaizing Calvin," in *Die Patristik in der Bibelexegese des 16. Jahrhunderts*, ed. D. C. Steinmetz (Wiesbaden, 1999), 135-45.

9. According to Steinmetz, *Calvin in Context*, 210: "The picture of Calvin that emerges from this book is of a theologian who extols the ancient Christian Fathers and is clearly influenced by them, but who also maintains a fierce independence of their authority."

investigation into both the quality and form as well as into the roots of its spirituality. This design is not entirely new. Interest in the spirituality of the Further Reformation may be found in various publications. Here its content and shape receive attention, as does the influence of the medieval devotional material. In this connection, the dissertation of I. Boot[10] and especially the extensive investigation of W. J. op 't Hof deserve to be mentioned with respect. This literature will be amply consulted in the course of this study. I have utilized its results. In two senses, however, I would also like to complement this research. The first way is by more explicitly surveying how this spirituality is interpreted formally and informally. The second way is by going more deeply into which medieval spiritual themes have worked their way into the Further Reformation legacy, and especially how these later writers integrated them into their own framework. I am well aware of the risks involved in the approach of providing extensive citations. Through repetition, interpretation can sometimes remain underdeveloped. When this pitfall is avoided, however, I think the advantage of providing generous quotations is large. By so doing, the flavor of the sources themselves is most purely protected. Precisely in the genre of spiritual texts, the idioms that they generally employ emerge in their uniquely characteristic significance.

The Main Question

The main question that plays an explicit role in this study is that of the continuity or discontinuity of the Further Reformation's spirituality with that of the Middle Ages. Are the frequently striking textual comparisons perhaps relativized by the differences in intervening time and context, or is it rather just the other way around, and are the temporal and contextual differences relativized by the agreement found in the textual material? The deeper question of whether a devout medieval person means the same thing as the paragon of pietism when they speak the same words is even weightier. I must admit that I am better at acknowledging this problem than at providing a definitive solution for it. Convinced that both drank from the same spring of word and Spirit, I am inclined to honor the textual analogies as substantive affinities. I will delve into this question only sporadically in the course of my investigation. But throughout it, the texts cited offer a cumulative basis for discerning whether through attentive interpretation a continuity exists that is unmasked as merely apparent, or whether—to turn matters just around—amidst all the apparent discontinuity there is still an actual continuity.

Choices

The number and selection of authors to which I have limited myself are not accidental. The criterion for choosing the medieval authors consists of the degree

---

10. I. Boot, *De allegorische uitlegging van het Hooglied voornamelijk in Nederland: Een onderzoek naar de verhouding tussen Bernard van Clairvaux en de Nadere Reformatie* (Woerden, 1971).

of their spiritual influence on the Further Reformation. W. J. op 't Hof, an exceptional expert in the field of pietism, has documented persuasively that in a selection of Further Reformation works an appreciable amount of material may be recovered from pre-Reformation literature.[11] His conclusion, which he establishes convincingly, is that among virtually all of the forty (!) pietists explored by him, Bernard of Clairvaux was quoted with the greatest affection and that Thomas à Kempis indisputably captured second place on the list of frequently cited medieval authors. This conclusion justifies my choices of Bernard and Thomas.

As far as figures of the Further Reformation are concerned, my eye fell on Willem Teellinck because he qualifies as the father of the movement; on Theodorus à Brakel on the basis of his decidedly meditative lifestyle; on Wilhelmus à Brakel on the basis of his widespread influence; on Herman Witsius because his devotional insights received expression in an academic setting. I included Guiljelmus Saldenus on the list based on personal preference. His style, mild in temperament and rich with imagery, appeals to me. The omission of men like Gisbertus Voetius, Jodocus van Lodensteyn and Simon Oomius—names that would have worked excellently in this study—are not in the least unqualified. To keep this book within its allotted limits, I had to restrict myself to the five people named. I consider them to be representative of the Further Reformation's spirituality.

Concepts

In the foregoing, concepts were used, two of which require some further explanation. I refer to the terms "spirituality" and "mysticism." Concerning the first concept, much could be said, but I will endeavor to keep it short. I will not get into the diversity of descriptions available.[12] I am content to clarify what I myself mean when I use the term in this book. Christian spirituality I summarize as the religious disposition that is worked in the heart by the word and Spirit, that is influenced by its time and setting and that takes shape in living before the face of God. I use the concept with a meaning that coincides with that of Christian piety.

Concerning the word "mysticism," I need to be more detailed. This is not to make the matter more complicated, but precisely to avoid the problematic associated with it. The term is both diffuse and loaded. Yet, in my opinion, it is useful as long as a person explains what he means by it. Also in this instance, it

---

11. W. J. op 't Hof, "Rooms-katholieke doorwerking binnen de Nadere Reformatie: Een eerste algemene verkenning," *DNR* 15 (1991): 73-120.

12. Among others, I point to C. Aalders, *Spiritualiteit: Geestelijk leven vroeger en nu* (The Hague, 1969); J. Beumer, ed., *Als de hemel de aarde raakt: Spiritualiteit en mystiek—ervaringen* (Kampen, 1989); C. Graafland, *Gereformeerden op zoek naar God: Godsverduistering in het licht van de gereformeerde spiritualiteit* (Kampen, 1993); W. H. Velema, *Nieuw zicht op gereformeerde spiritualiteit* (Kampen, 1990); W. van 't Spijker, ed., *Spiritualiteit* (Kampen, 1993); A. E. McGrath, *Christian Spirituality: An Introduction* (Oxford and Malden, 1999); K. Waaijman, *Spiritualiteit: Vormen, grondslagen, methoden* (Gent and Kampen, 2000). Further, see the various lexicons and handbooks cited throughout this study.

does not make a lot of sense to me to summarize this widespread, not exclusively Christian phenomenon here.[13] I restrict myself to a few basic observations.[14]

I consider the four-fold aspects that Otger Steggink proposes to be important for outlining the uniqueness of Christian mysticism. Phenomenologically, he regards the following elements to be constitutive. The first is when something other breaks through into everyday reality: a vertical intrusion into horizontal existence.[15] The second is an encounter with God which dominates the entirety of life. The third is a union (*unio* or *communio*) with God that is the result of the former and by which the soul is "immersed" in God. The fourth is the paradoxical interpretation of this experience, by which the person undergoing it attempts to put into words what essentially cannot be described. A person cannot express it, let alone explain it. But even less can a person resist attempting to give a stammering testimony about what is inexpressible.[16]

What is striking about this approach is that it is apparently not regarded as inherent in mysticism to relinquish the distinction between God and the person. The latter form of mysticism is not imaginary. In it, mystical union does not involve a faith-union with God, but a melting away of one's being into God. In it, the issue is no longer about a personal experience of fellowship with the God of revelation, but about the boundary-crossing deification of the person. This

---

13. Fuller treatments can be found in W. J. Aalders, *Mystiek: Haar vormen, wezen en waarde* (Groningen and The Hague, 1928); R. Otto, *Het Heilige: Een verhandeling over het irrationele in de idee van het goddelijke en de verhouding ervan tot het rationele*, trans. J. W. Dippel and O. Noordenbos (Hilversum, 1963); R. Hensen, et al., "Mystiek in de westerse cultuur," in *Rondom het Woord: Theologische Etherleergang van de NCRV* 2 (1973): 1-146; G. Quispel et al., *Mystiek en bevinding* (Kampen, 1976); H. H. Blommenstijn and F. A. Maas, *Kruispunten in de mystieke traditie: Tekst en context van Meester Eckhardt, Jan van Ruusbroec, Teresa van Avila en Johannes van het Kruis* (The Hague, 1990); "Mystik" in *TRE* 23: 533-97; K. Albert, *Einführung in die philosophische Mystik* (Darmstadt, 1996); F. Maas, *Van God houden als van niemand: Preken van Meester Eckhart* (Kampen and Averbode, 1997); Waaijman, *Spiritualiteit*. In addition, see the lexicons and handbooks cited.

14. Etymologically, the word "mysticism" is derived from the Greek word *mystikos*, that in turn comes from the verb *myoo*, which means "to close the mouth and eyes." It also appears to be related to *myeoo*, "to be initiated into mysteries." Otto, *Het Heilige*, 29, thinks that "mysticism" apparently comes from a Sanskrit root word, *moesj*, "to perform something mysterious." Early Christian usage covered three fields: the biblical, the liturgical and the spiritual. In the biblical area, the word "mysticism" was used, for example, by Clement of Alexandria (c. 200 AD) and Origen (c. 225 AD) regarding the Christ-mystery as the key to understanding the mystical sense of Scripture. Liturgically, it was customary to use it to designate the Lord's supper ("the pascal mystery"), especially the hidden presence of Christ in the bread and wine. The spiritual use had reference to the experience of Christ's presence in the word and sacrament—so used for the first time in Origen. He placed great emphasis on the mystical *theoria*, existential insight into Scripture that preceded ecstasy. See O. Steggink, "Mystik," in *Praktisches Lexicon der Spiritualität*, ed. C. Schültz, 904-5.

15. However passive a person might be in such an experience, for it overpowers him by grace, there is certainly a route of entry that leads to it. This is the route of aseceticism, meditation and emptying oneself. The threefold way (*triplex via*) is well-known, and Bonaventure (c. 1217-1274), consistent with an ancient tradition, gave it great weight: purification, illumination, unification (*purgatio, illuminatio, unio*). Compare F. van der Pol, "Spiritualiteit in de Middeleeuwen," in *Spiritualiteit*, ed. van 't Spijker, 118.

16. Steggink, "Mystik," 906-9. Compare Oberman, *Die Reformation*, 34.

construal of mysticism is neither required nor satisfactory.[17] What must actually be called mysticism is the faith-knowledge that comes over a person by the word and the Spirit and includes an intimate communion with God himself. One is inclined to speak here of a discovery. This is not unjustified, if only the person understands that the "discovery" covers a broader field than mysticism. The discovery involves not only direct communion with God, but simultaneously the experience that one is indirectly involved with him in the full breadth of one's existence, in one's trials and deliverances, one's cares and one's blessings. The vertical dimension, the heart of this discovery directly focused on God, is what is designated by the word "mysticism." Calvin at any rate, did not hesitate to speak of this central point in his pneumatology as the mystical union with Christ.[18] In this regard, he shows that he is in the company of Luther and Bucer.[19]

Now one can naturally observe that mysticism is a typically catholic and medieval phenomenon and be struck by the differences and even the contradictions between the piety of the reformers and that of Rome's medieval mystics. The points of difference are certainly there.[20] Whoever obscures them does violence to the historical facts. However, in addition to the gaps, undeniable points of contact between them can be identified. The rejection of mysticism by the reformers involved only a certain form of it. This form included, in the first place, a mysticism that functioned as an experiential union in which the boundary between God and humanity was obliterated. It included in the second place a mysticism that was prized and practiced as a meritorious pre-condition for salvation that ignored grace. It included, thirdly, a mysticism restricted to monastic observances. Fourthly, it involved a mysticism that upset the balance between faith and love at the expense of faith. These points of criticism did not produce a break with mysticism as such, however. The judgment of C. Aalders, in translation, seems right to me: "While the reformers strenuously opposed monastic mysticism with its dangerous, self-involved tendencies, it must never be forgotten that an undeniable mysticism also developed in the churches of the Reformation."[21] With the same author, it can be affirmed that all experience of a knowledge of God and of fellowship with God is mystical in nature. It involves what Thomas Aquinas designates as "cognitio Dei experimentalis,"[22] that is to

17. Compare W. J. Aalders, *Mystiek*, 68.

18. C. A. Keller, *Calvin mystique: Au cœur de la pensée du Réformateur* (Geneva, 2001), especially 85-143.

19. See W. van 't Spijker, *Geest, Woord en Kerk: Opstellen over de geschiedenis van het gereformeerd protestantisme* (Kampen, 1991), 118-19. Compare his "Spiritualiteit en theologie," in *Spiritualiteit*, ed. van 't Spijker, 389; and his *Calvin: Biographie und Theologie*, in the series *Die Kirche in ihrer Geschichte: Ein Handbuch*, vol. 3, ed. B. Moeller (Lieferung J 2; Göttingen, 2001), 101-236.

20. See, for example, K. H. zur Mühlen, *Nos extra nos: Luthers Theologie zwischen Mystik und Scholastik* (Tübingen, 1972), 198-203; Oberman, *Die Reformation*, 79-88; van 't Spijker, *Geest, Woord en Kerk*, 117; van der Pol, "Spiritualiteit," 114.

21. C. Aalders, *Spiritualiteit*, 196.

22. Ibid., 117. In *WA*, 9:98, Luther also makes use of this terminology. Compare K. H. zur Mühlen, *Reformatorisches Profil: Studien zum Weg Martin Luthers und der Reformation* (Göttingen, 1995), 89.

say, a knowledge that is not based on intellectual reflection, but on communion with God himself. It grips people at the deepest level of their existence.

God's revelation evokes a matchless experience that may be called "mysticism." Least of all does mysticism by definition stand in opposition to word-based faith, which was certainly Emil Brunner's position: "Entweder die Mystik oder das Wort."[23] But that hardly does justice to the sources. Albrecht Ritschl is no less guilty of this, when in his *Geschichte des Pietismus*[24] he accused both Lutheran and Reformed pietism of breaking the power of the Reformation by exchanging faith for mysticism.[25] On the basis of extreme examples that undoubtedly appeared, a contradiction was created that brought mysticism as such into discredit. I am of the conviction that we may legitimately speak of mysticism wherever the effect of the word of God is a personal encounter between God and the soul worked by the Holy Spirit.[26] The term "Mystik des Wortes" that K. H. zur Mühlen coined deserves approval.[27] A. A. van Ruler points to this experiential word as a movement that extends "from the verbal to the actual."[28] A person need not disqualify using the term "mysticism" as dubious or risky, therefore. But, I would like to plead for using the term sparingly, based on the conviction that it involves a valuable characterization of that which may be regarded as the very marrow of the faith-experience, namely fellowship with God in Christ through the word and Spirit. Whoever emphasizes the idea of mystery in the term "mysticism," in any case, is in step with an honorable tradition.

Route

I hope that by means of this introduction I have paved the way to a unique investigation. The route that I will follow is chronological in design. We first visit the twelfth-century Clairvaux in French Champagne. Then we make the transition to the fifteenth-century monastery of St. Agnietenberg near Zwolle. In what follows, we make stops at a number of places in sixteenth-century Netherlands: Middelburg and Makkum, Enkhuizen and Delft, Leeuwarden and Rotterdam, Franeker, Utrecht and Leiden. It is during this period extending from 1100 to 1700, and in this geographic region stretching from Champagne to

---

23. E. Brunner, *Die Mystik und das Wort* (Tübingen, 1924), could see nothing else in mysticism than "geraubte Unmittelbarkeit."

24. A. Ritschl, *Geschichte des Pietismus*, 3 vols. (Bonn, 1880-86).

25. S. van der Linde, "Mystiek en bevinding in het Gereformeerd Protestantisme," in Quispel et al., *Mystiek en bevinding*, 47.

26. Compare J. van den Berg, "Die Frömmigkeitsbestrebungen in den Niederlanden," in *Geschichte des Pietismus*, vol. 1: *Der Pietismus vom siebzehnten bis zum frühen achtzehnten Jahrhundert*, ed. M. Brecht (Gottingen, 1993), 58. The author wants to distinguish between mysticism in a narrower sense (spiritualism), which specifies the immediate union of the soul with God and to which all external types are relative, and the mystical element in all human longings for a personal experience of God's nearness. Also compare J. de Boer, *De verzegeling met de Heilige Geest volgens de opvatting van de Nadere Reformatie* (Rotterdam, 1968), 16-22.

27. Zur Mühlen, *Reformatorisches Profil*, 84.

28. A. A. van Ruler, *Theologisch Werk* (Nijkerk, 1971), 3:69.

Friesland, that these seven spiritual Christians experienced and recorded their sweet communion with God.

1

Bernard of Clairvaux (1090-1153)

The Twelfth Century

Bernard's century—the twelfth—is generally regarded as the era when medieval spirituality flowered. The period was characterized by a rapid increase in population, by advances in agriculture and trade and by the rise of cities. Equally typical are the founding of universities, monastic revitalization and the flourishing of gothic architecture, although it had not yet peaked. Moreover, what is of special interest as far as the theme of this book is concerned is the discovery of individuality with respect to personal emotional life.[1] This is a feature of the era that clearly emerges into social daylight in the period's spiritual writings. As far as spirituality is concerned, something more needs to be said in this brief introduction.

The great mystics of the twelfth century were oriented to the intellectual contributions of the early fathers, namely to the legacies of Augustine and Gregory the Great.[2] But they were not content merely to summarize or accurately repeat this classical inheritance. Their efforts were directed rather at advancing the tradition and completing it.[3] In this regard they reflected an ideal that can be considered characteristic of the entire social order of the high middle ages. This ideal is usually designated with the term "organizing principle." The impulse for order is manifested in the fields of politics and jurisprudence, and no less in the areas of church and theology. From a theological perspective, this orientation assumed two relevant forms. On the one hand it is seen in the form of the scholasticism promoted in the universities, and on the other hand in the form of the monastic theology followed predominantly in medieval cloisters. Although I will return to the methodological difference between these two parallel movements, a brief description is in order here. While the purpose of the scholastic method was to achieve a better conception of the faith, monastic mystical theology concentrated on striving for a deeper experience of that faith.

However, the monastics were no less attached to order than were the scholastics. Just as the ideal of courtly love was stylized and propagated in the secular literature of the twelfth century, in the mysticism of the day the love

---

1. See J. Le Goff, *De cultuur van middeleeuws Europa*, trans. Roland Fagel and Luuk Knippenberg (Amsterdam, 1987), 79-137; P. Dinzelbacher, "Die 'Bernhardinische Epoche' als Achsenzeit der europäischen Geschichte," in *Bernhard von Clairvaux und der Beginn der Moderne*, ed. D. R. Bauer and G. Fuchs (Innsbruck and Vienna, 1996), 9-53.

2. For a summary of Augustine's spirituality see B. McGinn, *Die Mystik im Abendland*, vol. 1, *Ursprünge*, trans. Clemens Maaß (Freiburg, Basel and Vienna, 1994), 330-80; and for Gregory, idem, vol. 2, *Entfaltung*, trans. Wolfgang Scheuermann (Freiburg, Basel and Vienna, 1996), 63-130.

3. *Die Mystik*, 2:238.

experienced between the church as bride and Christ the Bridegroom was glorified. "Die Brautmystik," says B. McGinn in his monumental study of mysticism, "war jedoch Teil einer umfassender *ordinatio caritatis*, die alle Anstrengungen und Kräfte der einzelnen Gläubigen und der gesammten Kirche auf die Liebe zu Gott und deren Freuden als letztem und wahrem Ziel richtete."[4]

The mystics did not only want to experience this love, but also to structure it. With this structure they naturally did not intend to control love, much less to repress it, but rather to give it full expression in complete submission to God. So the intellect was also assigned its place, by regarding it as subordinate to love and making it serviceable to it. Bernard did not have a high opinion of the intellect as autonomous. However, if the intellect had been purified through love for Christ and was combined with a humble self-knowledge, it became a real component in the knowledge of the divine mysteries.[5] In the forms of knowledge and discretion (*scientia* and *discretio*), the intellect was capable of guiding affective love down the right path and was in a position to avoid confusion (*confusio*) and to protect the unity of the church.[6]

The fact that experiential love transcended the intellectual idea did not signify a minimizing of the intellect as such. McGinn calls attention to the fact in this connection that it would be even less plausible to suggest that the twelfth-century mystics would have disdained or neglected the social dimension. Although they are often portrayed as "Privatleute mit solipsistischer Neigung," thus as people interested purely in their own personal experience of God, the reality is entirely different. Often the mystic provided the impetus for ecclesiastical and social engagement.[7] In the person of Bernard of Clairvaux this twofold dimension received its preeminent form. On the one hand he was introspectively spiritual, while on the other hand for almost twenty years he was the most important and influential church leader of the West.[8] That in his mysticism Bernhard transcended his own times, in no way implies that he stood outside his times. His ascendancy is not very conceivable aside from the twelfth century, and the twelfth century is even less conceivable without him. This is the case not only because besides being a mystic he was a polemicist and a church politician, but because as a mystic he transmitted a message to his century and to the following centuries. Here I emphasize the fact that the valuable insights that he discovered in the book of experience (*in libro experientiae*), as he calls it in his third sermon on Song of Solomon, he did not restrict to himself, but imparted to others in his sermons and writings. His intent in doing so was not to put himself on display, but to stimulate others to utilize the book of their own experience. In this way he wanted to act as a guide on the road of communal spiritual practice. McGinn is not mistaken when he calls him first of all[9] a

---

4. Ibid., 240.
5. Ibid., 306 and following.
6. Ibid., 332-34
7. Ibid., 241.
8. Ibid., 242
9. Ibid., 253. On Bernard's preaching, compare G. R. Evans, *The Mind of St. Bernard of Clairvaux* (Oxford, 1983), 72-107. The author notes, "Bernard's efforts as a preacher were always directed primarily toward the winning and above all the sustaining of souls" (99).

preacher and talks about the universality of Bernard's message, which had all Christians in mind.[10] In fairness the author adds that this line of thought in Bernard's spirituality is laced with an elitist tendency. The Abbot of Clairvaux accords every Christian, also the lay person, loving fellowship with Christ, but in practice he is inclined to regard the higher levels of this bridal mysticism as achievable only within the monastic setting.[11] In the cloister he could share his experiences with his brothers in every way. On the basis of his passion for this love and the stylizing of the love-experience, he qualifies as a proponent of twelfth-century culture.

Biographical Sketch

Bernard descended from a noble Burgundian family. He was born in 1090 AD at the Castle Fontaines near Dijon (Côte d' Or). During his eighth year the shy, highly gifted lad was entrusted to the care of the canon of Notre-Dame de Saint Vorles in Châtillon, where presumably he followed the usual education of the time in the seven liberal arts[12] and where he learned to master patristic Latin as his mother tongue. Noteworthy is that Bernard never sat at the feet of prominent masters and scholars. In a certain sense he was self-taught, and certainly at an exceptional level.[13]

While still in his school years, the thirteen-year-old Bernard lost his mother,[14] whose piety made a deep impression on his own life. This loss brought about an inner crisis and at the same time constituted the beginning of his choice for the monastic life.[15] After he successfully won also his brothers, several relatives and friends to this ideal and had gathered them as a circle around him— his shyness was not diminished by his influence—this society of about thirty individuals applied to the fairly recently organized reform-cloister at Citeaux (*Cistercium*, in Latin). It consisted of a monastic fellowship that, dissatisfied with the moral laxness of the Benedictine house in Cluny, had broken with it and

---

10. Ibid., 278. Also compare 302, where McGinn "perceptively" says of Bernard's rhetoric: "sie soll die Gotteserfahrung der Zuhörer fördern."

11. Ibid. 278-79.

12. In order to be able to pursue a university education (in theology, medicine or law), preparatory training in the liberal arts (*artes liberales*) was required. It included a threefold curriculum (*trivium*) of logic (dialectics), rhetoric and grammar, and a fourfold curriculum (*quadrivium*) of arithmetic, music, geometry and astronomy. On the university educational system of the Middle Ages, see P. Böhner and E. Gilson, *Christliche Philosophie: Von ihren Anfängen bis Nikolaus von Cues* (Paderborn, 1954), 408-13; L. M. de Rijk, *Middeleeuwse wijsbegeerte: Traditie en vernieuwing* (Assen, 1981), 117-31; D. Illmer, "Artes Liberales," in *TRE*, 4:156-71; G. van den Brink, *Oriëntatie in de filosofie* (Zoetermeer, 1994), 1:108-9; van Asselt et al., *Inleiding*, 54-57. On Bernard's education, compare Evans, *The Mind*, 38-44"

13. Compare G. B. Winkler, "Einleitung," in *Bernhard von Clairvaux: Sämtliche Werke* (hereafter, *SW*), ed. G. B. Winkler (Innsbruck, 1990), 1:31: "Er gehörte zu jenen Genies, die, mit hoher Sensibilität begabt, aus einem Minimum an quantitativer Anregung ein Maximum an qualitativer Bildung erzielen."

14. The timeframe is disputed. J. Leclercq, *Bernhard von Clairvaux: Ein Mann prägt seine Zeit* (Munich, Zurich and Vienna, 1997), 23, argues that it concluded "um 1103."

15 The customary term for entering a cloister was "*conversio*" (reversal, turning back, conversion). See G. R. Evans, *Bernard of Clairvaux* (New York and Oxford, 2000), 23-25.

in 1098 AD had formed a new monastery dedicated to strictly following the old rule of Benedict.[16] The admittance of this band of thirty led to the unexpected flourishing of the until then languishing monastery of Citeaux.

In 1115 AD Bernard, despite his youth and fragile health, received the mandate to establish a new monastery. Clairvaux (*clara vallis* or bright valley) was born, a center of light in the inhospitable region of Champagne. Until his death, Bernard was its abbot. However, in actuality his was not a life of isolation. On many occasions he left his domicile on trips into the surrounding region, with the result that he often returned with young nobles or students on whom his personality had made a substantial impact.

His influence was enormous.[17] In the first instance, this is obvious from the number of daughter houses, some seventy, which came into existence through his efforts. Beyond that, during his lifetime another hundred already existing cloisters spread throughout all of Europe joined his movement. In the second place, three times he traveled to Italy, where he played a significant role in church political developments. Moreover, he took part in various councils for the purpose of defending orthodox doctrine. His controversy with Abelard is well-known, as is his conflict with Katherine.[18] In the third place, he was entrusted by Pope Eugenius III with preparations for the third crusade. In addition, he visited Languedoc, the Rhineland and Bavaria.

Because within the framework of this study I am expressly concerned with Bernard the mystic, I will not give further attention to his public appearances. I am aware that this methodology is not without risk. Its consequence could certainly be that a somewhat truncated interpretation results. Bernard's portrait would then be less exact and would render my treatment suspect. He was not the saint that hagiography has made of him. In his contention with supposed opponents he could be merciless and implacable. In establishing or appropriating monasteries he could sometimes resort to questionable tactics. The abbot of Clairvaux was both a pious person and a fighter, both a monk and a manipulator. The tension that this duality caused he described himself, as when as a sixty-year-old he characterized himself as an elusive personality (*chimaera*) in his generation.[19] In any case, with A. H. Bredero there is reason to speak of Bernard's "double life."[20]

The abbot of Clairvaux displayed a degree of ambivalence in still another way. Living in the twelfth century, which is aptly described as a pivotal time for

---

16. Compare A. Angenendt, "Die Zisterzienser im religiösen Umbruch," in *Bernhard von Clairvaux*, ed. Bauer and Fuchs, 54-69; R. Fischer, "Kloster," in *TRE*, 19:275-81; McGinn, 2:192-94.

17. Leclercq, *Bernhard*, 43-47. The author speaks of an expanding influence: to 1130 AD on the religious and civil society of France, from 1120 to 1138 AD of Rome and from 1139 to 1148 AD of the entire church.

18. Ibid., 75-91. For the confrontation with Abelard, compare Evans, *Bernard*, 115-23.

19. Dinzelbacher, "Die 'Bernhardinische Epoche,'" 9; McGinn, *Die Mystik*, 2:336.

20. A. H. Bredero, *Bernardus van Clairvaux (1091-1153): Tussen cultus en historie* (Kampen and Kapellen, 1993), 309. Also compare Evans, *The Mind*, 218, where he speaks of "Bernard's duality in every department of his life."

Europe, he stood in the classical past in one sense and in another sense in the emerging modernity. So, we encounter a Bernard who is, in the words of Friedrich Heer, "zwei Menschen in seiner Brust trägt: den religiös-politischen Kirchenfürsten alten Stils und den Führer einer neuen spiritual-humanistischen Bewegung. 'Romanik' und 'Gotik' kreuzen in ihm ihre Klingen."[21]

The Monastic Context

Although Bernard, as indicated, led an eventful life, he was by nature an introspective monk. To be sure, he did not shun public life, but one gets the impression that he preferred staying close to home. His home was Clairvaux, or better stated, reading and reflecting on the Bible and the works of the church fathers was. He lived into them, and he lived out of them. What he encountered in them and ruminated[22] on in them he reproduced in what he said and in what he wrote. Bernard amassed knowledge of the Bible that bordered on the unbelievable. His language is saturated with Scripture and is literally strewn with biblical quotations and allusions. His 86 sermons on the Song of Solomon contain, in round numbers, some 6,000 Scripture citations! It has been strikingly observed that he speaks "Bible" like others speak French or German.[23] In this regard it must be remembered that for the monk the entire day, from early morning through the evening, was defined by the regimen of reading, praying and singing texts of Holy Scripture.

In the way in which Bernard understood and worked with the text of the Bible,[24] a handling of Scripture is seen that is characteristic of what can be called "monastic theology." Without suggesting a contradiction between this way of doing theology and the scholastic method—both approaches leavened one

---

21. Cited by Dinzelbacher, "Die 'Bernhardinische Epoche,'" 46. On Bernard's personality compare U. Köpf, "Die Rezeptions- und Wirkungsgeschichte Bernhards von Clairvaux: Forschungsstand und Forschungsaufgaben," in *Bernhard von Clairvaux: Rezeption und Wirkung im Mittelalter und in der Neuzeit*, ed. K. Elm (Wiesbaden, 1994), 27-28.

22. In the *Sermones per annum* (in "Epiphania Sermo 3," *SW*, 7:344) this "rumination [chewing cud] like the ceremonially clean animals" was a synonym for "careful reflection." On the term "rumination" (*ruminare*) see M. Nicol, *Meditation bei Luther* (Göttingen, 1991), 55-56; B. M. Lambert, "Ruminatio," in *Praktisches Lexikon der Spiritualität*, ed. C. Schütz (Freiburg, Basel and Vienna, 1992), 1072-73. Compare L. A. M. Goossens, *De meditatie in de eerste tijd van de Moderne Devotie* (Haarlem and Antwerp, 1952), 88-92. McGinn, *Die Mystik*, 2:213, describes ruminating meditation as the bond that connects lecture or sermon (*lectio*) and prayer (*oratio*). By reading a passage of Scripture slowly (often aloud), repeating it again and again, is its meaning personally appropriated and is the pathway to prayer opened.

23. M. A. Schenkl, "Bernhard und die Entdeckung der Liebe," in *Bernhard von Clairvaux*, ed. Bauer and Fuchs, 177. As far as authority is concerned, Bernard gave Scripture priority. See J. Leclercq, "Bernhard von Clairvaux," *TRE*, 5:648, where the author says, "Die Schrift ist [Bernhard] so unverzichtbar, daß alle anderen christliche Texte—liturgische, patristische oder monastische—sie nur kommentieren können, um ihre Botschaft weiterzugeben. Die anderen—philophischen, literarischen oder wissenschaftlichen—Quellen haben in dem Maße ihre Berechtigung, wie sie zur Deutung und Entfaltung der Schrift beitragen."

24. I will return to Bernard's exegetical method in a following section.

another, usually mutually—a definite difference in emphasis needs to be indicated.[25] While the theology of the schools labored with the assistance of the dialectical or logical method in order to bring systematic structure to the content of theology,[26] by means of prayer and meditation monastic theology was focused on the inner edification of the religious person. Its attention was directed not so much—at least not primarily—to insightful definitions of doctrines as to their existential significance for the heart. Its systematics was one of subjective order and was defined by the correlation of the knowledge of God with the knowledge of oneself.

Bernard also emphasized that this knowledge of God and knowledge of self belong together and that in their mutual dependence they are necessary for salvation. Without knowledge of God there is no road to salvation—much less to an understanding of oneself, and without self-knowledge one cannot travel to a saving knowledge of God. All meaningful striving for understanding involves both these components as the two foci of an ellipse. They constitute the points of orientation for the systematics that is definitive for monastic theology.[27] The role assigned to rational thinking here is something other than it receives in scholastic theology. It does not exclude reason, for monastic theology also draws conclusions and in doing so follows the laws of logic,[28] but its interest in logically coherent thinking is limited. For its primarily existential knowledge it appeals to a source to which scholastic theology assigns only a limited role, namely religious experience.[29] So, introducing a new element into tradition, Bernard opened and read alongside the books of Scripture and nature also the book of experience (*liber experientiae*). In this construct Scripture takes the lead and the book of experience acts as a clear mirror of the biblical message. By listening to the one book as well as to the other, one achieves a spiritual understanding of the text of Scripture.[30] In my judgment Bernard was concerned that his spiritual exposition of Scripture resonate with the personal experience of the listener and that this resonance would produce a personal appropriation of what Scripture has to say existentially to the listener. The basic significance of this *experientia* in no way implies that experience replaces or eliminates the

---

25. D. C. Steinmetz, "The Scholastic Calvin," in *Protestant Scholasticism,* ed. Trueman and Clark, 18.

26. De Rijk, *Middeleeuwse wijsbegeerte,* 108-138; Muller, *Christ and the Decree,* 1-13; van Asselt, et al., *Inleiding,* especially 54-66.

27. U. Köpf, "Monastische und scholastische Theologie," in *Bernhard von Clairvaux,* ed. Bauer and Fuchs, 128-29. Luther quotes Bernard with obvious agreement: "Sicut enim (ut Bernardus ait) cognitio sui sine cognitione dei desperationem, ita cognitio dei sine cognitione sui presumptionem operatur (*WA,* 5:508). Also, Köpf, "Die Rezeptions- und Wirkungsgeschichte," 46 and following.

28. That Bernard was in command of the dialectical method and when necessary utilized it, is convincingly demonstrated in Evans, *The Mind,* 91-97 and especially 141-47; idem, *Bernard,* 42-43.

29. Evans, *The Mind,* 133. Compare O. Langer, "Affekt und Ratio in der Mystik Bernhards," in *Bernhard von Clairvaux,* ed. Bauer and Fuchs, 141 and following.

30. McGinn, *Die Mystik,* 2:284-85. That the reformers, and preeminently Luther, also made use of experience as a hermeneutical key in their exegetical method is striking. In this regard consult B. Stolt, *Martin Luthers Rhetorik des Herzens* (Tübingen, 2000), 55-57.

authority of revelation, but it certainly does indicate that it is of vital and non-negotiable importance for the emergence of the understanding of revelation.[31] Bernard's spirituality is characterized by this emphasis on the experiential, heart-felt nature of faith-knowledge. It is an accent whose influence did not escape the Modern Devotion, the Reformation or pietism.

Not surprisingly, the monastic context with its unmistakable concentration on prayer and meditation formed the ideal setting for Christian mysticism, also that of Bernard.[32] Here his sensitive spirit could flourish. But the monastic life also had its downside. The care of his soul definitely had no comparable emphasis on attention to his physical health. Through a most rigorously driven asceticism, his stomach eventually could no longer tolerate solid food and Bernard grew visibly emaciated.[33] To be sure, his fragile appearance heightened his spiritual prestige,[34] but by this form of starvation his health was prematurely broken. While it had always been his custom to stand while praying, whether during the day or at night, his wobbly knees and swollen feet finally could no longer support his body.[35] However, Bernard would not have complained about his situation. For, the very reason why he valued his earthly existence was not based on his physical vitality, but paradoxically in his physical fragility and brokenness. Precisely his physical burdens provided added motivation for penance and turning to God in dependence. He wrote that in this way a weak body is "a good and reliable guide for a good spirit"[36] until the day dawns when full contrition is reached and God's beloved receives a glorified body with which she enters the life of his endless love. On August 20, 1153 AD, Bernard succumbed to his stomach ailments and laid down the burden of his earthly body.[37]

---

31. In this connection compare the informative analysis of D. E. Tamburello, "Bernard of Clairvaux," in *Historical Handbook of Major Biblical Interpreters*, ed. Donald K. McKim (Downers Grove and Leicester, 1998), 92-94.

32. McGinn, [2]:123; K. Ruh, *Geschichte der abendländischen Mystik*, vol. 1: *Die Grundlegung durch die Kirchenväter und die Mönchstheologie des 12. Jahrhunderts* (Munich, 1990), 208.

33. Dinzelbacher, "Bernhards Mystik," in *Bernhard von Clairvaux*, ed. Bauer and Fuchs, 186. Compare Leclercq, *Bernard*, 44 (also, 114).

34. According to a contemporary, his exhausted appearance and pallid face gave the abbot such an air of spirituality that people were persuaded before he ever uttered a word. See Ruh, *Die Geschichte der Mystik*, 1:251.

35. This is according to Bernard's friend William of St. Thiery in his biography of Bernard. See Dinzelbacher, "Bernhard's Mystik," 186. The earliest *vitae* or biographies, begun already in Bernard's time by Gottfried of Auxerre and William of St. Thierry respectively, are not strictly historical-biographical, but much more hagiographical in intent and highly idealized. See Leclercq, *Bernhard*, 9.

36. "Bonus plane fidusque comes caro spiritui bono." *De diligendo Deo*, 11:31, in *SW*, 1:126.

37. For an extensive biography, consult E. Vacandard, *Vie de Saint Bernard* (Paris: 1895); the 5th edition appeared in 1927. Of more recent date, but considerably less detailed, is the already indicated study of J. Leclercq, published in 1989. A concise survey is that by H. D. Kahl, "Bernhard von Fontaine, Abt von Clairvaux," in *Gestalten der Kirchengeschichte*, vol. 3, *Mittelalter I*, ed. M. Greschat (Stuttgart, Berlin, Cologne and Mainz, 1983), 173-91. Also see G. B. Winkler, "Einleitung," in *SW*, 1:15-37.

Writings and Influence

Bernard left behind a broadly encompassing body of work. The Bernard scholar Jean Leclercq asks himself how the abbot succeeded, despite his many travels and numerous ailments, in producing such an abundance of varied writings of high caliber in remarkably beautiful prose. His answer is, "Das kann nur auf eine Persönlichkeit, ein Talent und eine Gnade ganz aussergewöhnlicher Art zurückzuführen sein."[38] McGinn regards Bernard as the best stylist of his time.[39] Some of Bernard's most important publications are noted here:

De gradibus humilitatis et superbiae, a tract written before 1125 AD as an exposition of the rule of Benedict, with humility as its main theme.

De diligendo Deo, which appeared between 1126 and 1141 AD and treats the subject of the measure and levels of God's love.

De gratia et libero arbitrio, written before 1128 AD, in which the relationship between grace and freedom of the will is examined.

De consideratione, a tract that was drafted between 1145 and 1153 AD and was directed to Pope Eugenius III, who had been educated by Bernard as a fellow monk at Clairvaux.

Sermones per annum, 125 sermons for the church year.

Sermones super Cantica Canticorum, 86 sermons on the Song of Solomon—at least from 1:1 through 3:3—which appeared between 1135 and 1153 AD, generally esteemed as the high water mark in the history of mystical interpretation of Song of Solomon.[40]

In addition, about 500 of Bernard's letters have survived.

The spiritual influence of this "sweet-as-honey teacher" (*doctor mellifluus*)[41] extends deep and far. Not only contemporaries fell under his influence, but also, for example, the Brethren of the Common Life.[42] In Luther one finds hundreds of

38. Leclercq, *Bernhard,* 52.

39. McGinn, *Die Mystik,* 2:251. According to Evans, "Bernard was not a stylistic eclectic, but a stylist in his own right, who left his individual touch upon everything he wrote." *The Mind,* 43.

40. McGinn, *Die Mystik,* 2:253; S. M. Burgess, *The Holy Spirit: Medieval Roman Catholic and Reformation Traditions* (Peabody, 1997), 52. For an instructive consideration of Bernard's sermons on Song of Solomon, one is directed to Evans, *The Mind,* 107-31. According to Evans, Bernard found in Song of Solomon "a key to the life of faith and to the monastic life in particular" (110), and his sermons on this book constitute "a journal of his own spiritual pilgrimage" (113).

41. This honorary title indicates Bernard's position as a spiritual exegete of Scripture, who poured sweet honey out of the honeycomb and caused the Spirit to flow from the text. See T. Bell, *Bernhardus dixit: Bernardus van Clairvaux in Martin Luthers werken* (Delft, 1989), 328. According to Köpf, "Die Rezeptions- und Wirkungsgeschichte," 28: "In seinem Ehrentitel 'Doctor mellifluus' verbindet sich der Eindruck seines persönlichen Auftretens mit der Wirkung seiner Schriften."

42. See P. E. Mikkers, "Sint Bernardus en de Moderne Devotie," in *Cîteaux in de Nederlanden: Mededelingen over het Cisterciënzer leven van de 12de tot en met de 18de eeuw,* vol. 4 (Abdij Westmalle, 1953), 149-86.

quotations of Bernard.[43] Calvin makes repeated use of his writings,[44] and he was also held in high regard by puritanism[45] and Further Reformation pietism.[46] He has lifted spirits down to our own time.[47]

Now that the subject of Bernard's life, work and setting has been broadly surveyed, I direct attention to several aspects of his piety. I do so primarily on the basis of his tract *De diligendo Deo* ("On God's Love") and of his sermons on the Song of Solomon.[48] In doing so, I follow the sequence of God's love, meditation on Christ, bridal mysticism and union with God.[49] These four themes should certainly not be regarded as intending to provide a complete picture of

43. See Bell, *Bernhardus dixit*; B. Lohse, "Luther und Bernhard von Clairvaux," in *Bernhard von Clairvaux*, ed. Elm, 271-301. Lohse concludes that Luther, despite his reservations concerning Bernard's mysticism, "gerade durch die Christus-Mystik Bernhards eine nicht unbeträchtliche Hilfe erfahren [hat]." The author is for the rest of the opinion that Luther certainly appropriated from monastic theology the quest for the radical character of being a Christian, but that the answer it offered collapsed under the critique of his reformational position.

44. Cf. R. J. Mooi, *Het kerk- en dogmahistorisch element in de werken van Johannes Calvijn* (Wageningen, 1965), 320-27; D. E. Tamburello, *Union with Christ: John Calvin and the Mysticism of St. Bernard* (Louisville, 1994); A. N. S. Lane, *John Calvin: Student of the Church Fathers* (Edinburgh, 1999), 87-150. Compare idem., "Calvin's Use of Bernard of Clairvaux," in *Bernhard von Clairvaux*, ed. Elm, 303-32. Lane comes to the ultimate conclusion that Calvin "has followed the standard approach of the apologist, namely to quote what suits him and to pass over what does not," and that he "ably presents many of the more evangelical strands of Bernard's teaching." While Calvin frequently cites Bernard's sermons on the Song of Solomon, he passes over his "specifically mystical teaching."

45. C. E. Hambrick-Stowe, *The Practice of Piety: Puritan Devotional Disciplines in Seventeenth-Century New England* (Chapel Hill, 1982), 28, 36, 54. Compare G. F. Nuttall, *The Holy Spirit in Puritan Faith and Experience* (Chicago and London, 1992; reprinted from 1946), 148; G. S. Wakefield, *Puritan Devotion: Its Place in the Development of Christian Piety* (London, 1957), 89, 101-8, 158; S. Bush, Jr., *The Writings of Thomas Hooker: Spiritual Adventure in Two Worlds* (Madison and London, 1980), 199, 345 n.37; P. de Vries, *Die mij heeft liefgehad: De betekenis van de gemeenschap met Christus in de theologie van John Owen (1616-1683)* (Heerenveen, 1999), 20, 24, 330.

46. Close attention yields the observation that Bernard was not regarded as much as a medieval figure by the pietists as much as he was considered the last of the patristics (*patres*). See op 't Hof, "Rooms-katholieke doorwerking," 106. For that matter, it was the same for Calvin. See Tamburello, *Union*, 14. Compare as well G. B. Winkler, "Einleitung," *SW*, 1:23. Bernard's influence on German pietism seems to have been rather small. J. Wallmann, "Bernhard von Clairvaux und der deutsche Pietismus," in *Bernhard von Clairvaux*, ed. K. Elm, 374. At least Wallmann takes the position that strictly speaking, what Lutheran acceptance of Bernard's piety occurred, happened in seventeenth-century Lutheran orthodoxy and not in pietism.

47. J. Leclercq says, "Das erstaunliche Interesse, das Bernhard in der heutigen Forschung wieder findet, zeigt zur Genüge, daß seine Botschaft unter uns noch lebendig ist." "Bernhard von Clairvaux," *TRE*, 5:650.

48. The edition of the text of which I made use is the already cited, ten-volume *Bernhard von Clairvaux: Sämtliche Werke*, ed. G. B. Winkler (Innsbruck, 1990-). Among other works, *De diligendo Deo* appears in volume 1 (1990); the *Sermones super Cantica Canticorum* take up volumes 5 and 6 (1994). In our footnotes, these works are abbreviated as *DD* and *SC*, respectively. The numbers appearing behind them indicate the relevant paragraphs for *DD*, and the relevant sermon and paragraph for *SC*. These references are followed by the *SW* volume and page numbers. The Latin text in this edition of the collected works was reproduced photomechanically from *Sancti Bernardi Opera*, Editiones Cistercienses, vols. 1-8, ed. J. Leclercq, et al. (Rome, 1957-1977).

49. Ruh, *Geschichte der Mystik*, 1:229-75.

Bernard's theology, but they nevertheless comprise a selection that is useful for our purposes.[50] They involve components of his spirituality all four of which have left their imprint on the piety of the Further Reformation. And that is exactly my interest in this study.

God's Love

The love of God and the returning of love to God without any doubt constituted the secret of Bernard's religious experience. This pronounced attention to love was certainly tied to the cultural wrappings of twelfth-century human consciousness. The high Middle Ages are called the birth date of the individual. In this period individuality, especially in its affective and emotional dimensions, stepped into the spotlight. Humanity became freshly and strongly conscious of its emotional life and came to the discovery that it remained under-developed as long as it was impoverished with respect to love.[51] In Bernard we are dealing with a man who preeminently belongs to those who rediscovered God as Lover and Beloved.

Love (*caritas*) that does not seek self but the other he called the flawless law of the Lord (*lex Domini immaculata*). God himself lived by this basic principle. In the exalted, blessed Trinity an inexpressible unity is perfectly maintained through love.[52] It is not only a communicable attribute of God, but his very essence (*substantia divina*). What belongs to God as much as love? It is his nature to show mercy continually.[53] "For that reason it is correctly stated that love is God himself as well as God's gift; so Love bestows love."[54] The source of the love that we return to God can then be nothing other than the love that he first showed us (*Causa diligendi Deum, Deus est*).[55] Therefore, God is both the efficient cause and the ultimate cause of love (*causa efficiens et finalis*). He himself provides the occasion for it; he himself awakens the longing for it; and he himself also fulfills that yearning. "His love prepares ours, and he also rewards it. Filled with goodness, his love precedes ours."[56] According to Bernard, before anything else we must realize "in what measure, or better, how measurelessly, God deserves to be loved by us." He has first loved us. "He who is so immense has loved us so much that, though we who are so tiny and insignificant are undeserving, he loved us just as we are."[57]

---

50. A lucid analysis of Bernard's dogmatic starting points is presented by McGinn, *Die Mystik*, 2:254-76, which sequentially treats Bernard's anthropology, his soteriology and his ecclesiology.

51. M. A. Schenkl, "Bernhard und die Entdeckung der Liebe," 153-56; compare Dinzelbacher, "Die 'Bernhardinische Epoche,'" 35-36; P. Sheldrake, *Spirituality and History: Questions of Interpretation and Method* (London, 1991), 40-43.

52. *DD*, 12:35, in *SW*, 1:134.

53. *SC*, 69:6, in *SW*, 6:424. Compare *SC*, 36:6, in *SW* 5:568-69, where Bernard expresses himself in the same terms.

54. *DD*, 12:35, in *SW*, 1:134.

55. *DD*, 1:1, in *SW*, 1:74.

56. *DD*, 7:22, in *SW*, 1:110.

57. *DD*, 6:16, in *SW*, 1:100. "Prior ipse dilexit nos, tantus, et tantum, et gratis tantillos, et tales."

God's display of love is therefore strictly gracious in character and takes absolute priority.[58] God loved with undeserved love (*gratis*)—even his enemies. In free grace the Father gave his Son and the Son gave himself, the Righteous for the ungodly, the Almighty for the powerless.[59] Who could ever repay this precious and priceless love? Even if one would give all his "meager possessions" (*pulvis exiguus*) gathered by all his efforts, his returned love would be woefully inadequate. Divine majesty always precedes (*praeveniens*) these efforts in God's three-fold love: the Father in sending his Son, the Son in yielding himself, the Holy Spirit in his testimony in our hearts. "So, God loves, and he loves with his whole being (*ex se toto*), for the whole Trinity loves."[60]

The bride loved by God cannot put any stock at all in merit, then. She attributes everything to God's grace, without any restriction. It is completely impossible for grace to emerge where merit has already taken hold. Bernard regarded God's grace, therefore, not only as free, but also as abundant, complete. "Whatever you calculate on the basis of merit is lost to grace. I want nothing to do with merit by which grace is superceded. I shudder at everything that proceeds from myself (*de meo est*)."[61] In this connection the Abbot of Clairvaux forged the aphorism, "It is sufficient for merit to know that merit is insufficient."[62] To be sure, it was important for the believer to be concerned about being meritorious, but whenever he amasses merits, he must recognize them as gifts bestowed on him and must trust in God's mercy for his blessings on them.[63]

Bernard's position that we must understand two things—what we are, and what we are not in and of ourselves—breathes the same spirit. This excludes all attempts to make a name for oneself. Indeed, one ought to guard against neglecting inner gifts, but even more against attaching importance to that which is foolish. The latter occurs when we imagine that something good originates in ourselves.[64] In what follows Bernard goes a step farther when he poses the question of who, in reality, is at all able to attribute without reservation every good gift received only to God's grace. His answer is, "No one"—in their own strength or by their own free will (*liberi arbitrii*). Only believers learn this lesson. They understand how completely, also in this regard, they are dependent on Jesus and on him crucified.[65] The nature of true love for God is therefore as unpretentious as it is unselfish. To be sure, it enjoys the prospect of a rich reward, but it loves God not for the purpose of receiving a reward. Its reward is

---

58. McGinn, *Die Mystik*, 2:196.

59. *DD*, 4:13, in *SW*, 1:96.

60. *DD*, 4:13, in *SW*, 1:96.

61. *SC*, 67:10, in *SW*, 6:404. Compare ibid., 67:11.

62. *SC*, 68:6, in *SW*, 6:414. "Sufficit ad meritum scire quod non sufficient merita."

63. Ibid. Here Bernard reflects the sentiments of Augustine, who in his *De gratia et libero arbitrio* (Migne, *PL*, 44:891) explains: "Si ergo dei dona sunt bona merita tua, non deus coronat merita tua tamquam merita tua, sed tamquam dona sua." ("If, therefore, your good works are gifts of God, then God crowns your works not as your works, but as his gifts.") On Bernard's views on grace and merit, compare Evans, *Bernard*, 93-94.

64. *DD*, 2:4, in *SW*, 1:80.

65. *DD*, 2:6-7, in *SW*, 1:80.

the Beloved himself. Love loves. And if the loving soul looks for something more, it is certainly the case that it does not love God.[66] Undivided love is due him. God is always the true life of the soul (*vera animae vita Deus est*).[67]

Meditation on Christ

In the expression of love, estrangement from God gives way to the presence of God. In this exchange one returns to his Origin and his Savior, amazed by the mystery of the salvation that God has given him in Christ. Here we are definitely dealing with Christ the Crucified One, at least with the Christ who emptied himself and became flesh for the purpose of bearing our human miseries in his incarnate role. Reflection on Christ in his humiliation unmistakably forms the heart of Bernard's theology and spirituality.

This attention to the suffering Savior marks a new direction for the medieval mind set. Until the twelfth century people generally thought in strictly hierarchical categories, socially as well as religiously. This meant that in religious experience Christ was seen not as much as our Brother, but much rather as our strict Judge.[68] While early medieval Benedictine spirituality focused in large measure on the transcendent qualities of God the Son, in Bernard's time meditation was directed increasingly toward the Son of God who became flesh. In the history of spirituality, therefore, a form of devotion made its appearance that was especially typical of the later Middle Ages and that directed its attention to the life and sufferings of Jesus on earth, with all the human qualities uniquely associated with him in his proximity to us. This is a paradigm shift that might well be captured with the concept of "humanization."[69] The representation of a triumphant, divine King changed to one of a suffering, dying human being.

Ulrich Köpf does not hesitate to speak in this connection of a profound reorientation in the history of spirituality. Generalizing somewhat, he sees in the Christology of the early church a figure in whom Christ's sufferings lurked in the shadows of his glory.[70] The cross was understood as a sign of dominion over the cosmic powers. This was a long-lasting tendency. In Bernard, however, one encounters a completely different vision. For him the cross is not primarily a sign of miraculous power and victory, but a sign of suffering, pain and death that

---

66. *DD*, 7:17, in *SW*, 1:104. In *DD* Bernard distinguishes four levels in love generally: love of self, love of God for the sake of self, love for the sake of God and love of self purely on account of God's will. Compare Ruh, *Geschichte der Mystik*, 1:230-32; McGinn, *Die Mystik* 2:299-302; Schenkl, "Bernhard und die Entdeckung der Liebe," 164-70.

67. *Sermones per annum* (in "Psalmum 'Qui habitat' Sermo 10"), in *SW*, 7:624.

68. Dinzelbacher, "Die 'Bernhardinische Epoche,'" 11-12.

69. Ibid., 22-23: "Wenn er [Bernard] und so viele andere spirituelle Autoren sich damit jetzt auf die Menschheit Christi konzentrieren statt auf seine Gottesnatur oder die Gottheit an sich wie im Frühmittelalter, so ist dies ein zentrales Indiz für eine mentalitätsgeschichtliche Veränderung, die mit dem Begriff 'Humanisierung' angesprochen werden kann. Es geht um den *Menschen* Jesus, wie er auf Erden gelebt hat. Ein analoger Wandel vollzieht sich in der Kunst. . . . Christus etwa wird als Leidender unter der Dornenkrone, nicht mehr als Gott mit der Königskrone am Kreuz gegeben." Dinzelbacher develops the same idea in "Bernhards Mystik," 189-90.

70. For the alternative, however, consult A. van de Beek, *Jezus Kurios: Christologie als hart van de theologie* (Kampen, 1998), 30 and following.

gives rise to humbling and consoling meditation. Paul's theology of the cross made a deep impression on Bernard's writings. He cites the expression in Galatians seventeen times: "Far be it for me to glory in anything else than in the cross of our Lord Jesus Christ." In fifteen places one finds 1 Corinthians 2:2 invoked, "I have resolved to know nothing else among you than Jesus Christ and him crucified."[71]

In Bernard's mysticism, as we will show shortly, we are dealing with communion with the Logos, the eternal and glorified Son of God, but in practice his meditation revolves around Jesus' humanity. Behind this for him lies the Pauline notion that the natural, the creaturely, precedes the spiritual. People are bound by this sequence. But even God in his gracious accommodation restricts himself to this sequence and wants to reveal himself in the sphere of the creaturely. "Because his disciples were flesh and God is a spirit, and because flesh and spirit are in tension with one another, God adapted himself to them through the shadow of his body so that in the appearance of this concrete man they could consider God's Word in the flesh, the sun among the clouds."[72] The invisible God revealed himself in the child lying in a manger and resting on the lap of a virgin, and in the man hanging on a wooden cross.[73]

Jean Leclercq makes the remarkable observation that in his extensive portrayal of Christ's saving work Bernard not only calls attention to the exemplary nature of Christ's suffering, but that he powerfully emphasizes its actual saving significance. Christ's life, his teaching and his death all contribute to our salvation. He is the Way—the way in which God descends to us and the way in which we return to him. As Mediator he reconciles us to God, and as our example he shows us how we should follow him. In this connection Bernard is not interested in precise Christological theories, but he is much more interested in the practical benefit for the believer. Leclercq talks about a "practical Chrisotology" in which the "for our benefit" is dominant. For our benefit Christ assumed solidarity with our earthly, limited existence. For our benefit he ascended to heaven so that we might participate in his glory.[74]

Ulrich Köpf also draws attention to this soteriological tendency articulated in Bernard's writings. Christ came into the world for our benefit (*propter nos*); for us (*pro nobis*), through circumcision, he shed his blood; he was baptized in order to cleanse us; for our sakes he was willing to become poor and small, weak and lowly; for our benefit he allowed his side to be pierced. He completed his entire life of suffering for our benefit. In this interpretation Köpf sees the reformational *pro me* "bereits vollkommen ausgebildet."[75] It is indeed remarkable how often

---

71. Köpf, "Schriftauslegung als Ort der Kreuzestheologie Bernhards von Clairvaux," in *Bernhard von Clairvaux*, ed. Bauer and Fuchs, 196-98; idem, "Die Rezeptions- und Wirkungsgeschichte," 42 following.

72. *Ascensio Domini*, 3:3. Cited from Dinzelbacher, "Bernhards Mystik," in *Bernhard von Clairvaux*, ed. Bauer and Fuchs, 189.

73. Cited in McGinn, *Die Mystik*, 2:269.

74. Leclercq, *Bernhard*, 138-39.

75. Köpf, "Schriftauslegung," in *Bernhard von Clairvaux*, 194-95. He supports the analogy with thoroughly reliable Luther quotations. Compare his "Die Rezeptions- und Wirkungsgeschichte," 40-41.

and emphatically Bernard's meditations on suffering are imbedded in the context of application. In order to illustrate that fact, I produce several passages. With transparent clarity Bernard declares that the Savior humbled himself "for you, O man!" "He did not maintain being Lord in preference to becoming a slave, being rich to becoming poor, being the Word to becoming flesh, being the Son of God to becoming a human child. Remember that just as surely as you were created out of nothing, you are not saved without reason. In six days God created all that exists, including you. Just as surely, for more than thirty years he labored in the midst of this world for your benefit (*salutem tuam*). O, how much he has taken on himself, how much he has suffered! Has he not shouldered the impediments of the flesh and the attacks of the enemy through the shame of the cross and made full satisfaction by trembling in the face of death? How necessary (*necessarie*) all this was."[76] This necessity is undoubtedly soteriological in nature.

An impressive passage is found in the 67th sermon on the Song of Solomon. In it Bernard explains that in full confidence he appropriates to himself (*usurpo mihi*) from the inner life of the Lord that which is lacking in himself. He is able to do so because Christ's heart overflows with compassion (*misericordia*). "They nailed his hands and his feet and pierced his side with a spear. By means of these wounds ripped into his flesh, I am able to draw honey from the rock and oil from the hardest boulder. This is to taste and to see how sweet the Lord is (*gustare et videre quoniam suavis est Dominus*). The nail proclaims, the wound announces that in Christ God has truly reconciled the world to himself. . . What was hidden in the heart of God (*arcanum cordis*) lies exposed through the rending of his (Jesus') body; the great secret of his gentleness (*pietatis sacramentum*) has been disclosed; the bowels of our God's mercy by which he has sought us as a light shining from on high have been laid open. Through these wounds has his heart not been opened? Greater mercy has no man shown than he who abandoned his life to judgment and condemnation. My merit is nothing less than the mercy of the Lord (*Meum proinde meritum miseratio Domini*)."[77] Bernard did not hesitate to add, "What does it matter, then, that I am conscious of many transgressions?" God's grace is superior. And my own righteousness?—Christ alone is our righteousness! All this we owe to Jesus' wounds. "What abundant sweetness is contained in them, what fullness of grace, what perfection of virtues!"[78] In making this connection Bernard describes total devotion and a constant application (*tota devotio et iugis meditatio*) of Christ's wounds.[79] What is as effective (*efficax*) for healing the conscience as dedicated meditation on the wounds of Christ?[80]

---

76. *SC*, 11:7, in *SW*, 5:166.

77. *SC*, 61:4-5, in *SW*, 6:314-15. This last sentence Voetius quoted on his deathbed. See A. C. Duker, *Gisbertus Voetius* (Leiden, 1897-1915), 3:344-45; J. van Oort, "Augustinus, Voetius und die Anfänge der Utrechter Universität," in *Signum pietatis: Festgabe für C. P. Mayer OSA zum 60. Geburtstag*; ed. A. Zumkeller (Würzburg, 1989), 566.

78. *SC*, 61:5, in *SW*, 6:316.

79. *SC*, 61:7, in *SW*, 6:318.

80. *SC*, 62:7, in *SW*, 6:332.

That the divine Bridegroom became like us in all things was a source of amazement and adoration for Bernard. The Word became flesh. He stood behind the wall and watched through the windows, spying through the lattice (Song of Solomon 2:9). In Bernard's judgment these window lattices were meant to convey Christ's human emotions (*affectus*), through which he gained experience with every human need. He took our afflictions upon himself and he bore our sorrows. "Human feelings and physical emotions served as opportunities— windows—for him to come to understand experientially (*experimento*) human miseries (*miserias hominum*). These he certainly understood previously, but then in another way." What he first understood in his divinity—and for Bernard that meant spiritually and in no way on the basis of bitter, human experience—he came to discover in the body, in the reality of his impoverished humanity. Through his sufferings he learned obedience. In all things he was tempted as we are. By experience he felt all our weakness and vulnerability.[81] And the more the bride considers in her soul this emptying, the sweeter it tastes to her (*dulcius sapit*). For that reason she exalts Christ's grace all the more, gives his mercy preeminence and admires his self-effacing goodness (*dignatio*).[82] The bride does not intend to short-change his praise, therefore, whenever she praises his lovingkindness encountered through her consideration of his weakness (*consideratione infirmitatis*). For in this miserable condition he is preeminently the most beautiful of all people.[83]

In his famous sermon on Song of Solomon 1:13, where the bride compares the Beloved to a sachet of myrrh that nestles between her breasts during the night, Bernard explains that since his conversion, thus since he entered the monastery, he too has been concerned to put his confidence not in an abundance of meritorious works, which he lacks, but to tie (*colligare*) it to this sachet of myrrh that he desires will repose (*collocare*) in his inner being. What he means by this, he explains: "I associate it with all the fears and bitter sufferings of my Lord. To begin with, with the needs of his childhood, thereafter with the difficulties that he encountered in his preaching, with the weariness of his many travels, with the sleeplessness of his prayer life, with the temptations experienced while fasting, with his tears of compassion, with the cunningness encountered in his public teaching, and finally with the dangers presented by false brothers, the indignities, the spitting, the blows, the scorn, the reproofs, the nails and all such things. . . . By this I do not intend to overlook the myrrh that was given him to drink on the cross, nor that with which he was anointed at his burial. In the former he took the bitterness of my sins on himself, in the latter he pointed to my future immortality."

Bernard closes the passage with the following assurance: "Reflection on these matters I have characterized as wisdom (*sapientia*). Through it I have established the sufficiency of righteousness, the fullness of knowledge (*scientia*), the treasures of my salvation and the abundance of merit. Through it I am

---

81. *SC*, 65:1, in *SW*, 6:242-443.
82. On the significance of the medieval Latin word "*dignatio*," see E. Habel and F. Gröbel, *Mittellateinisches Glossar* (Paderborn and Zurich, 1989), s.v.
83. *SC*, 48:4, in *SW*, 6:152.

sometimes handed the cup of saving bitterness and through it on other occasions once again the soothing salve of sweet consolation (*suavis unctio consolationis*)." This saving mystery of the suffering Christ was for him a constant refrain, for it filled his heart. "As you know, I speak much about this. As God knows, it is always on my heart. As is obvious, this is my most trusted literary emphasis."[84] Then follows the confession that might be called the motto of Bernard's life: "This is the highly exalted philosophy of my spiritual life: to know Jesus, and him crucified ("Haec mea subtilior, interior philosophia, scire Iesum, et hunc crucifixum").[85]

Bernard knew, therefore, that all his hope and security were anchored in the crucified Christ. One could describe his devotion to Christ as a living, experiential commentary on the Pauline expression that Christ has become for us "God's wisdom, righteousness, sanctification and redemption, so that it is rightly written, 'He that glories, let him glory in the Lord'" (1 Corinthians 1:31). Yet, we would not entirely do Bernard justice if we did not add one more to this four-fold list of Christ's saving gifts, namely love. Peter Dinzelbacher is certainly correct when he names Paul as "Bernard's wesenverwandten Lieblingsautor aus der Heilingen Schrift."[86] In my opinion, John, the apostle of love, did not take a back seat to Paul in Bernard's judgment. For Bernard there would have been no talk of a tension between the two apostles in this regard. This much is certainly clear, that according to him faith-life culminates in the experience of God's love, which is for him met in part in Christ. The point of Bernard's meditation is directed particularly toward that end. This comes to light continuously in his writings. This is the case in a citation from *De diligendo Deo*. After Bernard has observed that one feels more love to the degree that one knows that one is loved to an even greater degree, he asserts that for that reason the church as bride (*ecclesia*) exclaims, "I am sick with love" (Song of Solomon 2:5). How does a person contract this "sickness?" Bernard explains, "She sees King Solomon with the crown with which his mother crowned him. She sees, namely, the Only Begotten of the Father as he bears his cross. She sees the Lord of majesty struck and spit upon. She sees the Creator of life and glory riveted to the cross, pierced with a spear, drenched with indignities, and she sees how he finally lays down his precious life for his friends." Then follows a climax of an explicitly existential nature: "She sees this, and the sword of love penetrates her own soul all the more deeply, so that she testifies, 'Strengthen me with flowers, refresh me with apples, for I am sick with love.'"[87] Lovesickness is an inevitable consequence of meditating on Jesus' *via dolorosa*.

The scope of Bernard's interaction with Scripture is shaped, therefore, by the experience of God's love in Christ. This does not mean that his sermons and

---

84. These three sentences contain a well conceived, undoubtedly intentional distinction: talking about Christ he does *often*; guarding him in his heart he does *always*; writing about him he does *continuously*. The first is known to his *brothers*; the second, to *God*; and the third to *anyone* who reads him.

85. *SC*, 43:3-4, in *SW*, 6:98-99.

86. Dinzelbacher, "Bernhards Mystik," 188.

87. *DD*, 3:7, in *SW*, 1:84. Bernard employs the Vulgate translation. On this subject, compare J. B. Bauer, "Bernards Bibeltext," in *SW*, 5:48-50.

other writings broach no other themes. The opposite is the case. The ethical dimension of discipleship in the practice of everyday, particularly monastic, life receives full treatment, for example. Above all, he does not sidetrack doctrinally complicated or controversial points and he can be sharply polemical. But Bernard's heart lived for the loving exchange between the Bridegroom and his bride. The name of Jesus was not only his light, but also his nourishment. All food for the soul is dry unless oil is added. It is tasteless if it is not seasoned with salt. When a person speaks about a subject, it has no flavor as long as the name of Jesus is not introduced into the conversation. "Jesus is honey to the mouth, a song to the ear, jubilation to the heart" ("Iesus mel in ore, in aure melos, in corde iubilus").[88] This affection for Jesus produces an interaction with Scripture that has its own, unique character.

That Bernard employs the allegorical method in his own biblical exposition is obvious. Given his education in the patristics and his own first love, as well as the context of the prevailing hermeneutics of the time, this is completely understandable. Characteristic of this method of interpretation is that the meaning of the biblical text is as completely reviewed as possible. To begin with, in that regard, one distinguishes between the literal-historical meaning and the spiritual or applied sense.[89] The latter does not depend on the former, but rather arises from what emerges. The main division, then, is that of *sensus litteralis* (*historicus*) and *sensus spiritualis*. Furthermore, the spiritual meaning is assigned three levels: an allegorical sense focused on the life of faith, a moral or tropological sense focused on conduct, and an anagogic sense related to future glory. In this triad the threefold Pauline sequence of faith, love, and hope was seen as being reflected.[90] Indeed, Bernard is content to function with three levels of meaning: the historical, the moral and the hidden or mystical sense.[91] What is decisive for him is that one always looks for the spiritual meaning in the literal.

---

88. *SC*, 15:6, in *SW*, 2:220. Using a rather free translation, Calvin incorporates this fragment into an important section of his Christology. See *Institutes*, II.16.i, in *OS*, 3:482-83. Voetius cites the same passage, possibly following Calvin, in his inaugural address, *De pietate cum scientia coniungenda* (1634). See Gisbertus Voetius, *Inaugurele rede over Godzaligheid te verbinden met de wetenschap*. The Latin text was recently republished with a Dutch translation, introduction and commentary by A. de Groot (Kampen, 1978), 70.

89. The distinction that the English New Testament scholar I. H. Marshall makes between "meaning" and "significance" is illuminating. The first concerns the exegetical question concerning what is written; the second, the question concerning the sense of the text for today's reader or listener. See A. Noordegraaf, *Leesbril of toverstaf: Over het verstaan en vertolken van de Bijbel* (Kampen, 1991), 54.

90. On the four levels of biblical meaning—the so-called "*quadriga*" (*sensus litteralis, allegoricus, moralis, anagogicus*), see H. de Lubac, *Medieval Exegesis*, vol. 1, *The Four Senses of Scripture* (Edinburgh, 1998), translated from *Exégèse médiévale*, vol. 1, *Les quatre sens de l'écriture* (1959); H. W. de Knijff, *Sleutel en slot* (Kampen, 1980), 28-38; R. A. Muller, *Dictionary of Latin and Greek Theological Terms, Drawn Principally from Protestant Scholastic Theology* (Grand Rapids, 1985), s.v. "*Quadriga*"; A. E. McGrath, *The Intellectual Origins of the European Reformation* (Oxford, England, and Cambridge, MA, 1987), 152-54; A. C. Thiselton, *New Horizons in Hermeneutics* (London, 1992), 179-94; Muller, *Holy Scripture*, 487-99; Köpf, "Schriftauslegung," 201-2.

91. *SC*, 23:3, in *SW*, 5:328. Compare Köpf, "Schriftauslegung," 202.

That this treasure hunt will not be in vain he sees as guaranteed by the illumination of the Holy Spirit himself. But, typically for Bernard, he knows that this work of the Spirit is totally grounded in the death of Christ on the cross. By it the curtain covering the dead letter is torn open so that now the *ecclesia* following the leading of the Spirit has the freedom confidently to enter the holy place of the deep, spiritual sense of Scripture.[92] This pneumatological-Christological conviction lays the foundation for his allegorical exposition of the Song of Solomon in particular, a book of the Bible that today is seldom if ever preached, let alone allegorically, but that in medieval monastic theology assumed a position of eminence. For eighteen years, although with extended interruptions, Bernard devoted 86 sermons to it—sermons that he revised for publication with great care.[93]

This allegorical interpretation of Scripture constituted the matrix for Bernard's meditative practice. In addition, the designation "allegorical" does not say everything, certainly not when one disqualifies this way of reading the Bible as the same as arbitrary *eisegesis*. While it cannot be denied that Bernard's allegorical approach sometimes yielded tortured, far-fetched interpretations, it must be said that for the most part his understanding of Scripture shows a constructive, directly personal relevance. It seems that for him exposure to Scripture yielded something more than explaining the text. The key to his approach lies rather in the opposite direction, namely in the amazing phenomenon that the expositor himself is exegeted by the text. The reason for this is that the Scriptures themselves are full of personal experiences with God. The reader and expositor come to understand that their own encounters with God, including being corrected and making spiritual progress, are recognizable in the text.[94] In this context Scripture does not function as the object of the interpreter's cool, workman-like, rational exposition, but rather as the point of encounter, where two subjects come together. The one subject is God in Christ, who discloses himself in Scripture through the work of the Spirit, and the other subject is the listener, who knows that in this encounter he is both known and loved.

Given this state of affairs, it is not surprising that for Bernard the line between exposition and meditation is fluid. Because the main feature of his engagement with Scripture has the character of encounter, his exposition has a strongly meditative quality and his meditations in turn are consistently vitalized by his understanding of Scripture. This weaving together of exposition and reflection produces a tapestry of spiritual encounters. We have already seen that Bernard primarily has his eye on the Word become flesh. The Savior drew closest to us in his love while on earth. The cross best expresses the depth of that love and is therefore the focal point of Bernard's meditation. This does not mean, however, that for him Christ's suffering is limited to his death on the cross. Rather, he considers all of Christ's earthly life to be suffering. He does so from

---

92. *SC*, 14:4, in *SW*, 5:204.
93. On the provenance of the Song of Solomon, consult Ruh, *Geschichte der Mystik*, 1:251-52; U. Köpf, "Einleitung," in *SW*, 5:27-32.
94. Compare Köpf, "Schriftauslegung," 204-8.

the basic idea that the incarnation as such consists of an emptying.[95] The pivot of salvation history is not the cross or death of Christ, but the humiliation involved in the Son of God becoming human. The entire life of Jesus on earth proceeding from that event provided Bernard with material for reflection and constituted the source of the love of Christ for him.

But the longings of Bernard's love had an even higher goal for him. To call to mind the suffering Christ, the *memoria passionis*, was in Bernard's view still only the lower rung on the ladder of loving God. He called this level physical love (*amor carnalis*). It ought to be immediately noted in this connection that by the adjective "physical" he did not intend in the least a negative connotation. What he wanted to convey by it is that this level of meditation dealt with the earthly Christ in the flesh, not the heavenly One.[96] That he regarded this phase of reflection as beneficial and essential is solidly established. But this *memoria* is of a relatively lower order in this sense, that it is the indispensable preparation for the level of *praesentia*, the endlessly contemplated spiritual presence of the heavenly Word, the Logos. To be sure, the *amor carnalis* also has its mystical highlights, but such experiences are, as we will learn shortly, not only occasional and short-lived in this fractured and impoverished state of affairs, but also partial and proleptic. They are, therefore, incomplete and temporary, and they reach out for that which is special and reserved for the eschaton.

In the coming glory the level of physical love will be superceded. In the present order it is at most just elevated and completed when it flows into spiritual love. But it is never overtaken, let alone eliminated.[97] The high voltage of the spiritual-mystical experience of God's love is short-lived for people of flesh and blood. They are not yet grounded in it. They need its energy. And they get this by descending in the *amor carnalis* to reflection on Christ's sufferings. Where this is lacking, love cools.[98] On the other hand, where it is practiced, the soul feels itself led in its yearning for complete satisfaction toward *amor spiritualis* for the heavenly Christ. No other admittance to contemplation of the glorified Christ is available than by way of *memoria passionis*. "The believing soul (*fidelis anima*) filled with longing yearns for his presence (*praesentia*) but also finds sweet peace in the contemplation (*memoria*) of his sufferings. And until he or she is in a position to contemplate the unobscured face of God's glory, they glory in the shame of the cross."[99]

So, people who love God make their way on earth by reflecting on what Christ once became for them and in longing for what he will always be for them, by moving from *memoria* toward *praesentia*. But Bernard knows, as already suggested incidentally, a mystical experience in which the "not yet" of life here

---

95. Ruh, *Geschichte der Mystik*, 1:235 and 244-45.

96. Boot, *De allegorische uitlegging*, 53 and following; especially, McGinn, *Die Mystik*, 2:270-71.

97. E. Gilson, *La théologie mystique de Saint Bernard* (Paris, 1934), 103: "La dépasser n'est pas la détruire, mais la conserver en la complétant par une autre."

98. Ibid., 104: "Il faut que la pensée se détende, et elle le fait en redescendant vers l'amour charnel du Christ. Ce recours à la méditation de la passion doit même être fréquent, si l'on ne veut pas que l'amour de Dieu tiédesse."

99. *DD*, 4:12, in *SW*, 1:94. Compare Ruh, *Geschichte der Mystik*, 1:238.

below is overwhelmed by the "already" of what lies ahead. How he gives expression to this experience will receive our attention in the section that follows.

Bridal Mysticism

Bernard's meditation on Christ tended toward mystical experience. It not only tended toward it, but it flowed over into it. While the line between the one and the other is not very sharply demarcated in my estimation, it seems to me, in agreement with scholars like I. Boot and K. Ruh, to be plausible to make some distinction between them. Ruh distinguishes between meditative Christ mysticism and bridal mysticism—also called nuptial mysticism—and he notes that the first is connected with love for the earthly Logos become flesh (*amor carnalis*), while bridal mysticism experiences loving communion with the glorified, heavenly Logos (*amor spiritualis*).[100] Boot underscores the preparatory character of *amor carnalis* and draws attention to the fact that in *amor spiritualis* Christ is in a real sense first called the Bridegroom (*Sponsus*).[101]

Indeed, this distinction has a repeated basis in Bernard's writings. This is especially the case in his famous passages in the sermons on Song of Solomon 1:2 (in the words of the Vulgate: "He kisses me on the mouth"), in which the exchange between the Bridegroom and the bride is depicted as a mounting emotion on the bride's part.[102] Stage-wise, she is led to the spiritual kiss (*spirituale osculum*) on Christ's mouth, which Bernard calls the "hidden manna" (*manna absconditum*) of Revelation 2:17.[103] This kiss on the mouth is preceded by two other kinds of kisses, however. The soul desiring communion with Christ will not rashly rise to the mouth of the exalted Bridegroom, but quivering like the publican and shyly, with eyes looking down, will first throw herself at his feet. This kiss on the feet Bernard understands as penitence (*poenitentia*). This is followed by a kiss on Christ's hand, which Bernard associates with the self-control (*continentia*) of actual conversion.[104] Both levels still express love for the incarnate Word. The highest level, however, relates to the glorified Logos.

---

100. Ruh, *Geschichte der Mystik*, 1:267.

101. Boot, *De allegorische uitlegging*, 58-60.

102. The question of who is to be identified as the bride (*sponsa*) receives somewhat varied answers. According to Boot, it is in principle the church, but in practice it is the individual soul. Ibid., 68. M. Verduin maintains that it is "both the individual soul as well as the church." See his *Canticum Canticorum: Het Lied der liederen, Een onderzoek naar de betekenis, de functie en de invloed van de bronnen van de Kanttekeningen bij het Hooglied in de Statenbijbel van 1637* (Utrecht, 1992), 218. Dinzelbacher, "Die 'Bernhardinische Epoche,'" 39, and Schenkl, "Bernhard und die Entdeckung der Liebe," 152, are of the opinion that the emphasis should be placed on the individual. Dinzelbacher expresses himself more carefully in his "Anmerkungen," in *DD*, in *SW*, 1:148, where he—like Verduin—speaks of "both . . . and." McGinn, in *Die Mystik*, 2:272, concludes that the ecclesiastical perspective constitutes the presupposition for the personal. Bernard himself seems not to make an issue of the matter. In *Sermones per annum* he writes that we all together are the bride and that the soul of each believer individually is regarded as the bride. See "Post Octavam Epiphaniae Sermo 2," in *SW*, 7:376.

103. *SC*, 3:1, in *SW*, 5:76. For other ways in which Bernard describes this ascent, see McGinn, *Die Mystik*, 2:280-83.

104. *SC*, 3:2-5, in *SW*, 5:76-82. Boot, *De allegorische uitlegging*, 58-59.

Whenever one has first implored for forgiveness at his feet and then has reached for his hand extended to those staggering toward holiness, and when through much prayer and many tears one has received both, then one might perhaps venture to lift one's head to the mouth of his glory—"I say this with fear and trembling"—not just to gaze on him, but also to kiss him ("non solum speculandum, sed etiam osculandum"). By clinging to him (*adhaerere*) in this holy kiss, the bride becomes one spirit (*unus spiritus*) with him as he stoops down.[105] In this way union is achieved between two completely dissimilar parties: an earthly being and the heavenly Christ.

That this ascent of the bride is due purely to the gracious condescension of the Bridegroom himself is apparent not only from Bernard's formulations, but also from the subtle way in which he wants to understand "the kiss on the mouth." When we review his convictions about this, it becomes clear immediately that the heavenly Logos is the Glorified One, to be sure, but that he still is definitely none other than the Logos become flesh, the Mediator between God and humanity. Bernard is impressed that the bride does not long to be kissed by his mouth, but to be kissed by *the kiss* of his mouth. What is the difference? Bernard distinguishes three components: the mouth that kisses, which is the divine Word, the Logos; the mouth that is kissed, which is the human flesh that he has assumed; and the kiss that unites them both, that is, the Mediator between the divine and the human, the Man Jesus Christ. In his incarnation the Logos forever united the divine nature with human nature and became our peace. And so, as the Incarnate One, the Logos is the kiss of God.[106]

The meaning of this interpretation is not unimportant. For it allows us to see that the mystical union, however immediate and intimate it is represented in Bernard's consideration, nevertheless implies positively no unmediated union with God, but much rather is achieved through the Logos, who is the Mediator. The bride is kissed by the admittedly glorified Logos, but he is nevertheless tied to his limited human nature. The heavenly Logos never undoes his incarnation, but as the Glorified One he remains the Incarnate One. In that capacity he kisses the soul that thirsts for him.[107]

If one inquires about the spiritual content of this mystical experience, then Bernard seems to describe it as being overwhelmed by the Holy Spirit ("non est aliud nisi infundi Spiritu Sancto"), who is sent by Christ and who in turn reveals both the Father and the Son.[108] Briefly stated, the kiss is the Holy Spirit, who on the one hand is poured out by the Son and on the other hand also reveals the Son and in him, the Father. A little further Bernard interprets this interaction of Christ

---

105. *SC*, 3:5, in *SW*, 5:82.

106. *SC*, 2:3, in *SW*, 5:66. Compare *SC*, 2:7, in *SW*, 5:72: "Osculum, id est incarnandi Verbi mysterium." By employing this motif, Bernard stands in an ancient tradition. It emerged already with Gregory the Great (d. 604). See Verduin, *Canticum Canticorum*, 149, and D. Turner, *Eros and Allegory: Medieval Exegesis of the Song of Salomo* (Kalamazoo, 1995), 119.

107. Gilson, *La théologie mystique*, 132-34.

108. *SC*, 8:2-3, in *SW*, 5:122. Schenkl, "Bernhard und die Entdeckung der Liebe," 170; Dinzelbacher, "Bernhards Mystik," 184. The kiss as being filled with the Spirit is a tradition that also has a long history. It appears already in Hippolytus of Rome (d. 235). See Verduin, *Canticum Canticorum*, 66.

and the Spirit as simultaneous: through the gift of the Spirit Christ reveals himself, and through the revelation of himself he imparts the Holy Spirit ("dando revelat, et revelando dat"). This is a revelation that not only enlightens us with knowledge, but also inflames us with love.[109]

However involved the soul of the bride is in these intimate events, their occurrence is not the result of cooperation but of unilateral grace. In them the soul is not productive, but receptive. It is also fully aware of this fact. Bernard regards this gracious encounter as impossible, then, without humble self-knowledge. As we already have seen, humble self-knowledge is the condition for and the non-negotiable other side of knowing God.[110] Bernard understood that he was heir to a long tradition with this interweaving of knowledge of God and knowledge of self. For it he was indebted, namely, to Ambrose and to Augustine.[111] Within this correlation Bernard generally accorded priority to self-knowledge. The spiritual house could only stand firm on the solid foundation of humility.[112] He even allowed the formulation that un-coerced humility justifies and that it merits the grace of God's strengthening and glorifying work.[113] Precisely in the same context the idea also emerges that the humility of self-knowledge indeed precedes the saving knowledge of God, although not God's efforts. The origin of humility lies with God, not with people. He is always the one who humbles human beings by means of trials.[114] Above all, humility emerges clearly in the searchlight of God's truth.[115] If God rewards humility, he is simply blessing the fruit of his own effort.

Authentic humility, therefore, is the best fruit of grace. But above everything else, this posture depicts grace. The gracious love of the Bridegroom is more strikingly portrayed against the background of humility. We are dealing here with an entirely dark background. "Whenever the soul perceives itself in the clear light of truth, it will consider itself as belonging to the realm of the unlikely and will sigh under the weight of its misery." The truth of revelation exposes the nakedness of the human debacle as not being conformed to God. And in this disclosure, who would not be humbled in genuine self-knowledge ("in vera cognitione sui")? One sees oneself laden with sins, blind, deformed, weakened, entangled in many errors, vulnerable to a thousand dangers, trembling with a thousand fears and inclined to wickedness and incapable of virtue.[116] This humility (*humilitas*) of self-knowledge Bernard calls the mother of salvation

---

109. *SC*, 8:5, in *SW*, 5:124. On this passage, see Burgess, *The Holy Spirit*, 55.

110. Köpf, "Monastische und scholastische Theologie," 122.

111. Gilson, *La théologie mystique*, 92.

112. *SC*, 36:5, in *SW*, 5:568. Compare E. Kleineidam, "Ursprung und Gegenstand der Theologie bei Bernhard von Clairvaux und Martin Luther," *Dienst der Vermittlung* (Festschrift Priesterseminar Erfurt), ed. W. Ernst, K. Feiereis and F. Hoffmann (Leipzig, 1977), 222-35.

113. *SC*, 34:1-3, in *SW*, 5:538-42.

114. *SC*, 34:1, in *SW*, 5:540.

115. *SC*, 36:5, in *SW*, 5:568.

116. Ibid. The analogy between the last sentence and the formulation in the Heidelberg Catechism, Lord's Day 3, Question and Answer 8, is striking.

(*mater salutis*).[117] It smoothes the way to the amazement produced by knowledge of God.

The bride cannot glory, then, in her external beauty. Her beauty is entirely of an inner nature, not something to display ostentatiously, but a gift that by contrast lies hidden in the soul beneath external appearance. In this hiddenness the Abbot of Clairvaux saw conformity (*similitudo*) to Christ. Whenever the bride declares concerning herself that she is "black but lovely" (Song of Solomon 1:5), she is obviously not ashamed of the color of her skin. The reason for this is that she knows that also the Bridegroom wants to share in this "blackness" (*nigredo*) by means of the self-emptying of his becoming human. "Is there greater glory than to be like (*similari*) him?" For Bernard this meant nothing less than to bear the reproach of Christ, the Man of Sorrows, who was wounded for our transgressions and was made sin on our behalf. "In himself he is beautiful; black for your sake."[118] Likewise, the bride is weak and black externally, but inwardly she is strong and beautiful, so that Christ's strength is made manifest in her weakness.[119] Her virtues are not her achievements, but reflections of the Eternal One.[120]

In the humility and concealed virtues motivated by a comparison with Christ, the condition is laid for what Bernard considers the provisional fulfillment of loving fellowship with the Bridegroom. He describes this as a marriage. For this to occur, however, not only is similarity (*similitudo*) with the Word become flesh necessary, but also conformity (*conformitas*) with the heavenly Logos. Conversion (*conversio*) does not produce this state of affairs. This approach to the Logos is a deeply moving event, particularly in light of the radical nature of turning away. Humanity, created in the image and likeness of God, always turns away from God and bows, crooked and warped, to self. From an "upright soul" (*anima recta*) one becomes a "warped soul" (*anima curva*).[121] Through this warping process one loses one's God-likeness and simultaneously one's own self-likeness, that is to say, the state for which one was originally created.[122] On the strength of the grandeur of their origin, people maintain the image (*in imagine*) of God throughout their lives, it is true. But as far as their uprightness (*rectitudo*) is concerned, they make their way limping through life, estranged from God's image (*deturbatur ab imagine*).[123] After the fall into sin, the human soul is constantly entangled in vices, vulnerable to temptations, imprisoned in exile (*in exsilio captiva*), incarcerated in the body, compromised by filth, anxious in its cares, driven by heresies, in short, an alien in enemy territory and living as though dead.[124] Such passages are not an exception in Bernard's works. McGinn

---

117. *SC*, 37:1, in *SW*, 5:572. McGinn, *Die Mystik*, 2:265-66.
118. *SC*, 25:8-9, in *SW*, 5:382-83.
119. *SC*, 25:7, in *SW*, 5:382.
120. Ruh, *Geschichte der Mystik*, 1:261-62.
121. *SC*, 80:3, in *SW*, 6:572.
122. *SC*, 82:4, in *SW*, 6:604.
123. *SC*, 80:4, in *SW*, 6:604.
124. *SC*, 83:1, in *SW*, 6:610.

does not even hesitate to assert, "Es findet sich kaum eine Seite ohne pessimistische, oft wehmütige Auslassungen uber die sündige Menschheit."[125]

However damned and desperate (*damnata et desperata*) a person might be, however, the confidence is still given him on the basis of his exalted origin (*de origine*) that he may return to fellowship with God.[126] To the extent that she has maintained her elevated status as God's image-bearer, she retains the possibility (*capax*), despite her perverted nature, of eternal blessing.[127] This return of the soul (*animae reditus*) represents nothing less than its conversion to the Word (*conversio ad Verbum*), by whom she is transformed and with whom she is conformed.[128] Conformed in what way? In love![129] This conformity (*conformitas*) unites the soul with the Logos in a marriage (*maritat animam Verbo*).[130] "What offers one more joy than this conformity? What is more worthy of desiring than this love?" It creates a reliable approach to the Word in which the bride continuously adheres (*inhaerere*) to the Word and confidently (*familialiter*) seeks his counsel, just as open to understanding him as she is unfettered in her desires for him (*intellectus capax, audax desiderio*). "This is a truly spiritual and holy marriage contract (*contractus*). A contract? That is too weak. It is an embrace (*complexus*). Frankly, it is an embrace that forms one spirit from two (*unum spiritum de duobus*) in which they want the same things and reject the same things."[131]

In this spiritual marriage the responsive love of the bride can never be measured in terms of the Bridegroom's love. They differ as much as thirst differs from a spring of fresh water. The spring, the Word, loves first and loves spontaneously. And he, who himself is Love, loves in matchless measure. At the same time, this difference in the levels of the two loves does not impede their loving communion. Although the love of the bride is significantly smaller, she lacks nothing if she only loves with her whole being (*ex tota se*). "Blessed is the soul that is so favored as to experience such a sweet embrace."[132] It consists of nothing less than a holy, sober intoxication.[133]

Clearly, the emotional character of this loving exchange is pronounced. It is not a matter of rational deliberation, but of inner conformity that comes down to a matter of feelings! ("Res est in affectibus.")[134] Here the soul that is loved is

---

125. McGinn, *Die Mystik*, 2:264.

126. *SC*, 83:1, in *SW*, 6:610-11.

127. *SC*, 80:3, in *SW*, 6:572. Compare Böhner and Gilson, *Christliche Philosophie*, 326-27; Ruh, *Geschichte der Mystik*, 1:246. How the "receptivity" that Bernard examines here is related to the freedom of grace, is not expressed. See A. de Reuver, "Zo'n trotse titel voor een zo geringe zaak," *TR* 37 (1994), 265-89.

128. *SC*, 83:2, in *SW*, 6:612: "reformandae per ipsum, conformandi ipsi."

129. Ibid.

130. Of interest in this connection is the consideration of Turner, *Eros and Allegory*, 153-56.

131. *SC*, 80:3, in *SW*, 6:612. A little further, on page 612, this marriage is called an "intertwining" (*nexus*).

132. *SC*, 83:6, in *SW*, 6:618.

133. *SC*, 49:1-2, in *SW*, 6:160-61. Ruh, *Geschichte der Mystik*, 1:262. The idea of holy and sober drunkenness Bernard seems to have borrowed from Augustine. See T. J. van Bavel, *Als je hart bidt . . . Augustinus' leer over het gebed* (Leuven, 1996).

134. *SC*, 67:8, in *SW*, 6:400. Boot, *De allegorische uitlegging*, 88.

oblivious to the level of objectivizing and intellectualized knowledge and is so overpowered by the love of God that she experiences him in her deepest being.[135] This explains the frequency of terms often used synonymously in Bernard's writings such as "loveliness" and "sweetness" (*suavitas, dulcedo*).[136] This shows that the emotional character of experiencing union with Christ extends right to Bernard's vocabulary.

The question can arise how he thinks about the place and significance of faith in this connection. As far as I am able to tell, his perspective on faith is ambivalent. On the one hand he can critically fence faith (*fides*) off from feeling and experience. Faith comes only in response to the Word heard, and this Word is the irreplaceable truth.[137] It is reserved to this faith to embrace the invisible things (*invisibilia comprehendere*). It is not hindered by the deficiency associated with feeling (*sensus*) and it transcends the limits of human reason (*finis rationis humanae*) and even the boundaries of experience (*experientia*). One must learn, therefore, to place more confidence in faith anchored in the Word and to follow it with more certainty than one does other sense perceptions.[138] Whenever the subject of truth is under consideration, therefore, faith receives exclusive primacy as the basis for Christian existence.

But Bernard is just as apt to choose another approach. He does this whenever the perspective shifts from the subject of truth to that of the ultimate purpose of human existence. With this point of attack he emphasizes the provisional nature of faith. It is one step on the ladder of contemplation ("Gradus est auditus ad visum."). It is preparation (*praeparatio*) for the latter—essential, but nonetheless provisional.[139] From this perspective one can legitimately speak of greater value placed on experience than on faith. J. Schuck gets it positively right, therefore, when he summarizes Bernard's slogan as, "I believe in order that I may experience." ("Credo ut experiar.") What Schuck adds is equally interesting, however, namely that for Bernard it is not the case that experience replaces faith, but that experience arises from faith.[140] One could call experience the affective

---

135. Langer, "Affekt und Ratio," 148; L. van Hecke, *Bernardus van Clairvaux en de religieuze ervaring* (Kapellen and Kampen, 1990), 48-55.

136. B. Vosicky, "Bernhards Leben mit der Eucharistie," in *Bernhard von Clairvaux*, ed. Bauer and Fuchs, 218. The vocabulary of the Psalms and the Song of Solomon (Vulgate version) is undeniably mirrored in Bernard's use of language. For example, note Psalm 34:9 (Psalm 33 in the Vulgate): "Gustate et videte, quoniam suavis est Dominus"; Song of Solomon 2:3: "Fructus eius dulcis gutturi meo"; Song of Solomon 5:16: "Guttur illius suavissimum, et totus desiderabilis." On Bernard's perceptively considered borrowing of vocabulary, see McGinn, *Die Mystik*, 2:286-88.

137. *SC*, 28:7, in *SW*, 5:442.

138. *SC*, 28:9, in *SW*, 5:444. The same is true in *Sermones per annum* (in "Quadragesima Sermo 5," *SW*, 7:484): "Ergo iudicium fidei sequere, et non experimentum tuum, quoniam fides quidem verax, sed et experimentum fallax." ("Follow, therefore, the judgment of faith and not your experience, for faith is reliable but experience is deceitful.") According to McGinn, *Die Mystik*, 2:284, "Im Diesseits dient der Glauben vorrangig zur Öffnung der inneren, geistigen Sinne."

139. *SC*, 41:2, in *SW*, 6:72. Compare *SC*, 48:7-8, in *SW*, 6:156-60; and *SC*, 84:7, in *SW*, 6:626.

140. J. Schuck, *Das religiöse Erlebnis beim hl. Bernhard von Clairvaux* (Würzburg, 1922), 95-102, as cited in Boot, *De allegorische uitlegging*, 83.

point of faith's penetration. The pinnacle of this experience is the blessed contemplation of God in glory. This does not preclude the fact, however, that this experience can sometimes befall the believer who has not yet reached his heavenly home (*in patria*) but who is still en route (*in via*).

Union with God

Bernard saw the object and highlight of the spiritual union of love with God while one is still on earth as contained in contemplation, the mystical consideration of God's glory. By this he meant a visual experience of God's presence.[141] The close connection between contemplative love and the presence of God constitutes, according to McGinn, "das Herzstück von Bernhards mystischer Theologie."[142] This does not yet involve, as already noted, the beatific vision (*visio beatifica*) destined for the eschaton. Of this it is only anticipatory, a pledge and a foretaste. But the provisional and partial nature of this experience does not detract from its special quality. To a significant degree, the truly amazing part of this contemplation by the one loving God occurs in a spiritual ecstasy (*excessus mentis*)[143] that Bernard, following 2 Corinthians 12:13, called rapture (*raptus*).[144] With an affectionate predisposition toward it, he described this event as rest or peace (*quies*).[145]

K. Ruh calls attention to the fact that in Bernard, as with all important mystical writers, one does not find an extensive discussion of this extraordinary experience. The abbot mentioned it only sporadically, and then he spoke of it only with a degree of modesty. This is the case, for example, in his 85th sermon on the Song of Solomon. There he explains that in spiritual meditation it sometimes (*interdum*) occurs that the soul is transported out of the physical-sensual so that it no longer experiences the self, but only the Word (*Verbum*). This happens whenever the spirit, enticed by the sweetness of the inexpressible Word, as it were withdraws (*furator*), or better, is snatched (*rapitur*) from itself in order to enjoy the Word (*ut Verbo fruator*). In this context the word "embrace" (*amplexus*) again emerges. But, Bernard asks, when does this occur and how long does it last? He answers this by citing Johannes van Fécamp (c. 990-1078).[146] "Sweet communion, but what a momentary and a rare

---

141. McGinn, *Die Mystik*, 2:321.

142. Ibid., 290.

143. For the patristic, specifically the Augustinian, source of this term, see ibid., 323.

144. Gilson, *La théologie mystique*, 130, underscores the passive quality of this *raptus*: "Il veut donc dire, que l'âme ainsi ravie n'a rien à mettre du sien dans une telle opération, qui s'opère en elle sans elle et à laquelle elle ne coopère pas." According to Gilson, the terms "*excessus*" and "*raptus*" overlap one another: "Je n'ai réussi à trouver aucun texte qui autorise à les distinguer nettement, moins encore à les hiérarchiser." Ibid., 131. McGinn, *Die Mystik*, 2:323, takes this position. Ruh, *Geschichte der Mystik*, 1:272, however, is of the opinion that in Bernard a higher function is assigned to "*excessus*." Moreover, Ruh suspects that the term "*excessus mentis*" is basically of Augustinian origin. This point is confirmed by McGinn.

145. McGinn, *Die Mystik*, 2:323.

146. McGinn, *Die Mystik*, 2:224 and 290.

experience!"[147] And whenever someone asked him what this enjoyment of the Word exactly involves, his reaction was that in order to receive a clear answer they should seek such an experience (*expertum*). "Or, when I would be permitted to have such an experience, do you believe that I would be capable of explaining what is unexplainable?" ("Eloqui quod ineffabile est?") Whoever wants to know will open not only the ear to the Word, but also the heart. "This is taught not by the tongue, but by grace."[148]

Bernard provided an account of this secret also in his work "Concerning God's Love." It constitutes the highest level of love, in which one loves oneself for the sake of God. ("Diligit se propter Deum.")[149] This specific version of self-love obviously has nothing to do with trivial self-love. Bernard means by it that in it a person knows that he is entirely caught up in God's love for him and thus loves himself purely because God loves him. He loves the God who loves him. Then the soul gets drunk on divine love and "forgets itself." It clings to God (*adhaerens Deo*) and becomes one spirit with him (*unus spiritus*). "Blessed and holy, I say, is he who in this life that is a constant death very seldom, perhaps only one time and then only fleetingly (*raptim*), as it were in a single moment, is given this experience. For, to lose yourself in a certain sense, as though you were nothing, entirely unable to feel yourself anymore, to be emptied (*exinaniri*) of yourself and almost to become nothing, is something of what heavenly conversation (*conversatio*) means (both in its sense of 'communion' and of 'transformation') and is not a purely human experience." Bernard calls it holy and pure love. "O sweet and lovely affection (*affectio*). O clean and purged intention of the will, certainly more fully purged and pure to the extent that nothing of self (*de proprio nil*) remains mixed with it; all the sweeter and lovelier when what is experienced is completely divine." Every human affection then loses itself in the will of God and is poured into (*transfundi*) his will. This can be compared to a small drop of water that, dripped into a large quantity of wine, seems to disappear completely, assuming both the aroma and the color of the wine; and to iron, when heated in the fire, glows and seems to become entirely

---

147. *SC*, 85:13, in *SW*, 6:646: "Dulce commercium, sed breve momentum et experimentum rarum." Also see *SC*, 23:115, in *SW*, 5:344: "Sed, heu! Rara hora et parva mora." And compare *SC*, 32:2, in *SW*, 5:502 and *SC*, 41:3, in *SW*, 6:74. Ruh, *Geschichte der Mystik*, 1:232 and 271; Dinzelbacher, "Bernhards Mystik," in *Bernhard von Clairvaux*, ed. Bauer and Fuchs, 185. This saying of Bernard, borrowed from Johannes van Fécamp, is not unfamiliar in the Second Reformation. See A. de Reuver, *"Bedelen bij de Bron": Kohlbrugge's geloofsopvatting vergeleken met Reformatie en Nadere Reformatie* (Zoetermeer, 1992), 167 and 174. In pietist circles, two expressions were still in vogue that recalled Bernard's proverb: "Short and sweet!" ("Uurtjes van korte duurtjes!"), and "Good times go fast!" ("Zo genoten, zo toegesloten!"). See van de Ketterij, *De weg in woorden*, 327.

148. *SC*, 85:14, in *SW*, 6:646. Compare *SC*, 31:6, in *SW*, 5:494: "The divine Word not only resonates, but also penetrates ("non sonans, sed penetrans"); is not loquacious, but efficacious ("non loquax, sed efficax"); is not noisy to the ear, but soothing to the emotions." Did Bernard have in mind Augustine's *Confessions* (11.8.10), where this church father talks about the word that sounds in the ear externally ("foris auribus"), in order that it would be believed, sought and found internally ("intus")? This analogy has been suggested by G. B. Winkler, "Anmerkungen," in *SW*, 6:621. However, it occurs to me that here Augustine ties the inner and outer working of the word together more tightly.

149. See n.66.

like the fire, having lost its own earlier, unique form; and to air that permeated with the light of the sun seems to be transformed (*transformatur*) into that same clear light.[150]

This transformation into the eternal Word, into inner and heartfelt conformity to the Logos, defines union (*unitio*) with God. Bernard also called this union "deification,"[151] but only by way of exception. "To have this experience is to be deified."[152] What he intended by this he explained by referring to Paul's pronouncement that God will be all in all (1 Corinthians 15:28). Very significantly, however, he added that in this "deification" the unique substance and being of a person's humanity continues to exist. The person does not become God by being taken up into him, but the matter has to do with a change in form, glory, and power (*forma, gloria, potentia*).[153] Union with God does not involve any melting down of the person's being, but a fellowship of the will and a harmony of love.[154]

In order to avoid a pantheistic misunderstanding, Bernard explained that this unity is least of all similar in character to that of the Father and the Son. In Song of Solomon sermon 71 he made this plain in some detail. The Father and the Son are "in one another" (*in sese*). They are one in being (*consubstantiale*). By contrast, a person may by grace become one in spirit with God, one in purpose (*consentibile*), one in love. Although the Father and the Son are one (*unum*), one and the same common being, God and a human person can never be called one (*unum*), for they are not of the same being or the same nature. That they nevertheless become one in spirit (*unus spiritus*) is due to the bonding agent, literally the glue (*glutinum*), of the love that holds them together. This unity (*unitas*) does not yield, as Bernard explained with detailed precision, a coherence in essence (*essentiarum cohaerentia*) but an agreement of will (*conniventia voluntatum*).[155] When God and a human person are so entirely and completely

---

150. *DD*, 10:27-28, in *SW*, 1:120-21. P. Dinzelbacher, "Anmerkungen," in *SW*, 1:150, notes that these are traditional metaphors and appear to have been borrowed by Bernard from Duns Scotus Eriugena (*Div. nat. 1:10*, in *PL*, 122:450).

151. Ruh, *Geschichte der Mystik*, 1:273.

152. *DD*, 10:28, in *SW*, 1:122: "Sic affici, deificari est." For the term "*deificatio*," see R. Williams, "Deification," in *A Dictionary of Christian Spirituality*, ed. G. S. Wakefield (London, 1983), 106-8; and *The Study of Spirituality*, ed. C. Jones, G. Wainwright and E. Yarnold (London, 1992), 158, 161-62 and 235-36.

153. Here Bernard makes use of the scholastic distinction between "*substantia*" and "*forma*." See Muller, *Dictionary*, 123.

154. Evans, *The Mind*, 122-23; Dinzelbacher, "Bernhards Mystik," 185; W. van 't Spijker, "Experientia in reformatorisch licht," *TR* 19 (1976), 240-41.

155. *SC*, 71:6-7, in *SW*, 6:450. Gilson, *La théologie mystique*, 41 and especially 142-46: "Mais quelle est la nature de cette union? . . . L'union mystique respecte intégralement cette distinction réelle de la substance divine et de la substance humaine, de la volonté de Dieu de la volonté de l'homme; elle n'est ni une confusion des substances en général, ni une confusion de la substance de deux volontés en particulier; mais elle est leur accord parfait, la coïncidence de deux vouloirs" (146). Compare Ruh, *Geschichte der Mystik*, 1:273; McGinn, *Die Mystik*, 2:327-28; M. A. Schenkl, "Bernhard und die Entdeckung der Liebe," 152 and 169-70. Also see *SC*, 71:10, in *SW*, 6:456: ". . . communio voluntatum et consensus in caritate."

bound together by heartfelt, reciprocal love (*intima mutaque dilectione*), Bernard did not hesitate to posit that God is in the person and that the person is in God.[156]

Concerning his own ecstatic, mystical experience Bernard can be remarkably modest. "I do not want to speak about it as one who has experienced it, but as one who longs to experience it."[157] We may undoubtedly regard this reserve as an expression of humility that veils reality. In every way his works breathe the spirit of such experience. With Dinzelbacher we affirm that in Bernard's writings we need to recognize an autobiographical undercurrent.[158] Ruh, likewise, does not have the slightest hesitation in asserting that the Abbot of Clairvaux speaks from personal mystical experience.[159] As if Bernard had forgotten the reticence he expressed elsewhere, he could in fact on other occasions certainly point to his own experience.[160] But even then, his tone remained modest. "I recognize that the Word [i.e., the Bridegroom] has also come to me—in fact, often [*pluries*]. I admit this in foolishness!" This arises "not from my inner being, for the Word is good, and I know that in myself there is no goodness."[161] This awareness would not have been the least consideration motivating him not to put his own experiences on display but to treat them with sobriety. The deepest motive for his reserve, however, seems to me to lie in the conviction that the mystical experience is actually incapable of being described in earthly categories. Rather, they belong much more to the potential than the actual. This feature of what one could describe as eschatological reserve comes to light only indirectly in the foregoing. However, it deserves further, explicit attention.

Precisely on account of the highest order of loving communion with God here on earth, Bernard remained keenly aware of its provisional nature. However highly he valued this fellowship with God, it should in no way be confused with the everlasting beatific vision (*visio beatifica*).[162] The instances when he indicated its provisional nature were numerous. Often he even went so far as to regard the highest level of this love *purely* as reserved for the hereafter. The church first participates in it in immortality, when death is swallowed up in victory and when in every way the everlasting day overcomes the night.[163] Although sometimes the Exalted Majesty stoops to favor us mere mortals here, proleptically, with the experience of heartfelt, sweet fellowship (*consortio*) in

---

156. *SC*, 71:10, in *SW*, 6:456.

157. *SC*, 69:1, in *SW*, 6:418. Compare *SC*, 23:9, in *SW*, 5:336, where he says, not to arrogate it to himself, to have experience in such an exalted matter as is presented in Song of Solomon 1:3. Compare *SC*, 74:1, in *SW*, 6:494.

158. Dinzelbacher, "Bernhards Mystik," 182.

159. Ruh, *Geschichte der Mystik*, 1:274.

160. The solution that Bernard could have achieved the mystical experience only in a later phase of his life does not strike me as tenable.

161. *SC*, 74:5, in *SW*, 6:498-99. On this passage also consult McGinn, *Die Mystik*, 2:294.

162. See Gilson, *La théologie mystique*, 113-15. Gilson notes that people often call the ecstatic experience a foretaste of heavenly blessedness, but that this is nothing more than a metaphor. "Il est de l'essence de la béatitude d'être eternelle, car qu'est-ce qu'une béatitude que l'on serait menacé de perdre à tout instant, sinon une misère?" (113). And precisely this makes all the difference. Although all earthly enjoyment is temporary, that of heaven is marked by the endlessness of eternity. See McGinn, *Die Mystik*, 2:318.

163. *DD*, 10:29 and 11:30, in *SW*, 1:124-25. Compare *DD*, 15:39, in *SW*, 1:142.

order to consummate a marriage (*connubia*) with the soul in exile (*animae exsulantis*), the full reality of this union will only blossom in heaven.[164] As long as we continue to live the life of faith and the essence of the inner light is not yet revealed to us, we are left with only a fragmentary sample of contemplating pure Truth.[165] Here on earth the road is still a path of thorns and one must endure the burden of temptations and the sting of adversity.[166] Growth and progress consist in never allowing ourselves to believe that we have already reached the goal.[167]

Meanwhile, the bride of Christ languishes for the kingdom of God. This is a longing that Bernard explained gladly and often. Everyone who, moved by the promise of the heavenly kingdom, no longer confuses this place of captivity on earth (*exsilium*) with the fatherland (*patria*), makes his pilgrimage through this world as a stranger (*peregrinus*) and begins to look for the city of the future (*futuram civitatem*) with great expectation. He endures the absence of that kingdom only with difficulty and hails the desired fatherland with groans and sighs (*gemitibus et suspiriis*).[168] The bride is comforted by two things in the land of her estrangement (*peregrinatio*): from the past (*de praeterito*), by recalling Christ's sufferings (*memoria passionis Christi*), and from the future (*de futuro*), by the thought of the glorified state of the saints that is received in the conviction of faith. Both perspectives fill her with longings that cannot be quieted. This joyful expectation, furthermore, is never in doubt, since it is established by the death of Christ (*Christi morte firmata*).[169] On the deepest level, Bernard's longings were not fixed on heaven, but on Christ himself. He truly considered it better to be with him in the fiery furnace of hell (*in camino*) than to be without him in heaven (*in caelo*).[170] For Bernard, heaven is the fulfillment of everything that God has promised: "I will show him (i.e., the believer) my Jesus so that for eternity he sees him in whom he has believed, him whom he has loved, him whom he has desired."[171]

So, Bernard ached to realize the vision that leads to the eschaton (*in novissimis*). Only then will we see him as he is (1 John 3:2). Now he only shows himself as he chooses, not as he is (*sicuti vult, non sicuti est*).[172] The person who is justified still lives by faith (*iustus ex fide vivit*), but the person in glory exalts in what is seen (*beatus exsultat in specie*), face to face (*facie ad faciem*).[173] Bernard portrayed the blessedness of heaven in effusive language rich in imagery. At the wedding of the Lamb, the Bridegroom gets those he loves

---

164. *SC*, 52:2, in *SW*, 6:196.

165. *SC*, 41:3, in *SW*, 6:74. On the Augustinian background of this idea, see the German translation of Augustine, *Über Schau und Gegenwart des unsichtbaren Gottes*, trans. with introduction by Erich Naab (Stuttgart and Bad Cannstatt, 1988), 60-61.

166. *SC*, 48:1, in *SW*, 6:148: "Donec ergo in carne est anima, inter spinas profecto versatur, et necesse patiatur inquietudines tentationum tribulationumque aculeos."

167. McGinn, *Die Mystik*, 2:330.

168. *SC*, 59:4, in *SW*, 6:288. Remarkably, Calvin in *Inst.* 3.9.5 renders the longing for Christ's return and for eternal blessedness in the same words: "gemitu ac suspiriis," *OS*, 4:176.

169. *SC*, 62:1, in *SW*, 6:324.

170. *Sermones per annum* (in "Psalmum 'Qui habitat' Sermo 17"), *SW*, 7:712.

171. Ibid., 716-17.

172. *SC*, 31:2, in *SW*, 5:488. Compare Boot, *De allegorische uitlegging*, 86.

173. *SC*, 31:8, in *SW*, 5:496.

thoroughly intoxicated. Then he pours them the drinks of his free-flowing delights. "Hence, complete satisfaction without interruption; hence, everlasting and insatiable desire that lacks nothing; hence, that sober drunkenness (*sobria ebrietas*) that refreshes itself with the Truth and not with drink (*vero, non mero*), drenched with wine, but radiant with God (*non madens vino, sed ardens Deo*)."[174] He was positively lyrical when he described this state: "O, true noon-day, fullness of heat and light. . . . O, everlasting sunshine, when daylight will never die. O, midday light; O, springtime softness; O, pleasantness of summer; O, fruitfulness of autumn; and, to overlook nothing, O, rest and freedom of winter!"[175]

The pinnacle of all this heavenly pleasure is nothing less than to contemplate (*contemplari*) Christ in all his light and beauty (*lumine et decore*). "When will you satisfy me with the joy of your presence (*cum vultu tuo*)?"[176] In this eschatological perspective, it is understandable that Bernard relativized even the highest delights that he experienced in his union with God here below. They were sweet to him, but they could not quiet his hunger for complete satisfaction. Tasting was, simultaneously, yearning. Bernard's mystical experience, therefore, was an indication of his longing and sense of the provisional. It is mysticism in the light of eternity (*sub specie aeternitatis*).

Evaluation

I am conscious of the fact that this sketch does not in the least offer a complete picture of Bernard's piety. For that, deeper research would be required into his epistemological, theological and anthropological starting points. The intention here was only to bring to light some key ideas that, at least in part and eventually in modified form, have worked their way into the spirituality of the Modern Devotion as well as the Reformation and pietism. What comes to mind in this connection is Bernard's Christological emphasis, his meditative disposition, his yearnings to experience God's presence, his realistic perspective on human sinfulness, his interweaving of knowledge of God and knowledge of self, his emotional interpretation of fellowship with God and his deep conviction concerning the transitory nature of earthly existence, tied to the longing for the perfection of heaven.

In several regards Bernard is timeless, or rather, for all times. This in no way indicates, however, that his appearance and his contributions should be interpreted outside the contexts of his own time and his own tradition. Bernard was not Augustine *redivivus* nor a literary innovator, let alone a forerunner of the Reformation. He was a devout child of the twelfth century, completely involved in the contemporary developments of the Roman papal establishment. What particularly characterized him is his monastic frame of reference. The monastery was also his spiritual home. Preeminently there he practiced his meditative

---

174. *DD*, 11:33, in *SW*, 1:130.

175. *SC*, 33:6, in *SW*, 5:522.

176. *SC*, 33:7, in *SW*, 5:524. The last quotation is virtually a literal citation of Psalm 16:11 (in the Vulgate, 15:11).

exercises and had his mystical experiences. There he preached his allegorical sermons. These monastic surroundings offered Bernard the shelter for separating himself in stillness and developing his literary creativity. The rhythm of set hours created the space in which his knowledge of Scripture achieved such astounding allure.

At the same time, the monastic climate contributed a somewhat elite dimension to Bernard's mysticism. Like his lineage, his spirituality took aristocratic form. As far as that form is concerned, its nature was strengthened by his aesthetic ability and his poetic, image-rich use of language. His literary expression is rich and graceful, his style polished and vibrant. But content-wise as well, this signal vitality set a stamp on his work. The spiritual experiences that he described are part of that special spirituality. By this I do not mean in any way to retract what I observed about Bernard's deep longing that all his listeners and readers would be included in the experience of God's love. That which he himself had gained in his life with God, he desired for everyone. Least of all did he consider himself to be an exceptional, especially favored individual, but rather as a companion of all who share in God's grace. McGinn's judgment deserves total approval when he emphasizes Bernard's continuing appeal to his listeners and readers in order "seine Lehren am Buch ihrer eigenen Erfahrung zu messen."[177] This ideal does not deny, however, that his sermons and writings in actual practice were aimed at his monastic brothers and spiritual family. He described experiences that were hardly threatened by the pressure and busyness of a worldly, unruly lifestyle, but ones that were encircled by the set hours of the breviary and safeguarded by the solid walls of the monastery. Here the goodness of God's love and the sweetness of the love returned to him could flourish. Bernard's fragile health caused no interruption in these inner pursuits, but rather intensified them.

Apparently this sphere of monastic serenity is primarily the source of a difference that emerges between it and the piety characteristic of the Further Reformation.[178] One could posit the thesis that the spirituality of Bernard turns on the axle of love, while that of the Reformation turns on that of faith. Yet, that thesis seems too absolute to me. It requires some nuancing. For, even Bernard recognized the principle of *extra nos* as the irreplaceable foundation of faith, and the reformers also embraced the inalienable love that springs from faith. One can certainly agree with Gilson: "La *fiducia* luthérienne est une foi, qui permet au pécheur de se sentir pecheur et de se sentir néanmoins sauvé par Jésus-Christ. La confiance de saint Bernard est une charité. . . ."[179] At the same time, Gilson admits that Bernard does not represent a purely forensic form of justification. Whether one is compelled to follow him when he suggests that Luther's doctrine of justification is purely forensic remains to be seen. Good grounds exist for rejecting that "purely." Although Luther considered of primary and determinative importance that in justification by faith alone the righteousness of

---

177. McGinn, *Die Mystik*, 2:340.

178. The figure for whom this distinction least applies is Theodorus à Brakel, whose meditative lifestyle hardly fits that of the monks.

179. Gilson, *La théologie mystique*, 169, especially n.1.

Christ imputed (*imputatio*) to believers is an alien righteousness (*iustitia aliena*), he forcefully posited at the same time that this imputation is inseparably tied to effectual justification that takes the form of love and obedience that are worked in us by the renewing power of the Holy Spirit and the indwelling Christ. The Christ beyond us cannot be separated from the Christ within us. Luther repeatedly spoke in this connection about the "two parts" of justification, namely reconciliation and cleansing. For that reason he never hesitated time and again to characterize the Christian life as one of faith and love.[180] To call attention to differences makes sense, but one must not make them absolute.

Furthermore, whenever Bernard accorded the human will meritorious cooperation in the process of salvation, that seems at first glace to clash diametrically with the position of the Reformation. But when he added with emphasis that this will originates purely from God, for it is from God both to will and to bring to completion, and when in conclusion he explained, "Finally, those whom he has justified, he has also glorified, and not those whom he has encountered as (self)righteous" ("non quos iustos invenit"), then under closer scrutiny the conclusion comes out a little differently.[181] According to Bernard, all merit rests on this: that people fix their hope completely on him who saves the whole person.[182] The Abbot of Clairvaux, therefore, considered God's grace so surpassingly sweet (*dulcissima*) because it is entirely free (*gratis*).[183]

A question with which people in doubt can be occupied is hermeneutical in nature. Is the allegorical method of scriptural exposition that Bernard applied with verve and candor not a long way removed from the Reformation's high regard for the literal interpretation of the Bible? This is not the place to discuss this question at length. That one needs to be attentive in this connection to both straightforward and to rash approaches appears in Calvin's understanding of the exposition of Song of Solomon. Interestingly enough, he considered it inadvisable on this matter to disregard the continuing—thus, allegorical—testimony of the universal church.[184] Meanwhile, it is striking that neither Luther

---

180. For more expanded treatment, see de Reuver, *"Bedelen bij de Bron,"* 254-60; R. Prenter, *Spiritus creator: Studien zu Luthers Theologie* (Munich, 1954), 73-74; W. von Loewenich, *Luther als Ausleger der Synoptiker* (Munich, 1954), 185.

181. As given in the closing sentence of *De gratia et libero arbitrio* (59), in *SW*, 1:249. Compare *SC*, 22:7, in *SW*, 5:314, and particularly *SC*, 23:15, in *SW*, 5:344-45: "Omne quod mihi ipse non imputare decreverit, sic est quasi non fuerit. Non peccare, Dei iustitia est: hominis iustitia, indulgentia Dei" ("All that he does not charge against me by virtue of his sovereign council, is as though it had never happened. God's righteousness is that he does not sin; human righteousness is found in God's forgiveness"). A brief overview of Bernard's doctrine of grace is presented by B. Hamm, *Promissio, Pactum, Ordinatio: Freiheit und Selbstbindung Gottes in der scholastischen Gnadenlehre* (Tübingen, 1977), 20-22.

182. *Sermones per annum* (in "Psalmum 'Qui habitat' Sermo 15"), in *SW*, 7:692.

183. *Sermones per annum* (in "'Circumcisione' Sermo 3"), in *SW*, 7:302.

184. Verduin, *Canticum Canticorum*, 349. That Calvin, *Inst.* 3.16.4., in *OS*, 4:252, calls the Song of Solomon 5:3 allegorical is striking. To illustrate the connection between justification and sanctification, he appeals to the *"fidelis anima,"* which states, "I have washed my feet, how could I defile them again?" In general, for Calvin's critical opinion on the unmanageable and arbitrary allegorical method, see Thiselton, *New Horizons*, 185; P. Opitz, *Calvijns theologische Hermeneutik* (Neukirchen, 1994), 197-99; D. L. Puckett, *John Calvin's Exegesis of the Old*

nor Calvin produced an allegorical, mystical commentary on the Song of Solomon. Luther gave it a political application.[185] Calvin did not touch it at all.[186] In marked contrast, for Bernard the Song of Solomon filled a pivotal and key function in his own experience as well as in his account of fellowship with God. This gives his spirituality a different timbre than that of the reformers, without challenging the fact that not infrequently striking material analogies appear between the two. With the pietistic writers of the Further Reformation this agreement increases in the sense that their spiritual terminology is graphically colored by the language of the Song of Solomon, just as is the case with Bernard.

Testament (Louisville, 1995), 106-13; W. de Greef, *"De Ware Uitleg": Hervormers en hun verklaring van de Bijbel* (Leiden, 1995), 198-205.

185. Verduin, *Canticum Canticorum*, 258-326.

186. In contrast to Calvin, his successor in Geneva, Theodore Beza, gave extensive treatment to the Song of Solomon. Its translation into Latin verse appeared from his hand in 1584; and three years later, his 31 typological-allegorical, although not specifically mystical, sermons on the first three chapters saw the light of day. See Verduin, *Canticum Canticorum*, 351-81. Vincent Meusevoet, minister in Schagen, translated the work into the Dutch language (Amsterdam, 1600).

Super omnia, et in omnibus requiesces, anima mea —
in Domino semper, quia ipse Sanctorum æterna requies.
de imitatione Christi. Cap. 21.

2

Thomas à Kempis (c. 1379-1471)

The Modern Devotion

The spiritual atmosphere in which Thomas à Kempis breathed was that of the Modern Devotion, a reform movement that had its origin in the century in which Thomas was born. It was a movement whose emergence is inseparably joined to the life and work of Gerard Groote (1340-1384).[1] Groote came from Deventer. After an extended period of interdisciplinary study in Paris and other European cities, and after commencing a career in canonical orders when he was more than thirty years old, his life took a new spiritual direction. He not only distanced himself from his position as canon, but also from the house that he had inherited from his parents. He designated it for the use of indigent women desirous of serving God. Subsequently, the movement's first convent would blossom in this dwelling. By late 1374, he himself entered the Carthusian order in Munnikhuizen, a fellowship that in many respects served as a model for the later Modern Devotion. Here his ideal of world-denial, his consciousness of sin and his longing for union with God matured. Because his health was too fragile to sustain the rigors of monastic life, he left the Carthusians and established himself in Deventer. From there he traveled throughout the Netherlands for a time as an itinerant preacher. A circle of followers sprang up rather spontaneously around Groote, and among them emerged a desire for their own expression of communal life. They found shelter in the home of Florens Radewijns, one of Groote's spiritual associates in Deventer. In 1384, the year of Groote's death, a few of his followers in Zwolle built a communal house at Nemelerberg, north of that city. In 1398 it was reconstituted as a cloister for full-fledged monks and was renamed St. Agnietenberg, the well-known daughter house of the Convent of Windesheim, that was founded in 1395 south of Zwolle. While Groote promoted the development from a lay movement to monastic life, he had to leave the realization of this transition to his disciples. Not yet 44 years old, he died in 1384, a victim of the plague raging in Western Europe.

---

1. I limit myself to an abbreviated review. For fuller information see J. G. R. Acquoy, *Het klooster te Windesheim en zijn invloed*, vol. 1 (republished from the original, 3 vol. edition, Utrecht, 1875-80; Leeuwarden, 1984), 13-58; A. Hyma, *The Christian Renaissance: A History of the "Devotio Moderna"* (New York and London, 1924), 9-40; S. Axters, *Geschiedenis van de vroomheid in de Nederlanden*, vol. 3, *De Moderne Devotie 1380-1550* (Antwerp, 1956), 27-58; R. R. Post, *The Modern Devotion: Confrontation with Reformation and Humanism* (Leiden, 1968), 51-196; M. de Kroon, "Gerard Groote," in *Gestalten der Kirchengeschichte*, ed. Greschat, 4:234-50; A. G. Weiler, "Leven en werken van Geert Grote," in *Geert Grote en de Moderne Devotie*, ed. C. C. de Bruin, E. Persoons and A. G. Weiler (Zutphen, 1984), 9-55; P. van Geest, *Thomas a Kempis, 1379/80-1471: Een studie van zijn mens- en godsbeeld* (Kampen, 1996), 35-36; Waaijman, *Spiritualiteit*, 185-88.

Cloisters in the Netherlands attached
to the Chapter of Windescheim

● Men's Cloisters
★ Women's Cloisters

NORTH SEA

Anjum

Bergum

Ludingakerk

Sneek /*Thabor*

Haske

★ Brunnepe

Heiloo
Hoorn/*Nieuwlicht*

ZUIDERZEE

Agnietenberg
Zwolle /*Bethlehem*

Frenswegen ●
WINDESHEIM

Beverwijk/
Sion

Haarlem/*O.L.V. Visitatie*

Albergen

Amsterdam/ *St. Jan Evangelist*
Amsterdam/*Mariënveld*
Leiden /*St.Hiëron.dal*
Naarden

Diepenveen ★

Leiderdorp/*Engelendaal*

Amersfoort/ *Mariënhof*

Birket

Vredendaal

IJssel

Utrecht/*O.L.V. en 12 Apostelen*

Bredevoort/
Nazareth

★ Utrecht/*Jerusalem*
Renkum

Arnhem/*Mariënborn*
Arnhem/*Bethanië*

Rugge

Dordrecht

Waal

Kijfhoek
Zaltbommel

Maas

Nijmegen/*St.Catharina*
Nijmegen/*Mariënburg*

Eemstein

Gaesdonk

Uedem

Rijn

Reimerswaal

Eindhoven/*Mariënhage*

Straelen

★Oostmalle

Weert

Antwerpen ★*Facons*

Korsendonk

St.Elisabethsdal

Neuss

Grobbendonk / *Ten Troon*

Roermond/*St. Hiëronymus*

Gent ★/*Galilea*

★Mechelen/*Bethanië*

Keulen ●

Melle

Herent/*Bethlehem*

Leie

Leuven/*St. Maartensdal*

Schelde

Oudergem
★Tienen/*Barberendal*

Aken

Elsegem

●St.Genesius-Rode/*Zevenborren*

Tongeren/*Ter Nood Gods*

Bonn ★

Hoeilaart/*Groenendaal*

Ophain/*Bois-Seigneur-Isaac*

Luik/*St. Leonard*

Not without reason is Geert Groote considered the spiritual father of the *Devotio Moderna*. Yet, it was not only due to his personal influence that the movement was born. The times were ripe for it. The fourteenth century was characterized by a set of factors that influenced the emergence of the Modern Devotion. Four factors are especially important.[2] In the first place, the hopelessly confused practice of church discipline needs to be mentioned. From 1309 to 1377 the seat of papal authority—from antiquity located in Rome—was located in Avignon. This era is generally designated as the "Babylonian Captivity" of the papacy. This situation resulted in the papal schism, 1378-1417, a period of almost forty years characterized by a dual papacy. Little imagination is required to understand the earth-shaking consequences this crisis had for the Roman establishment. It is aptly described as the heaviest trial that the medieval church had to endure.[3] The two rival popes excommunicated one another's followers. The crisis was so pervasively damaging that even resolving the schism at the Council of Constance could not remove the poison affecting the church's authority. The secularization of its leadership only strengthened the perception of the institutional church's unworthiness to provide spiritual direction. Many yearned for religious renewal.

A second factor that should not be underestimated concerns the consequences of the plague, which afflicted the European population during the Middle Ages. On the one hand, fear of "the black death" caused massive displacement of people. They moved in groups through many countries, giddily dancing in despair or scourging themselves in penance. On the other hand, the plague also led many to personal conversion. The last instance came to expression also in the aspirations of the Modern Devotion, which became a nursery for reflection and introspection.

A third factor is social and economic in nature. About 1400, the overwhelmingly agrarian social order of the Middle Ages gave way to an increasingly urban social structure created by the growing importance of trade. The city became the center of commerce.[4] This process was coupled with the rise of a self-conscious middle class. This changing situation was accompanied by the emergence of religious societies in and around cities that intentionally cultivated a mediate position between monastic life and lay status. Throughout all of Europe organizations of religious women (*mulieres religiosae*) were created. The women lived with one another in urban homes and distinguished themselves by their precisely regulated daily lives, strict chastity and voluntary poverty. When Gerard Groote designated his home for poor, godly women, he must have had this quasi-religious lifestyle in mind. "Here the unpretentious seed of the Modern Devotion sprouted."[5]

The fourth factor is theological. While not exclusively so, to be sure, the Modern Devotion must be regarded as a reaction to the prevailing scholasticism.

---

2. This summary of contributing causes is borrowed primarily from van Geest, 27-34.

3. W. Lourdaux, "Zur Devotio Moderna," in *Studien zur Devotio Moderna*, ed. K. Egger, W. Lourdaux and A. van Biezen (Bonn, 1988), 3. Also, Axters, *Geschiedenis*, 3:2-10.

4. For a description of this process see Le Goff, *De cultuur*, 98 and following.

5. Van Geest, *Thomas*, 32.

In the minds of its devotees, the practice of academic theology with its abstract and rational method was alien to authentic faith-life. Speculation for the sake of speculation they considered meaningless. In their estimation scholastic theology, with its strongly intellectualizing features, lacked the elan to be meaningfully innovative. In contrast, they pleaded for a renewed appreciation for the experiential dimension in theology.[6]

These contextual factors abetted the birth of the Modern Devotion. For that reason the movement can scarcely be characterized as one of the heretical groups isolated from reality that emerged from nowhere.[7] It is far more preferable to regard it as a development entirely in rapport with the needs of the time. The celebrated historian J. Huizinga may, then, have somewhat sarcastically characterized the spirit of the Modern Devotion as "the comforting spiritual activity, pursued in quiet intimacy, of simple little men and women, whose huge heaven arched above a miniscule world where all the powerful currents of the age simply flowed right past them."[8] This judgment deserves to be challenged. Huizinga's comment that a prior of Windesheim bore "the honorable name 'John-I-Don't-Know'" is certainly witty, but is per se a deficient characterization. C. C. de Bruin does more justice to the movement when he locates it entirely in the context of its time.[9] The times definitely did not merely flow past these so-called Brethren of the Common Life,[10] whose simplicity is not to be confused either with inanity or illiteracy. Their ideal of devotion contains a perspective that was a critical corrective in an epoch of pervasive decay within the clergy, when religious ceremony was externalized and scholastic theology was intellectualized. In reaction to this bastardization, they sought an authentic spirituality that could satisfy the heart and that therefore simultaneously both opposed the times and met them.

In striving for renewal they were anything but alone. The Modern Devotion formed a variant within a widely flung network of renewal movements produced in the twilight of the Middle Ages.[11] In several European areas the same pressure for a total rebirth of church and society was manifest: in Bohemia and in England, in cities like Prague and Oxford, and far beyond. The Modern Devotion was the form taken in the northern Netherlands by this widespread, deeply rooted yearning for a revival of Christendom.[12]

---

6. See H. A. Oberman, "Fourteenth-Century Religious Thought: a Premature Profile," in *Speculum* 53 (1978): 93. "The warning against *vana curiositas* and academic speculation gave weight and new authority to *experientia*," (quoted in van Geest, *Thomas*, 34). Compare H. A. Oberman, *Werden und Wertung der Reformation: Von Wegestreit zum Glaubenskampf* (Tübingen, 1989), 59-60.

7. According to van Geest, *Thomas*, 32.

8. J. Huizinga, *Herfsttij der Middeleeuwen*, vol. 3 in *Verzamelde Werken*, 9 vols. (Haarlem, 1949), 3:232.

9. De Bruin, "De spiritualiteit," 102.

10. Van Geest, *Thomas*, 36, indicates that this name radiates the desire for communal life—the fellowship of the early church.

11. Ibid., 25.

12. De Bruin, "De spiritualiteit," 102.

The name of the movement, "Modern Devotion,"[13] at the same time connotes a program. Adherents strove for "devotion" in the sense of a pious fervor and of introspection that reacted to the aforementioned formalization of religious life. They pursued practical devotion in the exercise of meditation and sanctified living that was in sharp contrast with pretentious speculation and abstraction. Their devotion was called "modern" not because it endeavored to be contemporary—even though they espoused a break with the spiritual and doctrinal legacy of the classical tradition—but because they aimed, in the spirit of the times, at a renewed spirituality that endeavored to dispel the prevailing spirit of religious laxness.[14] That to which they aspired was a pronounced, personal communion with God.[15] Although this concept in itself was not new, but was connected to the tradition of Augustine and Bernard, it received a contemporary, popular content that produced renewed vitality. Along the lines of the lay movements in Germany and Switzerland like the *Gottesfreunde* and like the *mulieres religiosae*, the Brethren consisted of a fellowship that from the outset was open to the laity.[16] It thereby produced a definite democratizing of spirituality.[17]

Nevertheless, their pattern of communal life from the outset was consistent with that of the cloister, even before they opted for monastic life. The difference was that the Brethren maintained their communal life entirely on the basis of free choice, without binding commitments. The only demand for admission was that their life together would be based on a genuine fear of the Lord and on the yearning for the salvation of their souls.[18] But their lifestyle itself displayed a strong similarity to that of the monastery: study, meditation, fasting, vigils, periods of silence.[19] The intent was personal reformation, the reshaping and equipping of one's life through concentration on the inner life.[20] Concentration on the inner life was at the same time not an end in itself. The object was rather God and the soul.[21] The concept of direct, personal relationship with God colored

---

13. Perhaps the name was applied by Johan Vos van Heusden, the prior at Windesheim from 1391 to 1424, by whom Gerard Groote was always characterized as the "primus pater huius nostrae reformationis" and as the "origo totius modernae devotionis." See A. J. Jelsma, "Doorwerking van de Moderne Devotie," in *De doorwerking van de Moderne Devotie, Windesheim 1387-1987*, ed. P. Bange, C. Graafland, A. J. Jelsma and A. G. Weiler (Hilversum, 1988), 17; de Kroon, "Gerard Groote," 247, reports in the same vein as É. Brouette, that the expression should be traced back to Henricus Pomerius. É. Brouette, "Devotio Moderna (I)," *TRE*, 8:605.

14. Post, *The Modern Devotion*, 680; Lourdaux, "Zur Devotio," 4.

15. This is the opinion of L. J. Richard, *The Spirituality of John Calvin* (Atlanta 1974), 34. The author appeals the possible influence of the *via moderna's* intellectual legacy with its emphasis on the individual. Ibid, 36.

16. De Kroon, "Gerard Groote," 248. On the *Gottesfreunde* see F. Rapp's article in *TRE*, 14:98-100.

17. Richard, *The Spirituality*, 33.

18. E. Persoons, "De verspreiding van de Moderne Devotie," in *Geert Grote*, ed. de Bruin, et al., 73.

19. Ibid., 76.

20. Brouette, "Devotio moderna (I)," 605.

21. Augustine's adage was central, "Deum animam scire cupio." *Soliloquia*, 1.2. For text in both Latin and German see Aurelius Augustinus, *Selbstgespräch: Von der Unsterblichkeit der*

their entire devotional life: their continuous striving to direct all their activities toward God, their spiritual exercises as well as their daily, manual labor. Guiding principles in this regard were humility, obedience, purity, self-denying and submissive service—all arising from love for God. Besides, this emphasis on the inner life did not produce de-emphasis on ecclesiastical, liturgical rituals, such as confession and communion. Devotees held these in high regard. Their critique was directed not toward the ceremony as such, but toward its externalization.

Without here going into the significance that the Modern Devotion had for education and publication[22]—although not to forget it—I conclude the review of this movement with special attention to its spiritual practice. The biblical text, particularly the Psalms, was very dominant in the daily spiritual experience of the movement's devotees. De Bruin mentions striking examples. While working in the fields, the brothers recited Psalms. The sisters did the same while spinning and weaving. If a sister lay on her death-bed, others supported her with penitential Psalms. One of them reported that they prayed the Psalms reverently, as best they could, including the words, "May your good Spirit lead me on level ground," (Psalm 143) after which she "sweetly" yielded her spirit. A chronicler reports concerning the sisters that they knew entire Bible passages by memory. They immediately knew where to locate an obscure text, and they identified every mistake made during the oral reading of the Word. Some of them always carried hand-written portions of Scripture with them in a little receptacle.[23] The way devotees handled the Bible was marked by a combination of respect and intimacy. For them, the Scriptures were not an object of scientific investigation, but rather a source of support and a companion on the road of life. On this last point they stood in the tradition of Augustine, who regarded the Bible as a letter from his heavenly home.[24]

In this connection it is interesting that all members of the congregation were skilled in the use of *rapiaria* (literally, "frequently consulted little books"), writings containing personal notes and striking quotations from the Holy Scriptures as well as from the works of the church fathers and later devotional writers.[25] The words of the Bible received the most prominence.

The main course in their devotional diet, if one can put it this way, consisted of meditative engagement with Scripture. The content that they gave this activity was different from that of their contemporaries. While meditation according to contemporary patterns is tied to stipulated times, the meditation of the Brothers occurred at every possible moment of the day. Special times were not provided for it. At every hour of the day, even during the tedious work of copying, one considered the great mysteries of salvation, alternately directed to pericopes that

---

Seele, text in both Latin and German (Munich and Zurich: 1986), 18. Also see Migne, *PL*, 32:872.

22. Oberman, *Werden und Wertung*, 58; van Geest, *Thomas*, 40. For the significance of the Modern Devotion for the earliest Dutch Bible translation, see C. C. de Bruin, *De Statenbijbel en zijn voorgangers: Nederlandse bijbelvertalingen vanaf de Reformatie tot 1637*, ed. F. G. M. Broeyer (Haarlem and Brussels, 1993), 28-34. According to Weiler, "Leven en Werken," 106.

23. De Bruin, "De spiritualiteit," 106.

24. A. van Biezen, "Zur Spiritualität von Windesheim," in *Studien*, ed. Egger, et al., 30.

25. Ibid., 32; Post, *The Modern Devotion*, 542 (compare 314).

condemned the conscience and ones that reassured it. To meditate was synonymous with "tireless rumination" (*indefesse ruminare*).[26] Living and breathing in the state of *ruminatio* was considered of greater value than all the programmed meditative exercises combined. This "rumination in one's heart" (*in corde ruminare*) is accurately designated as an orientation of one's life. Florens Radewijns interpreted this attitude toward life as follows: "It is useful for a person, therefore, to recall daily—at whatever hour—the blessedness of his salvation."[27]

The meditative devotion of the Brothers revolved especially around what the Bible records about Jesus' life on earth, namely in the passages on his suffering and crucifixion. Not only the canonical gospels served as the main thread of this emphasis, but also the various, freely reworked "lives of Jesus," that include elements of early Christian apocryphal literature.[28] Above all, use was made of Bernard's devotional tradition, in which the love for and toward the Man of Sorrows is so glowingly extolled. Most dominant was the affective devotion of the movement nurtured by Carthusian spirituality,[29] in which, consistent with the examples of Bernard and the Franciscans,[30] remembrance of Jesus' life and suffering carried the melody.[31] The deep purpose that stirred devotees can scarcely be more strikingly typified than with the words, inspired by Bernard, from the Brothers themselves: "That humble and loving life of Jesus Christ, who was crucified for an unshakeable foundation laid in the deepest recesses of our hearts, God also desires from us as a sachet of myrrh offered exclusively in a grateful love."[32] With similar words Gerard de Groote had already written that this is the way of Christ-likeness. He considered meditation on Christ's sufferings to be of little value if this was not accompanied with intense longing to follow him in his humiliation. For this reason, in meditation one must always hear his call, "Behave and live like this: I have suffered for you and with you in such a way that you might follow in my footsteps."[33] According to de Groote, this concentration on Jesus' passion was the source of power that enabled one to bear the cross of discipleship.

---

26. Post, *The Modern Devotion,* 235. Also see Goossens, *De meditatie,* 88-92; Nicol, *Meditation bei Luther,* 55-60. A contemporary appeal for internalizing texts by means of stipulated exercises can be found in R. Bohren, *In der Tiefe der Zisterne: Erfahrungen mit der Schwermut* (Munster, 1990), especially 58-74.

27. Cited in Post, *The Modern Devotion,* 325: "Ergo expedit ut homo cotidie aliqua hora recordetur de hoc beneficio redemptionis."

28. De Bruin, "De spiritualiteit," 112.

29. On the Carthusians, see Axters, *Geschiedenis,* 3:198-225.

30. For Franciscan spirituality, see J. A. W. Hellmann, "The Spirituality of the Franciscans," in *Christian Spirituality: High Middle Ages and Reformation,* ed. Jill Raitt (London, 1989), 31-50; E. van den Goorberg and T. Zweerman, *Was getekend, Franciscus van Assisi: Aspecten van zijn schrijverschap en brandpunten van zijn spiritualiteit* (Assen, 1998).

31. De Bruin, "De spiritualiteit," 117.

32. Cited in de Bruin, "De spiritualiteit," 117-18. The passage reminds one of Bernard, *SC,* 43:3, where he explains the sachet of myrrh (*fasciculum myrrhae*) in Song of Solomon 1:13, *SW,* 6:98.

33. Ibid., 118.

One cannot escape the impression that reflection on the suffering Christ was more a journey than a destination for adherents. For them faith achieved its certainty not as much in him who perfected it, as his support and stimulus to move it toward completion through discipleship. Yet, one ought not to absolutize this interpretation. When it was reported concerning a sister belonging to the Master Gerard House that she called Christ's sufferings a precious treasure "with which we might pay for all our guilt,"[34] this needs to be nuanced. One understood and considered not only what Christ did before us, but also what he did for us. But, something needs to be added. Namely, Groote valued meditation not only as a means for following Christ, but also as a means for union with him. "It is important, therefore, that we always endeavor to live in his presence and always conduct ourselves accordingly, for in this way we will be fused with him and become one in spirit with him."[35] Besides the exemplary dimension, the mystical dimension comes to expression here.

This is not to deny that the exemplary purpose of meditation generally predominated. What might well be considered characteristic is what is read in the *Epistola de Vita et Passione Domini*, an influential Windesheim treatment of meditation: "The life that our Lord lived, lifting it up before us, is both a fountain and an example of all virtue and all holiness, and following it is the chief means for achieving true virtue."[36] For each of the seven days of the week, the writer considered another aspect of Jesus' life. A fragment from one of the surviving addresses states exactly what meditation comes to: "We should keep his holy life before us, since he preceded us and held his life up as an example for us—in humility, in endurance, in mercy, in obedience and in love; how little he spoke and how he kept silence, how he neither laughed nor mocked, how fervent he was in prayer, how longsuffering and patient in his fasting and in his vigilence, in hunger and thirst, in cold and in heat, in poverty, in fatigue because of his preaching, and especially in the suffering of his bitter passion—in all of this he gives us the example that he would have us follow." [37]

In summary, it should be stated that meditation as institutionalized in the Modern Devotion was marked by a well-defined purpose. It came to expression not in extensive memorization, but in as thorough a digestion as possible of the pondered texts. Three components can be distinguished, namely feeling, understanding and action. Gerard Zerbolt of Zutphen, the theoretician and systematician of the movement, formulated nicely what its intent was: through rumination on what is heard and read, feelings are ignited and the understanding is enlightened, with the result that discipleship is practiced in conformity to Christ.[38] In this spiritual climate the writings of Thomas à Kempis were

---

34. Ibid., 122.

35. Ibid., 118.

36. Ibid., 121.

37. Ibid., 121-22. The citation is from Johannes Brinckerinck, poet of the women's cloister at Diepenveen.

38. De Bruin, "De spiritualiteit," 121. On Zerbolt see Post, *The Modern Devotion,* 326-30.

produced. Among them *The Imitation of Christ* was the most renowned. After the Bible, it was always the most widely read book in the world.[39]

Biographical Sketch

Because principally *The Imitation of Christ* will engage our attention, a review of à Kempis' life makes sense only if he is actually the author of this work. For this reason we first give some attention to this matter. However reliable and self-evident his authorship usually seems to us, it was already contested early on. At least forty other candidates have been mentioned, sometimes not without chauvinism. Italian historians, therefore, have attributed the *Imitation* to a Benedictine monk from northern Italy. French intellectuals considered the Parisian Jean Gerson as the possible author. The Nijmegen professor J. van Ginneken defended with some force Gerard Groote as its author. The long-standing case surrounding authorship seems at present to have been settled in favor of Thomas.[40] À Kempis himself would conceivably have considered all the commotion about authorship a waste of time. He would rather have remained anonymous. What he recommended to others, he practiced himself: "Prefer to remain anonymous." ("Ama nesciri.")[41] He never published anything mentioning his name. He assumed the position borrowed from Seneca: "Don't pay attention to who said what, but concentrate on what was said."[42] In light of this adage, I can be brief about his life.[43]

Thomas Hemerken à Kempis was born in Kempen in 1379 or 1380, not far to the east of Venlo. His father was a blacksmith named Johan Hemerken (or, Hamerken). Apparently on the advice of his considerably older brother Johannes, who played a pioneering role in the Windesheim movement by establishing a number of cloisters,[44] Thomas went to Deventer when about thirteen years old in order to pursue an education at the cathedral school of the Lebuinus Church. There he made contact with Florens Radewijns, the successor of Gerard Groote who was then the leader of the Brethren of the Common Life. Thomas was accepted into his tutelage. His association with Radewijns, who became his

---

39. De Bruin, "De spiritualiteit," 136, correctly notes, "It no longer holds this position. This title is absent from the current list of the world's bestsellers."

40. For a detailed treatment of this subject see Hyma, *The Christian Renaissance*, 176-90; Axters, *Geschiedenis*, 3:175-85; Post, *The Modern Devotion*, 524-33; de Bruin, "De spiritualiteit," 136; van Geest, *Thomas*, 59.

41. *Parvum alphabetum monachi in schola Dei*, in *Opera*, 3:317: "Ama nesciri: et pro nihilo reputari." I am making use of the authoritative edition, *Thomae Hemerken a Kempis, Opera Omnia*, 7 vols., ed. M. I. Pohl (Freibourg, 1920-1922). Henceforth, *Opera*.

42. De Bruin, "De spiritualiteit," 136.

43. The biographical details here are drawn from Hyma, *The Christian Renaissance*, 166-70; C. C. de Bruin, "Thomas a Kempis: *De Imitatio Christi*," in *Kerkelijke Klassieken*, ed. J. Haantjes and A. van der Hoeven (Wageningen, 1949), 79-114; Axters, *Geschiedenis*, 3:171-87; Post, *Thomas*, 521-23; de Bruin, "De spiritualiteit," 133-35; E. J. Tinsley, "Thomas à Kempis," in Wakefield, *A Dictionary*, 378; O. Davies, "Ruysbroeck, à Kempis and the Theologia Deutsch," in *The Study of Spirituality*, ed. C. Jones, G. Wainwright and E. Yarnold (London, 1992), 321-24; van Geest, *Thomas*, 42-57.

44. Acquoy, *Het klooster*, 246-48.

fatherly friend and defender, apparently had a definitive influence on Thomas' later life. As a choirboy he fell deeply under the influence of this respectable figure. Florens' school stood for nothing less than an education in Christian discipleship. It is reasonable to assume that in the library of the Florens House Thomas was influenced by the prominently represented writings of Augustine, Bernard and Rysbroeck.[45] Concerning Thomas' education R. R. Post judges that he had a good foundation in Latin, possessed some knowledge of philosophy, but remained a layman in theology.[46] On the last matter, judgment needs to be adjusted in the sense that it applies to systematic theology;[47] he thoroughly appropriated as his own monastic, spiritual theology.[48]

In 1399 Thomas moved to Zwolle, where he sought admission to the neighboring cloister of St. Agnietenberg, which for a year had been attached to the congregation of Windesheim. Seven years later he renounced his vows, and after another seven years, in 1413 or 1414, he was ordained to the priesthood. Perhaps this long postponement was the result of inner reluctance and his predisposition toward perfection. Apart from a three-year stay in the cloister of Ludingakerke near Haarlem, to which the entire Agnietenberg community had to retreat under pressure of church political conflicts, a brief visit to Arnhem in order to lend support to his dying brother Johannes, and a trip to Halle in connection with an assembly of the chapter, Thomas did not leave Agnietenberg. There for more than half a century he combined the contemplative life with the active existence of overseer of novices and of subprior, of a pastor and preacher, of a writer and copyist, and of a musician and hymn-writer.

However quiet and solitary his existence must have been, he did not escape the tensions of the monastic organization. He witnessed first-hand and up close the suffering imposed by the plague. His own writings make obvious how familiar he was with the fragility of human existence. Yet, this scarcely impeded his energetic work. He devoted a great deal of his time to writing tracts and copying books, including the works of Bernard and the entire Bible four times. This work of transcription was hardly a leisurely pasttime. It had both an economic as well as a spiritual and apostolic motive. With the income derived from this work, the treasury of the cloister was replenished. But more importantly, this literary output was seen as a form of spiritual exercise and at the same time as an indirect form of apostolic witness. Personal edification was not the least of the motives involved. In his *Breve epitaphium monachorum* Thomas writes, in connection with entering through the narrow gate, "Fellow monk, what are you doing in your cell? I read, I write, I gather honey-dew; and

---

45. On the collection in this library see Mikkers, "Sint Bernardus," 154. Ruybroeck's works are published by the Ruusbroec Society in Antwerp: Jan van Ruusbroec, *Werken, naar het standaardhandschrift van Groenendaal*, 4 vols. (Mechelen and Antwerp, 1932-1934).

46. Post, *The Modern Devotion*, 521.

47. Indeed, it is questionable whether one can accuse Thomas of ignorance on this score. Perhaps it is better to speak of indifference. In the scholastic enterprise he simply saw no possibility for inner reform. For him *fides quaerens caritatem* replaced *fides quaerens intellectum*. See van Geest, *Thomas*, 51 and 53.

48. On this distinction see Köpf, "Monastische und scholastische Theologie," 96-135.

these are consolations for my soul. Well stated! For the monastic cell is useful for inciting work and the study of books."[49]

Thomas continued working on the last treatise from his hand, *Chronicon Montis Sanctae Agnetis*,[50] until just several weeks before he died. After what for his day was an exceptionally long life, he died in 1471 at the age of 91. For a person who had always characterized himself as "a brother in the company of strangers, who endures his days in a vale of tears,"[51] this departure can not have been unwelcome.

Far and away the most well-known writing of à Kempis is the *Imitation*. But it is not his only one. It constitutes no more than a tenth of his literary legacy. Apart from the immense amount of time devoted to his work as a copyist— publishing appeared largely after his death—he composed a number of hymns, wrote a series of historical works, among which were the *Vitae* or biographies of Gerard Groote, Florens Radewijns and Johannes Brinckerinck, and produced the aforementioned chronicle of St. Agnietenberg. He earned the most notoriety for his devotional writings, however. These were all little tracts written in Latin.[52] Several important ones are *Orationes et meditationes de vita Christi*, *Meditatio de incarnatione Christi*, *Sermones de vita passione Domini*, *De elevatione mentis*, *Hortulus rosarum*, *Vallis liliorum* and *Soliloquium animae*. The most loved and influential was certainly the *Imitatio*.

The *Imitatio*

Whoever reads Thomas' *Imitation of Christ* receives the impression of having laid eyes on a work by a mature man with extensive experience in life. Yet, it belongs to his earliest writings, and in any case was written before his fortieth birthday. The book that enjoys world-wide notoriety bears the simple title *The Imitation of Christ*. For that matter, it is not a coherent whole, but consists of a collection of four separate tracts which are designated as Book I through Book IV.[53] The name "*Imitatio*" is clearly the name of a collection and is incorrect to

---

49. *Opera*, 4:143: "O monache, quid facit in cella? Lego scribo colligo mella. Haec animae meae solacia. Bene dixisti. Nam cella monachorum in labore et studio librorum flagrare debet." In expressing the idea that the transcribing of books has spiritual benefit, Thomas stood in a long tradition. See R. Schaab, "Bibeltext und Schriftstudium in St. Gallen," in *Das Kloster St. Gallen im Mittelalter*, ed. P. Ochsenbein (Darmstadt, 1999), 123.

50. *Opera*, 7. It has been translated in U. de Kruijf, J. Kummer and F. Pereboom, *Een klooster ontsloten: De kroniek van Sint-Agnietenberg bij Zwolle, door Thomas van Kempen* (Kampen, 2000).

51. *Sermones ad novicios regulares*, prologue, *Opera*, 6:3.

52. The title is "Van goeden woerden te horen ende die te spreken," *Opera*, 3:325-29.

53. These books are organized into short little chapters, consistently only one or two pages long. Respectively, they contain 25, 12, 59 and 18 chapters. Book 1 is known by its opening words as *Quis sequitur me* ("Whoever Follows Me") and bears the subtitle, "Useful Insights for Spiritual Life." Book 2 is also defined by its opening words, *Regnum Dei intra vos est* ("The kingdom of God is within you") and bears the title "Insights concerning the Inner Life." Book 3 begins, *Audiam quid loquatur in me Dominus Deus* ("I will listen to what the Lord God says to me") and is called "Inner Assurance." Book 4 commences with *Venite ad me* ("Come to me") and has as its subtitle "A Divinely Productive Incentive to Holy Fellowship." Consistent with the original manuscript, Pohl places Book 4 ahead of Book 3.

the extent that Thomas attached it only to the first tract, and strictly speaking, only to its first chapter.[54] The tracts appeared at intervals for a number of years, and like most of Thomas' works were intended for the instruction of young people.[55] Also, the tracts separately were in their earliest form fragmentary rather than an integrated whole. What Thomas presents is not a systematic exposition of a designated topic, but the precipitate of a number of reflections often clustered around a central theme. The differences among the first three books are thematically small. All three treat ideas that were current and cherished by the Brothers of the Common Life: devotion, humility, discipleship, world-denial, silence and reflection on Christ's sufferings and on the life to come. Compared with the first book, Book II gives more attention to the inner dimensions of devotion and to fellowship with Christ. But Book III, which takes the form of a discussion between God or Christ and the soul, is filled with the same ones. The fourth book delves into a special, specific topic, namely participation in the eucharist As an aside, I note the striking fact that Willem Teellinck incorporated various fragments from this chapter into his book "*Sleutel der Devotie,* even though in the sixteenth- and seventeenth-century Reformed editions of the *Imitation* it was intentionally omitted.[56] This is also the case, albeit to a lesser extent, with Thomas' *Soliloquium.*

The esteem with which the book was received is all the more remarkable given its fragmented composition. De Bruin correctly attributes this to the "deeply perceptive, coherent vision" it bears.[57] Post also moves in this direction. He is of the opinion that its tracts excel in the depth of thought and the warmth of love expressed in them, but also in their unaffected and rhythmic style. These features have contributed to the recognition of the *Imitation* as belonging to "the masterpieces of the world's religious literature."[58]

Not only does the Roman Catholic medievalist Post place a similarly high value on the book, the Reformed theologian B. Wielenga is equally laudatory. He thinks that the book's prominence is tied to its "pure piety, namely the experience and expression of communion with the living God," heart-felt and genuine. "The secret charm of Thomas' language lies in this, that it consistently gives the impression of welling up from springs that are pure and unfathomably deep. Thomas expresses nothing that he has not felt in his deepest self. For him writing is to express the harvest of his soul. For him speaking is to share what he had first received."[59] Post travels in what for him is the unlikely company of Ignatius Loyola, founder of the Jesuit order, who was accustomed to reading a

---

54. Compare Thomas a Kempis, *De navolging van Christus, naar de Brusselse Autograaf,* trans. G. Wijdeveld, with an introduction and commentary by B. Spaapen and A. Ampe (2nd edition; Antwerp and Kampen, 1985), 7 and 15.

55. Van Geest, *Thomas,* 49.

56. W. J. op 't Hof, "Eenen tweeden Thomas à Kempis (doch ghereformeerden)," in *De Doorwerking,* ed. Bange, et al., 160.

57. De Bruin, "De spiritualiteit," 139.

58. Post, *Thomas,* 523.

59. In Thomas à Kempis, *De navolging van Christus,* translated with an introduction by B. Wielenga (fourth edition; Delft, [n.d.]), 9.

chapter in the book daily.[60] Wielenga may know that in this regard he is supported by Reformed pietists like W. Teellinck, G. Voetius, G. Saldenus and numerous others.[61]

As far as the character of the *Imitation* is concerned, it should be noted that the work is not as much a textbook as a devotional book.[62] Thomas writes not only about devotion, but as an act of devotion. His work requires that it not be read rapidly. For that its style is too profound and aphoristic, despite its simplicity. Aphorisms require reflection. And Thomas excels at aphorisms. He knows how to write seminally, how to say a lot in just a few words. The most fruitful and singular method of approaching the *Imitation* appears to be the method of *ruminatio*, as the devotees themselves practiced it: examination and rumination. That Thomas' primary intention was to apply sacred Scripture is obvious from the way his work breathed the Bible. The Bible is cited perhaps a thousand times in the *Imitation*, whether literally or in paraphrase.[63] His familiarity with Scripture is reminiscent of Bernard, to whom he must have seemed closely related.[64] Aside from the Bible, Thomas drew heavily from the sources of the church's spiritual tradition, in which Augustine—the *doctor gratiae*—assumed the most prominent position. That a number of important streams and themes from medieval spirituality converge in the *Imitation* has been accurately observed.[65] In short, one hears in the work of à Kempis not just the

---

60. Jelsma, *"Doorwerking,"* 11; van der Pol, "Spiritualiteit," 138; G. Maron, *Ignatius von Loyola: Mystik—Theologie—Kirche* (Göttingen, 2001), 16. Compare A. Adam, *Lehrbuch der Dogmengeschichte*, vol. 2 (Gütersloh, 1968), 157; Post, *Thomas*, 548. For Ignatius' spirituality see Ignatius of Loyola, *Geistliche Übungen*, trans. Peter Knauer, S. J. (Würzburg, 1998); Maron, *Ignatius*, 48-98.

61. C. Graafland, "De invloed van de Moderne Devotie in de Nadere Reformatie, ca 1650-c. 1750," in *De doorwerking*, ed. Bange, et al., 53 and 65; op 't Hof, "Eenen tweeden Thomas," 153; idem, *Voorbereiding en bestrijding: De oudste gereformeerde piëtistische voorbereidingspreken tot het Avondmaal en de eerste bestrijding van de Nadere Reformatie in druk* (Kampen, 1991), 51, in which study, among others, J. Van Lodensteyn, W. à Brakel, S. Oomius and H. Witsius are also reviewed. Above all consult his "Rooms-Katholieke doorwerking," 73-120. Indeed, W. à Brakel was too ambivalent in his assessment for him to be included in that line of pietists who were highly dependent on the *Imitation*. For Voetius' appreciation of Thomas' *Imitatio*, consult Gisbertus Voetius, *De praktijk der godzaligheid*, 2 vols., translated with an introduction and commentary by C. A. de Niet (Utrecht, 1996), 1:20-22, 58, and 340. The original, Latin title was *Ta Asketika sive Exercitia pietatis* ([n.p.]: 1664). According to Voetius, in many ways the *Imitatio* left its stamp most importantly on the ascetic writings that appeared under the papacy, due to Thomas' vision of "the all-embracing grace of God that excluded human abilities and works" ("cum exclusione virium et meritorum hominis"). Idem, 2:8.

62. Compare à Kempis, *De navolging*, trans. Wielenga, 15.

63. De Bruin, "De spiritualiteit," 139.

64. Richard, *The Spirituality of John Calvin*, 45, n.97, "The first thing that strikes us in reading the works of the medieval monks is their familiarity with the Bible. St. Bernard, William of St. Thierry, Richard of St. Victor and others lived in a scriptural atmosphere—their thinking was molded by Scripture."

65. Richard, *The Spirituality of John Calvin*, 21: "The book serves as a channel through which Augustinian, Bernardian and Franciscan spiritualities influenced the sixteenth century and those which followed." Compare Ruh, *Geschichte der Mystik*, 4:189-90.

heartbeat of the Modern Devotion,[66] but also the echo of 1400 years of Christian piety and wisdom.

To trace Thomas' spirituality in greater detail, I will now examine individually a number of salient motifs in his *Imitation*, drawing incidentally also from his *Soliloquium*.

Discipleship

The title that the collection of Thomas' four tracts received refers to a theme that appears consistently and with emphasis in the history of Christian spirituality.[67] As was the case for many, although not for all spiritual teachers in the Middle Ages, for Thomas the *imitatio Christi* motif was the standard for spiritual vitality.[68] What is the secret of this emphasis? In one word: Jesus—or, more precisely defined: *in vita Jesu Christi meditari*, to steep oneself, through reflection, in the life of Jesus.[69] Thus, "to imitate" (*imitari*) does not have the meaning of external mimicry. Above all, it is a matter of the heart. It depends on entering cognitively and emotionally into the life and work of Jesus, and especially into his sufferings. The kernel of Thomas' program of discipleship can be summarized in a few words: "Keep the image of the Crucified One in front of you."[70] The etymological connection between *imitari* and *imago* (image) is not only philologically interesting, but has theological weight as well. The heart of *imitatio* is nothing less than one's inner focus on the image and form of the Man of Sorrows, or as Thomas expresses it, to discipline oneself to live into the most sacred life and suffering of the Lord. By this means the *religiosus*[71] finds in abundance everything that is useful and necessary. Aside from Jesus, he or she has no need to seek anything better.[72]

Clearly, for Thomas Jesus comprises the norm for discipleship. But at the same time he considers him as its source. Whenever he exclaims, "Oh, if only the Crucified One would come into our heart, how quickly and fully we would be instructed [*docti*],"[73] it is obvious that discipleship is no feat of external display, but that it is nurtured and protected by the inner working of the in-dwelling Christ. It takes concrete shape in denying oneself, not in discovering

---

66. Mikkers, "Sint Bernardus," 151, considers the *Imitatio* "de onovertroffen samenvatting en bekroning" ("the unsurpassed summary and culmination") of this movement. Also compare Acquoy, *Het klooster*, 327.

67. See K. S. Frank, "Nachfolge Jesu (II)," *TRE*, 23:686-91.

68. Richard, *The Spirituality of John Calvin*, 21; compare especially 42, n.53, where the author recalls the vital role that Augustine and Bernard have played in this regard.

69. *De Imitatione Christi*, 1.1, 5, in *Opera*, 2. Unless otherwise indicated, in the rest of this chapter references are to the book, chapter and page in volume 2 of the *Opera* edited by Pohl. For the Dutch translation I made use of the already cited edition of G. Wijdeveld (Antwerp and Kampen, 1985).

70. 1.25, 54: "Imaginem tibi propone Crucifixi."

71. Intended here is the monk or nun. Thomas has primarily this group in mind.

72. Ibid. "Nec opus est ut extra Iesum aliqua melius quaeret."

73. Ibid. Here Thomas was apparently inspired by Bernard, according to Ruh, *Geschichte der Mystik*, 4:248.

and developing oneself.[74] This comes down to radical abandonment of self-will, an abandonment—as we shall see—that implies submission to God's will and that is characterized by humility. Discipleship and humility are inseparable companions in the sense that humility is determinative of the spirit in which discipleship is realized. Thomas grasps deeply that this way of discipleship is not an ideal to be achieved by one's own sheer effort, but is rather a gift to be obtained from no one other than from Christ. From this conviction he prays, "Let your servant be shaped by your life, for in it lies my salvation and true blessedness."[75] What he hears or reads elsewhere has no appeal for him.

Given Thomas' theme being considered here, it is not surprising that the Christological accent falls on the exemplary dimension of discipleship. In discipleship Jesus is simply the perfect pattern. But, whenever Thomas at any given moment treats the fullness of salvation governed by Christ's exemplary significance, he raises the question of what the soteriological position looks like. According to Thomas, Christ has descended for our salvation. He understands that included in this salvation is the fact that in suffering Christ took our misery (*miserias*) on himself so that we could bear in the state of suffering our misery unto our salvation (*pro salute*). The burden of the present life à Kempis considers not only more bearable through Christ's example, but also very meritorious (*valde meritoria*) through his grace—undoubtedly the grace through which discipleship was created.[76] On the one hand, therefore, salvation consists of Jesus' exemplary endurance, on the other hand this exemplary-Christological salvation receives its continuation—its effect?—in meritorious discipleship, also by grace.[77] Still considered from the angle of the one-sided, exemplary content that salvation receives here,[78] the question presses on us how this relates to Thomas' train of thought developed elsewhere, in which he regards more highly God's overflowing mercy (*copiosa misericordia*) for the remission of sins than his own reputed righteousness (*opinata iustitia*).[79]

This appeal to God's superior grace appears to be in tension with the meritorious value of discipleship. Does this ambivalence elude Thomas, or rather does he consciously build it into his treatment? My impression is that he very consciously opts for both lines, and in doing so he connects with the conception current in the late Middle Ages that it is exactly God's prevenient grace that via habitual grace renders a person pleasing to God so that he or she is worthy of eternal life.[80] À Kempis displays a comparable dual track when he implores God for saving grace and for the salvation of his soul freely purchased by the precious

---

74. 3.56, 253.

75. Ibid. "Exercreatur servus tuus in vita sua: quia ibi est salus mea, sanctitas vera."

76. 3.18, 176-77.

77. Obviously Thomas here means the so-called *gratia praeveniens*, the antecedent grace that precedes all human response. Compare Muller, *Dictionary*, 132.

78. A. E. McGrath, *Iustitia Dei: A History of the Christian Doctrine of Justification*, vol. 1, *The Beginnings to the Reformation* (First edition, 1986; Cambridge, 1994), 171; idem, *The Intellectual Origins*, 82-83.

79. 3.46, 228.

80. Hamm, *Promissio*, especially 246-49, 438-45; McGrath, *Iustitia*, 166-72; McGrath, *The Intellectual Origins*, 75-85. Compare Oberman, *Spätscholastik*, 1:166-69.

blood of Christ, and in the same breath declares that he is ready to make full satisfaction (*satisfacere*) to the best of his ability.[81] With every acknowledgment that discipleship arises from grace-filled fellowship with Christ, Thomas maintains the apparently unqualified position that it is precisely this grace that lends discipleship its meritorious, satisfactory value. It occurs to me that in this à Kempis is following the emphasis of Augustine so dominant in the Middle Ages. That emphasis posited that all merit is nothing else than a gift of God and that whenever God ascribes merit, he is crowning his own gifts.[82]

Cross-bearing

Thomas is deeply convinced that cross-bearing cannot be absent from the path of discipleship. He devotes a separate chapter to the subject: "On the Royal Path of the Holy Cross."[83] In this longest section of his entire *Imitatio* he develops the following ideas.

In cross-bearing conformity to Christ, who did not live for one hour without the pain of suffering, comes to full expression. Thomas knows that a joyful spirit, the pinnacle of virtue, as well as attaining the holy life, lies in the path of cross-bearing. There is neither salvation of the soul or hope of everlasting life apart from the cross. No other way of life or path to true, inner peace (*internam pacem*) exists. Christ preceded us and, before he entered glory, died on the cross so that we in partnership with him—as his companions (*socii*)—might bear our cross in daily mortification (*mortificatio*) and might enter glory. Thus, the way of death promotes life. Accordingly, the more one dies to self, the more one begins to live for God.

Thomas views this life of continuous dying as filled with crosses (*circumsignata crucibus*). "And the more advanced one is in spiritual living (*in spiritu*), the heavier one will find the crosses become, for the pain of one's exile increases in proportion to one's love." In passing, it appears in this connection how concretely Thomas portrays cross-bearing. He thinks in terms of submitting the body to manual labor, of eschewing recognition, of willingly enduring indignity, of self-abasement and of suffering adversity.

Nevertheless, arching over this dark picture of Christian existence is a rainbow of joy. For, whenever we willingly bear our cross, it will lead us to the desired goal (*desideratum finem*). Light glows at the end. But that is not all. Now comfort (*consolatio*) descends on us. And this is no small thing. If only it amounted to the discovery that the greatest fruit is produced in the tested person

---

81. 4.9, 114. A kindred dual track is present in his conception of the Lord's supper. On the one hand he believes that no greater satisfaction exists for the expunging of sins than for him to offer to God the sacrifice of Christ in the mass (4.7, 111), and on the other hand that one can never receive the sacrament on the basis of their own worth, even if one possesses the purity of angels and the holiness of John the Baptist (4.5, 106), but that one must depend on Christ who suffered and died, hanging on the cross for peoples' salvation (4.2, 100).

82. Hamm, *Promissio*, 16, n.37, which cites Augustine's *De gratia et libero arbitrio*: "Si ergo dei dona sunt bona merita tua, non deus coronat merita tua tamquam merita tua, sed tamquam dona sua" (Migne, *PL* 44, 891). Bernard also takes this line of thought, see page 32.

83. 2.12, 82-88: "De regia via sanctae crucis."

(*afflictus*) by the bearing of one's cross (*ex sufferentia suae crucis*). Whoever submits with a good disposition experiences that the load of suffering is transformed into confidence in divine consolation. The greater the oppression is, the greater the inner grace (*gratia interna*). If one progresses to the point that testing for the sake of Christ is sweet, one may conclude from this that it is well for him, because he has found paradise on earth. It is no surprise that love for conformity to the cross of Christ can become so powerful that the cross-bearer would not want to live without adversity. She is always aware that she is well pleasing to God to the degree that she is able to bear (*perferre*) heavier sorrow for his sake. À Kempis appears to attribute cross-bearing here to human ability. Apparently he feels that to be true in his own case. By way of explanation, at least, he continues: "Not human virtue, but the grace of Christ so empowers and transforms frail flesh that, driven by the power of the Spirit, it takes initiative and finds enjoyment in things where by nature it earlier shuddered and shrank back." It depends on being armed with faith and marked with the cross of Christ (*fide armatus et cruce Christi signatus*). Whoever relies on self is equipped with neither of these. But whoever relies on the Lord, will receive strength from heaven.

At other places in the *Imitation* cross-bearing repeatedly receives attention, at least materially. This occurs whenever à Kempis discusses trials. Their purpose he locates prominently in a three-fold blessing. To begin, difficulties and opposition (*gravitates et contrarietates*) summon us back to our heart (*ad cor revocant*), that is to say, to the heartfelt conviction that we live in exile (*exilio*) here and that we do not pin our hopes on what is transient.[84] Further, through trial and temptation (*tribulatione et tentatione*) one is protected by humility. Pious people who are held in high regard cannot do without temptations. It is salvific when they are assaulted so that they will not become too confident (*securi*) or too exalted by pride (*superbia*).[85] Finally, temptation constitutes a test case. It makes obvious to what extent a person has progressed in the virtue of perseverance.[86] As iron is tried by fire, so is a righteous person tried by temptation.[87]

What remains to understand is that Thomas declares that he thanks his God both for the fruit that cross-bearing yields and for the comfort with which it is encircled.[88] God is not to be loved or praised (*diligi et laudari*) less during trials than under heavenly consolations.[89] Moreover, à Kempis knows that often Christ is closest when one experiences him as farthest away.[90] One then finds that all is not lost when a situation ends in adversity (*accidit in contrarium*).[91] So, Thomas seems to have an eye for the paradoxes that crisscross the Christian life. These do not happen beyond God's purpose and governance. Through adversities

---

84. 1.12, 20.
85. 1.20, 36.
86. 1.13, 24.
87. 1.13, 23: "Ignis probat ferrum, et temptatio hominem iustum."
88. 3.50, 238-39.
89. 3.59, 262.
90. 3.30, 200: "Quando tu putas te elongatum a me, saepe sum propinquior."
91. Ibid.

(*adversis*) he wants to train us precisely in a persevering dependence and to sharpen us in thankfulness that God counts us worthy of suffering. Moreover, they will not last forever. Christ himself assures us: "I can speedily lift you up again and turn all your burdens into joy."[92]

À Kempis knows a refuge where through trials one discovers great strength (*confortatio*), namely the wounds and precious scars of Jesus (*vulnera et pretiosa stigmata Jesu*).[93] Oppression befalls us in Christ's stead. We receive the way of the cross from his hands. These are the same hands by whose wounds, impressed on them, we are strengthened. One would like to know what Thomas means by this. Do Jesus' wounds constitute the guarantee of his substitution, by which salvation is once and for all fulfilled? Perhaps he would also reject this dilemma. But the accent which he lays falls unmistakably on the paradigmatic side of cross-bearing.

Humility

Humility (*humilitas*) is, due to Augustine's influence, one of the key words in the literature of medieval spirituality.[94] À Kempis is no exception to this rule.[95] Because God alone is great and good, the only attitude appropriate for a servant of God is that of self-abasement. For this reason Thomas esteems a lowly farmer (*rusticus humilis*) who fears God more highly than a proud philosopher who shows no self-awareness.[96] This attitude of modesty receives more attention in the *Imitation* than any other virtue.[97] What is the source of this foundational concept and what is its meaning?

Humility is born in sustained and completely candid self-knowledge (*cognitio sui*).[98] This requires a daily incursion into oneself.[99] The result is

---

92. Ibid., 201.

93. 2.1, 61.

94. Richard, *The Spirituality of John Calvin*, 44, n.83, offers a cryptic but substantive generalization. He calls *humilitas* one of the kernels of medieval spirituality. Compare P. C. Böttger, *Calvins Institutio als Erbauungsbuch: Versuch einer literarischen Analyse* (Neukirchen, 1990), 46, "Einer der wichtigsten Mahner zur humilitas war Augustin."

95. Richard, *The Spirituality of John Calvin*, 24.

96. 1.2, 7.

97. In the little pamphlet *Recommendatio humilitatis*, *Opera*, 2:377, he posits: "Humilitas cordis quasi fundamentum omnis virtutis." ("Humility is the foundation of every virtue.") It is noteworthy that Chrysostom identified humility as the "foundation of his philosophy." According to Augustine, it constitutes the first, the second and the third rule of the Christian religion. Calvin refers to both sources and identifies with the latter (*Institutes*, 2.2.11, in *OS*, 3:253). On Augustine, compare *Augustinus van Hippo: Regel voor de gemeenschap*, translated with a commentary by F. J. van Bavel (Averbode and Kampen, 1982), 50-51.

98. 1.3, 10. See Ruh, *Geschichte der Mystik*, 1:86 and 260-61, respectively, concerning Augustine and Bernard on the knowledge of self.

99. 1.19, 33. The motif of self-examination is similarly characteristic of, for example, Johannes Tauler (1200-1361). See A. M. Haas, *Nim din selbes war: Studien zur Lehre von der Selbsterkenntnis bei Meister Eckhart, Johannes Tauler und Heinrich Seuse* (Freiburg, 1971), 89-90. Tauler speaks of "nacht und tag studieren und ymaginieren und sich selber visitieren und sehen was in (sic., ihn) tribe und bewege zuo allen sinen werken." Compare A. M. Haas, "Zur Einführung," in *Johannes Tauler Predigten*, 2 vols., trans. and ed. Georg Hofmann (Einsiedeln,

nothing less than a shameful verdict concerning the self.[100] Nevertheless, one may not avoid this self critique. Whoever evades the verdict against one's own failures makes it known thereby that he is not yet truly humble (*verus humilis*).[101] Self-indictment (*accusare*) is the road to forgiveness. "It is for me to accuse, for you to forgive."[102]

Thomas does not hesitate to delve deeply into self-assessment. "Oh, how low and how little (*humiliter et abiecte*) I am compelled to regard myself. How insignificant I must consider it when it seems that I possess any good. Oh, how deeply I am forced to bow under your dire judgments (*abyssalibus iudiciis*), by which I perceive that I am nothing, and once again, nothing (*nihil et nihil*). Oh immeasurable burden, Oh unfordable waters, in which I am incapable of finding myself again, except as one who is entirely worthless."[103] What Thomas intends to express with this nihilism is not a misunderstanding of created reality or of his own creatureliness, but rather the recognition that now as a sinful creature he cannot stand in the bright light of God's judgment. *Coram Deo* fails to boast in any virtue. This anti-triumphalistic motif contains a profound awareness of complete dependence. In the same spirit that Tauler did a century earlier,[104] and that Schortinghuis would do three centuries later,[105] à Kempis professes: "I can think and say this with certainty: Lord, I am nothing; I can do nothing; I possess no good in myself, but fall short in all my endeavors; I am always inclined to futility (*ad nihil semper tendo*). And if I had not been helped by you and instructed in my inner life, I would be entirely lukewarm and indifferent."[106]

A related idea that Thomas uses is repentance or brokenness (*compunctio*). One has to train oneself in this regard.[107] This exercise consists of self-examination (*considerare sese*), through which one discovers one's own sins and lack of virtue (*peccata et vitia*), which contain the causes (*materia*) of genuine sorrow and inner brokenness (*iusti doloris et internae compunctionis*).[108] This sense of futility appears not to lie in creatureliness as such, but is based in the perversion of our humanity. Thomas' position is not to be taken as anthropological pessimism, therefore, but as a theological realism in which the self by contrast with God is revealed in all its naked reality. In the context of this

---

1987), vii (verso); K. Ruh, *Meister Eckhart: Theologe, Prediger, Mystiker* (Munich, 1989), 34-35; and idem, *Geschichte der Mystik*, 3:493-94.

100. 1.2, 7, "Whoever comes to understand himself well begins to esteem himself less." Compare 3.46, 226, "Examine yourself more fully, and you will note that the world still lives within you."

101. 3.46, 226.

102. *Soliloquium*, 6, in *Opera*, 1:216.

103. 3.14, 170-71.

104. Haas, *Nim din selbes*, 122 and following. Tauler recognizes besides a *gebrestlich nicht* ("deficient nothingness") in an ethical sense also a *natürlich nicht* in an ontological sense. The last dimension was not apparent to Thomas, it seems to me.

105. W. Schortinghuis, *Het innige Christendom* (republished from the 1740 edition; Nijkerk, 1858), 349.

106. 3.40, 216.

107. 1.20, 37: "Nemo dignus est caelesti consolatione: nisi diligenter se exercuerit in sancta compunctione."

108. 1.21, 40.

reality, humility applies. The actual occasion for it is the sinfulness remaining in the life of the saint. "Oh, how immense is the human frailty that is always inclined to evil. Today you confess your sins, and tomorrow you again commit what you have confessed. Now you put yourself on guard, and an hour later you act as though you had made no resolve." To this à Kempis attaches the admission: "We may rightly humble (*humiliare*) ourselves, therefore, and never hold ourselves in high regard, for we are weak and unstable."[109]

In spite of this, Thomas speaks positively about progress (*profectus*) in the Christian life. But the nature of this improvement intensifies humility rather than weakens it. He describes that progress as an intense conflict (*certamen*) in which we try to conquer ourselves and to make daily progress in what is good (*in melius aliquid proficere*).[110] All perfection (*perfectio*) in this life still bears the features of imperfection within it.[111] It comes down to this, that actual perfection is not attained. If we could only expunge one vice each year! But just as certainly, we often come to the realization of the contrary (*e contrario sentimus*), namely that we were better and truer in the early stages of our conversion (*in initio conversionis*) than we were after many years.[112] We make progress, therefore, in the intensification of our sense of our sin.

In the light of this discussion, it is understandable that Thomas considers it safest to conceal the gifts of grace beneath the shelter of humility.[113] One must definitely not exalt in the grace evident in the fruits of godliness, nor even talk about it often, but rather conceal it and especially not attach too much significance to it. To think little of oneself is advisable, and it is well to remember that all grace is a gift and that we are unworthy of it.[114] "In thinking about grace, remember how miserable and incapable (*misere et inops*) you are disposed to be without grace."[115] The conclusion seems justified that Thomas considers the brokenness of sanctification from two angles. On the one hand, he experiences it as painful and unbearable, on the other hand as ineradicable and in a certain sense useful, for it fosters the beneficial cautions of humility and hope.

The emergence of a knowledge of sinfulness, and along with it of humility, à Kempis also approaches from two vantage points. To begin with, it comes to serious expression not only in the presence of God, but also by the hand of God. It does not flow from the spring of one's own inner life and insight, but it depends on revelation, however profound experiential knowledge might be. God himself is the One who brings a person to the sense that he or she is of no value. In this way he graciously guards a person against vain glory. The voice of The Truth, of Christ himself, warns Thomas, "Remember your sins with great sorrow and displeasure, and regard yourself as though you were nothing (*aliquid esse*) on account of your good works. You have nothing in which you could glory, but

---

109. 1.22, 43-44.

110. 1.3, 10.

111. Ibid.

112. 1.11, 19-20. *Conversio* usually meant admission or entrance to a cloister.

113. 3.7 carries the subtitle, "De occultanda gratia sub humilitatis custodia."

114. Compare *Soliloquium*, 8, in *Opera* 1:228: "Non est hoc suum sed Dei munus gratuitum." ("This is not his work, but the unmerited grace of God.")

115. 3.7, 157.

you certainly have much that you must disparage, for you are needier than you yourself realize."[116] On account of this immeasurable poverty, Thomas heard the same voice say: "Glory in nothing you do, therefore. Above all else, find (*placeat*) your glory in the eternal Truth (*veritas*); always be displeased (*displaceat*) with your own unworthiness (*vilitas*)."[117]

At the same time, however, a second dimension must be added, namely that the humility that is unique to self-knowledge does not consist of a static achievement, but rather of a dynamic process requiring its own content. At least, it is as much an obligation as a gift. Meeting the obligation requires exertion against one's own resistance. Whenever I regard myself of little value, says Thomas, have distanced myself from all self-conceitedness (*propria reputatione*), and consider myself as but dust, which is what I really am (*sicut sum*), then God's grace will favor me and the last vestige of self-exaltation will sink away into the valley of my own self-abnegation (*in valle nihileitatis*) and perish eternally.[118]

The voice of Christ teaches and inspires, but it also claims all human activity. This claim requires an action of an entirely unique kind. Thomas views it in terms of the well known idea of death (*mortificatio*).[119] This consists of dying to all self-love, which he considered as the cradle of all vices. One is commanded to die to this root sin. Unfortunately, few take the trouble to do so.[120] But it requires diligence (*studium*) to die to one's self-interests and earthly desires. But only then can one cling to (*adhaerere*) God with all of her inner being. If we were truly dead to self and less entangled (*implicati*) within ourselves, we would be able to experience godly things (*divina sapere*) and would be able to experience heavenly contemplation (*de caelesti contemplatione aliquid experiri*).[121]

Fundamental for mortification is the renouncing of one's own will, which is the essence of self denial.[122] In this self-abnegation (*abnegatio sui ipsius*) lies one's true advancement.[123] À Kempis hears God telling him that he still had much to learn. When he asks about this, "What then, Lord?" he receives this answer: "That you would direct all your desires fully and entirely toward what pleases me (*beneplacitum*) and would not be a lover of self, but a fervent follower of my will (*voluntas*)."[124] Thomas takes the summons to heart. Renouncing himself, he prays, "Lord, you know what is best for me; whatever happens, happens according to your will. Give what you will, as much as you will, whenever you will. Do with me what you know to be best and what is most pleasing to you. . . . Behold, I am your servant, prepared for everything, for I desire nothing for myself except to live for you—Oh that it may be (*utinam*)

---

116. 3.4, 149.

117. Ibid., 149-50.

118. 3.8, 159-60.

119. 3.31, 202. Here Thomas blames the fact that many pay lip service to *contemplatio*, but neglect what is required for it. In this connection he has *mortificatio* in mind.

120. 3.53, 245.

121. 1.11, 18-19.

122. 1.3, 11; 1.11, 20; 3.17, 175.

123. 3.39, 215.

124. 3.11, 165.

worthy and acceptable."[125] For Thomas it amounts to unreserved capitulation, in which one's own will is folded into the will of God: "Let your will be mine, and let my will always conform to yours and follow it perfectly. In willing and in not willing, let me be one with you . . . . Above all, let my wishes rest in you."[126] This is strikingly analogous with Bernard.[127] He himself undoubtedly knows, as is apparent not just here but in the whole body of his writing, that in large measure his spirituality was tied[128] to that of "the most devoted Bernard" (*devotissimus Bernardus*), as he repeatedly calls him.[129]

Here there is no hint of coercion or desperation, but rather, joy and spontaneity dominate. Nothing pleases one who loves God as much as God's pleasure in his everlasting determinations (*beneplacitum aeternae dispositionis*). However God guides and determines, life is good. For, as Thomas assures, God's will and our love for his honor (*amor honoris*) must be more important for us than all else.[130] He says this devoutly, not fatalistically, like a person who has lost his heart in the love of God. This fellowship of love implies complete submission. "For, how otherwise can you be mine and I be yours," is what Thomas heard God asking, "unless both in your inner and in your outward life you are completely emptied of your own will?" Without this complete abandoning (*resignatione*) and daily sacrifice (*immolatione*) of oneself, the enjoyment of fellowship (*unio fruitiva*) with God cannot exist.[131] Humility receives its positive content in the transfer of the will entirely to God.

This strict relinquishing of our own interest and desires, this attentiveness to God, is otherwise joined to an equally stringent obedience to those, specifically in the monastic community, who have been placed in authority over us. "Whoever is not freely and from the heart subjected to those over him shows that his flesh has not yet been completely subordinated."[132] As our Master taught, we must bow to every authority. "Purge yourself . . . and demonstrate that you are so submissive and small that all can walk over you and can tread on you as though walking on dirt on the street."[133] Such a bearing involves powerful conflict. These are life and death blows by a grim and unruly enemy. This enemy is none other than our own ego. "No more exacting and malicious enemy of the soul exists for the self than oneself when one is out of harmony with one's own spirit. You must develop genuine contempt (*contemptum*) for yourself, if you would be

---

125. 3.15, 172.

126. Ibid., 173. "Sit mihi unum velle et nolle tecum."

127. Bernard explains the embrace (*amplexus*) of the Bridegroom as an "idem velle et nolle idem," by which those who were two become one in spirit. *SC*, 83:3, in *SW*, 6:612.

128. For this connection consult the convincing study of Mikkers, "Sint Bernardus," 164-65. The author identifies Thomas as "of all the Windesheim writers, the one most inspired by Bernard." According to his research, a number of passages in *The Imitation* were either taken over from Bernard's works or were inspired by them.

129. *Sermones ad fratres*, "Sermo octavus," in *Opera* 1:125; *Meditatio de incarnatione Christi*, in *Opera*, 3:44.

130. 3.22, 187-88. Compare 3.25, 192.

131. 3.37, 212-13.

132. 3.13, 168. Compare 3.32, 205. Also compare Augustine, *Augustinus . . . Regel*, 140-41; Benedict, *De Regel van Sint-Benedictus*, trans. V. Hunink (Amsterdam, 2000), 23-24.

133. 3.13, 169.

a match for your own flesh and blood."[134] What Thomas is recommending here has nothing to do with an unhealthy feeling of inferiority. Rather, his plea is for a healthy opposition to egoism and conceitedness, ailments that infect life.

In this connection à Kempis offers valuable advice on the respect that we must show for others. He presses the point that we regard the self as nothing (*de se ipso nihil tenere*) and that we think of others not just fairly but with high regard. That requires wisdom (*sapientia*) and perfection (*perfectio*). "Suppose you should see someone else sinning openly or being completely misguided, then you should not consider yourself to be superior, for you do not know how long you will maintain your good behavior." We are all weak, but we should consider no one weaker than ourselves.[135] If we possess any virtue, let us ascribe more to others and in so doing guard humility (*humilitas*).[136] Another man's failures we should bear patiently, in the realization that we have many of our own that others must endure. Thomas knows human cunningness: regarding others we are demanding, but regarding ourselves are highly tolerant. We seldom measure our neighbor with the same yardstick with which we do ourselves.[137] We rebuke trivialities in others, but excuse our own major failures.[138] When we ask for a defining theme for esteeming our neighbor, Thomas responds, "No creature is so small or lowly that it does not confront (*repraesentet*) you with God's goodness."[139]

Thomas is convinced that the quality of life does not suffer from the humbling of oneself that he is considering. The poor and humble of spirit, on the contrary, live with abundant peace.[140] As anyone knows, the exhausting pursuit of one's own interests becomes a redemptive journey through being submissive to God, who grounds all of life's guarantees in his own being. Inherent in humility is the idea of leaving life completely to God's determination. For this reason, Thomas can recommend without reservation not relying on one's own knowledge (*scientia*) or on the astuteness (*astutia*) of any other person, but rather on the grace of God, who supports the humble but humbles the proud.[141] With this kind of trust in God, a person is well off. For, whoever glories in God alone, glories in the Giver of all things who above all gives of himself.[142] Here we encounter the dialectic character of Thomas' *humilitas*: in forgetting self life is not impeded but reaches precisely its intended purpose. The other side of

---

134. 3.13, 168.

135. 1.2, 8. Compare 2.2, 63: "Do not think that you have made any progress as long as you do not feel that you are the least of all others." ("Non reputes te aliquid profecisse: nisi omnibus inferiorem te esse sentias.")

136. 1.7, 15.

137. 1.16, 27-28.

138. 2.5, 67. Calvin develops the same idea in *Inst.* 3.7.4 (*OS*, 4:154).

139. 2.4, 66. Here we are also struck by Calvin's analogy, when he posits that God himself designates an undeserving person in his place ("in vicem suam substituit") so that we may recognize the mercies shown that person as those that God also shows us. *Inst.* 3.7.6, in *OS*, 4:157.

140. 1.6, 13.

141. 1.7, 14.

142. Ibid.

calculating a radical reduction in self-fulfillment is the liberating idea that life belongs to God and is firmly anchored in him.[143]

This weaving together of one's own insignificance and of God's favor Thomas presses to the point of yearning to be found, by grace, increasingly more humble and more godly.[144] And as is always the case with grace, it will also apply to this manifestation of grace that one handles it most safely when one keeps it to oneself and takes no pride in it at all.[145] Thomas believes that the greatest saints in God's eyes are the most unworthy in their own.[146] His view of humanity is not related to that of the Renaissance. It is squarely opposed to any idea of autonomy. This is not to say that it would be identical with that of the Reformation. But that it has important parallels with the anthropological perspective of that movement seems obvious to me.

The Inner Life

Although discipleship takes an unmistakably outward form, it is primarily a matter of inner content. Like all spiritual writers, à Kempis knows, in the manner of Augustine, that the essence of humanity lies on the inside. As a typical representative of the Modern Devotion, he subjects the externalizing of life that he observes to heavy criticism. He is hardly satisfied when those who are still considered spiritual leaders (*spirituales*) are ostensibly focused on the inner life. About them, himself included, he writes, "I do not know . . . by what spirit we are driven and what we who pass for spiritual leaders actually think we are when we are so involved with transient and worthless matters (*transitoriis et vilibus rebus*), while we scarcely and rarely think with introspective substance about our inner life (*interioribus nostris*)." After a fleeting visit, we immediately return to the external order of the day, without subjecting our deeds to a searching investigation (*examinatione*) and laying them on the scales.[147]

Of what does this self-examination consist? It involves riveting attention on one's own inclinations and feelings. When the inner disposition (*interior affectus*) is corrupted (*corruptus*), it cannot be otherwise than that the activities that proceed from them bear their marks. To cite one of Thomas' numerous aphorisms, "A pure heart yields the fruit of a good life."[148] He is compelled to state for the record, however, that much attention is given to someone's achievements but, unfortunately, scarcely any to the inner attitude that is their foundation. The disposition that he scrutinizes is of a qualified kind. That becomes obvious when he writes, "People inquire whether someone is strong, rich, beautiful, and accomplished; or whether he is a good writer (*scriptor*), a good singer (*cantor*), or a good worker (*laborator*). But how poor in spirit (*pauper spiritu*) he may be, how patient and mild mannered, how pious and spiritually vital (*devotus et internus*)—many are silent about such things." His

---

143. See especially 2.2, 63.
144. 2.10, 78.
145. 3.7, 156-57.
146. 2.10, 79: "Summi sancti apud Deum: minime sunt apud se."
147. 3.31, 203.
148. Ibid., 204: "Ex puro corde procedit fructus bonae vitae."

complaint—which at the same time is intended as an appeal—he closes with the thesis that nature pays attention to human externals, while grace focuses attention on the inner life.[149]

The term "inner life" receives specific content here, therefore. It functions not so much as a designation of a place as of a quality. It is the equivalent of "piety." The combination of words "a person's inner life" not only designates in part an inner compartment of a person, but in its totality the complete person insofar as he is spiritually and piously constituted. Whoever lives the inner life lives with heart and soul in a personal, existential relationship with Christ. "Some keep me in the mouth (*in ore*), says he who is the Truth to Thomas, but have precious little of me in the heart (*modicum in corde*)."[150] To merely mouth piety verbally Thomas classifies in the same category with piety expressed in books (*in libris*) or in external signs and symbols (*signis et figuris*). Do not such utterances probably amount to concealed criticism of the not infrequent externalization of the ecclesiastical sacraments of his day? In that connection one does well to consider that à Kempis definitely does not reject the sacraments as such—Book IV speaks lovingly and with high regard for the Lord's supper—but that he is apprehensive about the loss of their spiritual connection with one's inner life. He raises his voice against mere formalism. As far as the positive side is concerned, as appears from the immediately following quotation: "There are others, possessing enlightened minds and pure motives (*intellectu illuminati et affectu purgati*), who are always interested in eternal matters. Minding earthly matters they consider to be burdensome, and they meet natural demands only as needed. But they are focused on those sentiments that the Spirit of truth works within them, for he teaches them to disdain the earthly and to love the heavenly (*amare caelestia*), to esteem the world but little and to long for heaven day and night."[151]

From this it appears that the inner life as such does not preclude the external and physical, but that this happens best when the understanding and the desires are illumined and purified. Only that, arguably, lends the inner life its high value. It is dominant, therefore, not merely by virtue of the simple fact that it is "inner life," but by virtue of the fact of its connection with a reality that in principle rises above inner life, namely the testimony of the Spirit. Positively, that voice is heard in the inner life in such a way that the heart is turned inside out, as it were, in its attentiveness to the Word. One could call this the auditory aspect of Thomas' view of the inner life.

Book III is entirely in this vein. It is entitled "On Inner Consolation" (*De interna consolatione*). The first chapter is called "Christ's Inner Communication with the Believing Soul."[152] In its opening words, "Blessed is the soul that hears the Lord speaking within and learns consolation from his mouth." What function Holy Scripture has in this regard is obvious. That role can hardly be insignificant in a book that quotes the Bible approximately a thousand times. But, what

---

149. Ibid.: "Natura exteriora hominis respicit; gratia ad interiora se convertit."
150. 3.4, 150.
151. Ibid., 150-51: ". . . caelum tota die ac nocte desiderare."
152. 3.1, 143: "De interna Christi locutione ad animam fidelem."

precisely is the relationship between the biblical word and the word spoken to the inner self?

To clarify that question we must insert a short excursion on à Kempis' use of Scripture. Thomas considered the importance of reading it so obvious that he did not actually expand on the subject itself, not even in his chapter "On Reading the Holy Scriptures."[153] He pays more attention to the precise intent and purpose attached to it. Truth, not eloquence, must be sought in the Scripture; one can better look for usefulness than for polished prose.[154] He immediately explains the connection in which this ought to occur: "Every Scripture must be read in the Spirit through whom it was written."[155] Here Thomas not only expresses his conviction that Scripture is the creation of the Holy Spirit, that it is "God-breathed," but above all that one understands the sense of Scripture only when one reads it in and through the same Spirit who is its primary and proper author. What this hermeneutical principle entails, he does not develop. He is concerned with three aspects of the subject

In the first place, Thomas finds that a needy and prayerful attitude is required. He reflects this himself. Humbly and longingly (*humiliter et desideranter*) he implores God for true understanding and for a yielded heart.[156] For Thomas humility functions as the key that gains access to productive reading of Scripture. He puts it this way, "If you want to receive a benefit, then read humbly, simply, and believingly (*humiliter, simpliciter et fideliter*), and never strive for the fame of the learned (*scientia*). Whoever is motivated by curiosity (*curiositas*) will intellectualize and rationalize (*intelligere et discutere*) Scripture and stands in his own way."[157] True knowledge is the result of submissive listening. It is acquired in simplicity.

This brings us immediately to the second aspect, in which the inner life receives explicit attention. Thomas prays for the presence of God himself and for the inner working of the Spirit, who is in the position to apply the Word to the heart. He formulates it this way: "Let not Moses or one of the prophets speak to me . . . , for without them (*sine eis*) you alone can instruct me perfectly, while without you they are of no avail." By this he intends to emphasize that the writers of the Bible by means of the written text "can certainly sound out words, but can never impart the Spirit." They certainly speak beautifully, but if God remains silent, they are in no position to kindle the heart. They transcribe the letters, but he reveals the meaning (*sensum*). "They deal only with the external,

---

153. 1.5, 12-13: "De lectione sanctarum scripturarum."

154. Ibid., 1.5, 12: "Veritas, non eloquentia; potius utilitatem quam subtilitatem sermonis."

155. Ibid.: "Omnis scriptura sacra eo spiritu debet legi quo facta est." This classical maxim has been attributed to Augustine, then again, to Gregory the Great or to Jerome. See à Kempis, *De navolging*, trans. Wijdeveld, 23.

156. 3.2, 144.

157. 1.5, 13. Also in this regard Thomas identifies with the patristic tradition. For Athanasius' perspective, for example, see P. F. Bouter, *Athanasius van Alexandrië en zijn uitleg van de Psalmen: Een onderzoek naar de hermeneutiek en theologie van een psalmverklaring uit de vroege kerk* (Zoetermeer, 2001), 62-68. How rooted in the classical tradition the theme of *curiositas* is, is apparent from the study of E. P. Meijering, *Calvin wider die Neugierde: Ein Beitrag zum Vergleich zwischen reformatorischem und patristischem Denken* (Nieuwkoop, 1980).

but you instruct and enlighten the heart. They water the surface, but you produce the fruit. They call out with words, but you turn hearing to understanding." Unless God himself is at work, one is only outwardly admonished but not inwardly inflamed.[158] In this way à Kempis emphasizes the prestige of the Spirit, in the same way that it would be recognized without exception in the doctrine of Scripture identified with the Reformation[159] and Pietism.[160] This implies no neglect of, let alone diminished regard for, the written Word. Rather, it clearly articulates the conviction that Scripture is only understood when its own author, the Spirit of God, blows on us and illumines our hearts.

The third aspect concerns the effect and implications of the approach to Scripture. For Thomas it is indisputable that the writers of the Bible prescribe commands, but that they cannot help us keep them; they certainly point the way, but do not give the power to actually walk that road. For that reason he asks: "Lord God, Eternal Truth, let me hear you yourself speaking so that I may never be judged for having only heard the Word and not keeping it, knowing it but not loving it, believing it but not safeguarding it." Only if God himself applies it, is life touched and healed to his own glory.[161]

Following this digression I think it is possible to shed some light on the issue of the relation of reading the Bible to God speaking to the inner self. That this speaking does not need to be tied verbally to Scripture is evident repeatedly in the *Imitation*. In his heart Thomas hears things that seem to come directly from Jesus' mouth but do not constitute a literal quotation of Scripture. What should one make of this? Has he received a second source of revelation alongside and above the Bible? That conclusion is premature. I think that he knows that the inner voice is completely tied to the external Word. While he is meditating on the biblical word, Jesus draws so intimately near that a dialogue can develop between him and Thomas' soul. In it he hears the voice of the One he meets in Scripture and who discloses himself, in the most literal sense of that word, with a person-to-person intimacy. The nature of this exchange is one of an indirect, although indispensable, rather than a direct relation to Scripture.[162] But in the encounter itself we are dealing with a direct exchange. Thomas is obviously speaking from his own experience when he testifies: "His visits with the inner person are frequent, and then the conversation is sweet (*dulcis sermocinatio*), pleasant and reassuring; peace overflows; and the familiarity (*familiaritas*) with him is wonderful beyond measure."[163] Thomas calls the ears blessed that receive

---

158. 3.2, 144-45: "foris admonitus et intus non accensus." The affinity with Augustine is evident.

159. Luther develops this insight when he profiles the word-based character of the Spirit. See de Reuver, *"Bedelen bij de Bron,"* 36-37. On Calvin, see ibid., 49-50.

160. Compare C. Graafland, "Schriftleer en Schriftverstaan in de Nadere Reformatie," in *Theologische aspecten van de Nadere Reformatie,* ed. T. Brienen, et al. (Zoetermeer, 1993), 29-97.

161. 3.2, 145.

162. Perhaps this way of encountering God is comparable to the experience one has when one understands the preaching of the word as being "from the mouth of God." Just as in this construct preaching is the medium of God's speech, for Thomas meditation is. Remarkably, William Teellinck in *Het Nieuwe Jerusalem* (1652) also makes use of this form of dialog.

163. 2.1, 59.

the breath of divine whispers, blessed the ears that ignore the clanging of outside (*foris*) voices but are instructed by the Truth heard within (*intus*), blessed the eyes that focus on inner realities (*interioribus*).[164] Thomas is not dealing with his own inner voice, but with that of the Spirit wafted for him in Scripture. But this voice is heard only by the inner self.

According to Thomas this inner knowledge requires assiduous concentration by way of preparation. Thomas calls "blessed" those who penetrate to the inner realities (*interna penetrant*) and who are committed through daily devotions to put themselves in a position to grasp the heavenly mysteries (*arcana caelestia*).[165] In this way he keeps his eye on the quest for silence and for shaking off worldly impediments. This longing constitutes the other side of yearning to be free and open before God (*Deo vacare*). "Concentrate on these things, Oh my soul, and close the door of your physical desires (*ostia sensualitatis*) so that you may hear what the Lord your God is saying within you."[166]

An attendant consideration that Thomas does not want to ignore is that this preoccupation with the inner life, and therefore with God and eternal matters, produces a certain detachment from the largely positive judgment that others fail us. "If your attention is directed toward what is going on in your own inner life, then you will not be concerned with what others say about you externally." People always see the outside. God sees the heart. People examine the deed. God knows the motive. If only this liberating concept is joined to a low opinion of oneself! It is a sign of inner trust (*signum internae fiduciae*) and an evidence of true submission to God, when one is not intent on being flattered by others. This is Thomas' ideal: "To walk with God in one's inner being and not to be bound by any external concern (*affectio foris*)—that is what it means for a person to live the inner life (*status interni hominis*)."[167]

Loving God

À Kempis' writings are permeated with heartfelt love for God, and especially for Jesus. It is a love that is the reflection of him who is love, and whose love completely preceded ours. While in the *Imitation* Thomas speaks almost continuously about our reciprocated love for God, he is deeply conscious of the priority and gratuity of the love shown by God. "In this you have shown me most clearly the sweetness of your love, that before I ever existed, you fashioned me, and when I wandered far from you, you brought me back to serve you and moved me to love you. Oh, Source of Eternal Love (*fons amoris perpetui*)! What can I say about you? How could I ever forget you, who regarded me as so precious even when I was so miserable and lost? You have demonstrated mercy to your servant beyond all expectation and shown him grace and friendship beyond anything that he deserves."[168] It is this love that ignites the response of

---

164. 3.1, 143.
165. Ibid.: ". . . per quotidiana exercitia se student praeparare."
166. Ibid., 143-44.
167. 2.6, 69.
168. 3.3, 162-63.

love. This causes him to reflect that this secret is, in part, imparted in the lush pastures of his time in the Scriptures (*in uberrimis pascuis scripturarum*), as the prologue of his *Soliloquium* states—times that are and remain his most cherished pleasures (*carissimae deliciae*) until the day of everlasting light.[169]

Now I want to examine one of the most specific features of Thomas' love for God, specifically its mystical hue. P. van Geest called attention to the fact that whenever Thomas speaks about the mystical union (*unio mystica*), he always uses the subjunctive or future tense and refers to this union with words conveying expectation rather than actual experience. This author comes to the definitive conclusion that in the corpus of Thomas' writings there are no testimonials to mystical experience, only aspirations to them.[170] I suspect, however, that this characterization is too hasty. To substantiate this suspicion, I point to a passage from the tract *Soliloquium*, in which the union of the soul with God is discussed. Thomas explains this union as a loving fellowship in which the soul dwells with Christ under his wings; or, as a grace-filled union filled with the love and sweetness of the Holy Ghost that one can feel better than one can explain.[171] As far as his own experience is concerned, he is, as usual, highly modest. He recognizes that the subject is obscure for him to the extent that he has had little personal experience of it (*non magnam experientiam*).[172] But he immediately adds that it reflects a reality not unknown to those who love God (*nec amanti ignota*). Because Thomas without a doubt falls into the category of those who are lovers of God, he implies thereby that he himself is not entirely a stranger to union with God. His characterization that this rare occurrence is still obscure (*obscurius*) even to him, does not constitute in my judgment a denial of his own mystical experience, but gives evidence, in Thomas's characteristically restrictive manner, that his experience still bears the fingerprints of tentativeness and brokenness. This eschatological reserve is in my opinion the reason why he is not quiet about the high points of his own experience (*experientia*) as much as he relativizes them. This attitude, it should be added, is an expression of the humility (*humilitas*) necessary for embracing the gifts of grace.[173] The subjunctive voice expresses a paradox: what he has, he needs just as much. He possesses it, but in hope. I believe that one should regard Thomas as a spiritual person who was able to sample something of the mystical love for God.[174] That he expressed himself consistently in terms of his longings is not in the least inconsistent with this. This is exactly the kind of love that, for all mystics, is always hungry for more.

---

169. *Soliloquium*, prologue in *Opera*, 1:192.

170. Van Geest, *Thomas*, 268.

171. *Soliloquium*, 13, in *Opera*, 1:253-54: "O dulcis societas: cum Christo et sub alis Christi. O gratiosa coniunctio; plena dilectione et suavitate Spiritus sancti: quae melius sentitur quam dicitur."

172. Even Bernard explains that he does not want to speak as an expert (*expertus*) but as someone who yearns for this experience. *SC*, 69:1, in *SW*, 6:418.

173. Compare n.113.

174. Mikkers is also of the opinion that for Thomas the "union of the bride with the Word" is the pinnacle of what is attainable here on earth. Mikkers, "Sint Bernardus," 179.

Factors that intensify this love more deeply are its provisional and anticipatory character. Whenever it pleased God, the holy Lover, to visit Thomas' heart, everything within him jumped for joy.[175] He makes generous use of Bernard's affective vocabulary. He says, in the chapter of the *Soliloquium* entitled "On the Great Loveliness and Comfort One Has in God,"[176] "Oh, how pleasing (*pius*), how lovely (*dulcis*), you are for those who love you, how satisfying for those who taste you (*gustantibus te*)."[177] Obviously, a line from Bernard's sermons on Song of Solomon comes to his mind when he exclaims: "What a great thing love is!"[178] He regarded nothing sweeter than love, nothing higher, nothing wider and more pleasant, and nothing fuller or better in heaven or on earth. "For love is born of God, and it finds no rest except in God alone, far above all that has been created." In this love one is focused not on the gift but on the Giver—far above all gifts.[179] The fervent desire of the soul (*ardens affectus animae*) is like music to God's ears when it says: "My God, my love, you are entirely mine and I am completely yours." From that testimony Thomas prays that he might be consecrated in love. For then he will taste in his inner being how sweet it is to love God and to melt into and to swim in that love (*liquefieri et natare*). "Let me be held by love, transcending myself in overflowing fervor and delight (*fervore et stupore*). . . . Let my soul love you in perfect submission, jubilant in its love."[180]

The beneficent affection that one now and then experiences is the fruit of the presence of grace (*effectus gratiae praesentis*), but then of a proleptic sort. It consists namely of a certain foretaste of the heavenly home (*quidam praegustus patriae caelestis*).[181] To be sure, a person should not become overly dependent on it, for it is something that comes and goes (*vadit et venit*). But meanwhile Thomas esteems it highly.[182] The sweetness of contemplating God (*contemplationis*), he considers totally indescribable, for God is the Fountain who lavishes never-ending love on those who love him.[183] According to van Geest, the context of this passage proves that this sweetness does not have its genesis in Thomas' own mystical experience, but in his understanding of God's omnipotence and goodness.[184] At first glance his argument seems defensible. Thomas always speaks in direct succession of God's love by which we are

---

175. 3.5, 151.

176. "De magna dulcedine et consolatione in Deo."

177. *Sililoquium*, 11, in *Opera*, 1:238.

178. 3.5, 152. For Bernard, see *SC*, 83:5, in *SW*, 6:616: "Magna res amor."

179. Ibid.

180. Ibid., 153.

181. One encounters a related theme in *Soliloquium*, 10, in *Opera*, 1:236, where Thomas makes mention of his otherwise unique reflection on the matters of eternity (*rara aeternorum cogitatio*). With unmistakable allusion to Bernard's *rara hora, parva (brevis) mora*, he exclaims, "And while time is short, it is still the hour of grace." ("Et licet brevis sit mora; est tamen gratiosa hora.")

182. 3.6, 154-55.

183. 3.10, 162.

184. Van Geest, *Thomas*, 269.

created and further by which we as wayward children are found.[185] After further consideration, however, one is compelled to ask van Geest whether this amazement over God's creating and saving love in Thomas' thought includes more than it excludes the contemplation of God. In my opinion there are good arguments for proposing that contemplation is not inconsistent with astonishment, but is simply nuanced by it. The mystical quality is not thereby diminished.

In so many words, even if only sporadically, à Kempis mentions an ecstatic spirit (*excessus mentis*), an inalienable motif in mysticism. He finds that it is definitely no fantasy (*illusio*) when the loving soul suddenly is transported to a state of ecstasy (*in excessum subito raptus*).[186] On the contrary, it is simply a situation of transcending (*supertransire*) all that is created and abandoning oneself entirely (*deserere*), to be caught up in sheer delight of spirit and to see that God, the Creator of all things, cannot be compared in any way (*nil simile habere*) with his creatures. As long as a person is not lifted (*elevatus*) in spirit, freed from all creatures and entirely united with God (*Deo totus unitus*), all that he knows and possesses is of little consequence. Whoever still regards anything else more highly than the one, infinite and eternal Good, at heart (*coram Deo*) does not meet God's standards.[187] The ecstatic experience does not consist of great, hedonistic delight, therefore, but of a person achieving his or her ethical identity and purpose. It is a position of worship, where God alone is exalted. Thomas' mysticism is not isolated from everyday living before God's face, but it deepens this living until it becomes a love song to God. Should this living achieve such contemplative experiences, they are exceptions according to Thomas. That is so because they are but few who fully understand how to free themselves from transitory things. At the same time, he realizes that no one controls this himself. Great grace is needed for the soul to forsake and escape itself.[188]

For the rest it is characteristic of à Kempis—and this is the element of truth in what van Geest wants to say—that most of the time he talks about these experiences in terms of desires and anticipation. Although this wishful emphasis repeatedly functions as an expression of modesty, at other times it is meant literally. The last is the case when in his *Soliloquium* he explains: "This one thing I seek, this one thing I desire. . . . My God is the One to whom it is good for me to cleave and to cling (*adhaerere et inhaerere*). To him I say, to him I

---

185. When van Geest says that we are "created and led" by God, he mistakenly limits Thomas' expression to God's providence. Thomas speaks emphatically about "those brought back" (*reduxisti*), and therefore has in mind God's saving work, by which the fallen creature is led back from estrangement from God to fellowship with him.

186. 3.6, 155. Van Geest's psychologizing interpretation seems arbitrary to me. Van Geest, *Thomas*, 269.

187. 3.31, 202-3. In my opinion, van Geest, in *Thomas*, on page 269 errs when he suggests that with the contrast made in this passage Thomas emphasizes the unique position of humanity in creation. Rather, Thomas is concerned with the unparalleled uniqueness of the Creator in contrast to all of created reality—unless by the unique position of humanity van Geest has in mind the magnanimous attitude with which only humanity regards God as good.

188. Ibid., 202.

call, 'Speak to my soul, you are my salvation.'"[189] A glowing example of longing for God and Jesus is likewise found in the chapter of the *Imitation* bearing the title, "Above All that is Good and above All Gifts, We Must Repose in God."[190] Here Thomas asks his sweetest and his most fully loving Jesus (*dulcissime et amantissime Iesu*) that he may always repose in him above all creatures, above all health and beauty, above all sweetness and comfort, above all wages and desires, above all joy and jubilation that the soul can experience. Thomas' longings find no satisfaction in any sort of experience, therefore, but reach out to his God as the only One who can satisfy his hunger. He wants only to contemplate God himself. For his heart, he says in conformity with the opening of Augustine's *Confessions*, is restless until it finds its rest in God. "When will I be completely absorbed in you, so that in my love for you I am no longer aware (*sentiam*) of myself, but only of you, above all awareness and all other ways (*sensum et modo*), in a way unknown to all others?"[191] It is a prayer that Willem Teellinck would appropriate literally by repeating parts of it.[192]

Union with Christ receives attention especially in Book IV of the *Imitation*, which treats the sacrament of communion and from which Teellinck likewise lifts substantial passages.[193] Here again it is a desired benefit. In the language of the Song of Solomon, Christ is spoken of as the Lover and as the Bridegroom (*dilectus, sponsus*).[194] Thomas calls him the "well head" (*fons*) that is always full and that overflows (*superabundans*), the fire that glows and never dies out. One drop or one spark from it is sufficient.[195] "You only are my sweetness, now and for the future, even to eternity. For you only are my food and drink (*cibus et potus*), my love and my joy, my sweetness and my every good." To this exclamation Thomas firmly attaches the prayer that he might always and entirely be received by him. Longingly stated in Bernard's style, it says: "Oh, by your presence may you set me completely ablaze, purified and transformed in you (*in te transmutes*), so that I become one spirit (*unus spiritus*) with you through the grace of inner union (*internae unionis*) and through the refinement of your intense love (*liquefactionem ardentis amoris*)."[196]

From his *Soliloquium*, it seems that Thomas can also speak of this union outside the context of the fellowship of the Lord's supper. He never doubts that a person can be united with God, however unworthy he might be. To test this (*probare*), he appeals to a two-fold witness (*testimonium*) in Scripture. The first originated in the book "of the law," the Old Testament, when it says: "My

---

189. *Sililoquium*, 12, in *Opera*, 1:245. A few pages further he says, "The intensity of love knows no rest and pursues its lover relentlessly . . . , for love desires to possess completely what it desires." ("Vis etenim amoris quiescere nescit; sed de suo amato incessanter quaerit . . . , quia amor omnino possidere vult quod concupiscit." Ibid., 249.)

190. *Imitatio*, 3.21, 182: "Quod in Deo super omnia bona et dona requiescendum est."

191. 3.21, 183. This passage demonstrates a strong affinity with Bernard's *DD*, 10:27, in *SW*, 1:121. Agreement is also suggested by Gerlach Peters, *Soliloquium ignitum cum Deo*, trans. A. Bellemans (Bussum, 1947), 118.

192. Op 't Hof, "Eenen tweeden Thomas," 162.

193. Op 't Hof, "Rooms-katholieke doorwerking," 96.

194. 4.3, 103.

195. 4.4, 105-6.

196. 4.16, 133. Compare Bernard, *DD*, 10:28, in *SW*, 1:122.

Beloved is mine and I am his" (Song of Solomon 2:16). The second is from another book, in the New Testament: "Father, my will is that they may be one, as we are one" (John 17:22). Thomas calls this "obvious testimony from the two testaments," which proves that the bride and the Bridegroom are united.[197]

If one asks in amazement how it is possible that a beggar (*pauper*) who lacks everything can be united with him who lacks nothing, the answer comes, "If you are looking for an explanation based on merit, you will only find the good pleasure of his own will."[198] Although Thomas is flexible in his view of merit, he considers the fertile ground of loving fellowship with God as clearly lying in God's gracious good pleasure. He knows only too well (*scio, scio et vere scio*) that his life and his walk are not of such a nature that he dare trust in any measure in himself. His entire hope and trust rest on the price of Christ's precious blood (*in pretio pretiosi sanguinis*). In this he abandons himself, with all his deeds and misdeeds, all he earned or forfeited.[199] He takes refuge therefore, also with any merit he possesses, in Christ alone. For when it comes down to it, he finds nothing good in himself (*nihil boni in me*).[200] This understanding forms the backdrop for his passion for Jesus: "For this reason I will read about you, my sweetest Jesus, write about you, sing about you. I will think about you, talk about you, work for you and suffer for you. I will rejoice in you and praise you. . . . For you are my God in whom I have believed, with whom I have fallen in love and whom I have sought and desired all along."[201]

Heavenly Matters

After everything that has preceded, it should be no surprise that à Kempis substantially relativizes this world—not to deny that on one level even writes it off. In the first chapter of the *Imitation* he immediately sets aside the explanation that the most profound wisdom consists in moving toward the heavenly kingdom with great respect for this world.[202] He explains that this world is always marked by vanity (*vanitas*) and from the outset has been of limited duration. "Oh, how soon the glory of this world passes."[203] For that reason one must be careful not to cling to earthly things. For then one would be swept along and as a result be lost.[204] When a person longs for the things of the present life (*praesentia*), he gambles away the things of eternal and heavenly life (*aeterna et caelestia*).[205] With sighing, therefore, he desired that his interest in the world would wither and that only his immortal Bridegroom (*sponsus immortalis*) would remain sweet to him. "Truly, the fleeting pleasures of this life are but a deceitful cup of bitterness." Whoever trusts in them will perish with them. Thomas made his

---

197. *Sililoquium*, 13, *Opera*, 1:253.
198. Ibid.: "Si meritum quaeris; invenies beneplacitum suae voluntatis."
199. *Sililoquium*, 22, in *Opera*, 1:316.
200. Ibid., 317.
201. Ibid., 315.
202. 1.1, 6: "Ista est summa sapientia: per contemptum mundi tendere ad regna caelestia."
203. 1.3, 11: "O quam cito transit gloria mundi."
204. 2.1, 61.
205. 3.16, 174.

choice. In his heart he despised (*abiectio*) worldly pomp and remembered his status as a stranger (*peregrinatio*) here.[206] He longed fervently that God would allow his heart to drink the dew of heaven and would fasten all his desires on heavenly matters, so that he would develop a taste for the lovely blessedness of things above and a deep sense of disappointment with the earthly things here below.[207]

With respect to earthly life, one ought to consider oneself an exile who is making a pilgrimage through this world (*exulem peregrinum super terram*).[208] This holds true particularly for those living the monastic life. Our dwelling place (*habitatio*) ought to be in the heavens, and everything earthly ought to be regarded as transient (*sicut in transitu*). We have here no abiding city, and wherever we linger, we are strangers and pilgrims (*extraneus et peregrinus*).[209] Thomas pleads for merely using earthly things (*temporalia in usu*), but to concentrate on longing for heavenly things (*aeterna in desiderio*).[210] The reason why temporal things cannot satisfy is not a problem for him. We simply have not been created to enjoy (*frui*) them as the highest good. One literally hears here the echo of Augustine's distinction between the use (*uti*) of earthly things and the enjoyment (*frui*) of God. À Kempis also knows that true blessedness (*beatitudo*) is found in God alone.[211] For that reason his searching heart cries out for eternal rest (*requiem*), that as a needy pilgrim he might return from his place of exile (*exilium*) to him who purchased him with his precious blood.[212] Then all seeking will come to an end; then the time of enjoyment will arrive, when God is all and in all. He alone is the One in whom each and every one is satisfied.[213]

Thomas reserves a separate chapter for the subject of meditating on death (*meditatio mortis*).[214] In it he gives advice on how a people can comport themselves in all their thinking and behavior as though they were going to die today (*quasi hodie moriturus*). In the morning one ought to consider that one might not see the evening, and when evening arrives, "it does not pay to promise yourself tomorrow morning." Blessed is he who considers the hour of his death, so that he remains prepared, day after day, for the time of his death. Thomas leaves no doubt about the nature of this state of readiness. It consists of despising

---

206. *Sililoquium*, 5, in *Opera*, 1:213.

207. 3.23, 190.

208. 1.17, 29.

209. 2.1, 60.

210. 3.16, 174.

211. Ibid. For Augustine's frequently misunderstood distinction, see *De Doctrina Christiana*, 1.22.20 and 1.4.4. Compare Böhner and Gilson, *Christliche Philosophie*, 221; J. van Oort, *Jeruzalem en Babylon: Een onderzoek van Augustinus' De stad van God en de bronnen van zijn leer der twee steden (rijken)* (The Hague, 1986), 119-22; V. Brümmer, *Liefde van God en mens* (Kampen and Kapellen, 1993), 121. By *"frui"* Augustine means to love the object for its own sake, and by *"uti"* to love out of some other consideration. So, a person may love created things—and people, but not to find salvation in them. That kind of love is to be directed toward God alone. See van Oort, ibid., 121.

212. *Sililoquium*, 6, in *Opera*, 1:218.

213. *Sililoquium*, 12, in *Opera*, 1:246-47: "Erit autem finis quaerendi cum venerit hora fruendi. Tunc enim erit omnia in omnibus: ipse solus unus sufficiens omnibus et singulis."

214. 1.23, 44-48.

the world in repentance, self-denial and suffering for the sake of Christ's love. Whoever dies to the world begins to live with Christ and sees through his tears the hour of his transition (*transitus*), his crossing over to the Lord. In his *Sililoquium*, he calls death better than life. This is so not because death in itself is desirable, but because when death removes all that is transitory, including death itself, eternal life first comes to light.[215]

Thomas' *Imitation* makes the case for a powerful yearning for that day. He has his own reasons for doing so. "Oh, whenever that blessed and desired hour arrives when you, Oh God, shall satisfy me with your presence, you will be my all in all."[216] Thomas, whose trust is deepened through his exile, hungers for the inner enjoyment of Jesus.[217] The fire of his desires burns. But no flame rises without smoke. Similarly, the desire for the heavenly home is not hindered by the desires of the flesh. But one day these trials will also be gone, and the hunger of the heart will be quieted. That satisfaction Thomas regards as a complete union of our will with God's.[218] He is definitely concerned with God himself.[219] However intensely he may yearn for heaven, he would rather walk with God as a stranger on earth than to inherit heaven without God. "Where God is, heaven is. And death and hell are where you, Oh God, are not present. You are my deepest desire."[220]

Certainly it cannot be said too often that the driving force of Thomas' spirituality is his emphasis on love for him who first loved us.[221] This love for God is what ignites his heavenly longings.

Evaluation

I do not want to close this consideration of Thomas' spirituality without an assessment. I provide it in a critically positive—and admittedly, anachronistic—way from a reformational perspective. To begin, I indicate a number of points from this perspective on which one would wish for more clarity.[222]

---

215. *Sililoquium*, 6, in *Opera*, 1:218.

216. 3.34, 208. Thomas' prayer recalls a line from a hymn ascribed to Bernard: "I long for you a thousand-fold, my Jesus. Oh, when will you come to me, gladden me? Oh, when? When will you satisfy my deepest longings?" ("Desidero te millies, o Jesu, quando venies? Me laetum quando facies? Me de te quando saties?") See J. C. Trimp, *Jodocus van Lodensteyn: Predikant en dichter* (Kampen, 1987), 178. Trimp relies on the Dutch translation of F. van der Meer.

217. 3.48, 231: "Desidero te intime frui."

218. 3.49, 236.

219. Compare *Sermones ad novicios*, "*Sermon* 13: 'Soli Deo adhaerere cupiens,'" in *Opera*, 6:91.

220. 3.59, 261: "Tu mihi in desiderio es."

221. Compare Oberman, *Die Reformation*, 39. Oberman calls the "*via amorosa*" the core of Thomas' mysticism.

222. I restrict myself here to these points, whether explicitly or implicitly handled in the foregoing discussion, and pass over, for example, Thomas' Marian devotion as that appears in a pronounced way for his day in his *Sililoquium*, while developing those that by reformational criteria are in tension with the uniqueness of Christ's mediatorship. I give even less attention to Thomas' view of the sacrificial character of the Eucharist, which is generally present but certainly not dominant, but in which the once-for-all nature of Christ's sacrifice is minimized. See, for example, 4.5, 107.

What comes to mind in the first place is Thomas' concept of grace. While in reformational thought grace, no matter how much it might be experienced by the inner self, still consists primarily of God's favorable disposition (*favor Dei*), Thomas almost always means by "grace" inner grace or graces (*gratia interna* or *gratiae internae*).[223] He talks readily, therefore, about the "gift of grace."[224] When he is concerned with the indispensability of the demonstration of God's grace, Thomas does not take a back seat to the reformers. His deep dependence on grace comes to expression more than once.[225] On this basis T. F. Torrance comments on the sometimes "remarkable approach to the *sola gratia* of the reformers."[226] But as surfaces incidentally, à Kempis at various times does not rise above the axiom that typifies the medieval doctrine of grace. I mean that the notion, otherwise variously interpreted, that the person who does what lies within his power (*faciens quod in se est*), will receive grace.[227] In the *Imitation* Thomas handles at least the first half of this expression repeatedly.[228] That the second half is missing in its precise expression is possibly not accidental. Does he want to avoid the impression that a person's good works could be the basis of God's (initial) expression of grace? In any case, as appears from the context, he thinks that "doing what a person can" is never, in semi-Pelagian style, contingent on a person's own ability residing in his fallen human nature, but depends on a capacity that is given by unmerited grace and that puts the recipient of grace in a position to perform "meritorious" works.[229]

The second matter that attracts our attention is in connection with Christology. That the main line of Thomas' piety is unequivocally Christocentric is beyond doubt. Even less dubious is the fact that the atoning significance of

---

223. The synonymous use of *"gratia"* and *"dilectio"* (love for God) in 3.55, 25 is very significant.

224. For example 3.7, 157, in comparison with the gift of devotion; 3.10, 163, in comparison with the monastic life; and 3.31, 202, in comparison with the *excessus mentis*.

225. For example, 3.14, 170; 3.23, 190; 3.46, 228; 3.55, 250-51. Compare T. F. Torrance, *The Hermeneutics of John Calvin* (Edinburgh, 1988), 75-78. Particularly significant is 3.55, 251: "O, how absolutely essential your grace is to me, Oh Lord, in order to begin anything good in me, in order to progress in it, and in order to bring it to completion. For apart from that grace, I can do nothing. . . . Oh, true heavenly grace, without which I have no merit of my own!" ("O quam maxime est mihi necessaria Domine tua gratia, ad inchoandum bonum, ad proficiendum, et ad perficiendum; nam sine ea nihil possum facere. . . . O vere caelestis gratia; sine qua nulla sunt propria merita.")

226. Torrance, *The Hermeneutics*, 182, n.56.

227. On the proposition, apparently inspired by Ambrose, "From the person who does what is possible, God does not withhold his grace" ("Facienti quod in se est Deus non denegat gratiam"), see among others F. Loofs, *Leitfaden zum Studium der Dogmengeschichte*, vol. 2 (7th edition; Gütersloh, 1968), 158-59; Oberman, *Spätscholastik*, 1:126-29; idem, *Die Reformation*, 103-4; C. P. Carlson, Jr., *Justification in Earlier Medieval Theology* (The Hague, 1975), 126-28; Hamm, *Promissio*, passim; McGrath, *Iustitia Dei*, 1:83-91; idem, *Reformation Thought: An Introduction* (Oxford, 1988), 57-60; idem, *The Intellectual Origins*, 81-83; Muller, *Dictionary*, 113. For various interpretations of the proposition, see B. Hamm, *Frömmigkeitstheologie am Anfang des 16. Jahrhunderts: Studien zu Johannes von Paltz und seinem Umkreis* (Tübingen, 1982), particularly 251-59; A. Zumkeller, *Johannes von Staupitz und seine christliche Heilslehre* (Würzburg, 1994), 151-54.

228. For example: 1.7, 14; 3.7, 157; 4.7, 111; 4.10, 118; 4.12, 125.

229. Compare the text of note 82.

Christ's work is overshadowed by the exemplary perspective. To be sure, one cannot posit that for à Kempis salvation depends entirely on Christ's example and our discipleship. But, that his restrained concentration on this matter tilts toward a reduction of the biblical witness concerning the sufficiency of Christ's atoning work, seems to me to be indisputable. (That his restraint is for didactic reasons does not obviate the distortion.) On this crucial point, he is mostly disappointing.[230] At the very least, this means that he would deny the crucial importance of Christ's mediatorship and sacrifice.[231] This certainly means that the Christ who is our substitute and whom no one can or may ultimately imitate often recedes into the shadow of the Christ who calls us to follow him.

In the third place, I reflect on the matter of justification by faith. Among reformational convictions it without a doubt assumes the cardinal place. Although Calvin, who may well serve as the model, regards justification as inseparably tied to discipleship by virtue of believing fellowship with the one Christ, who is simultaneously committed to both our justification and our sanctification, he nevertheless expressly regards justification as the most important pillar (*praecipuum cardinem*) of religion and piety.[232] Without asserting that this sentiment is entirely strange to Thomas,[233] one must nevertheless maintain that his position concerning it is ambivalent. Justification is not central, but the sanctified life of discipleship is. Wilhelmus à Brakel is not entirely wrong when he notes concerning "that most excellent tract on *The Imitation of Christ*"[234] that it has little to say, as does Tauler's writing, "about the Lord Jesus as a ransom and as our righteousness, and how he is instrumental in the justification of a true believer."[235] Whenever à Kempis ascribes some meritorious value to the practice of discipleship, therefore, the relationship of justification and sanctification is out of balance. In this regard a century later, Luther, and the entire Reformation with him, turned the rudder in a radically different direction. This heaving around of the theological bow is expressed in

---

230. Compare I. van Dijk, *Gezamenlijke Geschriften*, vol. 4 (Groningen, [n.d.]), 34-42.

231. See, for example, *Sililoquium*, 15, in *Opera*, [2]:268), where Thomas testifies to the great love with which Christ bore him on his shoulders when he, carrying his cross, made his way to the Place of the Skull, where he was crucified. "For, there it was more I than the cross that was carried to that place. And my sins were a heavier burden on his shoulders than was the wooden cross. For, on my account that cross was carried, not on his account." ("Ego enim ibi portabar ab ipso magis, quam crux ipsa. Et erant onera graviora umeris eius peccata mea, quam hoc lignum crucis. Nam propter me portata est crux illa, non propter se.")

232. *Inst.*, 3.11.1, in *OS*, 4:182. Compare his sermon on Luke 1:5-10, in *CO*, 46:23: justification is "le principe de toute la doctrine de salut, et le fondement de toute religion." In his *Responsio ad Sadoleti Epistolam*, in *OS*, 1:469, Calvin calls it the "summum in religione."

233. 3.46, 228 is especially significant. Compare 3.52, 242.

234. À Brakel records emphatically that here he has in mind the first three books, for the fourth he considered to be tacked on by someone else ("van een ander daer by gelapt").

235. W. à Brakel, *Redelyke Godtsdienst*, vol. 1 (12th edition; Rotterdam, 1733), 43.4, 1081; hereafter abbreviated as *RG*. According to him, it is astounding that à Kempis had even less to say about Jesus' "approach to God, in order to contemplate God's glory in his presence, and from him and in union with him to display true holiness." (". . . toenaderinge tot Godt/om in zijn aengesichte Godts heerlijkheyt te aenschouwen/en uyt hem/en in de vereeniginge met hem/de ware heyligheyt te betrachten!") He thought that as long as the reader of *The Imitation* kept these reservations in mind, he could derive profit from reading it (". . . kan men er profyt uyt halen.").

Luther's motto, "Discipleship does not make us God's children, but God's adoption of us as children makes us his disciples."[236] The antithesis captured in this conviction is strange to Thomas. For him synthesis is important. For Luther the two are exclusive, but for Thomas they are inclusive of one another.

The fourth point is closely related to the previous one. While faith is unmistakably central in reformational spirituality,[237] Thomas' spirituality obviously pivots on love. Thomas himself would certainly not want to acknowledge a dilemma here. Faith without love is as much an illusion in his conception of spirituality as the other way around. This is true for the reformers as well. The difference, however, lies in the distribution of weight, which in each case is driven by a different purpose. When the Reformation gives more attention to (clearly received) faith than to love, it does so with an eye toward justification by grace alone. Love adds no weight to the scale. But when Thomas on more than one occasion agrees with this perspective, he has another purpose. For him justification is seldom on his mind but is more or less on the sidelines. Much more prominent is the practice of piety (*praxis pietatis*), which is realized in fellowship with God and in following Christ. This specific perspective explains why for him love predominates. Both his mysticism and his ethics are always borne by this love. In this construction faith is implicit in the background. For him, faith operates through love (Galatians 5:6). One would like à Kempis to have brought faith more explicitly into the discussion and thereby done more justice to the structure of Paul's treatment in Galatians, indeed in all his writings. For it is certainly the case that faith works through love!

In the fifth place, I turn to Thomas' pneumatology. Although the Holy Spirit is not absent from the *Imitation*, it is noteworthy that throughout he remains unmentioned. His working ordinarily comes to light implicitly, and then in the various forms of internal grace (*interna gratia*). But once again one must say that that explication should have led to clarification. The misunderstanding that inner grace consists more of impersonal strength than of the personal working of the Spirit in the heart is always unimaginable. The reformers knew that grace is never transferred from God's hands to ours and in no instance is it at our disposal. Grace is always God's privilege. However inwardly it touches and renews us, it comes into us from above in a personal encounter with God through the Spirit. Thomas' writings awaken the suspicion that on this matter he in fact thought no differently. This makes it all the more regrettable that his thoughts in this regard were so seldom articulated in expressly pneumatological terms.

Sixthly, reformational spirituality is notably more afraid of legalism than Thomas is.[238] Naturally, the genre represented by the *Imitation* frequently injects the tone of admonition and exhortation, and the imperative could probably be more muted than it is. To be sure, spirituality involves conduct. But, the key to understanding it lies in the passivity of its receptiveness. Activity and receptivity

---

236. *Ad Galatas* (1519), in *WA*, 2:518: "Non imitatio fecit filios, sed filiatio fecit imitatores."

237. Calvin's statement in *Inst.* 3.1.4, in *OS*, 4:5, might well be considered as representative of this position: "Faith is the most important work of the Holy Spirit." ("Fides praecipuum est eius [i.e., Spiritus Sancti] opus.")

238. Richard, *The Spirituality of John Calvin*, 124; van der Pol, "Spiritualiteit," 137.

complement one another, but primary emphasis should be on receptivity. A man like Calvin knew how to protect this irreversible connection between promise and obligation. On the one hand he could write that the entire life of the Christian must consist of reflection on spirituality (*meditatio pietatis*), for he has been called to holiness. On the other hand, pastorally he just as emphatically added: "Whenever the conscience is unsettled over the question of how God will be gracious to a person . . . , one must not contemplate what the law demands, but one must always remember that Christ alone is our righteousness."[239] Thomas certainly understands this evangelical emphasis, but he is less attentive to it.

Finally, there is Thomas' monastic formation. Reformational piety understands seclusion and meditation, moderation and concern with eternity, but its asceticism is spiritual.[240] The reformers had their own monastic traits. Luther meditated for hours each day, and Calvin only slightly less. Their intimacy with God, however, detracted nothing from their solidarity with the world. Thomas' ideal consisted of world-flight. His spirituality was stamped by solitude. That of the reformers is characterized by solidarity. There were no closed windows in their monastic cells. Their windows were open to street noise. And their spirituality bore its marks. In this connection Luther recast the traditional medieval triad of *meditatio, oratio* and *contemplatio* (meditation, rhetoric and contemplation) as *oratio, meditatio* and *tentatio* (rhetoric, meditation and investigation).[241] À Kempis also had his temptations, but they were in a very real sense private and internal. Luther's were experienced no less internally, but they were fueled not so much in being shut off from his own existence as in the open air of public life, where loving faith could clash so painfully with the paradoxical realities of daily existence. The difference was substantial.

These seven important, critical factors render even more intriguing the question of why Thomas' *Imitation* and to a lesser degree his *Soliloquium*, received such a cordial reception in the movement of Reformed spirituality known as the Further Reformation.[242] I believe that this can be explained on the basis of a number of fundamental spiritual themes that cross confessional boundaries: heartfelt love of God, being humbled in one's guilt for sin, dependence on grace and longing for the glories of heaven. The passion of Psalm 27 burned in Thomas' soul: "One thing will I seek. . . ." Throughout this search he identified with the poet of Psalm 86: "Join my heart to the praise of your name." For à Kempis understood that while his longings were directed toward

---

239. From the 1536 edition of *The Institutes* (found in *OS*, 1:224), as cited from W. van 't Spijker's Dutch translation (Delft, 1987), 249.

240. The term "inner worldly asceticism" ("innerweltliche Askese") was coined by Max Weber and taken over by E. Troeltsch. See A. Bélier, *La pensée économique et sociale de Calvin* (Geneva, 1961), 477-97; J. Bohatec, *Calvin's Lehre von Staat und Kirche mit besonderer Berücksichtigung des Organismusgedankens* (reprinted from the 1937 edition; Aalen, 1968), 701-10; Richard, *The Spirituality of John Calvin*, 126.

241. Nicol, *Meditation bei Luther*, 91-101. On Luther's sympathy for as well as criticism of the brother-houses, see R. Mokrosch, "*Devotio moderna, II*," in *TRE*, 8:615.

242. W. J. op 't Hof, "Thomas à Kempis bij Willem Teellinck," *DNR* 13 (1989): 42-68; 14 (1990): 88-112; 15 (1991): 1-13. Compare idem, "Rooms-katholieke doorwerking," 75 and 96.

God alone, they were crisscrossed with the resistance of the flesh and threatened by the devil's enslaving power. Withstanding this siege depended not on his own power. The weakness that he readily confessed as a sin caused him to fall back on the chastening mercy of God. But, Thomas' intimacy with God never yielded the presumption of "a free ride." His devotion nowhere speaks of self, but was expressed as pure dependence on God. From a pietist perspective this forthrightly acknowledged weakness must be regarded as one of the strongest features of his spirituality.

This characterization of Kempian spirituality is intensified by its sustained sense of the provisional. To be sure, it allowed for those grace-filled times of delight and fellowship with God in the present, but these constituted exceptions to the rule. The rule consisted of the certainty of the "not yet." But Thomas did not passively resign himself to this reality. Rather, his ultimate longings smoldered in his unsettled heart. His devotion was permeated with an intense yearning for what was coming, and above all for the One who was coming. Pietism is intimately tied also to this kind of yearning.

À Kempis cannot be considered a fore-runner of the Reformation. In his case the basis for that status is too small. He stands completely, although not uncritically, in the late Middle Ages. Thomas brokers catholic ideas that are characteristically *Roman* Catholic. But, it is undeniable that his conceptual legacy lies embedded in a spirituality that reflects *Christian* catholicity. It appears to me that this catholicity of an experiential communion with God is what appealed to and attracted seventeenth century Reformed pietists. For that reason several of them could integrate Thomas' devotion with the piety that they advocated. Their Reformed convictions compelled them to do so critically in their writings and with corrections, but their sense of catholicity obviously accorded them enough room to make grateful use of this pre-reformational devotional legacy.[243] And it is understandable that for contemporary pietists, who have preserved this understanding of catholicity, the instances of estrangement do not eclipse those of recognizable unity.

---

243. In eighteenth-century Reformed pietism, according to C. Graafland, the connection with Thomas was pretty well lost. This author adduces two causes for this. First, the eighteenth century movement was less practically and more passively oriented. Second, it was less broadly catholic. Graafland, "De invloed," 67-68.

3

Willem Teellinck (1579-1629)

"A Steadfast and Experienced Practioner"

When a good two years after his father's death, Willem Teellinck's oldest son, Maximillian, wanted to publish from the extensive collection of manuscripts left in the older man's estate one entitled *De worstelinge eenes bekeerden sondaers* [*The Struggles of a Converted Sinner*], he asked Gisbert Voetius to provide an endorsement of the work. With obvious delight, the learned minister of Heusden responded positively to the request. Voetius would not have been true to his form, however, if he had expressed his praise in just a few words. He took the opportunity to craft an extensive preface of ten pages in quarto, in which he wrote a bird's-eye history of pietism and emphasized the importance of the authors who treat the practice of piety.[1] He then enumerated names of such medieval figures as Bernard, Tauler and à Kempis, and of Puritans like Perkins and Ames. Voetius also mentioned with respect Teellinck in this list of practical writers. Voetius noted that he would not easily forget the two or three times he had heard his colleague preach. Since then it had been his heartfelt desire that he himself "and all preachers here in our land would imitate a similar style and power in preaching." But, besides that, it was especially Tellinck's writings that aroused Voetius' admiration: "In them he has abundantly demonstrated how his mind was engaged with Scripture, his heart always deeply stirred by divine matters, and his spirit transported from idle preoccupation with the world to contemplation of heaven. In summary, what a steadfast and experienced practitioner of his profession he was, so that he may rightly be regarded as a second Thomas à Kempis (however, a Reformed one!) in our age." The highly gifted Voetius did not hesitate to declare that Teellinck in his writings, "as he has for countless others, has truly opened my eyes and my heart to God's grace, so that I understand many things more precisely and reflect on them more fully."

This quotation demonstrates that Voetius not only had a profound amazement for Teellinck's spirituality, but that this fascination also took the form of personal influence. Already from the time of his student days in Leiden, Voetius was inspired to deeper insight and further reflection by his colleague, who was ten years his senior.[2] Undoubtedly, this applies to the subject of the *praxis pietatis*, the ideal that characterizes the Further Reformation. Whenever one

---

1. Op 't Hof, "Eenen tweeden Thomas," 142-53.
2. Op 't Hof, ibid., 156, says, "Door het lezen van Teellincks boeken is Voetius gewonnen voor het ideaal van de praktijk der godzaligheid." See especially also op 't Hof, "Gisbertus Voetius en de gebroeders Teellinck," in *De onbekende Voetius: Voordrachten weten-schappelijk symposium Utrecht 3 maart 1989*, ed. J. Van Oort, et. al. (Kampen, 1989), 92-108.

recalls that Voetius—who on account of his piety, erudition and academic status is considered the pivotal figure of the Further Reformation—has Willem Teellinck (and also his brother Eeuwout, to be sure) to thank for the fact that he became the theologian of that movement, Teellinck's importance for this pietistic tradition is hard to overestimate. Not without good reason is he regarded as the father of the Further Reformation.

Voetius was indebted to Teellinck, in large measure, for his Further Reformation convictions, and in his own right became a resource for the riches of Anglo-Saxon Puritanism. Pre-eminently Teellinck's biography and body of work demonstrate that the pietistic movement in the Netherlands was intertwined with that of England and Scotland. What is just as clearly apparent from his writings is the unmistakable fact that the medieval devotional material—whether or not via Puritanism—penetrated the Further Reformation's realm of thought. It was not an empty claim, therefore, when Voetius called the author of *De worstelinge eenes bekeerden sondaers* a second, albeit Reformed, Thomas à Kempis.[3]

Biographical Sketch

That Willem Teellinck bears the honorary title "Father of the Further Reformation" has good reason.[4] He deserves the title not just because he stood at the beginning of the movement, but certainly also because of his wide public acceptance. The number of publications by this prolific author that appeared in print stands at about seventy-five, among which some twenty are extensive. He also left approximately fifty never-published works. Based on the scope and

---

3. For three reasons I forego a characterization or positioning of the Further Reformation. The first is that I already did so briefly in the "Introduction." The second is that its most prominent feature, in my judgment, namely its spiritual heart, is discussed in what follows. The third is that ample, accessible, recent literature on the subject is readily available. I provide a selection: W. van 't Spijker, "De Nadere Reformatie," in *De Nadere Reformatie: Beschrijving van haar voornaamste vertegenwoordigers*, ed. T. Brienen, et al. (The Hague, 1986), 5-16; C. Graafland, "Kernen en contouren van de Nadere Reformatie," ibid., 349-67; W. J. op 't Hof, *Engelse piëtistische geschriften in het Nederlands, 1598-1622*, Monografieën Gereformeerd piëtisme, vol. 1 (Rotterdam, 1987), 583-625; W. van 't Spijker, "Bronnen van de Nadere Reformatie," in *De Nadere Reformatie en het Gereformeerd piëtisme*, ed. T. Brienen, et al. (The Hague, 1989), 5-51; van den Berg, "Die Frömmigkeitsbestrebungen," 57-112; de Reuver, "Wat is het eigene," 145-54; Graafland, op 't Hof en van Lieburg, "Nadere Reformatie," 107-84. Of great interest for a review of Second Reformation study is W. J. op 't Hof, "Studie der Nadere Reformatie: verleden en toekomst," *DNR* 18 (1994): 1-50.

4. The following sources were consulted: W. J. M. Engelberts, *Willem Teellinck* (Amsterdam, 1898); H. Bouwman, *Willem Teellinck en de practijk der godzaligheid* (Kampen, 1928); P. J. Meertens, *Letterkundig leven in Zeeland in de zestiende en de eerste helft der zeventiende eeuw* (Amsterdam, 1943), 173-78; K. Exalto, "Willem Teellinck (1579-1629)," in Brienen, et al., *De Nadere Reformatie*, 17-21; P. J. Meertens, "Willem Teellinck," *BLGNP*, 1:373-75); M. Golverdingen, *Avonden met Teellinck: Actuele thema's uit zijn werk* (Houten, 1993), 17-31. For Teellinck's publications see J. van der Haar, *Schatkamer van de gereformeerde theologie in Nederland, c. 1600-c. 1800: Bibliografisch onderzoek* (Veenen-daal, 1987), 470-82; W. J. op 't Hof, *Bibliografische lijst van de geschriften van Willem Teellinck* (Rotterdam, 1993). Furthermore, according to the last source, see also the extensive list of 46 articles published to date in *DNR*, vols. 1-25, under the title *"Willem Teellinck in het licht zijner geschriften."*

especially the wide circulation and illustrious quality of his publications, this author's titles were in great demand, as is indicated by their frequent reprints.[5] Perhaps he ought to be regarded, therefore, as the most important representative of Further Reformation spirituality.

Teellinck was born at the beginning of January, 1579, in Zierikzee. His father, Joost Teellinck, wore the robes of the mayor's office and participated in various important ceremonial functions in the Province of Zeeland. Although Willem originally wanted to study theology, upon further reflection he followed in the footsteps of his older brothers, all three of whom pursued careers in law. Among them, his well-known brother Eeuwout became Procurer General of Zeeland. Choosing legal studies, Willem began his academic preparation in Leiden, continued it at the Scottish University of St. Andrews, and completed it in Poitiers in France. He graduated as a doctor of jurisprudence in 1603. Thereupon, the newly minted, 25-year-old "J.D." traveled to England. This visit marked the turning point of his life. While he was lodging with a friend in Bambury, he made contact with a circle of Puritan pietists whose lifestyle made a lasting impression on him. The deeply and quietly held quality of their spirituality captivated him from that time forward.

Because of the defining importance that this episode had for Teellinck's Further Reformation insights, it seems appropriate for me to summarize here his own account of it. He included this in the preface of his *Huysboeck,* 1618, which is addressed to "the heads of Christian homes" in Middelburg.

In order "to awaken upright hearts to discipleship," he recounts there how the family life of the English friend with whom he resided for a few months as a guest was structured. In the morning everyone in the home prepared for their daily work in a timely manner, so that no one began the day before they had called on the name of the Lord earnestly and had read a chapter of the Bible with serious inquiry. In this way they sanctified their daily activity by the Word and prayer. Even the servants were granted time for this activity. Thereafter, each went about their responsibilities until noon-hour. Then the entire family gathered, young and old, in order to read Scripture together once again. "Also, having been prepared by the reading of the Word, they called on the name of the Lord with one accord, on bended knees." Then, after offering a brief prayer for blessing on their meal, they discussed at table the points raised in their Scripture reading. After the meal a Psalm was sung and people returned to their work. The evening meal occurred in the same vein. At the time of retiring for the night, each person reflected "in private, between herself and God alone," on the course of the day and thus devoted herself in prayer to God, "as the occasion dictated."

The weekly church services were diligently observed. Saturday afternoons the children and servants were given catechetical instruction. On the Lord's day, everyone assembled for the reading of a chapter from Scripture and in order to

---

5. Apparently the verbosity of his style did not damage his popularity. Otherwise, his stylistic deficiency was compensated for by its vivid imagery. See Meertens, *Letterkundig leven,* 178, on Teellinck's linguistic style. This source for the most part presents a rather negative judgment, but it makes an interesting connection between Teellinck's artless style and the Puritan ideal of sobriety.

pray together. Afterwards, they attended church and listened attentively to the spoken Word as people "who knew that they would have to give an account of the demands made by whatever they had heard." Some transcribed the sermon they had heard. At home, individuals personally applied it to themselves and prayed for God's blessing. At noon, while seated at table, they discussed the sermon. Then each one found a spot "in order, through prayer and solemn meditation, to renew their readiness to obey the Word." Attendance at the evening worship service followed the same pattern. The day closed with the entire family gathered to reflect on the content of the sermons and to receive an admonition "to overcome what was still lacking" in their lives. In this way, preaching was for them "a lamp to their feet and a light upon their path."[6] One's entire daily walk was stamped and defined by "spiritual exercises" and the call to discipleship. "Thus, they served the Lord with steadfast endurance and demonstrated that in fact one did not have to crawl into a cloister with the superstitious papists in order to lead a religious life."

The Puritan spirituality that Teellinck came to know in Bambury and that he described with such great affection would leave a deep impression on his life and work.[7] This English retreat also had profound consequences for his vocational choice. During this period his slumbering desire to enter the ministry awakened. Overcoming his original hesitation, he divulged his desires to a few godly friends. After a special day of fasting and prayer, they were able to help him overcome his hesitation. Rather quickly thereafter, already in 1604, he left for the Leiden Academy in order to prepare himself theologically under professors Lucas Trelcatius, Jr., Franciscus Gomarus, and Jacob Arminius. There Gisbertus Voetius, ten years younger than he, was his fellow student. Here the eventual father of the Further Reformation and the future pivotal figure of the movement found themselves in the same setting.

Meanwhile, Teellinck was married to Martha Angelica Greendon, an English woman, who in the Dutch language went by the name Martha Grijns. Upon completing his studies,[8] he received a call in 1606 to "Haemstede and Burcht" on the island of Schouwen, where the famous Godefridus Udemans had served before he had left for Zierikzee in 1604. Prior to his ordination, Teellinck and his wife made a trip to France. In French Angers their first child, Maximillian, was born. He would be followed by two daughters and four sons. The second of Teellinck's five sons died very young. The others—Maximillian, Justus, Theodorus, and Johannes—all studied theology, and all but Justus became ministers.[9]

For seven years Teellinck served in Haamstede. According to Maximillian, the people were known as "the most foolhardy of the entire island." To what extent Teellinck's Puritan ideals made an impression on them, I have not been

---

6. Ps. 119:105, according to the Deux-Aes version employed by Teellinck.

7. According to W. van 't Spijker, R. Bisschop and W. J. op 't Hof, *Het puritanisme: Geschiedenis, theologie en invloed* (Zoetermeer, 2001), 247-50.

8. For a two-year curriculum in theology see H. H. Kuyper, *De Opleiding tot den Dienst des Woords bij de Gereformeerden* (The Hague, 1891), 531.

9. On Justus see W. J. op 't Hof, *"Een onbekende zoon van Willem Teellinck,"* in *DNR* 25 (2001): 84-89.

able to determine. Concerning his stay in his first charge there is little to report. What is known is that he paid another visit to England in 1610, and that in 1612, together with his colleague Hermannus Faukelius of Middelburg, was delegated to The Hague to put pressure on the States General to convene a national synod. The following year he was called "to the leading mercantile city of Middelburg." He accepted this call. After he had preached a "sample sermon" in all four of the Dutch-speaking churches of the city, he was installed in November. Among his ministerial colleagues, besides the already mentioned Faukelius, were Antonius Walaeus and Franciscus Gomarus, the last of whom had left the Leiden Academy and in 1615 would became a professor in Saumur. Teellinck faithfully served his Middelburg congregation for the rest of his life. For sixteen years he pursued his official duties with great blessing. Despite his frail health—every year he was incapacitated with some severe illness—he displayed remarkable diligence in his daily duties regarding preaching, catechism instruction and pastoral care. That he found time and energy for sustained publishing is cause for amazement.

The practice of piety that he introduced from England and propagated in various ways he himself pursued scrupulously. Especially in his book *Noodtwendigh Vertoogh* [*An Essential and Earnest Testimony*], 1627, which came to 500 pages in quarto format, he laid out in great detail his all-encompassing, Puritan-pietistic program of reform. That it was not merely a theoretical ideal but a living reality for him is illustrated by the pattern of his own life. He was regarded as a simple, open, friendly person. By nature he was peace-loving and possessed a forbearing manner, at least to the extent that God's honor was not short-changed. In his own family, where he took personal initiative, devotions three times a day were strictly observed. Already early in the morning, at the breakfast table, he led in prayer as head of the home. Idle conversation was taboo. Each evening father Teellinck catechized his entire household from an open Bible. Saturday was devoted entirely to the task of preparing for the sabbath.[10] On Sundays the Teellincks usually invited the Middelburg poor to a (somber) meal. This was a characteristic of Teellinck's social compassion, which also came to expression in his sharp critique of the wealthy aristocracy. At least once a year the family observed a day of fasting, although Teellinck himself fasted more frequently.

One could call certain positions held by Teellink "rigorous." He was undoubtedly no stranger to the appearance of moralism. However, if one is in any way knowledgeable about the licentiousness that characterized early seventeenth-century society, one can appreciate Teellinck's strictness.[11] He was

---

10. In the first section of his *Noodtwendigh Vertoogh*, Teellinck calls attention to five "remaining sheets" (apparently blank pages provided by the publisher) on which the reader could record his reactions pointedly and extensively. These were preceded by an "explanation" of his "opinions on sabbath observance."

11. A. T. van Deursen, *Mensen van klein vermogen: Het kopergeld van de Gouden Eeuw* (Amsterdam, 1992), 117-36.

very disturbed by the coarsening of Dutch social life. What necessarily followed for him was his serious pursuit of the sanctification of church and society and the formation of souls characterized by the inner, mystically tinted piety in which the love of Jesus predominated.

By the time he was a good fifty years old, Teellinck sensed the end of his life approaching. It was March, 1629, at the time when Prince Frederik Hendrik was preparing for his successful conquest of Den Bosch. Teellinck's former fellow student Voetius was at the time active as the prince's military chaplain and the fame of his illustrious academic career still lay ahead of him. He would outlive Teellinck by almost half a century. The Middelburg pastor had run his race. He was prepared for the end. Gathering his somber friends around him, he assured them that he desired to enter his heavenly home, if   God so willed. At peace, he died in the Lord on April 8, 1629. He was buried in St. Pieterskerk—demolished in 1838—and mourned by the Middelburg congregation; it was the church in which pietistic spirituality had blossomed, not least of all because of his influence. In the dedication of selections from Teellinck's publications that he edited, Franciscus Ridderus wrote, "Where others desired to soar like eagles, his aspiration was to turn his face toward Christ, the Sun of Righteousness, like a sunflower, and to wait with the bride while the Bridegroom tarried, in order to follow in his footsteps and to encourage others to do so as well."[12] This citation aptly portrays Teellinck.

A Selection

Teellinck was not only a prolific but also a many-sided writer, at least as far as the *praxis pietatis* is concerned. His conviction was that this spiritual practice should simply cover all of life: hearth and home, church and civil government, education and medical care, vocation and spare time, Sunday and the workday. From his writings it appears that scarcely any area escaped his attention or was not illumined by his insight. Just as obvious is the fact that for him the fullness of life had one, single center, namely personal communion with God. For him, as it must be for every Christian person, everything revolved around this center. One can characterize Teellinck's life as both a quest for this center and as a flight to it. On the one hand he sought this center with an enduring desire, and on the other hand this secret and private refuge was simultaneously the source of his inspiration that bore fruit for others. This concentration on God—Teellinck called it "devotion"—is what I want to draw out and emphasize from the body of his work. Accordingly, I allowed myself to be led mainly and extensively through three of his publications, namely *Sleutel der Devotie* [*The Key to True Devotion*] (1624, volume two published posthumously in 1656),[13] *Soliloquium*

---

12. From *De Mensche Godts* (Hoorn, 1656), as cited in Engelberts, *Willem Teellinck*, 38.

13. I used *Sleutel Der Devotie Ons openende De Deure des Hemels* (improved, last edition by T. and J. Teellinck; Utrecht, 1655), and idem, vol. 2 (Utrecht, 1656). [Trans.: *The Key of True Devotion Opens Heaven's Door*.]

$(1628)^{14}$ and *Het Nieuwe Ierusalem* (published posthumously in 1635).[15] In the context of this selection from his works, I make another choice. I choose a number of themes that seem to me to be the most relevant and the most representative for explaining his views on personal piety.

Teellinck's Sources

The point Teellinck raises about communion with God does not rest on theoretical knowledge, but was nurtured by personal experience. He handles the subject not like a crass salesman, but his writings simply radiate his own personal experience. Yet, he makes explicit mention of them only relatively infrequently. Therefore, it is an exception to hear him say in the introduction of his *Soliloquium* that in these "tracts" he wants to commit to writing the experiences "that we to some degree have experienced ourselves."[16] He immediately adds that these "stirrings" are ones that he has "detected, furthermore, in many others." But this in no way detracts from his own personal engagement. It only emphasizes that he did not hold himself up as the spiritual model, but as one of many who speaks from experience. Teellinck writes not to put himself on exhibit, but "to motivate" others to this kind of devotion, or at least "to make progress" toward it. He wants to recognize that his piety is shared with many others.

In yet another very specific way, how indebted his faith-life was to that of others comes to expression, namely to devotees who had preceded him. What role these played in his thinking on the theme of piety he explains in the preface of his voluminous *Sleutel der Devotie*. There he clarifies that he took the trouble "to work through all sorts of books on devotion by as many spiritual kinsmen as we could recover (down to the most unsavory ones who went by the name 'Christian')." Exactly whom he had consulted he does not disclose, but that he did this on a large scale and that in so doing he did not hesitate to cross confessional boundaries is as clear as daylight. His explicit qualification shows, however, that he had not read the mentioned authors uncritically and that he had

---

14. I used *Soliloquium ofte Betrachtingen eens sondaers/ die hy gehadt heeft inden angst zijner Weder-gebeboorte. Dienstich om te voorderen de Bekeeringe van de doodelijcke wercken tot den levendighen God; ende tot een hartsterckinghe tegen alle weereltsche droeffenisse* (reprinted; Rumpt, 1999, with an introduction by E. Stronks; Middelburg, 1628), and *Soliloquium, ofte alleensprake eens zondaers, in den angst zijner wedergeboorte,* a new edition of this work, with notes, by H. Vekeman (Erfstadt, 1984). [Trans.: *Soliloquies: Or the Experiences of a Sinner that He Had in the Fear Felt During His Spiritual Rebirth; Which Are Useful for Promoting a Conversion from Dead Works to the Living God, and for Strengthening the Heart against All Worldly Sorrows.*]

15. Use was made of *'t Nieuwe Jerusalem Vertoont in een t'samensprekinge, tusschen Christum en Mariam, sittende aen sijn voeten* (Utrecht, 1652). [Trans.: *The New Jerusalem Disclosed in the Dialog between Jesus and Mary while She Was Sitting at His Feet.*]

16. The three separately published volumes of *Tydt-winninghe* (Middelburg, 1629) constitute a spiritual diary of the last three months of Teellinck's life. Also in them he provides us with a window on the life of his soul. The same is true of the letter that he wrote in 1600 to Franciscus Junius, included as an appendix in Engelberts, *Willem Teellinck*, 224-27. I thank Dr. W. J. op 't Hof for calling my attention to this fact.

certainly not followed them gratuitously. What criterion he maintained in this connection comes to light in what followed. He writes pointedly that he drew not only from what he had learned about devotion from his own "investigation and experience" with Holy Scripture as well as from "the most prominent authors in the Reformed church," but that above all else he had adopted with thanks from the "aforementioned authors" only "that in them which was well-testified and that they had adopted from true religion and wholesome teaching." Accordingly, he only had use for what corresponded with Scripture and with Reformed religion. When necessary, he introduced his own "changes," undoubtedly in a Reformed sense.

While the authors in question were repeatedly identified by Teellinck as "aforementioned," they nevertheless remained anonymous. He made an exception for only one work, even though he did not mention the author's name; it is "the book called 'The Imitation of Christ.'" Especially from it, he says, he "drew" many passages. He had a special reason for this, and it was not because without exception he found himself in à Kempis' tract. Rather, it was simply because this little book was in so many hands, even though here and there expressions appear in it that are capable of leading "the simple" astray. Summarizing, he said that he was of the opinion that whatever in "the aforementioned authors" was useful for true devotion had been worked into his *Sleutel*. The conclusion that he drew from this is remarkable. He was of the opinion that his own writing would be able to replace "all other devotional books." Here Teellinck seems to be more than a little pretentious. But, that was not his intention. On the contrary, he frankly acknowledged that "among the thousands of our fellow-workers in the Reformed church" he certainly considered himself to be the least qualified for this task. Above all, one should not forget that he had just explained that he had drawn liberally from the work of others. That he pushed aside the earlier, pre-reformation devotional material as unusable is certainly not the case. He made grateful use of it, and whatever was of value in it he incorporated into his own project. But he aimed to transpose its form and flavor into a Reformed context. For he was convinced that "only the true and right religion, that we by God's grace confess, is well-suited to awaken one powerfully to true devotion and to the right pursuit of a religious life."

When W. J. op 't Hof concludes that Teellinck "recognizes and esteems"— within the framework of Reformed theology—the sources he considered useful, his conclusion contains a great deal of truth.[17] At the same time, it needs to be emphasized with the same author that for good reason Teellinck developed a responsible alternative. He did this because in his opinion those other works contained dangerous and unhealthy doctrinal elements.[18] In the already mentioned preface he identifies three "errors" by name: the "delusion of perfection," justification by or in conjunction with good works and "under-

---

17. Op 't Hof, "Eenen tweeden Thomas," 160.
18. Op 't Hof, "Rooms-katholieke doorwerking," 95-97; also compare 75-76. In this connection, of interest is also L. F. Groenendijk, "Opdat de mensche Gods volmaekt zy. Lectuur voor de religieuze vorming der gereformeerden tijdens de zeventiende eeuw," in *Pedagogische Verhandelingen: Tijdschrift voor wijsgerige en historische pedagogiek*, 9 (1986): 17-18.

valuing" Scripture. Their consequence is that one either maintains "erroneous" traditions of one's own devising or appeals to "unusual invasions" of one's own spirit.[19] With respect to Teellinck's dependence on Roman Catholic sources, it is useful to keep two considerations in mind. What K. Exalto expressed in a broader context strikes me as applicable also to Teellinck: "In our discussion of Reformed pietism, it will always be possible either to emphasize its affinity with medieval piety or to stress the difference between the two. But it will be necessary for us to keep *both* in mind and yet to discount *both* in our own appraisal of pietism."[20]

Teellinck's ambivalent assessment, however, does not detract in the least from the fact that countless times he quotes from Thomas' *Imitation*. Striking examples of this are, first that his main source consists of a Roman Catholic translation of à Kempis' well-known tract,[21] and second that in his *Sleutel* Teellinck not only quotes from its first three books, but cites copious passages from the fourth book, which deals with the eucharist, the section that in the Reformed editions of the day was intentionally omitted.[22] To be sure, not just the *Sleutel* contains a great deal of à Kempis' material. The same holds true for his *Soliloquium* and for his *Het Nieuwe Ierusalem*.[23] One hardly needs to guess at the cause and purpose of Teellinck's "ecumenical" endeavor. The cause is that he recognized himself in a mystical spirituality borne by experiential communion with God and a glowing love for Jesus. While he did not hesitate to cleanse this pre-Reformation spirituality of its "impure stains," his perspective nevertheless embraced a breadth that crossed its own confessional boundaries.[24] The purpose would have been none other than an evangelistic one. For Teellinck was certainly Reformed to the core, but at the same time he was also Christian to the core. As a Reformed Christian he accorded true devotion not just to Reformed people, but to the entire Christian tradition. He wanted to make this catholic breadth recognizable expressly by his ties to late medieval spirituality.[25]

---

19. In the "Aenhanghsel aen de Sleutel der Devotie" [i.e., appendix], he discusses in more detail the difference between true and false devotion, 2:265-305.

20. K. Exalto, "De Nadere Reformatie in de polemiek met Rome," in *DNR* 15 (1991): 130.

21. *Qui sequitur me, Dat is De naevolginge Christi, in vier Boecken bedeylt*, trans. Pauwels Stroobandt (Antwerp, 1615). See op 't Hof, "Eenen tweeden Thomas," 160; idem, "Rooms-katholieke doorwerking," 96.

22. See op 't Hof, "Eenen tweeden Thomas," 160-61. Op 't Hof offers an accurate summary of the pages on which the numerous quotations in the *Sleutel* and in the edition used are found. In my own research, that involved not only the *Sleutel* but also the two other works previously mentioned, this Antwerp edition was not readily at my disposal. I used the edition edited by M. I. Pohl: *Thomae Hemerken a Kempis, Opera Omnia*, 7 vols. (Freiburg, 1902-1922).

23. Boot, *De allegorische uitlegging*, 152-54; Vekeman, H. "Inleiding," to *Soliloquium, ofte alleensprake eens zondaers, in den angst zijner wedergeboorte*, by Willem Teellinck, published with an explanation by H. Vekeman in the series Veröffentlichungen des Instituts für Niederländische Philologie der Universität zu Köln (Erfstadt, 1984), xxxvi; B. Hollebenders-Schmitter, B. "Willem Teellinck: *Soliloquium*, mystisches Gebet im Zeitalter des Barock: Eine Analyse" (an unpublished manuscript, Cologne, 1989).

24. Graafland, "De invloed," 68, correctly regards this characterization as applicable to the first period of the Further Reformation in general.

25. Op 't Hof, "Rooms-katholieke doorwerking," 96, says: "In fact, in this way he wanted to promote evangelistic endeavors among those that did not adhere to Reformed doctrine." Perhaps

Devotion

Since the days of early Christianity, the term "devotion" has been in vogue as an expression of the worship of God. Although Augustine's preference seems to be for the term "*pietas*," the designation "*devotio*" assumed a dominant place in spiritual vocabulary, especially due to Bernard's influence. The abbot of Cluny reserved "*devotio*" for the inner contemplation of Christ, particularly of the suffering Christ. I need not go into the development of the term here.[26] I note only that this designation was much loved in the circle of the Modern Devotion. Teellinck attaches himself to this tradition. He describes devotion as "a conscious surrender of oneself to God whenever a person, living an aimless and uncommitted life, now commits himself totally and completely to the worship of God, and with heartfelt resolution lives close to the Lord."[27] For him this constituted the core of "the proper exercise" of religion. In other places he designates it "the unfeigned exercise of divine blessedness," or else "the practice of divine blessedness."[28] Of its benefit and enjoyment he had no doubt. Remarkably, he regarded it as situated in the first place in freedom. Although natural man lives in a freedom without God, such a person is "free and loose" from any constraint, but is called to obedience to the God who is "our Absolute Lord."[29] Whoever loses himself to God lives in a two-fold freedom: he is freed from the guilt of sin and freed for loving service. "The worship of you, O Sweetest Lord, is complete freedom," cries Mary in her conversation with Jesus.[30] The second "benefit" consists of the fatherly assurance that the vicissitudes of life ultimately, one by one, "serve our blessedness."[31] The third fruit that he noted was the durable trust with which a person awaits eternal joy.[32] Devotion, therefore, is not a matter of coercion or pretentious obligation, but much rather of freedom, certainty and joy.

Typical of Teellinck's spirituality is when he has Mary address her Master as the "God of my total delight and joyfulness."[33] This involves a joy that is the fruit of communion with God and the closeness of Jesus. Whenever a person communes with God "in stillness and in solitude," one can expect Jesus' refreshing entry. "Always be very humble," writes Teellinck echoing Thomas, "for then Jesus will draw near to you; be devoted, ardent and quiet, for then Jesus will remain with you and impart to you the flavor of sweetness."[34] Teellinck

---

this notion of catholicity is comparable to the high regard that the reformers accorded the patristic fathers. See W. van 't Spijker, "Reformatie tussen patristiek en scholastiek: Bucer's theologische positie," in *De kerkvaders in Reformatie en Nadere Reformatie*, ed. J. van Oort (Zoetermeer, 1997), 50-51.

26. For a concise review see Richard, *The Spirituality of John Calvin*, 79-86. Compare Hamm, *Frömmigkeitstheologie*, 159-60; and Waaijman, *Spiritualiteit*, 343-44.

27. "Voor-reden tot den Leser, *Sleutel*, 1: unpaginated.

28. *Jerusalem*, 2 vols., 1.2.

29. *Sleutel*, 1.4.3, 247.

30. *Jerusalem*, 1.2, 7.

31. Ibid., 8.

32. Ibid., 10.

33. Ibid., 1.4, 33.

34. *Sleutel*, 2.6.5, 235. *Imitatio*, 2.8, in *Opera*, 2:72.

describes his own such experience in *Soliloquium*: when he clung to the Lord and worshipped him for an entire day, then in the evening he was apt "to feel great joy."[35]

One cannot force devotion. The exercise of that "most profitable divine blessedness" is least of all the result of a purely external approach to God. The latter is only "the outline and shadow" of it, in which "the power, the kernel, the spirit" is lacking. Then one experiences nothing of the "heavenly incursions of the heart that come from spending time alone with God, from holy meditation, from the soul's deliberations, from inner concerns, from the wrestling against sin, from those sweet intimate consolations, pleasures and solaces that are worked in the spirit through spiritual rebirth, the fountain of all joy."[36] Teellinck's devotion, therefore, is an inner experience, but it does not originate from inside oneself. It has a "strange" origin and depends exclusively on the inner working of the regenerating Spirit. In the meanwhile, from this "fountain of all joy" comes not only comfort and pleasure, but also struggle and strife. The sin of self-love is a stubborn enemy. Against it God's Spirit does battle. At the same time, he does so not without requiring the full involvement of a person's spirit. Evil desires must be slain. In this connection two things are particularly commanded, namely that one resist the desires of the flesh on one hand and that one "force oneself to purse all the spiritual disciplines" on the other hand.[37] Teellinck was compelled to determine that for most people, alas, this was asking too much. On this subject he maintained that a spiritually productive person was an "entirely unusual creature." His estimation of the percentage of genuine Christians was not optimistic. "Frequently, among a hundred who bear the name 'Christian,' it is impossible to find three who are true Christians." Therefore, everyone must earnestly establish whether he belongs to this class, and above all also "pay strict attention to himself, that he might be found to be such a person."[38]

Also, whenever one can meet the test and may consider herself a true Christian, it in no way means for Teellinck that she can rest on her laurels. Spiritual life is marked by growth and vitality. "All nature teaches you this—all herbs and all vegetation do so; how would the same then not by the case for the entirely new creature?" Would a person who daily devotes careful attention to his body have no concern for his soul "and not take care that it also is improved day by day?"[39] Following this exclamation, Teellinck claims the patriarchs and

---

35. *Soliloquium*, 28.90.
36. *Jerusalem*, 1.7, 65.
37. Ibid., 1.7, 71.
38. Ibid., 74.
39. Ibid., 2.7, 180-81. As an aside, I note that with respect to punctuation seventeenth-century authors like Huygens, Hooft, Brederode, Vondel and Brandt in general made little use of the semicolon, but in its place often employed the colon. One can substitute a semicolon where we presently employ a colon, while the semicolon likewise can function like a comma. An exclamation that begins with a question (for example, "What a . . ."), is often followed by a question mark in place of an exclamation mark. See A. Weijnen, *Zeventiende-eeuwse Taal* (Zutphen, 1956), 15-16. These punctuation rules or conventions, which for the most part—like spelling rules—were applied without subsequent consistency, need to be kept in mind when

the prophets as examples. In a long and practically literal quotation from Thomas' *Imitation*, he then describes what "tribulations" all the "apostles and martyrs, confessors, virgins and all the other saints," as well as "the holy, ancient fathers in the desert," have endured.[40] Inspired by their exemplary devotion, a person will increase in dedication and virtue.

Teellinck is sober enough to realize that the degree to which a person is involved in devotions is dependent on the time available. In this regard he pleads for "discretion." A minister, for example, can and must be "more profuse" in "religious exercises" than someone in a secular profession. A well-off man who is "well cared for" can permit himself more time in this regard than "a needy man who must work hard for his daily bread."[41] But this graduated difference does not undermine the fact that all Christians are reasonably expected to engage in devotional exercises at home every day.[42] The question of exactly how much time these daily devotions should take he did not presume to answer with "a universally applicable rule." Just the same, it did not stop him from explaining that he identified with "an old little verse quoted by the faithful":

> Worship our God four hours a day,
>> Let three for food come into play,
> Sleep seven more, less if you can,
>> Give eight others to the work of man,
>> And two to help the mind to understand.
> If you, this way, your time so use,
>> You'll find your soul has none to lose![43]

By this Teellinck indicates, furthermore, that this division of one's time is not compulsory, since many need all of twelve hours simply to maintain themselves. What "in general" he does contend, however, is that every Christian, no matter in what situation he finds himself, must invest just as much time in the care of his soul as he does on his physical wellbeing. The soul is certainly "the most

---

dealing with the literature of the "old writers" of the Further Reformation. [Translator's note: we have modernized the older punctuation included in quotations by the author.]

40. Ibid. Compare *Imitatio*, 1.18, in *Opera*, 2:30-31. It is striking that Teellinck changes à Kempis' "sacrifices of prayer" to "prayers"; "contemplation" to "devotion"; "loved" to "chosen"; "example for monastics" to "example"; "monks" to "they"; "holy and perfect" to "holy." Among the little additions that Teellinck introduces, the expression "to become increasingly holy" is striking.

41. *Sleutel*, 1.4.17, 373.

42. Ibid., 375. In this connection Teellinck makes some interesting remarks of a social-critical nature. He laments the fact that so much time is spent working in jobs that cater to the luxurious lifestyle of the rich and the powerful. Here he has in mind silk and lace workers, confectioners and pastry bakers, and other unnecessary "superficialities." A poor "hair stylist" must sometimes slave the whole day, plus part of the night. If only people would keep busy with necessary activities, like "agriculture, sheep herding, and those that applied in earlier times!" Were people to devote themselves to agriculture, raising livestock, spinning and weaving, etc., they would be able "to meet their necessities nicely" in six to eight hours of work a day. Then what time would be freed for reading the Bible, prayer and meditation! Ibid., 1.4.18, 393.

43. Ibid., 1.4.18, 395.

valuable dimension" of our being! For that reason, it is advisable to turn aside from "all worldly concerns" at least once a day and to render oneself "entirely detached and free" from earthly cares, for the purpose of directing oneself "with understanding and affection" toward the Lord alone. Then one is involved in "offering himself as a sacrifice" (Romans 12:1), submitting to the will of our good God "without any reservation whatsoever."[44] In order "to win" the heart over to this task, Teellinck advises "loving reflection" on God's bounties bestowed on us, and especially on all the glory laid up for us in the future. In this way one will "touch and taste how merciful the Lord is." Teellinck called this a "powerful love potion, or loving compulsion." The "loving fragrance of his name" (Song of Solomon 1:3) will draw Christ's bride to follow her Bridegroom more readily.[45] By "following" Teellinck means nothing less than practical living in human society. The inner communion with God is expressed in the external sanctification of life. The fruit of devotion carries over into "every other endeavor," so that they all are directed according to the will of God.[46] For this reason, fellowship with God as the fount of sanctification cannot be neglected for a single day. Whenever circumstances so require, it can of necessity be conducted "quite quickly." Thus, it does not always require the same amount of time. It only need be accompanied with a "strong resolve of the heart and a yielding of self to God."[47]

This resolve Teellinck liked to call good or earnest intentions. It is a concept that repeatedly appears in Thomas' *Imitation* and also is the warp and woof of Teellinck's writings.[48] In the *Sleutel* he devoted a separate chapter to the subject. By it he understood an unfeigned desire and determination to exalt the Lord in all things: in family life and society, church and private matters.[49] A decision must always be made in a person's heart. But it is a decision that must be renewed and implemented every day. To illustrate the necessity of this, Teellinck appealed to the example of a timepiece. Just as the weights of a clock must be pulled up repeatedly, in the same way a Christian needs to renew continually his "holy determination." Otherwise it happens just as with the weights of a clock: it is drawn downward by its own weight. It is the same with the heart of a Christian. It always is pulled "down toward the earth." For that reason, a person must "be pulled back up toward heaven" with renewed determination on a daily basis.[50]

This resolve Teellinck definitely did not regard as a purely intellectual decision. Rather, for him it functioned as an existential motive, by which the

---

44. Ibid., 396. Here one hears in the background echoes of a passage in Thomas' *Imitatio*, 3.37, in *Opera* 2:213, where the daily offering of oneself to God is discussed.

45. Ibid. The image of the aroma of love recalls Bernard's "loving and sweet-smelling sachet of myrrh," whose content he gathered from Christ's saving work. *Sermones* 43.3, in *SW* 6:99. This metaphor borrowed from the Song of Solomon one encounters likewise in Gerard Zerbolt of Zutphen, one of the earliest representatives of the Modern Devotion. See Ruh, *Geschichte der Mystik*, 4:167.

46. *Sleutel*, 1.4.18, 397.

47. Ibid.

48. Boot, *De allegorische uitlegging*, 153.

49. *Sleutel*, 1.1.8, 39. A strongly related description can be found in *Jerusalem*, 1.9, 92.

50. *Sleutel*, 1.1.8, 43.

practice of one's way of life is determined from the inside out. It came down to this inner disposition. In order to underscore this, he appealed for help to a crucial passage from the *Imitation*.[51] Citing Thomas almost literally, he wrote: "Men usually ask what great accomplishments someone has achieved, and that is what they regard as important. But they do not investigate nearly as closely from what great love or from what intentions of the heart[52] such accomplishments were made or are being made. But that is what it all comes down to as far as God is concerned." People consistently pay attention to courage and beauty,[53] but hardly ever to the "heart and spirit" behind them. How poor in spirit someone is, how patient and devout, people usually pass over in silence.[54] In this context, in the tradition of à Kempis,[55] Teellinck intended to relativize the external exercise of devotion. A person cannot permanently live in prayer and meditation. Good judgment is required.[56] A person can also spend too much time fasting, weeping and praying. "In this regard, good proportion must be maintained." But as far as the inner dispositions of the heart are concerned, there a person should impose no limits. Our intention always and everywhere should be to serve God in everything.[57]

With à Kempis, Teellinck thought that the understanding as well as expression of this intention is strictly dependent on the grace of God and does not proceed from one's own power and wisdom.[58] He produced the same biblical texts in this connection that Thomas did: Proverbs 16:1 and Jeremiah 10:23. But aside from this, the Middleburg pastor emphasized grace and the leading of the Holy Spirit. For Teellinck devotion requires all our human capacities. For this he made a powerful appeal. Following the lead of Thomas, he said: "We must certainly renew our best purpose and intention every day, and we must daily endeavor to awaken ourselves to new intensity in our spiritual lives, even if we have begun the day on the wrong foot. We must do so as if we had never done so before."[59] However, this is a command that is encircled by the promise of God's

---

51. *Imitatio*, 3.31, in *Opera*, 2:204.

52. Thomas says, "from what virtue" (*virtute*).

53. Here Teellinck has in mind, respectively, the work of a general and a preacher; Thomas, that of a *scriptor* and a *cantor*.

54. *Sleutel*, 1.1.8, 40.

55. *Imitatio*, 1.19, in *Opera*, 2:32-33. This concerns the heading, "On the Devotions of a Good Monk." It is a chapter from which Teellinck quotes generously, for example, when he says that not all devotions need to be practiced in the same way by everyone; or, that communal exercises (for Thomas, the monastic; for Teellinck, the church-goer) must be observed; or, that when time allows, a person may devote oneself "to some special exercise according to their devotional inclinations"; or, that to be sure we cannot always be introspective, but nevertheless we must devote "some time" to this each day, concerning which his advice is to pursue good intentions in the morning and in the evening to reflect on what our conduct has been in thought, word and deed.

56. Thomas says, "Corporalia exercitia discrete sunt agenda." ("The physical side of devotions are to be done with discernment.")

57. *Sleutel*, 1.41.

58. Ibid., 42. Compare *Imitatio*, 1.19, in *Opera*, 2:33. "Iustorum propositum in gratia Dei potius quam in propria sapientia pendet." ("The intentions of a righteous person depend more on God's grace than on his own wisdom.")

59. *Sleutel*, 1.4.9, 295. Compare *Imitatio*, 1.19, in *Opera*, 2:32, also.

grace. For at the deepest level, true devotion is not awakened and kept alive by the spirit of the devotee, but by the Spirit of his God. It is the Spirit from Above who re-sets the completely descended weights of the clock.

Prayer and the Spirit's Movement

Teellinck considers an essential trait of a believer to be a continuous "movement toward God."[60] This movement finds its expression in prayer. Teellinck devotes a remarkably long chapter to the subject in his *Sleutel*.[61] Here he defines prayer as an "earnest, ascending desire of the heart directed toward the Lord God, in order to receive from him all that we need and to thank him for what we have already received."[62] Genuine prayers are intense, like fire, Teellinck found. For him this was not a cliché, but rather a metaphor in which he saw two important aspects of praying indicated. The first is that prayer has an upward direction. Just like the "unique feature and nature" of fire is to rise toward heaven, genuine prayers leave all earthly things behind. They "are lifted up to the Lord God." The second feature is that prayer ought to be intense. Just as a coal from a "blazing fire" has a wide reach, so a prayer intensely pursued with the fire "of holy desire and the Holy Spirit" penetrates to the throne of God.[63]

Yet, Teellinck only captures the direction and power of prayer with this image. For the act of praying itself, he depends on a construction which depicts not the intensity but the intimacy of prayer. He who prays enters "the council room of God," the private domain of the heavenly king. In those hallowed surroundings the person praying is permitted "to speak with him on a familiar basis."[64] There he may not only praise and exalt God, but also empty out all his concerns into the lap of God and invoke his help. The prayer, however, does not remain a monologue. It assumes a dialogical form. Teellinck calls it "a loving discussion between God and the Christian's heart."[65] In it a person may pose the question, but God gives the answer. According to Teellinck that arrangement is also a feature of prayer. By his Spirit God assures us that he will do what we ask. "The result is that there is no more friendly or loving exchange that can be held between one friend and another than the prayer that occurs between God and the Christian heart."[66]

To illustrate the life of prayer, Teellinck appeals for help to many images. Prayer is called a reliable message and "express letter" that speedily delivers our "message" to God and just as speedily delivers his response to our home address.

---

60. *Soliloquium*, "Dedicatie," 2.
61. *Sleutel*, 1.3.7, 178-217. Its length is exceeded only by the chapter on the sacraments. Ibid., 105-50.
62. Ibid., 178.
63. Ibid., 179.
64. Ibid., 199.
65. Ibid., 202. Teellinck's formulation recalls one of Calvin's descriptions: "Oratio familiare sit piorum cum Deo colloquium." ("Prayer is a confidential discussion of the pious person with God.") *Inst.* 3.20.16, in *OS* 4:320. The idea probably goes back to Augustine. See van Bavel, *Als je hart bidt*, 6.
66. *Sleutel*, 1.3.7, 202.

Prayer is the "sweet channel of grace" through which all good gifts flow from the heavenly fountain.[67] It is "like the vein of our soul" that carries the blood of life from Jesus Christ, "our Head and heart."[68] Prayer in the name of Christ is the key that opens the treasure chest of grace and locks "the warehouse of his wrath." It is the best and most willingly available friend that a person can ever have. Night and day this friend is ready to help us immediately. He stays awake with us through the night, and he allows himself no rest during the day; he never deserts us when we are underway, "either by land or by sea." He stands by us in sickness and in health, in life and in death. Prayer is, in one word, "our last and our best friend." To all of God's children prayer is a "universal medicine and catholic" potion against all ailments. Concerning this medication one may confidently write: "Probatum est."[69]

In light of the foregoing, it is understandable that for Teellinck no other spiritual discipline—whether it was reading, or reflection and meditation, or discussion—is "as welcome" to God as "the perfume of prayer."[70] The reason for this is undoubtedly that in it communion with God achieves its greatest intimacy. The distance between heaven and earth falls away. He considered prayer to be the ladder to heaven, the doorway to God's presence, the hand that carries from there whatever a person needs. By it our soul is lifted to heaven, and conversely, by it, "in a manner of speaking, we draw the Lord our God into our hearts." It creates the closeness in which one becomes aware of his saving power and by which spiritual life is strengthened. In prayer it is certainly true that "we embrace" our God, "lovingly kiss him, and draw all our salvation and confidence from him." Teellinck introduces all of this in order to give his definition of prayer its mystical hues: "in order that prayer might truly be a union of our souls with God, the principle of heavenly joy."[71] And yet, however much the distance between heaven and earth is bridged through prayer, Teellinck does not want to forget that a praying person can only appear before God's face "as a poor and needy beggar, that is, as an entirely empty vessel. For, he knows that the loving dew of heaven falls on the lowest valley.[72] Even in his most reflective moments he is conscious of the radical difference between creature and Creator. They are related to one another like a spring is to a thirsty soul, like fullness is to emptiness.

The fidelity with which Teellinck characterized prayer-life must certainly not be confused with boldness. One ought to approach prayer as a sacred matter. One cannot just haphazardly ask God about anything. Before one makes his questions known, one must judge in the light of Scripture whether they are warranted.[73] Above all, one must concentrate. Exceptionally helpful in this regard is that a person lifts "hands and eyes"—note well, hands too—toward heaven, bends the knees, speaks aloud so as not to be distracted, and retreats to "a quiet, dark spot."

---

67. Ibid.
68. Ibid.
69. Ibid., 199-200.
70. Ibid., 200.
71. Ibid., 200-201.
72. Ibid., 201.
73. Ibid., 208.

As an aside Teellinck advises that when less than full "attention" is possible, to keep prayers short. What in the last analysis it comes down to, however, is "one's own inner disposition." By this he has two things in mind. In the first place is that we do not restrict ourselves only to set times of prayer, but that "at all times in our lives" we practice making our hearts more and more "detached and free from the concerns of the flesh." In the second place is that at our times of prayer we not "tumble into prayer impulsively," but that beforehand we prepare out hearts and senses "for an encounter," in order to direct them to God, who is the One to whom we pray, and to Christ, who is the One through whom we pray.[74] Teellinck readily admits that in this connection a complication presents itself. We cannot bring our heart along without some pushing and shoving. It is not inclined toward God, but toward the earth. Teellinck meets this problem with pastoral temperateness. Let this hindrance discourage no one, he advises. Rather, let a person be encouraged by this, for in it he recognizes his own powerlessness. One should not be too vexed by this, but rather consider that the perfume of our prayers is like the smoke of a fire. Before smoke rises, it is often first blown down by the wind "so that it swirls and churns." In the same way our prayers can die. But God will not extinguish "the flickering wick"[75] and will bless our prayers, "however inadequate they may be."[76]

Teellinck expresses himself emphatically on the issue of written or set prayer and extemporaneous prayer. On this subject there is no dilemma for him. Set prayers he holds in high regard. To begin with, he commends the Our Father. He is quite definite on the subject. With as much "devotion and heart-felt emotion" as possible, we have "often called on God" by means of this prayer. For it was prescribed for us by the "Lord of the church himself." No prayer is as profitable as this one—at least, as long as we do not misuse it routinely and thoughtlessly. But in addition to this perfect prayer, other prayers are available to us. For "the convenience of right-hearted Christians," godly men, who by means of God's Spirit and the Lord's Prayer were experienced in the practice of prayer, have left behind a variety of prayers that can be of special benefit to us. Of which prayers Teellinck is concretely thinking here, he does not specify. But undoubtedly he has in mind those encompassed in the "devotional books by various spiritual leaders" mentioned in his "Preface"—at least insofar as he considers them useful when judged by Reformed criteria. In any case, the prayers of à Kempis would have assumed a prominent place in this list, as is testified by the fact that in his own writings he quoted them liberally.[77]

For praying people who are not able to "stand on their own two legs," these prayers constitute a staff on which to lean. Moreover, by using them the misguided heart is protected from "impetuous and impertinent fantasies and prayers that are entirely inappropriate." The "simple people" who allow themselves to be guided by the "bonds" of such "established formularies" should

---

74. Ibid., 211-12.

75. Isa. 42:3, according to the Deux-Aes translation.

76. *Sleutel*, 1.3.7, 212-13.

77. Ibid., 1.3.5, 144-49, where Teellinck writes out nine prayers for the Lord's supper that are either substantially developed in the spirit of Thomas or are entirely borrowed from him.

certainly not think that they "are doing a bad thing." This is hardly a bond that restricts, but one that protects. Moreover, these written prayers pave the way to the extemporaneous prayer. As soon as through our use of "these established prayers" the Holy Spirit renders us proficient to do so, we may pray in the words that he "brings to our senses." Teellinck compares this to children who take their first steps while holding chairs and benches, but who at a later stage do not need these "supports."[78]

In this way Teellinck comes quickly to his third point: extemporaneous prayer "from the heart." In this connection he cuts through to an emphasis that deserves attention. By this I have in mind the theme—undoubtedly borrowed from Puritanism[79]—of "the stirrings and movements of the good Spirit of God," to which he devotes the largest section of book three of the *Sleutel*. Already in the first chapter on it he attempts to explain what he understands by this theme. Now and then the souls that seek Christ are overcome with the "feeling and awareness"—they cannot explain how—that their thoughts are transported from earthly to heavenly things. In those moments they find themselves in a serene, "pleasing" peace, and they are freed from "painful distractions" and idle thoughts. They devote themselves entirely to spiritual exercises and are elevated with a burning zeal "above and beyond" themselves "to heaven itself, to Christ, to communion with the Most Highly Exalted One."[80] These "stirrings" cannot be sustained for very long. Unless God "tempered" them, they could not be endured.[81] But when they appear, one must take advantage of them without delay. Whoever ignores them behaves in the same foolish way as a blacksmith who allows his red-hot iron to cool off, or as a sailor who pays no attention to a favorable wind.[82]

In chapter 7, which is devoted particularly to the subject of prayer, Teellinck returns to that "stirring" and describes it as an activity of the Holy Spirit as the Spirit of prayer, who in "a very special way," according to time and circumstance, prepares the heart for prayer. Teellinck cannot explain this with great precision. That this work of the Spirit was also hidden, something of a secret, for him is apparent from his added observation: "I do not understand these secret movements." But this much he understands clearly, that a person must be totally attentive toward them and must "affirm their reality" when they present themselves. As soon as a person detects this movement, it is imperative that he isolate himself as soon as possible from all human contact and that he "pour out his heart in these holy movements" to the Lord. From this formulation it seems implicit that by the stirring of the Spirit Teellinck not only focuses on the inner stimulation preceding prayer, but also on the content or prayer itself. These spiritual motions of the soul one must always express or "pour out."

---

78. Ibid., 1.3.8, 214-15.

79. Nuttall, *The Holy Spirit*, 141. The author provides a quotation from Richard Sibbes: "Let us give him way to come into our souls when he knocks by his motions. Grieve not the Spirit by any means."

80. *Sleutel*, 1.3.1, 82. The terms "transported" and "uplifted" recall Bernard's terms *raptus* and *excessus mentis*.

81. Ibid., 84.

82. Ibid., 85.

Teellinck attaches unusually great importance to the sensation of this work of the Spirit. "See to it that you never disparage it, but that you always and in every way make serious work of it." He is certain that these stirrings will yield powerful prayer.[83] From his book *Het Nieuwe Ierusalem* it can be established that this work of grace can also emerge *during* prayer. There he describes this as a sweet experience of spiritual things. "Often when you were praying, as Mary heard from Jesus himself, have I inspired you so that you not only uttered mere words, but also poured out your heart to me with a flaming zeal."[84] That these things were not only expressed verbally, but also experienced in the heart, is purely to the credit of the Spirit's stirrings. A person cannot avail oneself of this Spirit simply as one pleases. He is sovereignly distributed to the believer. Spiritual stirrings come from the hands of Jesus. They enliven our prayers and promote, "as the wind of heaven," our progress on our journey toward our homeland.[85]

Although these heavenly experiences are not by our arrangement and while the Spirit blows where he wills, this does not mean that he works arbitrarily. The remarkable thing is that on the one hand these stirrings are totally a gift of the Spirit and that a person experiences a fervent prayer life *after* receiving them, but that on the other hand a person can prepare for them *ahead of time* by prayer and other spiritual exercises. Clearly, praying in the Spirit can be preceded by a prayer of the believer. A devout person can "have it that the same aforementioned stirrings and movements of the soul often appear and arise in his heart, and that he has them more frequently, slightly awakening and experiencing them by way of preparation, then buoyantly experiencing them in full force."[86] A person has to cultivate susceptibility to these stirrings, so that they are not the exception but become the rule and do not wither but flourish. Teellinck sharpens his point with the admonition that we must "always" be prepared to pay strict attention to the Lord's visitation that comes to us in these spiritual movements, so that we immediately open the door of our heart as soon as he knocks. "What secret things might not the Lord then have come to tell us?"[87] What these hidden truths are exactly, Teellinck does not explain here. In any case, we encounter them in Scripture, for the Spirit leads according by his Word,[88] and they amount to "the sweet experiences of God's grace."[89]

The means that is pre-eminently useful for awakening the movements of the Spirit is "the working of God's Word." By it Teellinck understood the whole sweep of contact with Scripture: personal reading, preaching, meditation and discussion. The Holy Bible is the point of contact with the Holy Spirit. It is certainly "full of references to God's Spirit." The breath of the Spirit is poured over it and has "permeated it." Every page and every verse as a result breathes out the sacred movements of the Spirit. Whoever disciplines himself in the Word

---

83. Ibid., 1.3.7, 216.
84. *Jerusalem*, 2.6, 151.
85. Ibid., 2.7, 171.
86. *Sleutel*, 1.3.1, 85.
87. Ibid. See note 39 above on the use of the question mark.
88. Ibid.
89. Ibid., 86.

becomes—"and I do not know how," Teellinck adds as an aside—ever increasingly a "spiritual participant" and assumes more and more "a spiritual identity," that is to say, a disposition of life that to a growing degree exhibits the image of Christ, his example. Christ's image is portrayed in the Bible for our reflection and imitation.[90] The person who interacts with the Bible in this affective as well as effective way and understands it in reliance on the Holy Spirit, its author,[91] according to Teellinck appropriates the most basic means by which the stirrings of the Spirit "are received, applied and also awakened."[92]

Concerning the correlation of Word and Spirit Teellinck has a great deal to say. He emphatically distances himself from experiences that pass as spiritual, but that are not because they lack biblical foundation. The movements of the Spirit never carry us above the Word, but arise exactly from the Word and bring us to the Word. The criterion for healthy spiritual movement—its touch-stone, actually—according to Teellinck is that the Spirit directs his inner working "to the Word of God," thus in dependence on Scripture and in harmony with it.[93] That some members are of the opinion that they have achieved such a high level of spirituality that they no longer have need of any external assistance, Teellinck calls an "idle delusion, an empty imagination." He has in mind those spiritual leaders, whom he does not specifically identify, who regard the Word as superfluous, like candlelight is to full sunshine.[94] These are "very dangerous" and shameful ideas that these "representatives of a higher spirituality" spread. Teellinck's rely is that it is the unique work of the Holy Spirit to open our eyes to what the candle of the Word brings to light.[95] When a person thinks that she has outgrown the biblical content of the Spirit's work, she stands exposed to the most terrible errors. Scripture is the boundary and the standard of the Spirit.[96]

The great extent to which Teellinck goes to clarify his position leads us to suspect that he wants to create a safeguard in this way against a spiritualistic misappropriation of the spiritual stirrings that he has in mind. When he pleads for being attentive to these stirrings and also to wait for them, he is fully convinced that that has nothing to do with quietism or false passivity, let alone with a devaluation of the Word. Rather, his intent is purely to emphasize that a

---

90. Ibid., 1.3.4, 95-96.

91. Ibid., 104-105. Compare *Imitatio*, 1.5 in *Opera* 2:12: "Omnes scriptura sacra eo spiritu debet legi quo facta est." ("All of sacred Scripture must be read in the Spirit through whom it has been given.")

92. *Sleutel*, 1.3.4, 96.

93. Ibid., 1.3.1, 85. Compare ibid., 1.3.4, 96.

94. Ibid., 1.4.15, 331.

95. Ibid., 332-33.

96. Ibid., 334. In the second volume of *De Sleutel* Teellinck defends at length (chapters 7-14!) his hermeneutical point of departure, namely that the "literal and grammatical sense" of Scripture is its correct and saving sense (2.52). Whoever plays fast and loose with this premise makes Scripture "a wax nose that a person can twist and turn whichever way he desires" (2.54). By the expression "the dead letter" is not meant the literal sense of the Old and New Testaments, but the covenant of works (2.59). The spiritual understanding of Scripture is, therefore, nothing other than the understanding of the literal sense as it penetrates to the heart (2.64). Indeed, it is not the "confirmation published in books" that in itself constitutes the rule of faith, but this rule is "the meaning" contained in them (2.84).

mysterious connection prevails between prayerfully meditating on Scripture and the working of the Spirit. Bible reading owes its impact to the Spirit, and at the same time it is the "exercise" that evokes "many stirrings of the Spirit" in the heart.[97]

From his own experience during times when the Lord in his sovereign freedom left him in a state of spiritual barrenness, Teellinck knew that God also withholds his spiritual "streams" and his "pursuing" grace.[98] When sailing, a person simply cannot always stay "ahead of the wind and the tide." The safe haven of blessedness cannot always be reached across the "sandbars and lulls." Often those regarded as God's dearest children experience many spiritual desertions and extended dry spells. But precisely at such times it is important to seek God's grace with all the more perseverance. "I cannot always do as I should, but I should always do what I can!" Then, "in hope against hope," it comes down to leaving it up to God. But Teellinck does not stop here. He adds two things. In the first place, he adds the confession that spiritual drought is his own fault, because the stirrings of the Spirit are not "taken seriously."[99] (Apparently, in Teellinck's opinion this contrasts not in the least with God's sovereign determination!) In the second place, he adds the determination "to listen carefully and learn" whether the flood of grace and the wind of the Spirit are not being announced. For what it ultimately comes down to is that "insensitivity" makes way for "new opportunities."[100]

The absence of the stirrings of the Spirit is not without meaning, therefore. It forms the incentive to watch all the more closely for the coming of the Spirit. This vigilance comes to expression via the ear. In order to detect the sound of the Spirit, one must tune his ears to listen to the Word. But in order to understand the Word, one cannot dispense with the Spirit. He does not allow himself to be commandeered. The Spirit only allows himself to be anticipated. The listening person who waits for him is already dwelling in his neighborhood; he places himself under his authority. For, if the Spirit is the author of the Word, the Word is the sound of his voice. One only needs to internalize it. That this gracious miracle of Word and Spirit will happen belongs at the very center of Teellinck's doctrine of prayer. At the same time, it constitutes one of the key themes of his whole understanding of true devotion.

---

97. *Sleutel*, 1.3.1, 82.

98. *Soliloquium*, 17.49. Compare *Imitatio*, 2.9, in *Opera*, 2:76: "Interdum in fervore et interdum in frigiditate sumus; quoniam spiritus venit et recidit secundum suae beneplacitum voluntatis." ("Now, at one time we are passionate, then again cold. For the Spirit comes and goes, according to the good pleasure of his will.") The entirety of the passage here shows striking similarities to the second half of the *Imitatio*, 2.9.

99. À Kempis espouses a similar thought in *Imitatio*, 3.51, in *Opera*, 2:241.

100. *Soliloquium*, 17.50-51.

God above All

For Teellinck God is "simply the very best," the Most Noble One without equal, without end, without measure.[101] He lacks the categories for explaining God's uniqueness. God is without equal and transcends every precise definition. Rather than resorting to concepts, Teellinck reaches for images. The metaphors that he uses in his *Soliloquium* to name God are filled with adoration. He calls him a "Spring," a "Fountain," a "Full Ocean" and also a "Sun."[102] He therefore seeks God with a burning desire, "more intense than whatever can be thought of in this world." He esteems but one friendly glance from his face more than all the "pleasures" of the world, even if these were to last for ten thousand years. A matchless God deserves matchless love. He himself evokes it. For this love is not produced by flesh and blood, but is "instilled" by God himself.[103]

Teellinck yearns for God, and for God alone. He longs for nothing less than that his love for God might "swallow up" all his other emotions of love as one huge passion, one "all-illumining brightness."[104] He knows well that he may and must love his neighbor, but also that this kind of love can never approximate the love for him who wants to be loved above all. Love for neighbor has its legitimate place, but it is only sanctioned when it is awash in the stream of love for God, "like the river running to the sea is lost in it . . . and like a lesser light is darkened by the light of the sun."[105] So, Teellinck's prayer is: "Let the sea of love for you swallow up all the brooks of my human love; let the passion of love for you consume all my misguided love, purify all my defective love, and become so singularly and increasingly my all-in-all, that I no longer love in any other way than that which worships you, is in you, and is for you."[106] He always wants to keep in mind that it is not the created and received things, but only the uncreated Giver of all good things who can be the proper joy and solace of the heart. "And let me at last, O Lord, come to the point that I no longer need ask either for heaven or for earth, since I have you alone, O Lord, who is better than both heaven and earth and all that is in them."[107]

Glimmering in the background of Teellinck's desires is undoubtedly Augustine's distinction between the enjoyment of God and the use of his gifts (*frui* and *uti*).[108] Teellinck wants to deny even less than Augustine does that we

---

101. *Sleutel*, 1.4.5, 264.

102. I refer to Vekeman's "Inleiding" to *Soliloquium,* xviii.

103. *Soliloquium*, 18.53.

104. Ibid., 28.90. The early seventeenth-century idea of "infusion" ("*verswelgen*"), just as in middle Dutch, means "to take up into," "absorb."

105. Ibid.

106. Ibid. Attention is called to this distinction: the love under judgment is caught up in the love for God; misguided love is consumed by it; defective love is purified by it.

107. Ibid., 27.85-86. A strongly related passage may be found in *Theologia Deutsch.* See *"Der Franckforter:" Theologia Deutsch*, ed. A. M. Haas (Einsiedeln, 1993), 126; as well as *Imitatio*, 2.8, in *Opera*, 2:72-73. Perhaps the "Frankforter" as well as à Kempis is indebted to *DD*, 8:25, in *SW*, 1:114.

108. For a lucid discussion of Augustine's position see van Oort, *Jeruzalem en Babylon*, 119-22. Compare van Bavel, *Als je hart bidt*, 28 and 108-9.

may love the things and especially the people that God has entrusted to us.[109] What Teellinck intends, as Augustine did, is that we not love any gifts for their own sake—for this is *frui* and God alone can be the object of this; we are to love them for God's sake. In the notion that it is God who "bequeaths" to him wife and children is the idea that he infuses this trust with joy.[110] In this way the "for the sake of, in and for God" receives concreteness. Nothing and no one equals God. Love for him is primary and unique, and as such it has the character of a source. Teellinck's love merely flows toward that source.

But perhaps the last point is saying too much. At least he himself is not so certain that his love for God is entirely pure. On the contrary, he often experiences discord between the ideal and reality. That his longing is for God is beyond doubt. He does not dare, however, to identify this longing with pure love. Teellinck is a lover who desires to love God, but who knows that this love is laced with paltry, fleshly desires that sway his soul back and forth "like tempestuous winds impede and shake a little boat."[111] What is remarkable is that Teellinck does not ascribe this complaint to the new convert, as he allows in the first chapter of his *Soliloquium*, but that it is uttered by a converted, sensitive, passionate and convicted sinner, as he subsequently applied the word in chapters 24-27. Maturing in spiritual life, as is so clearly revealed in *Soliloquium*, does not exclude the fact that the "convicted sinner" of chapter 27 must continually confess his complete imperfection. Obviously, progress in piety occurs in step with the knowledge and understanding of one's inability, considered from the point on which everything else turns, namely undivided love for God.

The same deficiency Teellinck confesses via the mouth of the "sensitive sinner." Actually, joy in the Lord should surpass all earthly joy. He should always be "the holy Fountain of everything that we desire," above health, peace and life itself. All these gifts are derived from God, but they are not God himself. They are "only little droplets in the whole ocean" and "rays of that marvelous Light."[112] But, he sighs concerning the subject, how then can it be that I do not yearn more intensely for God and that I still find so little joy in him? "O, what an earthly heart! O, what a barren soul! O, what poison of sin! O, what a hellish disposition!" It is just this many impediments that block the experience of joy in the Lord. In perceptive, affective imagery he complains that they rob him of all taste and smell, so that he is not able "to smell, nor to taste, nor to hear, nor to see, nor to feel, nor to touch" the joy that there is in God.[113] Only by God's grace do these impediments displease him. He humbly implores: "Lay this burden not

---

109. J. de Boer says: "What would Teellinck's spouse have thought if he passionately assured her that he loved her only because it was God's will and because he did so in the Lord, and absolutely not because of herself? Where does Teellinck come up with this language?" De Boer, *De verzegeling*, 96. When he does so, he misunderstands the Augustinian background of Teellinck's feelings as well as its positive intent.

110. *Soliloquium,* 27.86.

111. Ibid.

112. Ibid., 25.82. In *Sleutel*, 2.6.5, 235, Teellinck uses the same imagery, namely that the good things that we enjoy must lead us to their Source. If the "little droplets" already provide so much satisfaction, "how much more satisfying God himself must be."

113. *Soliloquium,* 25.82.

on me, then O Lord, but better and rather purge me of it through the costly blood of your Son, which is completely able to cleanse from all the poisonous dispositions of sin." At that moment, scattered remnants from à Kempis' *Imitation* apparently hit the mark. For the prayer that immediately follows is, while certainly not a literal quotation, unmistakably drenched with Thomas' glowing language:

> And would that you arouse in me warmth of love and a flame of zealous affection so that I might be wholly and completely consumed by your love and lose myself entirely in your affections. Yes, my Lord, let me possess your love—above the sun, the moon and the stars; above the earth and all that it contains; even above heaven itself and all your glory. May you be more precious to my soul, Lord, than all my dearest friends, than all my possessions, than all my pleasures, than my own joy, comfort, peace and life. For you, O Lord, are better than all that is—better than life itself. If only I have you, O Lord, my life will be sweet; but without you my life itself is no better than an accursed death and everlasting torment.[114]

The essence of this prayer, in which à Kempis is so prominently present, is already met much earlier in the *Soliloquium*. In chapter 12 it is expressed like this: "O, Lord! If I could but find you, so that I might lose myself in you . . . That I might be still within, that I might rest in you alone."[115] By the end of the book nothing has changed on this point. This establishes the fact that the nature of Teellinck's love for God is indeed intense, but at the same time this love is more desired than fully realized. In the course of his *Soliloquium* he never rises above this sense of incompleteness. This is not a stage beyond which he advances, but a life-long pilgrimage in experiencing the presence of God, a journey which by his growth in grace he would sooner see strengthened than abandoned.

The limitations of his love for God at the same time do not prevent Teellinck from admonishing others, and implicitly himself as well—in words that once again are borrowed from Thomas—to love this God "only and purely." Possibly love's incompleteness acts as precisely an added stimulus for this appeal. "Strive, endeavor, labor and apply yourself always and increasingly . . . to rest in God more than in all creatures, more than in all that is respectable and considered great, more than in what is powerful and valuable in this world, more than in all learning or all that is regarded as profound, more than in gratification of the flesh and solace . . . , more than in all things visible and invisible; and especially, more than in all that is not of God." God himself is simply "the all-sufficient; he is the all-pleasing; he is the all-satisfying; he is the all-beautiful;

---

114. Ibid., 82-83. Compare *Imitatio*, 3.21, in *Opera*, 2:182-83; 4.13, in 2:126; and especially 4.16, in 2:133. At the same time, the passage reminds one of Bernard, *DD*, 10:27, in *SW*, 1:121. The most remarkable thing, however, is that the union with God mentioned by both medieval figures is literally missing in Teellinck. On Teellinck's relation to Bernard, see Boot, *De allegorische uitlegging*, 145-55.

115. *Soliloquium*, 25.37.

and he is the most worthy of love."[116] By piling these superlatives one on top of the other, ones that item for item are found back in Thomas, Teellinck wants to exalt all-embracing love for his matchless God. That love may cost something, not because God's favor requires payment, but because it requires undivided submission. Therefore, whoever wants to sample the "sweetness of God" must resolutely take distance from "all that is contrary to [the love] of God and hinders it." In this way a person "places himself entirely in the will of the Lord."[117] That produces an unimaginable joy. Teellinck thinks that it "cannot be expressed" how much a person "is benefited in the school of Christ" when she decides to surrender her will without reservation to God's good will and pleasure. "For where God is present, there all is joy." He who loses his will to God, finds the willingness to serve him. "As soon as you . . . set the direction of your heart toward God above everything else, then through these spiritual disciplines the love of your heart and your will will be properly formed and purified."[118]

Love for Jesus

Teellinck knows only one form of love that may "compete" with love for God, and that is love for Jesus. But, here there is no thought of competition in the sense of rivalry. "Competition" needs to be understood here in the sense that it had originally: concurrence, companionship, coincidence. Everything that was said concerning the earlier stage of love for God exclusively, must be taken as always intended to apply also to the love for Jesus. Love for God aside from Christ is fictitious for Teellinck; love for Jesus is love for God. Behind this lies Teellinck's articulately Christocentric doctrine of God. Just as for him Jesus is no one less than God the Son in human flesh, so God is no one less than the Father who makes himself known in the Son. In the incarnation God draws extremely close to us. The Son's emptying of himself involves no loss of his divinity whatsoever, but rather it is its revelation and manifestation.[119] Indeed, it is from this perspective that Teellinck urges readers to set "the direction of the heart" toward God above all else, but then, and with just as much emphasis, he can admonish them to set "the direction, the focus, and the earnestness" of their hearts on nothing else than on the Lord Jesus.[120] In the same breath he speaks of his yearning to renounce everything in the interest of gaining God, and that he regards Jesus his Lord so highly and dearly that all things "must become loss and filth in comparison with him."[121] One thing that he wants to impress on the heart "again and again" is "that you must take this as sufficient and fully satisfying, as your best portion in this world, namely that you possess the Lord Jesus Christ, the Son of God given to you by God the Father." The soul's desire must ever

---

116. *Sleutel*, 2.6.5, 233-34.

117. Ibid., 234.

118. Ibid., 235.

119. Willem Teellinck, *Huys-boeck, ofte Eenvoudighe Verklaringhe ende toe-eygheninghe vande voor-naemste Vraeg-stukken des Nederlandtschen Christelijcken Catechismi* (Middelburg, 1650), 230. The work was originally published in 1618.

120. *Sleutel*, 1.1.4, 15.

121. *Soliloquium*, 14.40-41.

return exclusively to this: "to possess Christ and nothing but him." Everything a person does should honor him, ought to be a sacrifice to him.[122]

Within this framework, it appears again how much Teellinck finds himself in the piety of à Kempis as centered on Jesus. Passages resonate almost word-for-word with the *Imitation*, without acknowledging their source, whenever Teellinck writes that those that seek Jesus also find him, and in so doing possess all things. "But to be abandoned or separated from the Lord Jesus is an unbearable hell for the person who loves God. By contrast, to abide with him is sweet paradise. When Jesus is with you, no enemy can overpower you." Just as is the case with the love for God, so with the love for Jesus: one must love every other person for the sake of Jesus, but Jesus "for his own sake."[123] This love knows no equal. It surpasses all other love and pleasure.[124] For Teellinck there was not the least doubt that anyone who sees only "a glimmering" of Christ's glory "with the simple eye of faith," will immediately begin to regard everything else in this world "as insignificant by comparison with it." As long as someone "keeps that lively vision in mind," he will desire nothing other than "to read, to pray, to talk with Christ, and to be preoccupied with the things of Christ." The world and everything in it then becomes "nothing at all."[125]

When Teellinck writes about David the Psalmist, who clearly functions here for him as something of a model, it recalls Luther's preface in his commentary on Galatians: "All his endeavors conclude and end in Christ, to whom they all aspire, on whom they are all focused, and with whom his heart rises and falls."[126] Everything that the world considers important and illustrious dissolves into nothing in the light of Jesus' glory. Even though someone could "work all sorts of miracles and amazing feats, he could find no satisfaction in any of them—no more than in a dried up cabbage stalk—as long as Christ the Lord hid his friendly face from him—just as we witness with David all through the Psalms."[127] The total focus that Teellinck emphasizes takes the whole person into account, body and spirit. The eye desires to see nothing except what kindles love for Christ. The ear wishes to hear only what contributes to the knowledge of Christ's all-sufficiency. The mouth longs to taste only the goodness of the Lord in all his glory that awaits us in heaven. The nose wants to smell only "the sweet loveliness" of Jesus' "perfume." In short, the whole body longs to experience nothing except what contributes to the realization that "Christ the Lord is all in all." But it all comes down to a person "so binding and curbing his inner senses" that all his thoughts and desires depend entirely on Christ. The means for

---

122. *Sleutel*, 1.1.8, 45.

123. Ibid., 2.6.4, 230. Compare *Imitatio*, 2.8, in *Opera*, 2:71-72.

124. *Soliloquium*, 3 (Dedication).

125. *Sleutel*, 1.2.1, 49. The quote is from a passage that is almost identical with a section of *Jerusalem*, 1.7, 77-78.

126. *Sleutel*, 1.2.3, 55. On Luther, see the preface in *WA* 40:1, 33: "Nam in corde meo iste unus regnat articulus, scilicet Fides Christi, ex quo, per quem et in quem omnes meae diu noctuque fluunt et refluunt theologicae cogitationes. . . ." ("For in my heart this one thing rules, namely faith in Christ, from whom, through whom, and to whom all my theological thoughts flow day and night.")

127. *Sleutel*, 1.2.3, 55.

achieving this "external and internal"[128] concentration on Christ consists of prayer and fasting, "as our beloved Paul frequently admonishes."[129]

The question of whether the focus of this concentration is not perhaps the exalted Christ in his glory rather than the historical Jesus in his humiliation seems not to have occurred to Teellinck. In any case, the contrast between the two is not part of his discussion. The believer not infrequently finds "joy and contentment" in the contemplation of "Christ's unspeakable heavenly glory."[130] But Teellinck also emphasizes Jesus Christ "the crucified."[131] The heavenly Christ is none other than the Suffering One, the Bridegroom none other than the brother who made payment with his sacrificial blood. In the section where Teellinck discusses "the right knowledge and understanding of our Lord Jesus Christ," this comes across clearly. There he describes the scene of Christ "lifted up on the wooden cross." Through such contemplation that occurs with the "eyes of faith," the soul is healed from all its deadly diseases and is made "vital and alert" for the service of God. Whenever the Lord God opens our eyes in this way and shows us "the marvelous, loving sight of Jesus Christ," he motivates by means of that sight all the powers of our soul, turning them from the vanities of this life and directing them to Christ the Lord." Teellinck calls this "the contemplation and the consideration of the heavenly and spiritual things of Christ's kingdom." It is a "heavenly exercise" by which a person finds "more appetite, satisfaction, comfort and enjoyment" than is to be found in the world. The one who discerns Christ in this way is lifted above all earthly matters and is drawn to him.[132] That this contemplation involves the heavenly Christ is unmistakable. What is significant, however, is that a little further along Teellinck also applies the same experience to Christ's work of salvation in history. The heart of the Christian, in which the light of knowledge is shining on Christ, sees "simultaneously the excellent glory of Christ and also the satisfaction with God the Father that Christ has made for our sins."[133] If it is warranted to speak here of bridal mysticism in Teellinck, then we are concerned with a mysticism in which both the heavenly and the earthly Christ are central.

This mysticism has an explicitly ethical point.[134] In her way of life the bride desires to be conformed to the Bridegroom. Through love she is transformed into his image. Just as a lover "attracted by the sight of a beautiful doe who radiates her love for him is drawn away from all earthly matters and devotes himself to pleasing her," in the same way the Christian who has seen Christ in all his beauty begins to adorn herself or himself with Christian virtues in order to please him. It

---

128. Here is one of the numerous examples of inconsistent [seventeenth-century Dutch] spelling. [Translator's note: in the old Dutch cited, the ending of one word is old style, the second, new style.]

129. *Sleutel*, 1.2.7, 70-71.

130. Ibid., 1.2.3, 54.

131. Ibid., 12.1, 50.

132. Ibid., 1.2.2, 51-52. Mystical terminology is evident here. The delight, the sweetness or satisfaction and the process of being uplifted immediately remind one of the *excessus, dulcedo* and *raptus* in Bernard's mystical writings.

133. Ibid., 1.2.3, 59.

134. *Soliloquium*, 3 (Dedication).

is completely impossible that a person who wants to be the bride of Christ and the love of his life would not want to be conformed to him in his "mannerisms, virtues and qualities."[135] Teellinck is under-standably concerned here with virtues of which the *earthly* life of Jesus is an inspiring model and example. At the same time, one is impressed that the *heavenly* Christ, by whom this conformity is modeled, is also kept in view.[136]

Finally, of interest is Teellinck's vision of union with Christ (*union cum Christo*). He calls this a mystery that God brings to light for us "out of the rich treasure chest of his manifold wisdom." By a "wonderful working of the Spirit" all those that are reconciled to God are made one with Christ by means of faith and become members of his body. This union is close and intimate. It has a salvation-history component in the sense that all that Jesus did and suffered is also experienced and endured by believers. In and with him they put to death the curse of death. The applicatory aspect of this union is further indicated by the fact that believers feel and value the reality that he is the Vine and they are the branches, that he lives in them and that they have intimate fellowship with him.[137] The bond between Christ and them is closer than that between husband and wife, even than that between body and soul. Teellinck appeals in this connection to Bernard's image of a drop of water in a large vat of wine.[138] While the drop of water retains its own substance, it nevertheless assumes the color and aroma of the wine. "In the same way the Spirit of Christ and the spirit of men are joined to one another—though not in essence—in such a way that their spirits flow together or can be mingled with one another in such a way that a third reality also emerges, namely the hidden Christ. It consists of Christ the Lord as Head and the people of God as members of the body."[139] Teellinck emphatically distances himself from the mysticism of identification, in which man disappears into the being of God. But just as emphatically, he posits a union in which man finds his new identity in Christ. The center and fountain of his life lie no longer within himself, but in Christ. Heaven is his home. The secret of his life is there. There one finds his Head.

Whether or not one calls Teellinck's characterization of love for Jesus mysticism, that it takes on a mystical hue cannot be denied.[140] As he says in the dedication of his *Soliloquium*, it involves a love that awakens in the heart a "wonderful affection and passion for the Lord Jesus . . . that from the beginning are apprehensive."[141] This love for Jesus has meditative as well as ethical dimensions. It "produces beautiful and powerful attractions to Christ." All this is

---

135. *Sleutel*, 1.2.2, 51-52.

136. Ibid., 52.

137. Teellinck, *Huys-boeck*, 96-97.

138. *DD*, 28, in *SW*, 1:122.

139. *Nieuwe Historie van den Ouden Mensche* (Amsterdam, 1623), 96-100. Compare Boot, *De allegorische uitlegging*, 151.

140. The judgment depends completely on the definition that one has of the concept "mysticism." Oberman distinguishes the mysticism of identification from an "alternative Mystik," in which the *via amorosa* and meeting with God as a person is central. Teellinck's spirituality moves along these lines, I think. See Oberman, *Die Reformation*, 39.

141. *Soliloquium*, 3 (Dedication).

totally Teellinck. But it is not the total Teellinck. No less the case is that he remains persuaded that true conversion proceeds from this "affection for Christ."[142]

Sin and Grace

No one is born with love for God. Rather, "the natural man is much too happily married to sin." He loves it and he is tied to it "with such affectionate and pleasant ties that those chains can only be snapped by a Higher Hand. Sin is an atrocious matter, a supernatural evil. By this last insight Teellinck wants to indicate that natural forces offer no solution for it.[143] Precisely those who possess an intimate love for God come to the realization that sin is a treacherous and insurmountable power. "Yes, Lord, my Lord," confesses Teellinck, "sin wounds me so deeply in my heart that it flows in blue, red and rose-colored hues—all three. Because it cannot be expunged from the heart and because those abominable colors cannot be washed out, one would strip naked and pulverize his heart completely if only he could eliminate the sin that clings to him." Not a single capacity that God in his "common grace" has still left in us is able to withstand this terror.[144] Only God's "especially gracious hand" is able to break the power of sin.[145] This is a level of power that transcends Teellinck's comprehension. But it is not only his own powerlessness that he confesses. He is just as ashamed of the *stain* of sin that renders him guilty before God. Teellinck sees himself as "a vessel filled with filth" that deserves to be everlastingly cut off from God.[146] Quoting à Kempis, he laments, "O Lord, how immense human evil is, for it is inclined toward sin. Today I resolve to forsake sin, but then I commit the same sin that very same day; the hour I resolve to guard against this or that sin, an hour later I sink into the same ones again—as though I had never expressed such intentions."[147]

Despite this extremely sobering outlook on human nature, Teellinck attaches an important nuance to it. The human soul still possesses "some remnants of the image of the eternal God." As a consequence, people experience unbounded longings, longings that in this limited and perishing world can never be satisfied.[148] The entire scope of earthly reality is inadequate to satisfy the unending longing for the eternal.[149] Only the eternal God can satisfy the hunger for perfection.[150] True happiness can be found neither in the world "nor in our own selves." In our own understanding and senses, on the contrary, there dwells

---

142. Ibid.
143. Ibid., 21.67.
144. Ibid., 66.
145. Ibid., 67.
146. Ibid., 15.43.
147. Ibid., 6.24. *Imitatio*, 1.22, in *Opera*, 2:43-44.
148. Ibid., 2.14-15.
149. Vekeman, "Inleiding," xxxi.
150. Teellinck's vision appears to be related to Augustine's saying, "Our heart is restless until it finds its rest in you." Compare H. Veldhuis, "Onrustig is ons hart: Over onrust en verlangen naar God," in *Onrustig is ons hart . . . Mens-zijn in christelijk perspectief*, ed. H. Veldhuis (Zoetermeer, 1994), 14-15.

only "enmity toward God and toward our own selves."[151] Teellinck apparently thought that the desire for true happiness was contradicted and frustrated by this enmity. Ultimately, what is produced from what remains of God's image is dissatisfaction with everything under the sun. Examined closely, Teellinck's negative view of human nature is not compromised but refined by such nuances.[152] They are intended to emphasize all the more that people must abandon themselves, if they are ever to receive true "satisfaction." He means to repudiate his own will and his own understanding and to "rise above . . . the best" that remains in him."[153] Teellinck indicates by this formulation that people must live outside themselves, as it were. If they ever hope to satisfy their deepest longings, they must find the center of their existence outside themselves—will and deepest desires included. They will find peace only theocentricly, not self-centeredly.

This exchange of centers, however, does not lie within the grasp of one's natural capacities. For that one would have to have control over one's own heart. But that is not in the least the case. Teellinck cannot rule his own heart, at least as far as he is concerned. It produces "such a plight" for him that he takes no counsel from it and "can never be its master." Because it is "so slippery and so fickle" that he still does not know how "to comprehend and to understand" it, he implores God to "tame" it by his Holy Spirit and to master it. For, God alone can, "with a flick of the wrist," bring about a miraculous change in this "turbulent heart." In the same prayer he acknowledges that it comes down to a complete change of control: "I want, O Lord, to surrender my heart to you, and I renounce, O Lord, every right I have to it. I admit that for the future it rightfully belongs to you."[154] A life totally devoted to God is, on the one hand, exclusively a gift from God himself. He alone has the power to renew the "heart and conscience thoroughly," by his regenerating Spirit.[155] On the other hand, the subject of this renewal is apparently moved to this change "only" and totally by praying. This might raise the suggestion that the initiative for it lies only with the praying person. But that is only a mirage. For, we must not forget that already in the dedication of his *Soliloquium*, Teellinck understands that the entire beginning of the new life is anchored in God. Whenever our heart comes to the point of being "controlled" by spiritual realities and "affection for Christ," it is due entirely to God's "favorable disposition toward us."[156]

---

151. *Soliloquium*, 3.17.

152. On Teellinck's anthropology, see W. van 't Spijker, "Teellincks opvatting van de menselijke wil—Voornamelijk in verband met de uiteenzettingen van W. J. M. Engelberts en W. Goeters," *TR* 7 (1964): 131-32.

153. *Soliloquium*, [3].18.

154. Ibid., 15.43-44.

155. Ibid., 12.36.

156. Ibid., 3 (Dedication).

Not only the beginning of spiritual life, but also its progress is a gift of grace. All the "tossing and turning" in one's own strength yields nothing.[157] The only outcome is, testifies Teellinck, "that I now at long last, by your grace and my own inability, am made aware in all these matters that I must be yielded to your power from on high and look to receive the gift of your Spirit."[158] Apart from God's Spirit we act as foolishly as the captain who, ignoring "wind and tide," endeavors to "put the boat that has run aground back on course without regard to wind and water and to sail it nimbly once again." Only the Spirit can render our dull souls, "stuck on the sandbars of this world," nimble again by "the currents of his ever-flowing grace" and propel us forward "by the winds of his divine power."[159] For this reason it is Teellinck's prayer that "the Savior of the world" would apply to him the benefits of his merits and that the Holy Spirit, the "Purifier of all defiled hearts," would pour out his love on his heart. Only then "would all be well."[160]

Precisely here Teellinck faced a problem—in "the doctrine of predestination."[161] The question surfaces "repeatedly" of whether his entire quest for God is not completely futile, since with respect to salvation matters "do not proceed according a person's will or way of life," but "only" according to God's mercy. Already before the foundation of the world God decided "how things would go with humanity in eternity." He has mercy on whom he wills, and he hardens whom he wills.[162] The way that Teellinck proceeds with this extremely existential question in his own case is interesting enough to consider at this point.

When he honestly owns up to the fact that the idea of predestination worries him to such an extent that he loses courage and concludes that all his zeal for conversion is meaningless, he immediately admits his sorrow over "this vile decision." He calls that conclusion a "product" of his depraved flesh, by which he misleads his heart with "paltry objections and cavils." These are stirred up especially by Satan, who wants to entangle him in the snares of hellish and pernicious "sophistry." Without any attempt to make the matter comprehensible, Teellinck confronts his worries about predestination with the full scope of the gospel. Speculation he considers forbidden. We are commanded to think that God desires everyone's conversion and salvation, and that no one is lost "except the one who cast himself willfully into ruin." Teellinck says this not by way of doctrinal reflection, but rather by way of personal contemplation and prayer. "What on these occasions I am obliged to ponder deeply is that you love and defend all men as the Lover and Defender of men, and that you are so desirous of their salvation that you have given your only beloved Son to die in order to save

---

157. Ibid., 16.45.
158. Ibid., 46.
159. Ibid, 46-47.
160. Ibid., 22.74.
161. Ibid., 19.54-55. C. Graafland regards Teellinck as among those who operated as "critically positive" with the Reformed doctrine of election. C. Graafland, *Van Calvijn tot Barth: Oorsprong en ontwikkeling van de leer der verkiezing in het Gereformeerd Protestantisme* (The Hague, 1987), 216-22. Also compare de Reuver, '
"*Bedelen bij de Bron*," 578-81.
162. *Soliloquium*, 19.55.

those who are lost. Yes, you have truly sworn an oath that you have no pleasure in the death of the sinner, but that you desire that he turn from his ways and live. And you genuinely call all those to yourself who are weak and heavy laden." Teellinck wants to cling to the Word of promise "that stands fast." Over against his temptation to regard seeking God as futile effort, he decidedly asserts that God did not "futilely" command, "Seek me!"[163]

In his book *Sleutel*, Teellinck wards off in a similar manner those "negative, cackling folk" who "superficially" excuse unbelief with an appeal to predestination. He simply applies the subject of preaching in this instance. God's saving grace appears to all men to whom the "Son of God is preached as the Son of Righteousness." The intent of this preaching is nothing less than to illumine people unto salvation, unless men oppose it through the "stubbornness" of heart and do not want to "receive or admit into their lives" this revealed grace (based on an appeal to Matthew 23:37). That this divine appearing, "ready to shine its light," does not penetrate everyone's heart "is not the fault of the proffered grace of God, but of the overwhelming wickedness of men," who oppose the shining of the light of grace in their hearts. Theirs is an opposition that is created by resistance to God's renewing work. If he wants to come and demolish the old house of your existence, "and you call this 'murder and arson' and blame God for this effort, then he is not at work in you."[164] Teellinck calls the intended excuse "an entirely wicked and unbiblical pretension." The one who really longs to be saved, when he or she realizes that everything depends on God's mercy, will be all the more "prodded" to apply himself or herself to the greatest extent possible to pleasing God.[165]

At the same time, Teellinck is compelled to admit in his *Soliloquium* that he does not know how "to explain fully or to harmonize" both of the "foregoing, certain truths" of God's particular election and his universal call. His understanding "dies" and is "dumbfounded." The paradox simply concerns a point that reaches far beyond the natural mind and that is not made transparent in Scripture. However, God has a saving purpose in this last matter. For in this way he wants to test our "simple obedience" to his Word and our unconditional submission to his revealed will. The only existential conclusion that is permissible is that a person must restrain himself from rational conclusions. This is due to the fact that with respect to God's eternal decree "concerning the salvation or condemnation of his human children, some deep secrets lie buried, some unfathomable depths and heights that we poor, puny humans are unable to reach."[166] Teellinck has no doubts himself about the double predestination

---

163. Ibid., 55-56.

164. *Sleutel*, 1.3.9, 223-24. Compare 1.3.11, 231, where Teellinck gives this assurance: "this much is true, no man is separated so far from God by any sort of wicked will and sin, who could not again be restored to newness of life through God's grace, if only he will humble himself beneath God's will. . . ."

165. Ibid., 226.

166. *Soliloquium*, 19.56-57. Virtually the same formulation is encountered in *Sleutel*, 1.3.9, 228.

confessed by the Synod of Dort,[167] but the question of how this happens exceeds his understanding.

Besides, it is characteristic of Teellinck's position that in his *Sleutel* he develops a clearly asymmetrical approach to predestination. He writes that on the one side God, through whose pure grace one is converted, teaches that he will "show" his grace to all those who seek him and use the means he provides.[168] Therefore, it is entirely due to grace that people are converted and experience grace. On the other side of the matter, God testifies that he in his righteousness will harden and render obstinate those that despise the grace he offers and reject the means he provides, so that, stiff-necked, they heap up for themselves a reward of wrath.[169] Perhaps one can speak here of an actualizing tendency in the doctrine of reprobation.[170] The fact that God hardens a person is never casually connected with his reprobation from eternity, but it is attributed to the stiffnecked response with which one despises the grace offered him.

The formulation that Teellinck employs in his *Soliloquium* at first sight betrays nothing of this actualizing completion of reprobation. He places both poles of predestination above the denominator of God's eternal decree. What certainly is striking is that also here he does not speak of an election to salvation and of reprobation to damnation, but of a decree to salvation or to damnation. The context time after time makes clear that the basis of the decree to salvation is purely God's mercy. But about the basis for the decree to reprobation, as far as I can determine, he never expresses himself. Possibly Teellinck's reticence is significant here.[171] However that may be, despite all his caution, Teellinck still has to admit that he cannot fathom the twofold dimensions of God's

---

167. See his *Voorloper tot de navolgende Tweede Geestelijcke Couranten* (1655), 62, where he explains "with a straightforward and unpretentious opinion that he regards the Reformed churches, as they were profiled by the Synod of Dordt, as the "very best generation of Christians of which I am aware in all the world and in whose fellowship I experience the highest joy that I could ever have." This is quoted in van 't Spijker, "Teellincks opvatting," 125-26.

168. For Teellinck's appeal to use the means God provides, see van 't Spijker, ibid., 135-36.

169. *Sleutel*, 1.3.9, 226-27.

170. Compare de Reuver, *"Bedelen bij de Bron,"* 579. It is not accidental that it is the "vile person," who entrenches himself against the call to conversion by means of his own opposition, or that God has decided from all eternity who will be preserved and who will be lost, or that therefore "the reason for the exact number of both is fully known to God." The conclusion one consequently attaches to this is that it revolves around how a person lives, since it is inappropriate to meddle with God's decree. Without his tampering with this line of reasoning, it is still clear that Teellinck heartily detests such a construction. Over against it he posits that God indeed has taken a decision "concerning the disposition of the children of the human race," but that we in no way may doubt God's goodness that is so clearly revealed to us in his Word. In this regard, he avers earnestly "that sinful man must still accept Christ his Son in order to be saved by him. To all of this the wicked person cannot and will not pay attention. But he desires to continue in his sins and wicked ways, so that it is actually enough to justly condemn such a person and in this way he recklessly perverts all his willing and all his knowing, and his own soul perishes." *Sleutel*, 1.3.9, 228.

171. It seems as though, concerning the cause of being eternally lost, that for pastoral considerations Teellinck prefers what Calvin calls the evident cause recognizable by all of us, namely guilt for human wickedness, rather than the hidden and for us incomprehensible cause of God's predestination. Indeed, Calvin himself also notes that one must maintain the first point of view instead of inquiring about the second. *Inst.*, 3.23.8, in *OS* 4:403.

predestination. The pastorally edifying and non-dogmatic spirit in which he writes gives him the space not to delve into deeper reflection on the matter. He prefers to ponder predestination, at least its positive pole. The freedom of grace that comes to light in God's electing initiative restrains him, redemptively, from self-aggrandizement, writes Teellinck in his *Soliloquium.* For in this he realizes that everything rests "actually and only" on grace, and that no other way is open to him "to come, creeping with all possible humility and self-loathing, to the throne of grace."[172] In this way the predestination that had so often troubled him became, with deeper understanding, very "useful" for his salvation. It enabled him "to work it out further with fear and trembling." Were salvation still to depend in any sense on him, he would be exalting himself.[173] But now that everything depends on grace, there is no reason in the least to glory in his own abilities and he can only humble himself deeply before God. And this is precisely the way along which salvation is obtained. God always opposes the high and mighty, but pours out his grace on the lowly.[174] Teellinck's train of thought is therefore this: consideration of God's gracious election produces humbleness and this humility is "useful" for people in obtaining grace.

At this point something needs to be added. This display of unmerited grace intensifies thankfulness. Nothing need be written about one's own willing or striving, but much needs to be said about God's display of compassion. Precisely and only those who have felt the truth of God's everlasting grace "guaranteed in their hearts" commit themselves to serve the Lord "with all diligence." It cannot be otherwise, emphasizes Teellinck. For, the person that recognizes that the goodness received comes exclusively from God wants to give goodness back to him fully. Understandably, all the frustrated arguments about divine good pleasure that might once have been considered arbitrary are now silenced, and Teellinck resolves "to apply himself" above everything else to "giving God's grace its full due."[175] He follows this up with a remarkable sentence. After citing for the fourth time in the same context the Pauline saying that it is not to those that will or to those that work but to those on whom God has mercy (Romans 9:16), he asserts that God does not actually commit himself to have mercy on one to whom he has not beforehand given the "sense" both to will and to work.[176] Here Paul's expression receives a peculiar nuance. Teellinck sees our "willing and working" as definitely preceding God's display of grace, even if the willing and the working are provided by God. The conclusion that he draws from this implicitly contains an anti-passive position. Human activity is not paralyzed by God's good pleasure, but rather is stimulated by it. At any rate, what Teellinck expresses next is his vow that he will for that very reason not stop sighing and groaning in making his request that it might please God to grant him the willing and the working, so that he might receive "still more" of his mercy.[177]

---

172. *Soliloquium,* 19.58-59.

173. Ibid., 58.

174. Ibid., 20.60.

175. Ibid., 61.

176. Ibid., 61-62. Teellinck maintains the same formulation in *Sleutel,* 1.3.9, 227, the same idea in *Sleutel,* 1.4.7, 271.

177. *Soliloquium,* 19.62.

Teellinck apparently cannot conceive of experiencing divine mercy without it being preceded by our search for it, which is also provided by God.[178]

To round out both chapters in his *Soliloquium* that he devotes to the problem of election, Teellinck makes two more desires known. The first is whether God will allow him to understand that it is much more blessed to be assured that the entire work of conversion lies in God's "special grace" than that it is established "in part by his grace and in part by my free will and my own strength." Human power is always "frail and evil," but God's grace is "entirely good and powerful."[179] His second desire is that from that time forward he might praise all good gifts received from his good God, and that he might be persuaded in his own soul that God would not withhold his blessing from him "in the exercise" of salvation. And, so he continues, "that in this way (if it may be consistent with your eternal decree), I shall certainly be converted and preserved as though I held within my own hand the power to be converted whenever I so chose." For it is God's own command that we be converted by using the means he provides.[180] Teellinck, who was so often troubled about predestination, as appears here, seems to let God's actual and much loved command prevail with a completely untroubled heart over God's eternal and hidden decree.

Now the expression, "as if I had within my own hands the power to be converted," sounds rather optimistic. Time and again, however, it is made clear that this is not Teellinck's intention. He sighs and groans for God's grace and for God's (note well!) conversion.[181] While Teellinck might seem to be the subject of conversion here, the actual subject is none other than the God who grants conversion. Satan's shackles and the unruliness of sin are forces that can be broken only by God's overpowering grace, Teellinck assures his readers repeatedly. Otherwise, "nothing that is involved"[182] will come to anything through all our own sighing, wishes and struggles. For that reason, all upright seekers of God pray that above all the Lord himself will work in them the work of conversion by giving them the means of conversion, of which this prayer itself is one, and that he will so draw them that they follow him. If it is God alone who

---

178. It is not impossible that the background of Teellinck's sentiments was the Anglo-Saxon motif of preparatory grace, as William Perkins (1558-1602) developed the idea. Perkins had a major influence on Teellinck. See Engelberts, *Willem Teellinck*, 96; and J. R. Beeke, *Personal Assurance of Faith: English Puritanism and the Dutch "Nadere Reformatie," from Westminster to Alexander Comrie (1640-1760)* (Ann Arbor, 1988), 114. The idea is that by means of initial grace—therefore, there is no thought of synergism—certain preparatory activities such as contrition and longing precede a trusting dependence on God's promise. See C. Graafland, *De zekerheid van het geloof: Een onderzoek naar de geloofsbeschouwing van enige vertegenwoordigers van reformatie en nadere reformatie* (Wageningen, 1961), 131-32; and van 't Spijker, "Teellincks opvatting," 133-34.

179. *Soliloquium,* 19.62. Teellinck's insight here, and this applies to other themes in this chapter, is strongly related to the manner in which Voetius defends the Reformed doctrine of election against Daniel Tilenus (1561-1633) in *Proeve van de Cracht der Godtsalicheyt,* which appeared in the same year as Teellinck's *Soliloquium.* See A. de Reuver, "Dank en vreugde in de gereformeerde traditie," *DNR* 24 (2000): 82-87.

180. *Soliloquium,* 19.62-63. The last thought is repeated in *Soliloquium,* 21.69.

181. *Soliloquium,* 21.64.

182. Ibid., 65.

extends these means, but their "working out" is left to the free will of humans, then the result comes to nothing.[183] God not only must knock at the door of the heart, but he must break it down from the inside and "take possession of it."[184]

Perhaps the heart of Teellinck's concept of grace is expressed most clearly when he prays to God concerning his forbearance near the end of his *Soliloquium*, "If I neglect serving you, do not then neglect still caring for me; if I pursue the things of the flesh, send your Spirit after me; if I stray from you, pursue me nevertheless." Amazed, he asks himself, "Is that prudent behavior on the part of so great a God; is that any way to deal with a wicked man? You act, O Lord, not as if I am involved with you, but as if you are involved with me; not as if my blessedness lies in your well-being, but as if your well-being lies in my salvation." Teellinck calls God's grace enormous "in every respect."[185] It is motivated by nothing less than God's unconditional love. This is a love that gives; a love that wells up in a heart that has every reason to be displeased, but that obviously overflows with great delight. If anyone ever felt that God desires the salvation of humanity more than humanity desires this for itself, it would be Teellinck—as though God's well-being resides in ours! Certainly, such grace is enormous "in every respect."

Faith and Love

Teellinck sees the "essence" of being a born-again Christian as consisting in a continually "God-ward direction" of life that seeks salvation only in the Lord Jesus through faith.[186] Although faith is mentioned here as an aside, according to him it is nevertheless of fundamental significance. It is the instrument or only means that connects a person with Christ.[187] My impression is that Teellinck, in the spirit of Calvin, does not have a lot of interest in the question of the chronological sequence of faith and regeneration, although it is completely clear that he regards the entire process of a person's spiritual renewal—faith as well as regeneration—as an activity of the supernatural power of God's Spirit.[188] What interests him more is that the Spirit generally works through the instrument of the Word. For the believer, the Word is not only the source but also the single point of orientation and source of stability. He must never allow himself to be disengaged from it, whatever might be raised against it. This he must maintain above all in the face of evil distortions, heavy attacks and tests of his faith. Whoever would serve the Lord must place more trust in the promises of

---

183. Ibid., 68. The assertion by Engelberts that Teellinck would have accepted free will as a good thing, in contrast with Calvin, is in conflict with the sources and has been refuted by van 't Spijker in "Teellincks opvatting," 130-33. Before him, Bouman already demonstrated that Engelbert's thesis is untenable. See Bouwman, *Willem Teellinck*, 29 and n.69 on page 62.

184. *Soliloquium,* 21.69.

185. Ibid., 30.68.

186. Ibid., 2 ("Dedicatie").

187. Teellinck, *Huys-boeck*, 96. If we do not believe in Christ, he is of no benefit to us. Then he is like a deep well which definitely contains water, "but we have no implement for drawing the water out of it." Faith is the bucket by which we draw water from the fountain of salvation. Ibid., 97.

188. Ibid., 407.

salvation contained in the Bible than on a thousand unfounded testimonials of his own conscience or from the devil.[189]

Teellinck knows that it is namely the preaching of the Word that brings about "faith and spiritual life."[190] That faith and spiritual life function here as synonyms is related, it seems to me, to a second point that he gives special emphasis. The entire renewal of a person is the fruit of the believing union with Christ.[191] This "close and intimate union" with Christ is produced "by the Spirit of God through faith."[192] Here I skip the syllogistic construction by which Teellinck understands the way in which personal assurance of faith comes about.[193] The point that concerns me at present involves the close relationship between faith and love. Teellinck understands love to have both a vertical and a horizontal focus. By the latter he has good works in mind. He considers them to be inextricably bound to faith. In Calvin's footsteps, that in turn followed Luther's, Teellinck posits that a person is certainly justified through faith alone, but that faith is never "alone."[194] By this he does not mean that faith justifies us *because* it does good works, but *so that* it may do them. Faith justifies exclusively because it appropriates the satisfaction of Christ, who is our only righteousness. What Teellinck wants to say, however, is that no one can appropriate Christ as his righteousness unless he is united with him and receives a portion of his Spirit, and that this Spirit sanctifies him for works of love. In this way faith is never present without love, but love is a consequence of faith.[195]

In addition to the horizontal dimension that is concerned with interpersonal relationships, love also has a vertical dimension according to Teellinck—one that concerns the relationship with God. Although it is difficult to evaluate which of these two aspects is dominant in his writings—concurrence seems in any case to be out of the question for him—the intertwining of faith and love for God is a theme of the first order for him. After what we have learned about his love for God and for Jesus, that should not surprise us at all. Teellinck's conception of faith is above all, insofar as it is related to that of Bernard, that faith and love can hardly be distinguished. Although he grants faith undiluted primacy on the point of justification—he stands on the Reformation!—he immediately does all he can to articulate that this faith cannot proceed at the expense of love. Perhaps Teellinck's sentiments in this regard are not adequately qualified. The formulation that love is inherent in faith could certainly be more to the point.

---

189. *Sleutel*, 1.1.7, 35. Teellinck voices the same thought in *Jerusalem*, 1.9, 90-91.

190. Teellinck, *Huys-boeck*, 448.

191. *De Toetsteen des geloofs. Waer in De gelegentheyt des waren saligmakende Geloofs nader ontdeckt wordt soo dat een yder sich selven daer aen kan Toetsen of hy oock het ware Salighmakende Geloove heeft* (Amsterdam, 1662), 468. Compare *De worstelinghe eenes bekeerden Sondaers, Ofte Grondige Verklaringe van den rechten zin des VII. Capittels tot den Romeynen* (Vlissingen, 1650), 54: "Regeneration is the promise made in the covenant of grace, which we receive through faith in Christ."

192. Teellinck, *Huys-boeck*, 96.

193. Ibid., 100-102. See de Reuver, *"Bedelen bij de Bron,"* 406-8.

194. *Sleutel*, 2.5.15, 100. On Luther and Calvin, see de Reuver, *"Bedelen bij de Bron,"* 258 and 270, respectively.

195. Ibid.

H. Vekeman has also expressed himself on this relationship between faith and love. He correctly indicates that the language of faith frequently culminates in the language of love "with an explosion of images." But again and again, Teellinck emphasizes that faith is "the vital breath of mystical love." According to Vekeman this love is the fruit of faith alone. He adds, "Perhaps this is the fundamental difference with Roman Catholic mysticism."[196] Whether this generalized, yet careful, judgment also holds for the catholic mystic Bernard is an open question. Also according to him the experience of love always springs from faith. Indeed, it is its fruit, as long as "fruit" is not regarded as a product in the sense of faculty psychology, but strictly as the essential movement given with faith. In any case, Teellinck takes it in the sense of water belonging to a spring. His faith is affective in nature and is an extension of love.

Of great significance in this regard is the manner in which Teellinck in *Sleutel* describes the difference between a natural and a spiritual knowledge of God. The first kind of knowledge can also be achieved by unregenerate people. "Through mental agility" they often know how to "discuss all the fine points of religion" with insight and precision. But such knowledge is nothing more than "a vainly traced silhouette or shadow of the true knowledge of God." Teellinck's criterion for making this judgment is readily apparent. It is knowledge that lacks precisely the most important quality of spiritual knowledge, namely "the feeling of God's nearness" and the inner, "sweet taste of the one confessing knowledge of divine things." Teellinck compares this to someone who stands gazing at sumptuous food without tasting it. That does not satisfy the appetite. Therefore, he lays it on his readers' hearts to pray fervently that God will "clothe" such "naked" knowledge "with heartfelt love" and that he will "warm" such "cold knowledge" with "the flaming realities of the things pertaining to God's Spirit." For this is what the knowledge of faith comes to. Then it no longer remains an arms-length consideration, but it becomes an "amazing love, desire, appetite, and affection of our hearts." These affective experiences Teellinck develops in his continuing discussion when he says that the heart "anchors" itself in "the things that it knows," that is to say, in the divine realities that faith confesses on the basis of the Word, and that it is so disposed to cling to them that "the self is changed and transformed into the image and likeness of one who truly knows the things of God." In this way then, a person knows the things of God "through her own discovery and lively experience"—"and that with feeling."[197] Here Teellinck is clearly describing faith in which love is inherent.

The description is no different in his *Soliloquium*. How firmly established is the person whose faith rests on the Cornerstone? he asks. In the same breath he adds: "How secure and how well protected against all the waves and billows of this terribly turbulent and restless world is the one who with unfeigned love has fixed his heart on you, O Lord?" How sweet and calming God's love is! What peace its presence brings into the heart, and how "serenely the soul rests under the shadow of your wings when in love it relies on you." Love of earthly things is "unsettlingly vexing," beset with "storms and tempests." But the love of God

---

196. Vekeman, "Inleiding," xxxiii-iv.
197. *Sleutel*, 1.1.5, 22-23.

is one that "never vexes." By nature it is pure and purifies, and it is always answered with love returned.[198] Precisely because this passage demonstrates how intimately faith and love are connected, it is relevant to our discussion. The same interweaving of the two—one could almost say, the same union of the two—should be noted when Teellinck adds, "If you only had as much unfeigned faith as a grain of mustard seed to see the Lord Jesus Christ's coming to you, would his divinity not dazzle your eyes?" And, in the immediately following sentence he adds, "If you only had a small spark of divine love within you, would it not be ignited and burn like a huge bonfire for the Lord—one that could not even be doused with a huge flood of water?"[199]

We are undoubtedly dealing with faith primarily in the sense of that "true and precious faith" without which there can be no talk of surrender to God.[200] For that reason, Teellinck thanks God profusely for opening "the bosom" of his grace so cordially in Christ that it taught him to see Jesus as the most beautiful and "the only One." From this perspective Teellinck intends to portray nothing less than an acquisitive faith. But it is certainly a faith in which the love of God is reflected above all else. That is obvious from the immediate conclusion that Teellinck draws after explaining exactly what it is that he subsequently sees in Christ, namely God's undying "love of humanity." He adds a concluding clause that is very significant: "so that in Christ we possess such a compelling attraction powerful love, that we come to you." Teellinck experienced this himself, and thereafter his love for the world began to shrivel and his heart was directed increasingly toward God.[201]

On the basis of what I have found in the body of Teellinck's writings, I think I can conclude that in his spirituality faith, as a response to God's revelation, has the position of indisputable primacy, but that the love inherent in that faith predominates to the extent that it transforms faith into a thoroughly affective response.

Self-denial

The classical theme of *abnegatio sui* that throughout the ages has defined the shape of Christian spirituality is also prominent in Teellinck's writings. This self-denial is related to approaching God in Christ as warp is to woof. For the reason that salvation in Christ is everything, I must especially deny my own self. Boundless love of self Teellinck, along with à Kempis, regards as the root of our natural depravity.[202] At this point for Teellinck there exists a clear dilemma: heaven or hell. With an obvious allusion to the text of the man from Agnietenberg, he prays that he might consider from what a "huge peril of hell" he can yet be delivered and what his portion will be in so great a salvation, if he

---

198. *Soliloquium*, 28.88.

199. Ibid., 23.77-78. Elsewhere Teellinck makes similar sounding observations about hope.

200. Ibid., 21.65. See also 22.75, which emphasizes that it is only by faith that a person makes progress in spiritual life.

201. Ibid., 30.96-97.

202. *Sleutel*, 2.6.7, 241. Compare *Imitatio*, 3.53, in *Opera*, 2:245.

will but deny himself.[203] What does the short time of self-denial on earth amount to when compared with eternal salvation? Now sighing and weeping in the battle against oneself can be beneficial, but often this is too late, he says with Thomas' *Imitation*. Then an hour in hell will cause more severe "pain than a hundred years of self-denial here" on earth.[204]

But it is not the fear of hell that is determinative for Teellinck. The real dilemma is God or self. That is to say, concretely, God's will or my will. My will needs to be derived completely from that of God. On this point every semblance of compromise is fatal. It is all or nothing.[205] "Pay attention to no one as closely as you do to yourself," advises Teellinck in the spirit of Thomas.[206] Freedom from self-control produces slavery in the regime of one's own caprices and lusts. Giving oneself to God frees one from this land of compulsion.[207] Whenever a person is united with Christ and subjects herself entirely to God's will, she enjoys complete freedom for the first time.[208] That is the blessing that self-denial spreads already in this life. But what concerns Teellinck the most is the life to come. Without self-denial no prospect of participating in it exists. "I must give myself entirely and at all times to you, or I will not be preserved to the end."[209]

This complete devotion to God is inseparably tied, to be sure, to one's own preservation, but nevertheless it has above all a theocentric purpose. Insight into one's own "vanity and insignificance" opens one's eyes to the "all-sufficiency" of God. That is the positive impact of self-negation. Self-denial has no value in and of itself, but it serves the purpose of undivided devotion to God. It forms the flipside of such devotion, purely and simply. The awareness that all is vanity apart from God is lacking, therefore, as long as one does not see at the same time that full meaning is found in him alone, "so that men may learn entirely and completely and with every possible stirring of the heart to depend on you alone."[210] God, who gave his own Son up for us all, is entirely worthy of our surrender to him.[211] In this regard Teellinck finds it so bitter to recognize that so much self-love still resides within him. He does not hesitate to express himself in

---

203. *Soliloquium*, 10.31. In the original edition, this is wrongly numbered as "The Seventh Chapter." Compare *Imitatio*, 1.24, in *Opera*, 2:48-49. That this activity produces satisfaction (*satisfactio*), Teellinck nowhere indicates, as does à Kempis.

204. *Soliloquium*, 10.31. The same thought is expressed in 27.87. Compare *Imitatio*, 1.24, in *Opera*, 2:49-50: "Ibi erit una hora gravior in poena; quam hic centum anni in gravissima poenitentia." Teellinck changes "poenitentia" to "self-denial." Also the sentence with which Teellinck follows immediately is almost literally the same as that which appears in the same chapter of *Imitatio*: "If it is the case, then, that a little suffering now is so unbearable for me, what would the pain of hell be like?" Compare *Imitatio*, 1.24, in *Opera*, 2:51: "Si modo modica passio tam impatientem efficit, quid gehenna tunc faciet?"

205. This radical requirement is not to be considered as a demand for unnatural death. In the "Appendix" of *Sleutel* Teellinck gives numerous illustrations of "superstitious, explicit and reprehensible things" that have emerged in the history of spiritual devotion and from which he strongly distances himself.

206. *Sleutel*, 2.6.7, 240. Compare *Imitatio*, 3.13, in *Opera*, 2:168.

207. *Sleutel*, 2.6.8, 245.

208. Ibid., 1.2.9, 79.

209. *Soliloquium*, 11.34.

210. Ibid.

211. *Sleutel*, 2.6.7, 242.

strong language: "I esteem my own self as my god."[212] Here one looks deep into Teellinck's heart. It is a heart torn in half. He longs to give himself to God alone and in so doing to abandon all self-interest, but at the same time he recognizes the bitter opposite "at the bottom" of his heart.[213]

The experience of this dissonance is understandably a phase in the life of faith that belongs in the past. In Teellinck's *Jerusalem*, Mary, whose heart is filled with love for Jesus, learns from his own mouth that she still harbors within her "some uncontrolled passions, desires and affections that have not been put to death."[214] In *Soliloquium* Teellinck complains in chapter 27, after he has experienced many displays of God's love, about that "accursed indolence and cowardly compromise" that always still lurks in his heart. For that reason, he finds it "highly necessary" to "admonish" himself all the more to self-denial and not to gamble away eternal glory for the sake of passing trifles.[215] The last-named folly—he calls it a "raging madness"—he wants to fight with renewed strength. That sounds activistic. And on a certain level, it is. Teellinck regards the imperative with complete seriousness. But he knows enough to embrace this imperative on the basis of the indicative of God's grace. For he is not only aware of the necessity of self-denial, he is just as aware of its source. It is a disposition that he does not attribute to himself, but exclusively to God's grace.[216] His own will is so perverted—"twisted into a terrible shape and monstrous distortion"[217]—that only grace can bring about a change in it. Undoubtedly, he means special grace here. Only it possesses the power to recreate his perverse will and inclinations. He is in no position to do so himself. On the contrary, what he perceives in himself, as he also expresses in chapter 28 of *Soliloquium*, is the pressure to follow only his "own passions." What is so poignant about this is that he is completely persuaded that essential self-denial includes nothing less than that his own "passion" is broken and that he be able to will nothing else than what God wills.[218] As much as he knows and desires that things must be different, he bumps up against an inner conflict—he calls it "a troubling thing"— that he cannot exorcise. He knows even more. He knows that God can help him out of this impasse. And he considers knowing this to be something substantial: "And what a great thing it is, on the other hand, O Lord, that I know that you can easily tame my passion and set it straight."[219]

If God alone is the author of salvation, he is also the same for self-denial. Forsaking one's own will cannot possibly arise from our "old nature," but only from the "new nature," which the Spirit of Christ freely and graciously gives

---

212. *Soliloquium*, 11.34.

213. Ibid., 33.

214. *Jerusalem*, 1.2, 4. Compare 1.4, 36-37, where Teellinck compares depravities dwelling within to horses that fall into a hole and drag men into sin with them.

215. *Soliloquium*, 87.

216. Ibid.

217. *Jerusalem*, 1.7, 67.

218. *Soliloquium*, 89. The same idea appears in Bernard, *SC*, 83:3, in *SW*, 6:612, and in *Imitatio*, 3.15, in *Opera*, 2:173.

219. *Soliloquium*, 89.

us.[220] The spiritual exercises of prayer and meditation are certainly of instrumental value, but they take effect only when "the Spirit of God in his free grace desires to bless us and to accomplish his work in us." For that reason Teellinck's advice is to keep our eyes on God above all and to cling to his grace.[221] One must "look away from self entirely and completely and look to Christ" and depend on him alone. In light of this, it is understandable that for Teellinck self-denial coincides with "cleaving to Christ."[222] Self-denial blooms where life is rooted in Christ. Its source is grace.

Yet, it seems to Teellinck that this order can be inverted. Elsewhere he explains that we must empty ourselves in order for God to pour the oil of his grace into our hearts.[223] However, Teellinck places in our hands the key for unlocking this apparent contradiction. His statement does not pertain to the origin of self-denial, but to the "working out of God's salvation in our lives." In the actual practice of the life of faith, given purely by grace, one remains permanently under the direction of grace. In order to participate in this progressive display of grace, one must not ascribe anything to self, but deny and empty oneself. God pours his grace into that emptiness. That Teellinck has no other intent than this appears from a passage that displays the same progression. There he calls self-denial a pre-condition for following Christ. He develops this by positing that we must continually reflect deeply on our own insignificance and on Christ's all-sufficiency, and that in this reflecting we must "exalt" in Christ's power, for he will live in us.[224] In this way self-denial serves the practice of discipleship. Self-denial does not displace Christ and his grace from their rightful place, but it accords him the place that he deserves. In self-denial, then, we have something not of little value. A person properly regards herself as unworthy. Thus, self-denial is as indispensable as it is unworthy, for it accentuates the worthiness of Christ. With attention fastened on Christ's sufficiency, it does not add the slightest weight to the scales. From that perspective, one need not worry about her sins, her virtues or all her works, whether good or evil, for she fixes "the purpose of her heart on Christ the Lord" and his merits. It is as though there is nothing else in the entire world than Jesus, who is "all in all." On that basis a person takes courage and draws her strength from him, not because she herself can achieve anything, also not because she denies herself—"for that would be to rely on herself, and that is not acceptable"—but solely and only because it has been granted to her to rely on Jesus. This is the basis of Teellinck's salvation. It is this same vision of Jesus in which he knows the source of his self-denial lies. For the person whom God illumines with this knowledge of Christ is "prepared to forsake the world and to deny himself."[225] In the concluding chapter of his *Soliloquium*, he summarizes

---

220. *Jerusalem*, 1.7, 81.
221. *Sleutel*, 1.2.8, 218-19.
222. Ibid., 220.
223. Ibid., 2.6.8, 243.
224. Ibid., 1.2.5, 61.
225. Ibid., 1.2.4, 60.

this all in a single, complete sentence: "The work of my conversion began when the Lord Jesus began to be beautiful to me."[226]

Cross-bearing

Self-denial is tied very closely to cross-bearing, as the gospel of Mark says (8:34), and it is at the same time a central motif in the history of Christian spirituality. Teellinck calls for a willingness to bear one's cross and to suffer "a principal evidence" and "a special manifestation" of self-denial.[227] Pre-eminently in cross-bearing, therefore, the renunciation of oneself is manifest. The forms taken by cross-bearing are many, but they all have the same nature and quality. They bear the stamp of dying. Teellinck has in mind poverty, sickness, pain, bondage, loss of friends and status. In short, cross-bearing involves the putting to death of everything to which people are most attached.[228] He admits that "the things of the flesh are difficult to manage," but immediately adds that they become unusually "useful and expedient" occasions for restraining our fallen nature, "which would otherwise bring us to eternal death," and for increasingly making us participants in Christ.[229] For that reason the person who overcomes them must not "grumble, complain, mope around or be irritated about this," but "shut his mouth quite intentionally to such worldly cackling." It is much better that he says about himself, "O, you who are so poor and needy, 'I am not worthy that my God and Lord should give me a little piece of rye bread and some cold soup in order to fill my empty stomach; I am not worthy to receive a handful of straw on which to rest my head.'" As long as a person is provided with these basic needs, he has nothing about which to complain. On the contrary, he should be thankful for them. And whenever God sends him some "discomfort of the flesh," he needs to think of this primarily as a special favor. For by so doing, God always opens the way for him to crucify the old man, which Teellinck considers one of "the principal obligations" that a person has in this life. Therefore, he must "apply himself to this, his most important task, on the occasion of these inconveniences,"[230] says the man who himself was so frequently visited with sickness.

But yet, cross-bearing extends further than external adversity. It is required above all in the face of "inner vexations and tensions" such as profound anxiety and indecisiveness. One should not be especially "unsettled" by them, for this form of cross-bearing is also profitable. It helps us keep our feet on the ground and teaches us to be content with the smallest of gifts.[231]

The determinative motivation for willingly bearing one's cross, however, is the idea that it is inherent in following Christ. In part two of *Sleutel*, Teellinck readily quotes from the chapter of the *Imitation* in which Thomas commends

---

226. *Soliloquium*, 30.97.

227. *Sleutel*, 2.6.9, 247. Calvin calls the *tolerantia crucis* a part (*pars*) of self-denial. *Inst.* 3.8 in *OS*, 4:161.

228. *Sleutel*, 1.2.6, 65.

229. Ibid., 66.

230. Ibid., 66-67.

231. Ibid., 67.

cross-bearing. Just as it had for the devout medieval figure, the crucified Christ was the paradigm for the father of the Further Reformation.[232] That the soteriological dimension of Christ's saving work was overshadowed by its exemplary features for Thomas clearly did not upset Teellinck. For him there was no contradiction here. What Christ did for us is not entirely lacking, but to a great extent it does remain in the background. What he did as an example for us moves prominently to the foreground. With à Kempis, Teellinck says that it is all about a person taking up her cross and following Jesus. In this way she reaches eternal life. "Our dear Lord Jesus has gone before you, bore his cross for you and died for you on the cross, so that you might also bear your cross and that you might also be willing to die on the cross." Eternal joy awaits anyone who dies this death on the cross. For whoever joins Christ in his suffering, will also be with him "in his joy." Cross-bearing certainly yields wonderful fruit already in the present. No one can ever "have such heartfelt feelings concerning the sufferings of our Lord" as the person who has also experienced his sufferings. Their bitterness becomes sweet: "If it is the case that you willingly bear the cross, then the cross will also wholly carry you." The cross-bearer draws his strength from the cross itself, that is to say, from Jesus, by whom the cross is laid on the one who is the Lord's companion and participant. He did not live a single hour on earth without suffering and pain. Therefore, for all who would follow him he has prepared no other way to glory than "this way of the cross." And, the further one progresses in the spiritual life, the heavier the cross he bears.[233]

The complete passage from which I have just lifted the main ideas—all three columns of it—constitutes a virtually literal copy of the first half of Thomas' longest chapter in the *Imitation*, namely "Concerning the Royal Way of the Holy Cross."[234] Teellinck was apparently convinced that his own feelings concerning the benefit and necessity of cross-bearing were adequately represented in it. The same holds true for the manner in which, a little further along, he discusses the connection between the cross and comfort. Once again he follows in Thomas' footsteps by stating that the cross-bearer will not be without the illumination of divine comfort; Teellinck adds that this is so "even in the present miserable life." Whoever willingly bears his cross, already sees his burden turned to consolation. Unlike à Kempis, Teellinck clearly identifies this as the inner comfort of the Holy Spirit. Sometimes the cross-bearer is so strengthened in his suffering and so inspired by love for Christ and an intense desire to be conformed to his likeness, that he would not want to be without "suffering or tribulation." What the prior of Agnietenberg adds, however, Teellinck does not repeat: "because he knows that he is more acceptable to God to the extent that he is able to bear greater and heavier suffering for his sake." Apparently, for him that came too close to being meritorious. This is noteworthy, for Thomas explicitly states that this is not caused by one's virtue, but purely by the grace of Christ. When Thomas embroiders on this theme, Teellinck again agrees with him totally: "If we depend

---

232. Compare *Jerusalem*, 1.5, 39, where Jesus says to Mary, "My child, my example is your command."

233. *Sleutel*, 2.6.9, 250-51.

234. *Imitatio*, 2.12, in *Opera*, 2:82-85: "De regia via sanctae crucis."

on ourselves, we could never bear our cross or do any of these things in our own strength. But when you show us your faithfulness, dear Lord, then you lend us your strength from heaven on high and bring our sufferings entirely under your control." For that reason we shall "joyfully" bear the cross of him who allowed himself to be crucified for our salvation—Thomas says, "out of love for us"—for, as Teellinck adds, "then the Lord Jesus will be with you, wherever you may be." Whoever longs to be his friend must willingly drink the cup of the Lord, for then he will know that it is well with him. "Then you will have found paradise here on earth."[235]

The conclusion is that cross-bearing as a component of self-denial is an integral dimension of Teellinck's notion of spirituality. Although the weight of the cross radically disturbs the self-satisfied life, its intent and effect are nothing less than redemptive. The cross is not imposed heavy-handedly or coercively, but is extended by the hands of the Cross-bearer exclusively in a spirit of favor. In fellowship with Christ, his followers fall short, but their fellowship with him is safe-guarded and deepened by cross-bearing. Thus, cross-bearing is another sign of Jesus' love. Teellinck's spirituality turns entirely on that point.

Humility

To the great benefit contained in the cross and suffering, Teellinck adds humility. Whenever a person is under pressure or is tempted, he learns "in the best way possible" how insignificant he is.[236] For someone to live like a Christian, Teellinck thought that that realization was essential. Whoever aspires to the blessedness of salvation, which "lifts one to the heights of heaven," must unconditionally "plumb" its foundation in the depths of all humility. There is every reason to do so. For how enormous human frailty is cannot be overstated, Teellinck emphasizes along with à Kempis. Today we confess our sins, but tomorrow again we succumb to the same wickedness.[237] Therefore, we should never operate with any delusions. Rather, let the Christian consider himself the least of all, not only with respect to God, but also with respect to "the people in his guild, in any association of which he is a part, and in any contact he has with others."[238] He who really considers himself to be the greatest sinner before God will be gentle with others. He will be more disturbed by the smallest sin that he commits himself than by "the greatest fault" committed by his neighbor. Teellinck considers this to be "a very beautiful point about being humbled."[239] His conception of humility displays no trace of spiritualizing, therefore. However spiritually humility might be experienced, it has a decidedly practical

---

235. *Sleutel*, 2.6.12, 259-61. See *Imitatio*, 2.12, in *Opera*, 2:85-86. This passage and the one that follows—almost four columns in all—is a repetition of the second half of Thomas' chapter on cross-bearing, although with significant lacunae and variations.

236. Ibid., 2.6.10, 254.

237. *Sleutel*, 1.1.5, 27-28. See *Imitatio*, 1.22, in *Opera*, 2:43-44. As we saw, Teellinck weaves the same quote into his *Soliloquium* in 6.24. The same thought is reworked in *Soliloquium*, 14.41.

238. *Sleutel*, 1.1.5, 28.

239. Ibid., 29. Also see *Jerusalem*, 1.9, 88.

application. And it is this practical expression of humility that distinguishes it entirely from the mere appearance of humility. He illustrates this by pointing to those who, while admittedly showing some signs of humility, meanwhile are so "impressively well-connected" that they offer sharp criticisms of those "who are not precisely their equals in social status." They do this not only with respect to particular individuals, but also concerning "the whole church, fellowship of Christ," as soon as everything does not go exactly their way. These are people who "regard themselves alone as the holiest saints in the world."[240]

The attitude of meekness for which Teellinck pleads has an ethical dimension, therefore, that concerns one's relationship with one's neighbor. The strongest accent, nevertheless, falls on the spiritual dimension. *Coram Deo* requires of us no other attitude than that of humility. Its opposite lies in wait whenever God blesses us with unusual experiences of his favor. Precisely then it is important to remain lowly of heart and not to start talking about his gifts. Special vigilance is commanded here. For, it is a tactic of the devil to "sniff around in our hearts" at such well-chosen moments in order to see if he can find something "by which he can get a grip on us." That is the reason, Teellinck explains with à Kempis, why it is good "that a person maintain private devotions at these times of grace and not talk much or brag about them." One can better remember that she is not at all worthy of God's grace and that it was bestowed on the basis of "some unmerited favor of God." Above all, she should not stare herself blind at "that sweet experience," for it can easily go wrong. The best remedy Teellinck knows is, rather, to ponder how miserable and deficient we are without that grace.[241]

For Teellinck humility is nothing more than a validation of piety. He calls God's truth and our humility "sisters on friendly terms." Truth reveals "her secrets" to humility. "Humbleness" is the key to true understanding.[242] People are inclined to speak of it as a non-negotiable condition in this connection. However, it is better to think of it as a condition that they cannot satisfy in their own strength, but only by the grace of God. It is the case with humility that it is not only exercised in the presence of God, but that it is also caused by God. Teellinck is keenly aware of this. Humility does not consist of a virtue that he can present to God. He can only pray for it. In his *Soliloquium* he allows us to listen in: "May I always have, O Lord, a broken and a contrite heart in your presence; a humble soul in your eyes. May I always have, O Lord, an anguished spirit, a grieving conscience, eyes filled with tears and a mouth sighing over my deep feelings about my even deeper sinfulness."[243] In addition to prayer Teellinck has yet another way of finding humility. It is the way of meditating on Christ. Perhaps it is more accurate to speak here of one and the same way, by which humility is both prayerfully desired and believingly received. The person who earnestly—undoubtedly while praying—considers how humbly Jesus lived his life on earth and how humbly he conducted himself, will regard his own pride

---

240. *Sleutel*, 1.1.6, 32.
241. Ibid., 1.1.5, 25. Compare *Imitatio*, 3.7, in *Opera*, 2:156-57.
242. Ibid., 1.3.4, 101.
243. *Soliloquium* in 26.84.

as wicked in the light of "this humble image of Christ." By means of this "powerful example" the longing for humility worked by grace "will soak through" to one's heart and affections, and one will actually become humble.[244]

According to Teellinck an unanticipated blessing is imbedded in humility for God's children. While their humility is nurtured by the shamed awareness of their deficiency in what pleases God, he is well-disposed as to favor them in Christ by esteeming precisely their humility as the good that they lack. In this way humility becomes their jewel. Whoever has clothed himself with Christ by faith (Romans 13:14) and is clothed with the garments of humility (1 Peter 5:5) may know that this apparel covers the absence of all other virtues in God's eyes. That is why Teellinck also calls humility "a short, lovely and certain route . . . in God's estimation" for reaching all the virtues that we need.[245] What we see as empty, God regards as full.

The mystery of this paradox, pertinently enough, does not lie in the value of humility in and of itself. Humility as an internal virtue is not what is well pleasing to God, but rather the external activity that it produces. In the absence of virtue humility searches for all value outside itself and finds it in Christ. This is clearly illustrated by a scene in *Jerusalem* in which Mary humbly laments her own unworthiness, which envelops her like a dark cloud. The reaction she received from Jesus says a great deal. Her humility is not rejected, much less praised. It merely indicates the right direction. The cloud is simply caused by the fact that Mary only looks inside and does not at the same time pay attention to Jesus' completely satisfactory work. "Do you want to look for your salvation to yourself, or do you intend to be your own savior? Does the Lord your God bind himself to you on the basis of your own value and virtue?" Does Mary sometimes think that Christ's bitter suffering has become impotent? Is she of the opinion that her sin and unworthiness are so great that his worth would not be able to cover them and that his blood would be unable to heal them?[246] Through this exchange Mary's humility received its proper orientation, since by relying on her own feeling she was not sufficiently driven to a reliance on Christ's merits. Her deficiency was sanctified by his full satisfaction.[247] According to Teellinck this is how it is with true humility. As long as it only consists of introspection, it remains sterile. Its value is derived entirely in compelling one to turn to Christ.

That Teellinck rejects perfectionism as unworthy is not surprising, at least in the form where a person would be able to reach perfection "according to the demands of the law already in this life." No mortal, "with the exception of the Lord Jesus Christ," has ever perfectly kept God's law in his own strength. Perfection measured by the standard of the law Teellinck considered a deluded idea. But he immediately introduces an important distinction into his discussion. Satisfaction "according to the demands of the holy gospel" is always a different

---

244. *Sleutel*, 1.1.6, 32.
245. Ibid., 1.4.11, 310-11.
246. *Jerusalem*, 2.6, 139-40.
247. Ibid., 147-48.

matter. Certainly that is solidly achievable.[248] The explanation Teellinck gives this matter shows complete agreement with his understanding of external humility. Although the "truly born again person or believer"[249] is completely incapable in himself when held to the standard of the law, he is perfected "by the softening of the gospel," since Christ covers all his failings. To this objective reality Teellinck attaches a subjective component in what follows. Namely, God's children are also called perfect "with respect to the uprightness of their hearts," that is to say, concerning their unfeigned longing to keep all God's commandments and for the forgiveness of their sins.[250] The last thought is especially significant. As clear as daylight, Teellinck cannot conceive of perfection in any other way than with this polarity: in Christ it is absolute, in the Christian it bears the incomplete shape of pursuing sanctification and asking for justification. Perfection according to the letter of the law is stored up "for the hereafter, in heaven."[251] Then the bi-polarity disappears. Until that time, one has the merits and intercession of Christ "liberally applied to all our endeavors."[252]

Teellinck's view of evangelical perfection is in line with his understanding of humility. They are both strictly Christological in nature. To do justice to Teellinck in his often seemingly legalistic striving for salvation, one must always keep in mind this fundamental perspective of his. For him, striving yields the fruit of undivided longing to live according to God's Word, but it is always qualified by gospel-induced humility. This is the conviction that one must "cling to Christ" only. And it is precisely in this "cleaving to Christ" that the lesson of humility is best learned. For, to be sure, humility takes the least prominent seat "in the whole school," but it has "God the Lord himself as its school master and teacher."[253]

Longing for Jesus

The dominance of love that we have already encountered in Teellinck comes to expression pre-eminently in his frequently expressed affection for Jesus. This is love that strongly, perhaps even overwhelmingly, takes the form of yearning. Teellinck loves, but time after time he comes to the painful discovery that this inclination is far from what it should be. Accompanying this realization, however, is his hunger for a steadily increasing experience of that love. It seems, therefore, that the deficit of love and the yearning for love cancel one another out. But it only seems so. Teellinck cannot accept the deficit. Rather, he turns the deficit into desire. He reveals this in passionate images drawn from the Song of Solomon to represent his own situation. Jesus possesses the new wine that gladdens the heart. Jesus possesses the comforting apples that refresh the smitten conscience. If he would only slide his left hand under Teellinck's head and lay his right hand on his chest, then his soul would "recline gently, then he would be

---

248. *Sleutel*, 2.3.16, 347-48.
249. Teellinck uses these designations synonymously.
250. *Sleutel*, 2.3.16, 351-52.
251. Ibid., 357.
252. Ibid., 366.
253. Ibid., 1.3.8, 220.

transported beyond any earthly paradise." Look, he calls out, "this is my Friend, my Friend is like this!"[254] This last explanation is undoubtedly genuinely meant. One should not misunderstand Teellinck's use of the indicative, borrowed from his dependence on the Song of Solomon here. For immediately thereafter he again reverts to the subjunctive, when he asks himself whether such a Friend should not have to be sought with all the love of his heart.[255] And this is stated not by some new Christian, but by a mature Christian who obviously understands the heading of the chapter involved here, namely that his entire salvation lies in Christ.

However real Teellinck's love for Jesus is, he clearly assesses it as being so inadequate that he generally opts for an unrealistic tone when speaking of it. "Should the Lord Jesus obviously and properly not always be on my mind . . . ? Should all the intimate inner thoughts of my soul not be focussed on him, all my strength, all my affections, all the inclinations of my heart?" That this is not the case, he thinks is actually absurd. When a boy is taken with a girl, he emphasizes, it is completely unnecessary for someone to have to encourage him to think about her. That occurs automatically. But how can it be, then, that days pass in which he does not "yearn joyfully and passionately" for Jesus, the most beloved of all?[256] Teellinck does not leave matters with this shameful admission, however. "Be aroused then, O my soul, delay no longer; let all that you do throughout your entire life from this time forward be nothing other than a continual desire and constant yearning for the Lord God Almighty. May he cause you to give yourself to the Lord Jesus as your Bridegroom and to be betrothed to him in fidelity and trust."[257] This appeal to himself is not an end in itself. It presses him toward another end. In a passionate prayer he appeals directly to God and, in him, to Jesus Christ, although the latter more implicitly than explicitly. In effusive terms he addresses him as the joy of his heart, the "solace" of his being and "the great longing" of his mind. "That I might but find you, the Beloved of the depths of my being; that I might cleave to you, the Love of my soul; that I might embrace you, my Heavenly Bridegroom, would exalt me in every way, within and without." He wants to enjoy the Lord always. Finally, his only wish is this: "O Lord, be my God, my all and in all."[258] A progressive movement is inherent in such yearning. He wants to try daily to awaken more and more "fervent little outbursts of a flaming love of God that are expressed in intense desires and sighs." His desire is to continue doing so just as long as it takes for him to be entirely inflamed with love for God.[259]

That this spirituality may be regarded as bridal or marital mysticism seems to me to be undoubtedly the case. It is subject only to the qualification of being anticipatory and provisional. The most it can attain in this age with respect to attachment to the Bridegroom is betrothal. Marriage remains in the future.

---

254. *Soliloquium* 23.76. The repetition of Song of Solomon 5:16 is a slight variation of the Deux-Aes version.

255. Ibid.

256. Ibid., 77.

257. Ibid., 78.

258. Ibid., 26.83-84.

259. Ibid., 29.92.

However, what Teellinck desires in the here and now, is nothing less than a foretaste of that fulfillment—proleptic, to be sure, but experienced nonetheless. He yearns for this "inner communion" when he prays, once again imitating à Kempis, "O most sweet Bridegroom of my soul, O most sweet Lover among all creatures that have ever been created, who will provide me with the wings of total freedom with which to fly to you and to rest in you? O my, when will it be completely granted to me to taste how very sweet you are, O Lord my God, although I am empty and unworthy of heart? When will I be completely united with you? And when will it be that I feel only you within me with a greater love than I have or am permitted to have even for myself?"[260] That Teellinck is not alluding to the eschaton in this passage, but to the present age, is obvious from what immediately follows: "O, come Lord Jesus, for without you I will not longer experience a peaceful day or hour." From this time forward nothing can satisfy him except "my God, my hope and my eternal salvation."[261]

I want to add a few evaluative comments concerning this prayer, which is so typical of Teellinck. In the first place, I observe that it obviously breathes, by way of Thomas, the spirit of Bernard's bridal mysticism in which concepts like sweetness, taste, union, self-denial, love and yearning are characteristic. In the second place, just as was the case with Bernard and Thomas, union with the Bridegroom does not occur through one's own efforts, but entirely through his gracious initiative. In the third place, Teellinck's prayer has nothing whatsoever to do with the identification of a kind of pantheistic mysticism. This is entirely missing at this point, as it is from all his writings. The desire to lose oneself in divine love can at first sight remind us of this. But upon closer examination, it becomes clear that for Teellinck it does not amount to a loss of the subject in the being of God—as, for example, Tauler and especially Eckhart seem to describe in their idea of sinking into the divine abyss,[262] but rather the affective, intense experience of God's love that befalls the loving soul in its wholehearted devotion to the Lover. His personhood does not disappear in God. It is precisely the self that experiences God. Teellinck's prayer is the sighing of a person who yearns for the love of and a love for the Bridegroom by which his whole heart is overwhelmed. At the same time it is a love that realizes that it is painfully obstructed by life's brokenness. This brings me to a fourth assessment, namely, that Teellinck does not describe the climax of love's union with Christ as much as his desire for it. In this I see the insight reinforced, more consequentially than in Bernard, that his mysticism bears eschatological restraint. However far he may

---

260. Ibid., 93. On à Kempis see, again, *Imitatio*, 3.21, in *Opera*, 2:183. The same quotation appears in *Jerusalem*, 1.8, 85, as well as in *Sleutel*, 2.6.6, 238, where the material is amplified with a substantially longer citation that rather closely repeats the entire chapter in the *Imitatio*. Compare Bernard, *DD*, 27, in *SW*, 1:120.

261. *Soliloquium* 29.93-94.

262. For identity-mysticism see E. Vogelsang, "Die Unio mystica bei Luther," *Archiv für Reformations-Geschichte*, 35 (1938): 79-80; Oberman, *Die Reformation*, 38-39. Compare *Meister Eckehart: Deutsche Predigten und Traktate,* ed. J. Quint (Munich, 1985); J. Tauler, *Johannes Tauler: Predigten*, 2 vols, ed. G. Hofmann and A. M. Haas (Einsiedeln, 1987); Ruh, *Meister Eckhart*; and Maas, *Van God houden*.

have progressed in his spiritual life,[263] his experience of God remains partial and has the character of a pledge, an *arraboon*. Teellinck's experience also hungers for more.

At the same time, there is good reason to nuance the foregoing somewhat. That the pinnacle of this love remains to be experienced in the future, and that its present experience generally takes the form of a longing, does not detract from the fact that Teellinck also has moments when this longing comes to a present, although temporary but deeply felt, fulfillment. It is very significant that he closes the prayer just raised with an exclamation expressed not in a wishful but in a demonstrative mode: "O! I am sick with love; hold me in your arms; satisfy me with your apples."[264] Apparently the seeker experiences moments in which his yearning is quieted. However, these are moments which bear the features of Bernard's "rare hours with weak powers."[265] A significant insertion into an extended quotation from à Kempis that appears in his *Sleutel* points in this direction. When Teellinck prays along with the *Imitation* that he might no longer feel himself but only God in his experience of God's love, he adds this twist to Thomas' words: "although you have sometimes sought me, alas that has not happened very often."[266] The exceptional as well as the proleptic character of this experience comes clearly to the forefront also in *Jerusalem*. The lively and memorable "display" of joy that Mary is sometimes depicted as experiencing is a "foretaste" of heavenly glory. She is permitted "to already participate somewhat" in that joy and finds it "to be somewhat true now and then,"[267] but for the time being it is always piece-meal.

To summarize the result of this investigation, one can say that Teellinck primarily portrays his love for Jesus in terms of longing. But this longing comes to fragmentary fulfillment at special times as a foretaste of heaven.

Hunger for Eternity

Teellinck is unable to find satisfaction in what exists here below. This is not because he does not appreciate the earthly benefits that God gives him, but because they are inadequate for satisfying his deepest hunger. His aspiration is for God. He wants to enjoy him, and then not just temporarily and partially, but enduringly and fully.[268] For that reason everything that he enjoys on earth by way of foretaste has an ambivalent significance. On the one hand, as already noted, it gives life already now a certain joyful luster, but on the other hand it arouses a feeling of pain because its fullness has not yet come. One should not consider this outlook on life as tragic. It is not tragic, but providential. It has been

---

263. The prayer appears in the second-to-the-last chapter of *Soliloquium*!

264. *Soliloquium* [23].94. Compare Song of Solomon 2:5.

265. *SC*, 23:15, in *SW*, 5:344.

266. *Sleutel*, 2.6.6, 239. It is striking that Bernard also, when connecting with his source, John of Fécamp, precedes his "rara hora et parva mora" with "sed, heu" (but, alas). See McGinn, *Die Mystik*, 2:224.

267. *Jerusalem*, 1.2, 10-11.

268. Vekeman notes, "Whoever does not experience this aspiration, can never understand the *Soliloquium*." Vekeman, "Inleiding," xxxi.

so arranged by God in his painstaking wisdom. Teellinck believes that God has so arranged "the opportunities concerning the things of this world" that a person cannot possibly find any "constant satisfaction" in them. It is as though the Lord stretches out his arm from heaven in "this conviction," in order to draw humanity away from what is perishable and to lead them toward the true blessedness that is obtainable in God alone.[269] For that reason the Christian who would share in eternal salvation must only "use" the things of this world "for his needs" and for "Christian enjoyment," and he must direct the desires of his heart toward "eternal and heavenly things that are to be found in Christ Jesus." Humanity has been created for this purpose.[270]

Teellinck heartily agrees with the idea of *vanitas* that is so prominently present in Thomas' *Imitation*.[271] The things of this world are idle, empty and fleeting. So that we might not allow ourselves to be deceived by apparent beauty, God often places "some drops of bitterness in the sweetest things." Teellinck illustrates this with an almost trivial but compelling example: the purpose of "a toothache" is to remove all our enjoyment.[272] Or, said another way: all enjoyment without God is of only short duration. Ever-present is the "gnawing worm" of death. For one thing is certain: "that inexorable watchman of death is already coming to carry me away; he is hard on my heels; yes, he already stands knocking on my door."[273] In words taken from Thomas, Teellinck complains about the blindness and dullness of people who worry only about the present and neglect the future. Would they not be better off conducting themselves in all their thoughts and words as though they would die yet today and have to appear before God's face?[274] At the same time, with Thomas he esteems those as happy "who strive in their lives to conduct themselves in such a way that they are approved in the day of their death." He has no doubt that a person will begin to judge his life differently on the day of his death than he does during healthy times.[275] Only the "righteous person" has nothing to fear in death. For him death is never "a frightening master," but "a friendly messenger" who is sent by the heavenly Father "to call him home to take possession of everlasting joys."[276]

The basic motif in Teellinck's doctrine of eternity is not dissatisfaction, however, but intense longing. Just as consciousness of life's transience is nurtured by God himself, so is this longing. His method of dealing with all those whom he intends to bring into his "beautiful heaven" in the hereafter is to fill them already here on earth with "very beautiful desires, completely earnest and

---

269. *Soliloquium* 4.19.

270. *Sleutel*, 1.2.9, 30. On the Augustinian background of this idea, see note 108.

271. The titles of the first three chapters of *Soliloquium* all contain the word "idleness." Compare *Imitatio*, 1.1, in *Opera*, 2:6.

272. *Soliloquium* 2.12-13.

273. Ibid., 2.15.

274. Ibid., 7.25. Compare *Imitatio*, 1.23, in *Opera*, 2:44: "O hebetudo et duritia cordis humani; quod solum praesentia meditatur, et futura non magis praevidet. Sic te in omni facto et cogitatu deberes tenere; quasi hodie esses moriturus."

275. *Soliloquium* 7.26. Compare *Imitatio*, 1.23, in *Opera*, 2:45-46: "Quando illa extrema hora venerit; multum aliter sentire incipies de tota vita praeterita. . . . Quam felix et prudens, qui talis nunc nititur esse in vita; qualis optat inveniri in morte."

276. *Jerusalem*, 1.3, 13.

persistent longings for heaven."[277] Teellinck advocates maintaining "lively" meditation on it. In heaven the fullness of joy awaits him, as well as "a lovely existence always and for eternity."[278] He repeatedly describes everlasting joy as "a world without end."[279] Then, for the divinely blessed person God will be "all that is sweet, all that is lovely, all that is uplifting, all that is desirable." Whatever is still temporary and damaged here will belong to the past there. God will completely perfect a person's entire existence, including all his faculties. The blessedness for which Teellinck longs is not only a gift of God, it is God himself. "The Lord himself" will be "the blessedness and the life" of the soul. But not of the soul only, but God will "also be the life and the health" of the body: the beauty to the eye, the pleasing sound in the ear, honey for the mouth, a lovely aroma in the nose. God will be the light of the mind and the satisfaction of all desires, in short, the life in our lives, our "all in all." All that a person values highly here on earth—sweetness and beauty, virtue and strength in men and animals, in trees and vegetation, in food and drink, or in sun, moon and stars—is really only "a very small shadow and glimmer" of what God will be for us before very long.[280]

In the way in which Teellinck thinks himself into the heavenly life, two things are striking. The first is the idea of continuity. Heaven does not represent a radical break with earth, but much rather its glorification. What is only enjoyed sporadically and especially only in little bits and pieces here, will be relished there in unrestrained completeness. If glory here is only fleeting, there it will be an overwhelming flood. Nevertheless, it is an overwhelming flood of which a little trickle is already experienced here on earth. What appears immediately from this description is how little Teellinck spiritualizes his depiction of heaven. It has aesthetic features that appeal to the senses. The bodily dimensions of human existence are all included in it. The spiritual renewal of which Paul speaks in 1 Corinthians 15 is not at all shadowy for Teellinck, but it obviously has a concretely corporal character.

The second thing besides continuity that strikes us, however, is that Teellinck also speaks of a definite discontinuity. To put it in Calvinian terms, this does not concern inalienable human identity (*substantia*), but the quality (*qualitas*) of human existence.[281] Life will be clothed with the totally new quality of immortality. This aspect of the eternal, which is in sharp contrast with the transitory nature of this age, receives prominent attention in Teellinck's consideration. The youthfulness of humanity will blossom without changing; its

---

277. *Soliloquium* 22.74.

278. Ibid., 9.30. Teellinck concludes his *Soliloquium* with the same words. Ibid., 30.103.

279. Ibid. Compare 22.73; 23.78; 23.79; and *Jerusalem*, 1.4, 31.

280. *Jerusalem*, 1.4, 27-28.

281. *Institutes*, 3.25.8, in *OS*, 4:449. Calvin affirms, "Nos in eadem quam gestamus carne resurrecturos quoad substantiam; sed qualitatem aliam fore." ("We will be raised in the same body that we now bear insofar as its substance is concerned, but its quality will be something different.") Compare this with his commentary on I Corinthians 15:41 and 44. The same idea occurs in Augustine, *De Civitate Dei*, 13.23. See Aurelius Augustinus, *De stad van God*, trans. with introduction by Gerard Wijdeveld (Amsterdam, 1984), 611.

beauty will never again fade; life will be eternal and joy in the Lord unending.[282] The "short, transitory life" of this age will give way to the "beautiful, everlasting life" of the hereafter.[283]

The culmination of all this sensually enjoyed glory is obviously rooted for Teellinck in the enjoyment of Jesus' love. That is the goal of his hunger for eternity. If it is warranted to label and qualify Teellinck's spirituality as mysticism, it involves a mysticism not only of faith and love, but emphatically also of hope. He loves the Bridegroom with a heartfelt love. But his love comes wrapped in the cloak of hope. But it is still only an apron for the wedding to come. With a transported soul he depicts this appetizing expectation. Vekeman does not overstate matters when he observes that Teellinck's language has captured the hues of Bernard. "The soul speaking with the voice of Song of Solomon is love-sick," says Vekeman. "It is feverish and aching, but in no way and never having drank to satisfaction."[284] Satisfaction is still coming. "O Lord, when will that be, when will that hour come?" Only the expectation of that hour can already "exalt" his heart and "already" energize his soul. But precisely that "already" betrays a provisional nature. Hope certainly energizes, but only as a harbinger: "as a preoccupation and anticipation of your joyful wedding day." Then for the first time his heavenly Bridegroom, his soul's Beloved, will visit him and embrace him.   "O . . . , that I may find you whom I seek by day and by night . . . until I will find you and bring you into my mother's home and there embrace you."[285]

I conclude this section that is not only significant for the core of Teellinck's yearning for eternity, but that is just as important for his entire spiritual experience. In a quotation from his *Soliloquium* he says it this way: "If you only had a faint ray of heavenly hope and the weakest expectation that you would hereafter always and eternally enjoy the Lord Jesus Christ, and that you would pursue loving him as your most dearly beloved Bridegroom, and with a longing heart that you would always and eternally participate in the wedding of the Lamb in heaven, . . . would you not already in this world be busy your whole life long purifying yourself and preparing yourself for this glorious wedding with the Lamb, for whom you long so intensely?"[286] Following this rhetorical question he spurs readers on henceforth to concentrate "all their activity" in this life on an enduring quest for the Almighty, "that he might give you the Lord Jesus as your Bridegroom." And on the other hand, he urges concentrating all energies on adorning life with "all sorts of beautiful virtues" that will be well-pleasing to God, "so that you may not need to wait too long and may be assured that the Lord Jesus has become yours and that you have become his with the unbreakable bonds of love, for now and for eternity, world without end."[287] Teellinck experiences his time on earth as *sub specie aeternitatis*. His entire life, in his

---

282. *Jerusalem*, 1.4, 31.
282. Ibid., 2.6, 138.
284. Vekeman, "Inleiding," xxxvi-vii.
285. *Soliloquium* 29.91.
286. Ibid., 23.78.
287. Ibid., 78-79.

ethics and his mysticism, is regarded in eschatological perspective. In all its parts earthly existence is marked as transitory. But this is a qualified transitoriness. It is a life completed in the sanctification in which fellowship with Christ is established and preparations for the wedding are made. In this, it seems to me, the goal of Teellinck's spirituality is in large measure captured.

Evaluation

By way of evaluation I offer three comments. To begin, I note that in Teellinck we have an author who stands completely behind the affirmations of the Reformation. He has not the slightest doubt about salvation by grace, the uniqueness of Christ's sacrifice, the normative character of Scripture as divine revelation and justification by faith. At the same time his own context causes him to accent things in a way that implies a shift from some positions of the Reformation. In this regard I think of his emphasis on both sanctification and religious feeling. When it comes to the matter of articulating the doctrine of sanctification, Calvin certainly does not take a back seat to him. But on the matter of its emphasis, the two men part ways. Based on my study I find that the reformer is more intent than Teellinck on clearly striking the right balance between justification and sanctification as *gratia prima* and *gratia secunda*. With the later man, the scale easily tips toward sanctification. This difference in accent is not based on a doctrinal difference, however, but purely on situational considerations. In his response to what he regarded as a lack of holiness, he placed full weight on sanctification. Teellinck had no thought of a point of departure that was different in principle. If the "first acknowledged reformers,"[288] who in their day accentuated justification, lived in the present day, Teellinck thought, they would have "readily seen that it was absolutely necessary in light of the aforementioned circumstances to take another course by placing more emphasis on good works."[289] He himself is certainly clearly conscious of a certain shift of direction, but he regarded it not just as obligated by the situation, but also as completely in the spirit of the reformers. Whether this assessment stands up entirely remains to be seen. I will not get into that subject here, but rather turn to a second difference in accent. It concerns the subject of religious feelings.

Solidly in the tradition of such reformers as Luther and Calvin, Teellinck shares the conviction that the life of faith includes a deeply experiential fellowship of love with God in Christ, based on the inner working of the Holy Spirit. This experience amounts to a highly reliable, emotional encounter.[290] However, where Teellinck connects more with spirituality in the tradition of Bernard and à Kempis is in holding that affective love, however much it springs from faith and remains tied to it, is still dominant. Compared with the reformers,

---

288. On the high regard Teellinck had for the reformers, see van 't Spijker, "Teellincks opvatting," 136.

289. Willem Teellinck, *Noodtwendigh Vertoogh, Aengaende den tegenwoordighen bedroefden Staet van Gods volck* (Rotterdam, 1647), 85. The first edition appeared in 1627. [Trans. "A Necessary Discourse on the Present, Lamentable Condition of God's People."]

290. A. de Reuver, "Een mystieke ader in de Nadere Reformatie," *DNR* 21 (1997): 12-18.

Teellinck appears to overdose on religious feelings.[291] I am immediately compelled to qualify the force of this comparison, however. Teellinck did not live in the sixteenth but in the seventeenth century. To be sure, he carried the legacy of the reformers with him, but the mentality that he displays is primarily that of emerging pietism. And this brings me to my second comment.

Teellinck is an author of the Reformation who bears ecumenical traits. Like the reformers who, despite all their criticism of Rome, wanted to stand totally in the classical-catholic tradition, Teellinck understood that he was indebted to the legacy of the pre-Reformation period. Consistent with his interaction with the Puritans, he was also inspired by the spirituality of à Kempis and Bernard, the latter possibly via à Kempis. Its pre-Reformation derivation obviously posed no problem for him. In the first place, this was because wherever necessary he rebaptized it in a reformational sense without much difficulty, and in the second place, because he recognized that the *pietas* that he represented was of an earlier vintage than the sixteenth century. And it was exactly that piety that opened for him those perspectives that allowed him to reach across doctrinal differences for common spiritual values. With respect to spiritual devotion, matters always turn on *fides qua* and not primarily on *fides quae*, not on the content of the faith that people profess but on the fact of their believing. This is to focus attention on the *doctrina* that remains of fundamental significance, to be sure, but within which the practice of a life of faith is nevertheless central. With Teellinck this practice bore the name "devotion." In its exercise he felt with the majority of pietists that he was dependent on all those before him who loved God and waited expectantly for him. If the term were not so muffled by vagueness, one could call it an ecumenicity of the heart. With whatever name one characterizes this attitude, however, without some affinity for this idea one will not adequately understand Teellinck's predilection for à Kempis, much less appreciate it.

The third and last remark is that the father of the Further Reformation, in my estimation, may be called a mystical writer. While the complete Teellinck is not captured by this characterization—his mysticism is continually flanked by his ethics—his piety certainly bears mystical features. It is a mysticism that does not give rise to faith, but one which springs from faith and is always tied to faith. Teellinck's faith finds it purpose in love, but its boundaries in hope and faith. His mysticism is always an indicator of the provisional and inadequate. It is related to that of Bernard and à Kempis, but is more strongly tempered by a sense of being unfulfilled. What connects him with both men, however, is the yearning for fulfillment. Teellinck yearns for his Beloved, his "all in all." That is his soul's devotion. It is just as certainly the soul of his devotion.

---

291. On this matter, consult van 't Spijker, "Teellincks opvatting," 140-42.

4

Theodorus à Brakel (1608-1669)

"An Example of the Most Tender Fear of the Lord"

Of the two well-known à Brakels, the younger, who was the author of *Redelyke Godtsdienst*, is definitely the more renowned. Although Theodorus was the father and Wilhelmus was his son, the latter was given the honorary title of "Father à Brakel." This is not to say, however, that Theodorus was devoid of praise. He was also held in high regard. No one less than Abraham Hellenbroek is proof of this fact.[1] When Wilhelmus died on October 30, 1711, his Rotterdam colleague Hellenbroek addressed "an overflow crowd of interested people" on Sunday, November 8, in the New Church, giving an effusive eulogy on his "deeply beloved, fellow office-bearer."[2] An unusually large portion of this address, which soon appeared in print, is devoted to Wilhelmus' life. Here Hellenbroek extolled not only the sterling qualities of his mourned colleague, whom he knew so very well, but also the spirituality of his father, who by then had died more than forty years earlier. His characterization of Theodorus was more than a string of cliches: "By grace, he was a finer example of the most tender fear of the Lord than anyone in his day (as is demonstrated for us in the genius of his surviving writings, especially his *Geestelyk Leven* and his *Trappen van het Geestelyk Leven*), and particularly to the amazement of his descendents and to the blessing of all pious people."[3] The characterization of him as "an example of the most tender fear of the Lord" is certainly to the point. It touches the heart of à Brakel's spirituality. The way in which he served God was tender and intimate. One could add two other dimensions: his communion with God was intense and joyful. He breathed the presence of God.

Biographical Sketch

While Theodorus does not belong to the first generation of Further Reformation figures who were born already in the sixteenth century—men such

---

1. On him consult, among others, Boot, *De allegorische uitlegging*, 228-37; T. Brienen, "Abraham Hellenbroek (1658-1731)," in Brienen, et al., *De Nadere Reformatie*, 181-201.

2. Abraham Hellenbroek, *Algemeene Rouklagte in de straten van Rotterdam, over den Zeer Eerwaarden, Godvrugtigen en Geleerden Heere Wilhelmus à Brakel, voorgestelt uit het laatste gedeelte van Prediker XII:5* (7th edition; Amsterdam, 1737). The first printing appeared in 1711. See F. J. Los, *Wilhelmus à Brakel* (Reprinted with an introduction by W. van 't Spijker from the original, 1892 edition; Leiden, 1991). The citations are from the reprint, 18-19. [Trans.: *The Universal Outpouring of Grief in the Streets of Rotterdam Concerning the Death of the Highly Esteemed, God-fearing and Learned Gentleman Wilhelmus à Brakel, Depicted in the Last Portion of Ecclesiastes 12:5.*]

3. Hellenbroek, *Algemeene Rouklagte*, 14-15. See A. Ros, *Theodorus à Brakel, 1608-1669: "Een voorbeeld van allertederste Godsvrucht"* (Barneveld, 2000), 13.

as Willem Teellinck (1579), Godefridus Udemans (1581 or 1582) and Gisbertus Voetius (1589)—his birth-year of 1608 makes him one of the earliest representatives of those pietists born in the immediately following century. He cannot be called a leading representative of the Further Reformation for this reason. The theocratic spirit typical of that movement that was expressed in the actual attempt to reform church and state,[4] he always shrouded behind his almost exclusive concentration on sweet communion with the Lord—one could almost express it as an ascent to God. Because this experiential dimension is at least as definitive of the Further Reformation movement, however, Theodorus definitely qualifies as "a worthy representative" of it.[5]

À Brakel's youth coincided, generally speaking, with the period known as the Twelve-year Truce. He certainly would have been aware of the doctrinal contentions that unsettled the church during this era, but he could have hardly understood them at the time. The matter that was most deeply at issue in the controversy, however, the young Dirk (his baptized name of Dirck Gerrits was later Latinized as Theodorus Gerardi),[6] took to heart already at an early age: how can a person acquire peace with God?

Dirk spent his youth in Enkhuizen.[7] It was not only the city in which he was born and nurtured, but it was also the place, as he testifies in the dedication of the first fruits of his pen, of his "spiritual rebirth and formation in the spiritual life."[8] For that reason for his entire life he remembered the "glorious sermons" and "sweet comforts" that he had experienced there, and he was never able to forget what "satisfying and easy conversations" he was blessed to have with local believers there. In short, Enkhuizen had been the "school" where God had

---

4. Graafland, op 't Hof and van Lieburg, "Nadere Reformatie," 147 and 171-72.

5. Ros, *Theodorus à Brakel*, 15-16.

6. As far as the name à Brakel is concerned, Ros notes that this likely refers to an earlier, temporary stay his parents made in Brakel, an area in the province of Brabant to the southeast of Tilburg. Ibid., 17-18. Concerning the spelling of "à" Brakel, I note that Theodorus himself did not employ a grave accent sign above the letter "a," but used an acute accent mark: "á." See the facsimile of his signature in Ros, ibid., 96, and also compare that with the facsimile of the first page of the Makkum minute book, ibid., 58.

7. For this biographical sketch I have made use of Wilhelmus à Brakel, "De Laaste Uiren van den Autheur," in Theodorus à Brakel, *De Trappen des Geestelyken Levens* (7th edition; Groningen, 1739), 428-38; following the author's instructions, this material was appended only after his death and did not appear in the first edition, which is dated 1670. Additionally, I used: H. Heppe, *Geschichte des Pietismus und der Mystik in der Reformirten Kirche, namentlich der Niederlande* (Leiden, 1879), 173-85; Ritschl, *Geschichte des Pietismus*, 1:268-76; W. Goeters, *Die Vorbereitung des Pietismus in der Reformierten Kirche der Niederlande bis zur labadistischen Krisis 1670* (reprinted from the Leipzig, 1911, edition; Amsterdam, 1974), 93-98; de Boer, *De verzegeling*, 103-10; *BLGNP*, 1:55-56, article by B. W. Steenbeek; G. H. Leurdijk, "Theodorus à Brakel," in *Figuren and thema's van de Nadere Reformatie*, ed. T. Brienen, et al. (Kampen, 1987), 52-63; T. Brienen, "Theodorus à Brakel (1608-1669)," in *De Nadere Reformatie*, ed. Brienen, et al., 123-48; van den Berg, "Die Frömmigkeitsbestrebungen," 91-93; H. H. Langelaar, "'Krank van Liefde,' De gelukzalige ongezondheid van Theodorus à Brakel," in *DNR* 21 (1997): 67-76; Ros, *Theodorus à Brakel*.

8. F. A. van Lieburg, *Profeten en hun vaderland: De geografische herkomst van de gereformeerde predikanten in Nederland van 1572 tot 1816* (Zoetermeer, 1996), 317.

instructed him. For that reason he delighted in that city like "the hearts of the children of Israel did in the Jerusalem of their time, according to Psalm 137."[9]

He received the first impressions of spiritual life from his grandmother on his mother's side, in whose home he lived for a time after his mother's premature death. The protracted prayer-life of this woman left a deep impression on him. The fact that she often asked her grandson to read for her, since he had already mastered this ability, apparently also stimulated him to read privately. His reading material consisted of the Bible and various devotional books: "simple, blessed little books and small prayer books" whose identity—whether pre-Reformation sources or not—he unfortunately did not disclose.[10] In any case, it is clear that the roots of his later meditative lifestyle reached down into his earliest years.

Three events made a deep impression on him. The first was a stay in Vlissingen when Dirk was nine or ten years old. The proclamation of the Word that he heard there spoke to him in such a way that he experienced "a very great sweetness and pleasure from the sermons and in humbling himself before God."[11] Before that he had been unable to follow the ministers in Enkhuizen in the same way, either because he was "unable to hear" because he "sat too far away" or because of inattentiveness.[12] The second event concerns the time 2 Corinthians 6:14-16, which deals with the radical division between Christ and Belial and between light and darkness, hit him like a blow from a sword.[13] While one cannot speak here of a conversion experience, it was obviously a decisive event.[14] From that time on he dedicated himself all the more intensely to the only One whom he needed. The third experience seems to me to be even more determinative. It happened "at a certain time" when he was filled with a foretaste of heaven and his heart was "lifted up" to union with God. I will return to this event in a later connection, but call attention already here to the fact that the expression "lifted up" to union with God constitutes a definitely technical term for à Brakel that appears often in his writing and clearly reminds us of Bernard's idea of *"raptus."*[15] What is striking is that this heavily mystical experience happened to him already in his youth, the phase that Theodorus himself identified in a later stage with the first step in the spiritual life, namely that of our childhood in Christ.[16]

---

9. Theodorus à Brakel, *Het Geestelyke Leven* (newly edited, expanded and improved by the author during his life, 8th edition; Amsterdam, [n.d.]), "Dedicatie." I have made use of this edition.

10. À Brakel, *De Trappen*, 122. Whether Theodorus perhaps had in his possession prayer books that are mentioned by Voetius in *Ta Asketika*, 4:1, he does not mention. See *De praktijk*, 2:91-92.

11. À Brakel, *De Trappen*, 123. At this time the congregation in Vlissingen was served by the ministers Joos and Daniel van Laren and Jacob Hondius. See Ros, *Theodorus à Brakel*, 19.

12. À Brakel, *De Trappen*, 122.

13. Ibid., 124. Ros correctly observes in this connection that the 1637 *Statenvertaling* version of the Bible cited here by à Brakel would not yet have been in use during his youth. Ros, *Theodorus à Brakel*, 21. It is obvious that it was the Deux-Aes version that was available to him.

14. This is the opinion of Langelaar, "'Krank van liefde,'" 69.

15. Compare Boot, *De allegorische uitlegging*, 170.

16. À Brakel, *De Trappen*, 120.

While Dirk much preferred solitude for reading, reflection and prayer, this in no way estranged him from church attendance or the life of intimate Christian fellowship. His virtually ascetic devotion to spiritual life did not prevent him in the least from taking responsibility for his intellectual development. He attended the Latin school in the city of his birth, where he mastered the classical languages and steeped himself in the church fathers and classical historians.[17] What calling he pursued after completing his education is unknown. It is assumed that he maintained himself as a schoolmaster. In 1628 he married Margaret or Grietje Homma, extolled by Hellenbroek as "a pearl of godliness, a crown of glory among the women of her time."[18] Six years later à Brakel, his wife and their three little daughters—subsequently two more daughters and a son were born—moved to Leeuwarden. There he initially served as a school teacher. But that would not last long.

Two influential people, the minister Rippert Sixtus and the professor Meinard Schotanus, motivated the gifted teacher, who meanwhile had just made public profession of his faith at age 28,[19] to become eligible for a call to the ministry after successfully sustaining a church examination. In this case that could only happen by virtue of exceptional gifts, in the spirit and according to the provisions of article 8 of the church order of the Synod of Dordt, since à Brakel lacked the usual academic training.[20] His own uncertainty about his calling was soon removed, when one night the heavens opened and a voice spoke to him: "I have called you to this." That this was the voice of God, Theodorus never doubted. "With joy and confidence" he accepted his calling and submitted to the examination.[21] In the summer of 1637 he passed the exam and was declared "a German cleric," that is, a non-university-educated candidate eligible for a call to ministry.[22] In succession he served the congregation in Beers and Jellum, two villages in Friesland, for fourteen years;[23] that of Den Burg on the Island of Texel for a year; and from 1653 until his death in 1669, the church in

---

17. Ros, *Theodorus à Brakel*, 24-25.

18. Hellenbroek, *Algemeene Rouklagte*, 15.

19. Ros, *Theodorus à Brakel*, 28, supposes that timidity was the reason for this late date. The usual age for making profession was between the ages of fourteen and twenty. See W. Verboom, *De catechese van de Reformatie en de Nadere Reformatie* (Amsterdam, 1986), 139-40.

20. Opinions about an eventual, short period of study at the Franeker Academy are varied. See Ros, *Theodorus à Brakel*, 30-31.

21. "De Laaste Uiren van den Autheur," by Wilhelm à Brakel, appended to à Brakel, *De Trappen*, 432.

22. Goeters, *Die Vorbereitung*, 93 (also see page 30). On "De Duytsche Clercken" see Kuyper, *De Opleiding*, 399-422.

23. From this period à Brakel's first book is dated. It consists of two parts. It is entitled, *Het geestelijck leven ende de stant eenes gelovigen mensches hier op aerden; uyt Godes Heyligh Woordt vergadert ende by een gestelt* (Leeuwarden, 1649). To it was added as a third section, *Eenighe kenteeckens, waer uyt een geloovigh mensche hem can verseekeren dat hij van Godt is bemint* (Leeuwarden, 1649). Also during his ministry in Beers and Jellums there appeared *Eenige christlijcke meditatien, gebeden ende danckseggingen om 's nachts, 's middags en 's avonds te gebruiken* (Amsterdam, 1652). This work was also later added to *Het geestelijck leven*. In the edition which I used, the spelling has been changed to *Het geestelyke Leven*. More than forty printings of this work are known. See Ros, *Theodorus à Brakel*, 13 and 97-98. Also see van der Haar, *Schatkamer*, 52-53.

Makkum—initially in combination with that of Cornwert—that lay on the Friesian west coast.

Nothing of special significance is known about his official ministry, although it must have been that his sermons made a big impression[24] and that in his "interaction" he conducted himself in an "appropriate and friendly" manner and was known as a peace-maker of few words.[25] This is not to detract from the fact that he did not shrink back from being polemical, as is obvious from his dispute with his Makkum predecessor, the Anabaptist Hessel Ipes, concerning the human nature of Christ.[26]

His lifestyle was entirely characterized by godliness. Above all, he endeavored "to sanctify" Sunday "with great joy."[27] After all, it was a joy that was best fostered by rigorous precision. His friend Anna Maria van Schurman, who visited him in 1658—thus before the Labadistic period in her life—along with her brother Johan Godschalk and with Sara Nevius, who later became Wilhelmus' wife,[28] said with obvious approval that on Sundays à Brakel would not eat so much as a morsel of food that had been purchased or cooked after eight o'clock on Saturday evening—let alone on Sunday![29]

Theodorus' weekly life must also have been bound by set rules, given the rhythm of his practical meditation. From the time of his "youth in Christ," he always maintained three set times for meditation daily, which he called "exercises."[30] To these he added a fourth when he came to regard himself as a father in Christ. The first began very early in the morning. Three or four hours a morning was not exceptional.[31] The second fell immediately before noon, just

---

24. That the building of a new church building was necessitated by a large increase in attendance is not obvious. Already prior to à Brakel's arrival the church building had structural problems and was too small. He dedicated himself to the building of the new church. He borrowed 800 guilders for that purpose, which was a sizeable amount when one considers that his annual salary was about 200 guilders. See Ros, *Theodorus à Brakel*, 59-61.

25. À Brakel, "De Laaste Uiren," 433.

26. The publication that resulted from this is entitled *Disputatie ofte bevestigende de waerheyt, wederleggende de Valschheyt, toonende de nutticheyt der menschwerdinge Iesu Christi* (Amsterdam, 1664).

27. À Brakel, "De Laaste Uiren," 438. Compare à Brakel, *De Trappen*, 83-92, and the prayers for "The Sabbath Day" in *Eenige christelijke meditatien*, appended to à Brakel, *Het geestelyke Leven*.

28. On Theodorus' influence on her spirituality see J. M. D. de Heer, "Sara Nevius (1632-1703) and Personal Piety," a lecture in the 2000-2001 winter series of the SSNR, published by the Stichting Studie Nadere Reformatie in 2001.

29. A. M. van Schurman, *Eucleria, of Uitverkiezing van Het Beste Deel* (facsimile of the 1684 Amsterdam edition; Leeuwarden, 1978), 89. The certainty with which Langelaar states that à Brakel, if he had lived longer, would eventually have joined the ranks of the Labadists, is disputable. Langelaar, "'Krank van liefde,'" 74. The tension that this author suggests to have existed between father Theodorus and his anti-Labadist son Wilhelmus seems to me to be unsupported in light of the far-reaching affinity between the spirituality of the two men.

30. The term "exercises" is the Dutch equivalent to the Latin "*exercitia*," which from antiquity was the technical term for the set hours when devotions were held. See J. Sudbrack, "Exerzitien," in *Praktisches Lexikon*, ed. Schütz, 363. Compare Velema, *Nieuw zicht*, 128-43. Voetius adopted the term in the title of his famous *Ta Asketika sive Exercitia pietatis*. See the edition of de Niet, *De praktijk der godzaligheid*.

31. À Brakel, *De Trappen*, 135 and 325.

prior to the noon meal.[32] About three o'clock in the afternoon, meanwhile, he offered a short prayer.[33] The third began about twilight[34] and the fourth when it was actually bedtime—after a household service that included a Bible reading, a song, discussion and prayer.[35] This last exercise might last until midnight or even until two o'clock in the morning.[36] Given these times that each demanded an average of several hours,[37] Theodorus certainly spent a third of each day in prayer and spiritual reflection. He could not do without it. Meditating was his spiritual food. If it were absent, he would have been estranged from the "intimate presence" of God and would have "grown cold in his love for Christ." This is because for a regenerate person being "without spiritual exercises is like a fish being without water."[38] In introducing his own experience he wrote, "When I do my exercises . . . and apply myself solely to seeking God, to considering his love and kindness, to glorifying him for them, and to delighting myself in him, then I am thoroughly uplifted in an especially exalted state of grace, strengthened, and united with my God in a very sweet communion."[39]

À Brakel, who must have had a strong constitution, usually slept only a few hours. That is significantly less than even monks or nuns were accustomed to sleep. They certainly arose at least as early, but went to bed much earlier and could also get at least five hours of sleep after their nightly matins and lauds.[40] For that matter, Theodorus preferred to regard his sleep at night as sweet rest in Christ, with a wakeful heart.[41] Whether this pattern so consistent with monastic life with its established hours was compatible with his official responsibilities as head of the house and as pastor was not an issue for Theodorus. The exercise of personal communion with God was his breath of life. He was convinced that it alone made him productive with regard to God and his fellow man.

During the last three years of his life, the à Brakels were overwhelmed with sorrow. Within those few years all five of their daughters died.[42] Wilhelmus alone survived. It must have been a comfort for the parents that their son came to live nearby. He was installed as pastor in Exmorra already in 1662, and three years later he moved to Stavoren, from where Makkum was very accessible. Especially when à Brakel became sick, Wilhelmus became a strong source of support for him. The account that he gave of his father's illness and death is moving.[43] On Sunday morning, the 14th of February, 1669, Theodorus' yearning never to lose God his Savior from his heart was realized; it was a Sunday on

---

32. Ibid., 214.
33. Ibid., 222.
34. Ibid.
35. Ibid., 224. On à Brakel's idea of household worship see especially pages 92-99.
36. Ibid., 324 and 339.
37. Ibid., 157. Here he says that the morning exercises or devotions during his youth lasted "two or three hours"; on page 151 he speaks of "hours"; and on page 215 he says that the noon exercise was "ordinarily certainly an hour."
38. À Brakel, *Het geestelyke Leven*, 11.
39. À Brakel, *De Trappen*, 151-52.
40. De Kruijf, et al., *Een klooster ontsloten*, 30.
41. À Brakel, *De Trappen*, 182-83.
42. See Ros, *Theodorus à Brakel*, 75-76.
43. À Brakel, "De Laaste Uiren," 428-38.

which the Lord's supper was celebrated, and his son conducted the service for him. After he had commended his spirit into the hands of the Father, the Son, and the Holy Spirit, he was ushered into the joy whose foretaste on earth he had so amply experienced and that he had so remarkably often described in his works. "On the occasion when he wanted to enjoy the Lord's supper with his congregation, he instead sat down with Abraham, Isaac and Jacob at the wedding feast of the Lamb," wrote Wilhelmus.[44]

Theodorus left behind a few hand-written manuscripts as a spiritual legacy. His son had promised him that he would prepare them for publication. In the late summer of 1670, Wilhelmus made good on that promise and published his book *De Trappen des Geestelyken Levens*.[45]

De Trappen des Geestelyken Levens

After reading à Brakel's *Het Geestelyken Leven*, whoever then picks up and reads his posthumous *Trappen* discovers that both works display substantial agreement in content. In both writings, as the titles lead one to believe, attention is continuously fastened on the practice of communion with God.[46] The difference between them is that in *De Trappen* the theme is presented in a more organized way. The first section is brief and contemplative in nature, the second much more extensive and strictly autobiographical.[47] The entire work is presented in the much appreciated genre of the day, namely a dialogue, here between father and son. Readers naturally assume it is between Theodorus and his son Wilhelmus, although that is nowhere explicitly stated. The son plays an unmistakable but very modest role. His contribution to the dialogue is that throughout he raises questions purely for information, and the father uses these as the occasion to respond with his extensive monologue.

In my opinion this work presents the basis of Theodorus' spirituality, although now and then his first work will also be consulted. As the title shows, the author presents an account of the "steps," that is to say the levels, along which interaction with God develops. There are three. They do not reflect the threefold division of the Heidelberg Catechism, but the triad of childhood, youth and fatherhood, which is far and away the most extensive of the three.[48] Whoever is in any sense at home in the history of Christian mysticism, would be able to make the association with the threefold path (*via triplex*) popularized particularly by Dionysius the Areopagite (c. 500 AD), namely purification,

---

44. Ibid., 438.

45. Ros, *Theodorus à Brakel*, 82. More than thirty editions of this work are known, according to Ros, pages 13 and 99. See also van der Haar, *Schatkamer*, 53-54. On the several German editions of à Brakel's works see J. van der Haar, *Internationale ökumenische Beziehungen im 17. und 18. Jahrhundert* (Ederveen, 1997), 157.

46. Voetius includes the title of *Het Geestelyke Leven* in his summary of ascetic writings that treat the question of how a person should structure the day in a godly manner. See Voetius, *De praktijk*, ed. de Niet, 2:291. *De Trappen* is not mentioned by Voetius, since his *Ta Asketika* appeared in 1664.

47. The first volume consists of 117 pages, the second of 310, octavo.

48. While the level of childhood receives 10 pages, and that of youth a full 40 pages, that of fatherhood is explained in about 250 pages.

illumination and union (*purgatio, illuminatio* and *unitio*).[49] With them Theodorus' three divisions have little in common, however. His concern is the increase of "fellowship with God in Christ."[50] He borrows the three divisions from 1 John 2, although he gives them his own content that only resembles that of John partially. Using a different sequence, the apostle speaks of children, fathers and young people. This distinction according to à Brakel does not reflect only "years and age," although it includes that as well, but especially "the increase of grace in the born-again person."[51] That he does not have in mind so much three clearly traceable episodes but rather a gradual progression, is apparent from the illustration he uses: "A newly planted tree does not extend its roots as deep as one that has stood for a long time."[52] Indeed, not all believers have "been lifted to such a level of grace that they have become fathers in Christ." What it comes down to is that a person is "a child of God." But a person should not misuse this last thought as an alibi for spiritual laziness. "Whoever does not strive to increase, decreases, for with respect to spiritual life there is no standing still."[53]

While not everyone has reached the highest level, inherent in the life of faith is an ascending trajectory.[54] What is remarkable is that all three of the levels described by à Brakel receive at one and the same time the designation "in Christ." Just as significant is that he himself, as already mentioned, had a mystical experience on the first level. That a definite emphasis is placed on spiritual growth and deepening in his *Trappen* is beyond dispute. But the fact that the choronology of the Areopagite's *via triplex* plays no role here is just as clear. In a sense those are transcended, or at least penetrated, by Theodorus' steps or levels. The three steps that he describes are distinguished primarily in level and degree—and even that fact is not always equally recognizable—but they scarcely differ from one another as far as the content of faith is concerned. In the second, autobiographical section there is frequent overlapping of the three.

When à Brakel describes the three steps in the first, more contemplative section, he seems to distinguish them not only with respect to progress but also to content. Concerning the first category, that of "children in Christ," he says that, moved by the Spirit, they certainly cry "Abba, Father." He obviously considers this to be inherent already in the stage of childhood, but also thinks that here believers are not yet so illumined as to be able to understand "the higher dimensions of the Christian faith in its power." As though he had forgotten his own childhood experience, he adds the remarkable comment: "Therefore, the high level of communion with God in Christ and in the heavenly

---

49. See Böhner and Gilson, *Christliche Philosophie*, 139; Ruh, *Geschichte der Mystik*, 1:53-54; and *The Study of Spirituality*, ed. Jones, et al., 185-87.

50. À Brakel, *De Trappen*, 7.

51. Ibid., 10.

52. Ibid., 11.

53. Ibid.

54. Compare the foreword that Wilhelmus attached to *De Trappen*, in which he wrote entirely in the spirit of his father when he said, "all of God's children have not arrived at the same high level, and even on the lowest level can and may experience contentment and joy, while longing for more."

mysteries finds no place here."[55] As far as the "youth in Christ" are concerned, their knowledge and "grasp" of divine matters rises higher, and they are able "to rest on God's Word and promise to a greater and surer degree." But the conflict between flesh and Spirit is also more intense there. Longing for fellowship with God increases beyond what is experienced: "Then along with the Bride of Christ you become sick with love and lament that the Bridegroom is not with you." Nevertheless, in this stage one can be assured of God's love and grace, "although you cannot rise to the height that you wish."[56] Finally, the "fathers in Christ" are those whose knowledge rises even higher with respect to God's majesty as well as his eternal good pleasure. These are very closely bound to God and Christ in love, and they taste and experience "all the more" an inexpressible sweetness in God and have Christ's joy "all the more completely fulfilled in themselves." They are "more established and reliable" and experience less conflict. Pertinently, however, they are not perfected, "Oh no, the very best still know only in part." The sunshine of God's grace can be darkened even in them, so that they perceive no light at all and "for a time seem to have become only the Father's step-children."[57]

What is striking in à Brakel's explanation is that he characterizes the growth with the comparatives "more" and "greater." In principle the life of faith during the stage of childhood takes the same form as during the stage of fatherhood, but then is of less intensity, clarity, or dependability. Those who are children in Christ are not denied communion with God, but only a *higher level* of fellowship. Fathers experience "more" of its sweetness."[58] The only apparent difference in content lies in the understanding of "the higher matters." As we already saw, by this he means eternal election. Children still lack the proper perspective on this matter; fathers derive trust from it. What is striking is that even here Theodorus does not absolutize the difference: children do not understand the higher matters "in all its power." They grasp the idea, but its effect is still limited. My impression is, then, that the dynamic continuity in fellowship with God is at least as noteworthy as the difference between the levels. If this impression is accurate, the implication of the term "steps" is qualified more than a little. For it would indicate that in his book à Brakel, in spite of the first word in his title, is reporting more on the dynamic power of the daily exercises of prayer and meditation in all three stages than he is clearly delimiting three distinct "levels." To what extent my hunches are well-founded must still be demonstrated.

To distort the composition of Theodorus' account as little as possible, I refrain from clustering his thoughts thematically, but follow the progression of

---

55. À Brakel, *De Trappen*, 12-13.

56. Ibid., 14-16.

57. Ibid., 17-18.

58. Perhaps the solution to the dissonance between à Brakel's description of spiritual childhood in the first section and the account of his own experience that he presents in the second section is to be found here.

his three divisions.[59] I concentrate, therefore, mainly on the second, autobiographical part in the conviction that it provides a satisfactory basis for outlining his spirituality.

Childhood in Christ

When the son requests the father to say something about his own "exercises and practices in blessed fellowship with God," the father does not seem very eager to go into the matter: "I don't speak about that very willingly." He is certainly not ashamed of the gospel, but to speak about the experiences of his own soul gives him pause. Another consideration is that he does not want to discourage believers that have not yet experienced as much growth as he. Yet, he dare not refuse. He is not permitted to bury his talent in the ground. Above all, saints like Job and David, Heman and Hezekiah, and also a "church father" like Augustine and a reformer like Luther, have set an example in this regard. Finally, there is the consideration that he has felt compelled already for a long time to make notes on his religious experiences, "and now I am not content to keep these things to myself." For that reason he now honors his son's request with more freedom than reluctance, "for the purpose of spiritual awakening and comfort."[60] He begins with the first step, that of "Childhood in Christ."

In the same way that Theodorus saw spiritual childhood as coinciding with the early years of a child's natural life that in the first letter of John, in his own account he made clear that this synchronization was true in his own experience as well. "When I was a child in natural years, I was also a child in Christ." From what age he would actually date this phase, he does not say. In any case, he has his early childhood in mind: "from the time I began to understand and develop memory."[61] His account is remarkably sketchy about what occasioned this beginning. In any case he tells us nothing about a gap between his earliest days and his early conversion. All that he acknowledges is that from the time he can remember he was "inwardly" drawn to God and endeavored to serve him.[62] The role his father seems to have played in this appears to have been marginal. It is true that after his wife died, he bade farewell to "the Roman religion" in order to "become a member of the true Reformed church" and raised Theodorus "in a creditable and somewhat Christian manner," although this training in the faith left something to be desired.[63] Yet, it was not entirely without results. That "minimal training" by his father was blessed by the grace of God and the Spirit's application. Following the example of his pious grandmother,[64] he early on

---

59. The three stages were each again described in three sub-sections by à Brakel that I will not explain each time again: the time of the devotions, the exercise itself and the "state" (or status, or condition) of the soul in each with regard to both comfort or conflict.

60. À Brakel, *De Trappen*, 118-19.

61. Ibid., 120.

62. Ibid.

63. Ibid., 121.

64. Ibid., 123.

devoted himself to prayer,[65] reading Scripture, fasting and the reading of devotional materials. He pondered "the sufferings and death of Christ and the fact that he demonstrated such great concern for me." At such times he experienced "sorrow for the sins that caused this." He often sought the solitude needed in order "to lament his sins and to reflect on Christ's love toward me."[66] Obviously, Theodorus' "evangelical" sense of sin was awakened by meditating on Christ's passion and his freely given love.

In the biographical sketch it becomes obvious that à Brakel underwent three unusual experiences that deepened his piety. For the purposes of tracing the spiritual shape of his idea of childhood in Christ, the third one is especially significant. It concerns an experience of a mystical nature. At the same time, this had already been preceded by a great deal that Theodorus later came to describe in mystical terms. To the son's question of how his father felt concerning God's consolation in this earliest phase, the father responded: "When I served God in my childhood years, I was at peace with God, as memory serves me." To the degree that he then increasingly "served" him, that "peace and sweetness" became "heightened, livelier, clearer and more intense." Now that he thinks back on it after so many years, it is "still sweet" to him. When he entered God's house and heard his Word after his Vlissingen interlude, those consolations were at their strongest. Sometimes he had rock-solid confidence in God's grace, sometimes also brief times of a delight in God "that went a little higher."[67] Nevertheless, Theodorus thereafter described his original "knowledge of God, of the Holy Trinity and of Christ as still faint and pervasively dim." What he meant by this becomes clear in the immediately following part of his account. When he listened to ministers testifying of the "joy of the Spirit and the foretaste of heaven," he often thought, "What can this possibly be; what would it be like for me to experience this?"[68] His wish was fulfilled.

"On a certain occasion" it happened that when the young Dirk came home, he found no one there. Then it struck him: "Now I am free to pray without restraint." Immediately it occurred to him "that he wanted to pray" that God would give him the foretaste of heaven. He fell to his knees and prayed to be heard. But he did not stop there. He took the New Testament and, as he remembers ("as I recall"), eagerly opened it to John 12:3—or was it John 14:13-14?—where Jesus promises to give us whatever we ask in his name. While pointing to the passage with his finger, he made an appeal on the basis of that promise: "Now then Lord, according to your promise, let me for once feel the foretaste of heaven." During this prayer his heart and thoughts were "finally" so

---

65. For his thoughts on prayer, see the foreword of his *Eenige christelijcke meditatien*.
66. Ibid., 122.
67. Ibid., 125.
68. Ibid., 125-26.

"caught up" that he was filled with a "joy, peace and sweetness" that he "was incapable of describing."[69]

The experience that Theodore describes here is strongly reminiscent of the *raptus* and the *excessus mentis* familiar to us from the tradition rooted in Bernard. This is the case not only because of the terminology employed, but also on account of the content that he gives these experiences. For, while he recognizes that the intensity of the joy noted is beyond description—a stereotypical motif in mystical language, also in that of Theodorus—he at the same time talks about the experience itself. The experience of "being caught up" implies namely, that he *saw* "the Lord" (that is Christ, on whose promise he had pleaded) with the eyes of his soul and that he had been *united* with God, "brought into God, as it were."[70] At the very beginning of *Trappen*, fellowship with God is already identified as the "highest form of spiritual blessedness." Wherever this fellowship is "appre-hended, felt or believed,"[71] the true fruit of godliness flourishes and becomes "an unfailing incentive to even more explicit and fuller union."[72] Union with God seems to be not only the goal to which all piety aspires for à Brakel, but also the context in which it develops. And something of this experience of fellowship came over him already in his "childhood." That its full mystery defied an exact description moved him once again to borrow mystically flavored biblical language: "For it belongs to that manna that is concealed and that white stone on which a new name is written which no one knows except him to whom it is given (Revelation 2:17)."[73] In the spirit of Bernard, with this metaphor of hidden manna à Brakel means to show that the experience is strictly personal and on the deepest level is understood only by one who has been overwhelmed by it.[74] All he can say about it is that two or three days later his "feelings" were still in heaven, "as though I were gazing on the Lord, and that with a tranquil and joyful soul." Slowly that experience "began to ebb," however. What declined, he does not exactly say. He undoubtedly is referring to the overwhelming euphoria, for the sense of fellowship with God continued. At least he adds that he simply proceeded "like a child, as though with God alone," by "sweetly serving God with pleasure."[75]

When à Brakel was about sixteen years old, he lost "this sweet peace." What replaced it were "strong temptations." His sins became like high mountains for him and God disappeared from view. "I feared that I was not a child of God and that there was no grace for me." It seemed to him as though he had never had a

---

69. Ibid., 126.

70. Ibid.

71. Noteworthy is that à Brakel uses "perception," "feeling" and "faith" as synonyms.

72. À Brakel, *De Trappen*, 3.

73. Ibid., 127. See also à Brakel, *Het geestelyke Leven*, 195, where the same text is cited in a contemplative context.

74. Concerning Bernard on this matter, see *SC*, 3:1, in *SW*, 5:76. Bernard applies the image of the manna to a kiss from Jesus on the mouth. Also compare Bonaventure, *Itinerarium*, ed. J. C. M. van Winden (Assen, 1996), 154. Here the manna is tasted by those who travel through the wilderness in the company of Christ.

75. À Brakel, *De Trappen*, 127.

proper sorrow for his sins and that he had never truly served God.[76] The nature of his temptations arose from a sense of sin, and simultaneously from a doubt that his experience had ever been genuine—from the absence of feeling God's closeness and from fearfulness concerning his spiritual state. The Evil One made use of this lost condition by fueling the fire of his temptation. "The devil . . . so attacked my soul with his fiery arrows that I cannot and dare not describe it . . . . Heaven and earth were both too fearful and too oppressive for me." He often sought solace alone, far outside the city (at that time, Enkhuizen). There he cried out for God to appear. "And I often read the Psalms, for I always kept a psalter and several little prayer books with me—often the 143rd Psalm." Although sometimes he felt some "relief," he did not experience the former sweetness, when the Lord "dwelt" in him with his love. In short, "the clarity of spiritual sight was gone and stayed away for many long years, while the days of spiritual oppression held me in their grip."[77] Then, "after the passing of many years," that oppressive conflict began "to decrease somewhat" and his "faith became stronger." He also began to experience now and then "other joys and in quite another way than they first began in me, but I usually received them with much prayer and persistent attention."[78] With this, the section on childhood in Christ concluded.

Theodorus does not make it easy for us to determine at what age the transition from childhood to youth in Christ occurs. At first glance the question seems relatively simple to answer, since he spoke of "many years" after his sixteenth birthday. But I think that one should not take that chronology too literally. The fact is that he begins the second part on his youth with the report that by then he had become a youth in Christ, "as well as one in years."[79] Here, therefore, he makes his spiritual youth coincide with his natural adolescence. Also, even if that would have begun rather late, it nevertheless could not have been much later than approximately his eighteenth year. Then those "many years" would not have been more than two. How can this problem be resolved? I see two possibilities. The first is that Theodorus' subjective experience of time in his toddler years received the weight of many years because they simply seemed burdensome and prolonged to him. The second is of a completely different nature than a psychological explanation and seems more likely to me. It is very well possible that à Brakel never intended to limit the many years of conflict that he describes in the section on his spiritual childhood purely to that stage in his life, but rather that he wants to show that these struggles extend over the next phase as well. To be sure, a kind of chronology occurs in Theodorus' account, but its linear development is often unmistakably traversed by cyclic repetition.

A compelling illustration of this fact is found precisely in his "conflicts." In the days of his childhood it sometimes happened with him as it did with Job during his experience of God's hiddenness: "Behold, if I go forward, he is not

---

76. Ibid.
77. Ibid., 128.
78. Ibid., 129.
79. Ibid., 130.

there . . . (Job 23:8)."[80] And in the phase of his youth à Brakel had exactly the same experience so aptly portrayed in this biblical text.[81] And again during his fatherhood conflict returns that is illumined with texts from Job that convey the same meaning.[82] That Theodorus' spiritual autobiography also reflects progress and maturation is undeniable. But even less deniable is the fact that this dimension of his spirituality is drastically relativized by continuity, at least by the return every now and then of the same motifs.[83]

In any case, both of these considerations provide an adequate basis for not interpreting the "many years" between à Brakel's sixteenth year and the transition to his youth numerically and to make this transition, by his own account, coincide with the beginning of his adolescence. What is even more intriguing in my judgment, is the meaning of the sentence with which he closes his report on this first step. He says that after a long time another joy befell him than what he had previously experienced. What he meant by this will be explained in what follows.

Youth in Christ

Immediately at the outset of this section, Theodorus describes the change that emerges in this phase of spiritual life as gradual rather than instantaneous. "By degrees" he came to "deeper thoughts" concerning his solemn duty to serve God.[84] Simultaneously, this formulation conveys the idea that the transition into this phase also occurs gradually. What does he have in mind by a deepened sense of duty? He is thinking of nothing less than a set division of each day for the purpose of devoting himself "at fixed times" to prayer and meditation: early in the morning, at noon and in the evening.[85] In response to the question of how he came to this "apportioning of time," he points to Daniel and David, both of whom availed themselves of such a three-fold division.[86] À Brakel's mornings deliberately began early. And when he said "early," he meant early. To be sure, he left it to divine wisdom to awaken him at the time that God judged best—for Theodorus did not want to impose any "limits" on God. But this does not detract from the fact that he "did not like to stay in bed for more than three or four hours at a time." Sometimes he got up even sooner, sometimes a little later. Nonetheless, the earlier he began his morning devotions, the "easier" it was for him to find the Lord. The later he began, the greater was his sense of "estrangement from God in Christ" and the more effort he had to put forth to find him.[87] It was certainly not his own experience by itself that motivated his preference for these matins. He appealed to the biblical model in this regard. He

---

80. Ibid.
81. Ibid., 166.
82. Ibid., 390.
83. I already identified a potent sample of this in the preceding, specifically in connection with à Brakel, *De Trappen*, 18, where it is said that sometimes the fathers appear to be children.
84. À Brakel, *De Trappen*, 130.
85. Ibid.
86. Dan. 6:11; Ps. 55:18.
87. Ibid., 135.

referred to David, who in Psalm 119:147 testifies that he arose before dawn. But he appealed especially to what Mark 1:35 says about Jesus: "If the Son of God himself, who became flesh for our sakes, arose so early in the morning to pray for us, should I then lie in bed, or should I not also get up early in order to pray for myself?"[88]

He "discovered" that getting up early was very profitable for his spiritual life. "For along with the Bride of Christ, who according to Song of Solomon 3:1 and 4 arose in the night, I usually found my Lover then, and at those times I usually received such sweet peace and joy, such consecration of heart, such a joyful conscience, and such confident trust that they defy description." At that time he also found stronger resistance to the temptations by which he was originally, "at first," so heavily assailed.[89] One even gets the impression that these powerful temptations belonged to the earlier phase of his spiritual childhood. For, Theodorus follows with the explanation that whenever he "did not get up very early," a spiritual darkness and stupor enveloped him, a condition that was connected with strong and oppressive temptations, under which he felt "sad and estranged from God for the entire day."[90]

Concerning the subject of whether mornings were perhaps better suited to the worship of God than other parts of the day à Brakel offered a wise, pastoral response. He was convinced that the sanctity of "worshiping God" is definitely not dependent on the time when it is conducted. Whoever cannot bring himself or herself to get up early, whether that is due to working late the night before or to physical weakness, does not have to be discouraged by the notion that their meditation "is less pleasing to God because it happens later in the day." But he certainly finds that the morning hour is "very well-suit" for it. Then a person always has the time and is still fresh, and then quietness prevails. Above all else, a person must remember that God "will ease any physical discomfort with his inner grace."[91] While he would not impose it on someone else, he considers it absolutely necessary for himself to seek God early in the morning.[92] That certainly required some effort for him, especially "in the beginning." "I only overcame my natural sleepiness and the weakness and frailty of the flesh with great difficulty." But sometimes the Lord made him "so awake, and he gave him so much strength that he sprang up lightly and quickly."[93]

As time went by it did not seem as difficult for him anymore, since he had become "used to it."[94] It was an adjustment that definitely involved more than

---

88. Ibid., 132.
89. Ibid., 132-33.
90. Ibid., 133.
91. Ibid., 134-35.
92. Ibid., 136. See also 141, where à Brakel returns to the fact that "a great many people" are not permitted to observe a strict pattern of meditation for reasons of health or because of occupational obligations: "God does not lead all saints in the same way . . . He just will not put up with your laziness."
93. Ibid., 136.
94. Ibid.

mere force of habit. Rather, it was motivated by the "sweet and heavenly grace" that God consistently imparted to him early in the day. In a word, what stirred him most deeply was love. In this regard he offers a significant testimony: "For I could never adequately satisfy myself in serving my God."[95] In this sentence Theodorus allows us to look deep into his heart. He certainly enjoyed God's love, but he never experienced enough of it. It is for that reason that he wanted to find it early in the morning. Without imposing "hours or demands" on the Lord, he prayed that God would wake him up early for that very reason. But even that by itself did not satisfy him. He also prepared himself by not loading his body with food the night before and especially by "reconciling" himself with God in the evening in order "to sleep more peacefully in God, to awaken more refreshed with him, and also to be more prepared in both body and soul to arise early."[96]

The second "exercise" followed approximately at noon. What happened in the meanwhile remains entirely undisclosed in Theodorus' account. This is not because he regarded his daily work as merely marking time, but it is simply because this is not his purpose in writing. He only goes into the question of whether his study and "other aspects" of his calling are neglected by his spending so much time in meditation incidentally. This is an issue that does not embarrass him in the least. His response is that through these exercises God endows him with more wisdom for building up both himself and others than he could ever get from studying books, however essential he elsewhere finds that activity to be.[97] He regards this answer as adequate. The life of meditation was for his own benefit as well as for that of others, as far as he was concerned. And he does not restrict it only to the morning or the evening, but applies it to the middle of the day as well. He considers that to be a strategic interlude in the day, taken in order that a person may "stop the work of his calling for a little while in order to strengthen the body again with food and rest."[98] He gives the assurance that he does not "superstitiously" consider noon to be holier than other times of the day, but at the same time he indicates that anyone who neglects this noontime spiritual exercise "does not live close, in his emotional life, to his God and Savior Jesus Christ."[99]

Theodorus chose the evening as the third time of day for reflection, not just close to bedtime, but "somewhat earlier" since then he had less chance of being overtaken by sleep.[100] That this time early in the evening was also motivated by another consideration is worth noting. He explains that it put him in a good position to observe his devotional exercise "late in the evening" with less difficulty.[101] This indicates a fourth period of meditation, therefore. However, he only talks about a three-fold pattern in connection with his youth in Christ! Apparently while writing à Brakel was already anticipating his later custom of a four-fold pattern of spiritual exercises, whether the fourth occurred late in the

95. Ibid., 137
96. Ibid., 138.
97. Ibid., 157.
98. Ibid., 139-40.
99. Ibid., 140.
100. Ibid.
101. Ibid., 141.

evening or during the night. Once again, it seems to me to indicate that we should not assign too much precision to his chronology.

When asked about his experiences in connection with these exercises during his spiritual youth, Theodorus responded that his mood during the morning meditations was subject to "thorough and wondrous changes." At one time he might be enraptured by the love of God, at another moment beaten down by feelings of estrangement from God.[102] In the beginning of this phase he had "less light on feeling God's love and grace," and he allowed himself to be guided primarily by his own inner disposition. But "thereafter," he introduced more "structure" to them. He began by loving God for his grace and he followed this with a time of self-examination.[103] Despite the ambivalence felt in his morning reflections, no less than twice he acknowledged them as his "deepest" experiences: at those times he discovered "the highest and most special grace."[104]

In introducing the subject of how his meditating went when the feeling of "estrangement" dominated, Theodorus explains that he confessed the depravity of his heart and his deeds "with godly sorrow" and that he acknowledged that he himself was the cause of this distance between himself and God. This self-accusation was articulated in a prayer for forgiveness and for renewed clarification of his righteousness in Christ. "Thereupon I embraced Christ by faith and claimed this righteousness as my own." Sometimes that certainly required some extensive prayer-time. "But, throughout this process the Lord granted me his grace, assuring me of possessing a living faith and being righteous in Christ. . . . And in this way I again received that sweet sense of union[105] and fellowship with him."[106]

Three aspects of this passage deserve comment. In the first place, justification is represented here as a repeated event, just as is consistently the case throughout *Trappen*. In the second place, it was à Brakel's understanding that the active and the passive dimensions of faith evidently go together. On the one hand, he himself accepted Christ and he himself appropriated justification as his own. On the other hand, he knew full-well that living faith is a work of divine grace. What is striking in the third place is the connection between faith and feelings, perhaps with a definite emphasis on the latter. Faith's recognition that one is justified before God always develops into receiving sweet fellowship with God. Without this, therefore, the vital role of justification by faith is denied, and à Brakel's most intense longings are obviously for that emotional experience of God that is its fruit. This is obvious in what follows: "I prayed to God and beseeched him that he would not only renew his former grace in me, but that he would also impart more grace to me, more fully illumine my understanding, cause me to overflow with love, and lift me totally into fellowship with him that I might completely live in him, enjoy him forever . . . and participate in his divine nature (2 Peter 1:4), with the result that I might always will what he

---

102. Ibid., 142.
103. Ibid., 145.
104. Ibid., 160. Also compare 177.
105. The spelling of "union" vascillates in the Dutch: *"vereninge"* and *"vereniginge."*
106. À Brakel, *De Trappen*, 146.

wills."[107] Here the vocabulary is not only strongly dependent of Bernard, but the content is also reminiscent of his spirituality.[108]

How greatly salvation history and the appropriation of salvation—the objective and the subjective dimensions of salvation—affected one another during meditation becomes apparent whenever Theodorus provides somewhat more substantive information. After the prayer just indicated, his reflection develops "in about this way": I considered "that he had loved me in the Beloved (Ephesians 1:6) with an everlasting love (Jeremiah 31:3), and that when I lay in my own blood, he said to me, 'Live!' (Ezekiel 16) Then I began to be lifted up somewhat in my thoughts, and I considered how great that lovingkindness was that was applied to my soul, and in that way I came to reflect on my deliverance, especially on how great the love of my Heavenly Father is that he had given me his own Son as my Redeemer (Romans 8:32), since I was his enemy (Romans 5:10) and accordingly saw nothing good in myself. Next I considered how great the love of the Son is . . . that he so humbled himself . . . that he who was rich became poor for my sake. . . . Then I was again somewhat uplifted, considering these matters, and in my amazement I said along with the holy angels, 'Glory to God in the highest!'"[109] In his reflection, application occurred on the basis of what God had prepared for him in Christ. What is remarkable in this connection is the pervasive appeal to Scripture. This demonstrates that Theodorus' mediation was fed by his engagement with the biblical text. He seldom announces that explicitly. But to the somewhat strange question of his son of whether he had the practice of reading God's Word, the father responded, "That has always been my daily work; I devoured it and made myself thoroughly familiar with it; to me it was sweeter than honey. . . . God's Word never left my hands."[110] À Brakel's inner life was filled with the Word that came from the outside. For this reason his meditation was directly focused on the Christological basis of salvation as described in the gospel.

In *Het Geestelyke Leven* Theodorus also discusses, likewise in a meditative and reflective way, the road that Christ had to walk. Although the Son was "the Wealthy God," he became a poor human child whose glory was veiled behind his poverty and need. "For when he had been born, he had to endure being ignored and rejected, for there was no place for him in the inn. It was not his lot to be laid in an expensive, beautiful cradle, but he was laid in a manger and placed on hay for a pillow. And in his life he owned nothing, not even a place to lay his head. Naked, he was nailed to the cross, and when he died he had no clothing with which to cover his dead body. . . . And all this was for our sakes!"[111] Evidently Theodorus had familiarized himself with the passion meditations that Bernard provided in his sermons on Song of Solomon. He quotes from "the old spiritual father Bernard's" well-known "little jar," into which he had gathered instances of

---

107. Ibid.
108. *SC*, 83:3, in *SW*, 6:612. Compare à Kempis, *Imitatio*, 3.16, in *Opera*, 2:173, and Teellinck, *Soliloquium*, 28.89.
109. À Brakel, *De Trappen*, 147-48.
110. Ibid., 154.
111. À Brakel, *Het geestelyke Leven*, 67-68.

the Savior's "fearful circumstances."[112] To contemplate all of this amidst all his anxieties and temptations was for him many times like "the friendly embrace" of his Bridegroom. For this reason he admonished his readers "as strongly as possible," to observe these exercises daily.[113] Every day, but especially each morning, a person should ponder this "like he does a precious smell, for the quickening of the soul."[114] At the conclusion of this paragraph à Brakel addresses the timid who dare not claim salvation as theirs because of their sins: "Think about it! It is all about nothing but love. If God had calculated our worth, what would have happened? Simply believe, and your soul will be healed. And if it still does not penetrate your heart, take courage and say, when you are alone, 'I will simply throw myself on this love and, hopeful, will remain there.'"[115]

In the account of his meditation that à Brakel gives in *Trappen*, he tells how he proceeded with reflecting on Christ's sufferings, a genuine form of passion meditation. "Step by step" he reviews the Lord's progress on the road of suffering and applies it all to himself, "as happening because of my sins." On the one hand this awakened sorrow for his sins and on the other hand amazement over such love. "And this served more and more to awaken my love for him and through that love to be compelled to holiness."[116] The mystical and the ethical were interwoven for à Brakel. But the scope of his interest, at least here, lay with the mystical component. He closes the account of his meditation on suffering with the explanation that he was "completely overwhelmed" by the conviction of so much divine love in the face of so much unworthiness.[117]

However applicable all of this meditation on Christ had already been, Theodorus still wanted to devote attention particularly to the personal application of salvation during his spiritual exercises. At least he explains that after the foregoing he recalled how God "had made known those benefits for him by his Word and Spirit," how he had awakened him from spiritual death, had given him faith and had justified him from sin.[118] Something of the *ordo salutis* even shines through his account at this point.[119] In the previous section, remarkably enough we find little trace of this.[120] We certainly learn something about his renewed justification, but, as in the account of his spiritual childhood, not a word about

---

112. Ibid., 55. See *SC*, 43:3, in *SW*, 6:98.

113. Ibid., 59-60.

114. Ibid., 61-62. Compare Boot, *De allegorische uitlegging*, 165-66. A little further along (À Brakel, *Het geestelyke Leven*, 74) Bernard is again cited, here in connection with Jesus' meekness. See *SC*, 22:8, in *SW*, 5:316: "Omnino propter mansuetudinem currimus post te, Domine Iesu."

115. Ibid., 71.

116. À Brakel, *De Trappen*, 148.

117. Ibid. À Brakel is very brief at this point about meditation on Christ's exaltation (pages 148-49). He refers readers to his little tract *Het geestelyke Leven*, where he devotes "extensive" attention to the matter.

118. Ibid., 149.

119. The same thing is true on page 311: election, redemption, calling, justification, preservation and glorification.

120. This does not mean that à Brakel does not respect the order of salvation. In his tract *Eenige kenteekens*, its dimensions emerge vividly in his treatment of Romans 8:29-30.

his rebirth or initial justification.[121] It appears from the material just reviewed that he was certainly well aware of those benefits. But understandably, the genre of his material determines that he mentions them only in passing. He is not writing a history of his conversion to God, but rather of his inner life with God. Reflection on his justification is therefore followed, he explains, by amazement over God's comfort and faithful assurances. For him all of this constituted the occasion for pondering how from eternity God had shown him mercy.[122] The knowledge of the "great truth" of everlasting blessedness that à Brakel had originally reserved for spiritual fatherhood in Christ[123] appears here to have already received a place in the phase of his youth in Christ.

Furthermore, when Theodorus explains what the outcome of all this reflection was, the suggested chronological framework is once again eclipsed. While already in an earlier context he had announced that union with God is reserved for spiritual fatherhood, he describes the harvest of meditation during one's spiritual adolescence in unmistakably mystical terms. The shape of this experience is certainly also closely connected to what he experienced already in his spiritual childhood. At most one can perhaps speak of increased intensity. He writes the following: "And I also reflected on this and applied it to my soul, namely that my God permitted me to see so deeply into his love that I was almost consumed. Yes, my heart seemed too small to comprehend such endlessness, seemed to stop, even seemed as though it would burst and as though it were too weak to handle such a large portion of God's love; in this manner my soul was often brought to God himself, rested in his sweet communion and was united with my God and Savior who embraced me with a loving response that kissed me with the kiss of his lips (Song of Solomon 1:2)."[124] This all occurred during the morning devotions of his spiritual youth. That those exercises might even last for hours[125] did not bother him. "I was able to conduct them day or night without let-up."[126]

No wonder, then, that à Brakel also made time available during the middle of the day to have fellowship with his God. Often this lasted much longer than the time that he set aside for his meal, since he simply found more enjoyment in spiritual food than in "natural victuals."[127] Toward the end of the day two devotional exercises once again occurred: at dusk and before going to sleep. The latter consisted of forms of praise, humbling himself and prayer. He prayed on those occasions for the protection of himself and his family and made intercession for "God's church," especially for all those who had asked for his intercession and for "those who were suffering."[128] He writes that in addition to

---

121. When in ibid., 143, Brakel writes that God "sometimes" showed him that he was righteous in Christ, both the formulation and the context show that here the inception of justification is being considered.

122. À Brakel, *De Trappen*, 149.

123. Ibid. 17.

124. Ibid., 149. Bernard's singular for "kiss" (as in the Vulgate and Douai) is striking here.

125. Ibid., 151.

126. Ibid., 154.

127. Ibid., 159.

128. Ibid., 160-61.

his scheduled prayers he spontaneously offered "special prayers" as his soul was so moved.[129]

When Theodorus follows the account of spiritual youth with special attention to "exceptional grace," that is to say the special display of grace, he repeats that at times he felt as though he was being "consumed" by God's love. Then he felt so intimately one with Christ, his "Brother and Bridegroom," that he "seemed to be drunk" with his love. In that condition his body was sometimes "distressed and weakened," and he had to "interrupt" his spiritual embrace because his heart and his body could not sustain it. Then it seemed as though he certainly "could have died" from it.[130] On another occasion he was so "caught up" in God's loving fellowship that he stopped his meditating, maintained silence and allowed God to work in him. Only his yearning for eternal glory remained: "What a thing everlasting and complete communion with God will be!"[131] Then God allowed him to see once again how he had loved him with an everlasting love and had justified him, "yes had repeatedly, again and again, justified me." By this, his response of love was fanned into hot flames and by means of these noted mercies he ascended the steps to the eternal fountain of God's love, in order in reverse direction to descend again into himself, that is, into this freshly discovered grace. During "this climbing up and down with such an exalted view and such amazement," the flame of his own response of love "on the other hand" sometimes leaped so high that it almost seemed as though he was beside himself with love. His heart could not endure it and was far too small "to encompass the ocean of God's love." His soul "seemed incapable of dwelling in his body any longer." In this way the Lord led him "as it were into his bodega," an experience that he illustrated with some six passages from the Song of Solomon. À Brakel called all this merely "a tiny glimmer" of what he was incapable of describing "by even a thousandth!"[132] At the beginning of his spiritual youth, the "graces" were still not what they would later become, but "gradually they did increase."[133]

If one inquires whether à Brakel had experienced "a different joy," or had experienced it in "another way" than during the period of his spiritual childhood, the answer seems to be undeniable—as he had already stated.[134] The joy seems to be more intense, to be sure—even to the extent of being unbearable—but its nature and manifestation are no different. It still involves exactly the same contemplative fellowship with God that was his lot in his spiritual childhood. I also think, therefore, that by "another way" he does not mean another kind as

---

129. Ibid., 160.

130. Ibid., 161-62. He expresses the same thought on 149, repeats it on 163, and returns to it three times in the section on spiritual fatherhood: 318, 319 and 320. The motif found in Bernard that the experience of God's love transcends the strength to bear it is encountered likewise in such writers, for example, as Wilhelmus à Brakel, Witsius and Schortinghuis, as well as in Kohlbrugge. See de Reuver, "*Bedelen bij de Bron,*" 170. Also see *DD*, 10:27, in *SW*, 1:120, where for Bernard the corruption of the body receives more attention than its weakness: "defectus corruptionis non sustinet."

131. À Brakel, *De Trappen*, 162.

132. The archaic spelling of "*duizen*" for "*duizend*" ("thousandth") is used here.

133. À Brakel, *De Trappen*, 162-63.

134. Ibid., 129.

much as an increased measure and frequency. In our discussion of his account of his spiritual fatherhood we will have to explore whether there is any mention of "another joy" in that phase. But, before I turn to it, the concluding part of the section under consideration here deserves some attention. It focuses on conflict.

Theodorus' mystical raptures were interspersed with severe "temptations." This term functioned for him as a catch-all for "times of deadness," "periods of spiritual coldness" and "religious stupor," or also certainly "times of weak love," "emotional oppressiveness" and "spiritual uneasiness."[135] To dwell on this might "not be constructive, perhaps." Nevertheless, he wants to concern himself with the matter in order to say something to afflicted souls. Sometimes his sins seemed to him to be mountains; sometimes he doubted his spiritual condition. At times he felt "dead" and unfeeling; at other times he experienced a barrage from the devil. What was the worst was when "God was so far away from me and when his spiritual face was sometimes so darkened that I could not see his promises very clearly and that my faith endured many conflicts." At such times he relied on the divine promises and on "previous experiences of grace and on the signs of grace," but even that did not occur without conflict. It certainly happened that soon after he experienced "exceptional assurances," he entered into long periods of confusion, both day and night, when it definitely seemed as though he had never been united with God.[136]

I make three observations about this passage. The first is that the temptations that à Brakel describes here seem to a great extent to be like the conflicts of the years of his spiritual childhood. The second is that the oppressiveness that he associates with them is to a certain extent in tension with his earlier explanation that "after the passing of many years, that battle began to diminish somewhat."[137] Now, it might be that he had reference here to the phase of his spiritual fatherhood. But in any case, the temptations during the years of his spiritual youth seem to increase rather than decrease. Thirdly, I observe that its lengthy extent—"sometimes years long"[138]—is apparently difficult to harmonize with the abundance of spiritual pleasures of which he speaks. However, this is definitely to be interpreted to mean that enjoyment and oppression alternate continuously. He even writes that God always saves him from these "visitations" once again, "giving me relief consistently in my spiritual exercises."[139] Twenty-four hours seldom passed without a sense of great desertion and oppression, but again and again God gave him "exceptional grace and deliverance."[140] This was relief that followed a great deal of conflict, but also a great deal of time spent in prayer. Theodorus completes the account of his spiritual youth with two examples of such experiences. Because the passages are so significant for understanding his hungering after God, I do not want to ignore them.

---

135. Ibid., 164.
136. Ibid., 168.
137. Ibid., 129. This is from the concluding sentence of the account of his childhood.
138. Ibid., 169.
139. Ibid.
140. Ibid., 173.

Once he had spent "a fairly long time" without experiencing fellowship with God. On a given morning, "very early," he complained in prayer about his needs: "Lord, why have you continued to give me life when I cannot enjoy you as my God. . . . Lord, the earth and you yourself are too vast for me." However much the basis of his confidence was shaken, he was still not entirely without hope. He persevered. "I want to possess God, then, I will be satisfied." He prayed intensely to the Father as well as to Jesus and to the Holy Spirit, asking that he might experience their fellowship. He would rather die than live without God. "I cannot live without you, O God . . . ; I must be yours and you mine. . . . And although I am still on earth, let me live in heaven with you." Then he was finally "carried to God" and felt that his heart "was changed into his [God's] nature."[141]

On another occasion his experience was just as mystical. He had sought "to enjoy more" of God's grace day and night. One night he went to bed. While he was sleeping, the word of Song of Solomon, chapter 1, came to him: "namely the sentence, 'He kissed me with the kisses[142] of his mouth.'" At that very moment he felt in his soul that his Lover had kissed him with the kiss of his love. That was accompanied with such heavenly joy and such a clear vision in his soul—as though he were in the presence of his God and Bridegroom and were seeing him with his physical eyes—that he could not express "how divine it had been."[143] He awoke immediately "uplifted with a joyful soul." And he "remained" in that condition that night, the following day and "even longer." He walked joyfully with God and for a time his sadness disappeared.[144]

Once again, it needs to be said that Theodorus describes experiences here that, content-wise at least, harmonize closely with the "being caught up into God" from the phase of his spiritual childhood.[145] Also, he then lived for several days with his heart in heaven and as though he had seen "the Lord." One difference certainly is that in this instance the kiss of the Bridegroom is not mentioned. But it occurs to me that the union with God discovered earlier—"as though caught up into God"—was nothing other than the experience of the mystical union (*unio mystica*) of his spiritual youth. Most importantly, the motif of bridal mysticism has become more explicit.

Two questions cannot be suppressed. The first is what in fact constitutes the biggest difference between the level of spiritual childhood and that of spiritual youth. To the extent that I am able to discern, it is minimal. The second question is what the level of spiritual fatherhood can offer that is higher than the previous levels. We shall see. What can no longer be questioned, however, is that at all

---

141. Ibid., 170-71.

142. Different from the *Statenvertaling*, the Deux-Aes version, like Luther's translation and the Vulgate, uses the singular. Bernard also intentionally uses the singular in his sermons on Song of Solomon.

143. À Brakel here offers a compelling illustration of his custom of being able to sleep with a wakeful heart (*De Trappen*, 180—on spiritual fatherhood!). If one may speak of a dream in this context, this certainly says a great deal about Theodorus' "subconsciousness." Even in his dreams he could obviously be preoccupied with the love of Christ, for which he looked night and day.

144. À Brakel, *De Trappen*, 172-73.

145. Ibid., 126-27.

levels of his spiritual life à Brakel is less able to dispense with God than with his own breathing. God in Christ constitutes the soul of his existence.

Fatherhood in Christ

Theodorus' memoirs, meanwhile, have reached the point where he can write in the present tense. Both of the previous phases are written retrospectively, but now, as a spiritual father in Christ, he looks back on his earlier spiritual childhood and youth. In this third division he describes experiences from his current fatherhood, although he describes experiences in it that were also behind him. Precisely when à Brakel saw them as phase commencing, I have been unable to detect from the text itself.[146] What is certain is that their history belongs to the phase of his spiritual fatherhood that extends right to the time of his writing. When pressed by his son, he answered the question of whether he was presently of a different frame of mind than before, he responded without hesitation: "Yes, in my heart I am now usually not what I would like to be."[147]

His subsequent attempts to explain this change with precision seem to be more quantitative than qualitative in nature, based on the strength of the comparatives that he again employs at this point: his sense of grace is usually "much higher," his fellowship "closer," the view of God's love "firmer and clearer."[148] After all, he simultaneously uses expressions that capture the idea of total involvement. Admittedly, that touches not on the experience of God itself, but on its "duration." He presently lives in "continuous" communion with God; the Father and the Son have made their dwelling in him and remain with him "continuously;" he "always" trusts the forgiveness of sins now; he always feels God's love, without ever doubting it. He glorifies God "continuously:" "that is my preoccupation day and night."[149]

However, this continuity needs to be qualified not only on the basis of the adverb "usually," but especially based on the conclusion of the book *Trappen*. The suggestion of an unbroken fellowship with God is belied by à Brakel's own story. When right at the end of his account he reports opening a little book on the

---

146. An extremely vague indication might be the remark with which he concludes the section on his young manhood (ibid., 173): "And in this way, years passed." From the fact that a memorial volume entitled *Eenige Christelyke Meditatien* was written in 1650 during his Beers and Jellum pastorate and was published in 1652 (and later was appended to *Het Geestlyke Leven*) and identifies four times for meditation (night, morning, midday, and evening), it can be concluded that à Brakel's phase of spiritual fatherhood, in which the fourfold division originated, in any case dates from before 1650. But this latest possible date (*terminus ad quem*) does not say much about the date from which (*terminus a quo*) the phase can be dated. Concerning the duration of those "years" that passed between young manhood and fatherhood—at least if this is what was intended—one can only guess. In my opinion, à Brakel's vagueness on the matter once again constitutes evidence for the idea that his spiritual progress flowed smoothly rather than occurred as sharply distinguishable steps.

147. Ibid. 147. While the seventeenth-century word "*doorgaans*" usually means "continuous" or "enduring," à Brakel uses it almost exclusively—and certainly in this context (compare page 176!)—in the sense of "usually" or "mostly."

148. Ibid., 174-75.

149. Ibid.

conflicts that still overcome him in the phase of his fatherhood, he laments that his heart is sometimes completely unmoved and that he does not feel his faith, but is "just like the trees that appear to be dead during the winter." Then he is unable to pray and he sees himself as thoroughly impure and detestable before God. God seems to conceal himself in anger. All his religious striving seems to à Brakel to be only "bare mental knowledge."[150] Theodorus addresses these profound collapses precisely to avoid characterizing this spiritual fatherhood as a state in which the sense of God's love and of his own spiritual adoption is permanently present. He clearly experiences the problematic nature of this assessment on a personal level. Attached to these absolute expressions are formulations of a more cautious nature, and these qualify his assertiveness. On the one hand he says that he "always" feels like a child of God, but on the other hand he immediately recognizes that "various unbelieving thoughts and doubts assail him," although they never gain the upper hand.[151]

When one makes an attempt to explain the apparent contradictions in à Brakel's argument and to harmonize his statements, one might well reach the following solution. The change that emerges in his spiritual fatherhood involves neither the form of the experience of God nor its continuity per se, but an increase in the confidence of faith—one is inclined to say, in the "nevertheless" of faith—by which he knows that the not infrequently lost fellowship with God will be regained.[152] This shows progress when compared with what went on earlier. I reached this conclusion by analyzing all the relevant passages, starting with the opening of the section on fatherhood. There à Brakel begins with the explanation that he "always" trusts that he is made righteous and is being perfected in Christ. However, if he should stumble once again, he would certainly be "greatly" grieved. But, based on his faith, he understands that God's grace "always" remains the same and that the Savior is "with the believer . . . forthwith." "And in this way I am actually made righteous in him once again . . . and my God and Savior lets me feel his love and friendship once more."[153] Theodorus' "always" shows, therefore, not that he never loses God's grace, but that in faith he "forthwith" knows that he has found it again.

The same is true with respect to his unshakable confidence in being God's child. The faith-assuring function of the line of thought[154] seemingly dominant in the foregoing, à Brakel now seems to put entirely behind him. In his present "state" he does not attempt "to be assured by this or that proof or sign, as was certainly the case earlier." Apparently, in the thought pattern of the closing speech very little need exists anymore for a faith that is so closely tied to the emotions that seems to be interwoven with them.[155] He "always" believed and felt the certainty under consideration. But this "always" does not mean

---

150. Ibid., 395-96. Compare 341.

151. Ibid., 175.

152. Ibid., 343, 348, 350 and 359 provide examples.

153. Ibid., 175.

154. De Reuver, "*Bedelen bij de Bron*," 458-59.

155. That à Brakel otherwise thought that the syllogism was completely legitimate, appears from the tract that he devoted to this subject: *Eenige kenteekens, waar uit een geloovig Mensche hem kan verzekeren dat hy van God bemint is* (1649), appended to *Het Geestelyke Leven*, 351-95.

"permanently." For immediately afterwards he mentions "doubts that arise," doubts that sometimes creep in through the cracks of his heart. Because of the "inner grace" in his soul, however, these have no "power" to cause his faith to totter "even a little."[156] One notes how, taken literally, Theodorus contradicts himself: sometimes doubt is present, but it causes no wavering! He explains this, then, with the distinction that his faith is definitely "clouded" (smoky, darkened), but that certainty concerning God's love for him remains unwavering.[157] To my mind, he means that his faith certainly wavers but never collapses because he "forthwith" opts for the escape route of grace.

The speech just referenced is concluded with two qualifying notes that relate to temptation. The first strikes me as remarkable, and the second clarifies in that it sheds light on à Brakel's ambivalence. To begin with the latter observation: in the speech he advises his son to distinguish carefully between the beginning, the middle and the end of his spiritual fatherhood.[158] Here he apparently wants to indicate that during the mature phase of his fatherhood temptations are less intense in nature than previously. The period of fatherhood is not a static condition, therefore, but a process marked by gradual progress. This could well be an explanation of the fact that he speaks both of continuous fellowship with God as well as about its absence. That constancy would apply especially to the later period.

The other qualifying note is more surprising than clarifying. In it Theodorus relativizes the "severe temptations" that still afflicted him even during his fatherhood by noting that his account of those conflicts must be understood more in terms "of emotions and appearance than of their actual basis."[159] In other words, his perception was that they were certainly severe, but in actuality they were not serious. But this gives rise to the question of whether this distinction between the subjective experience and the objective meaning of the temptation only applied to the stage of spiritual fatherhood, or whether it could not also be just as relevant for both of the previous stages.

What is more, I see no basis for setting aside my interpretations that the stage of spiritual fatherhood does not in the least represent a break from the stages of spiritual childhood and spiritual youth, and that it involves even less a qualitative change in communion with God. It much rather consists of a phase in which faith yields the same experiences as before. The difference is that this faith has ripened to a maturity in which it is more prepared to defy opposition. My judgment is that this maturation is what à Brakel in fact had in mind.

In this third phase Theodorus broadened the times of his meditation to include an "exercise" at night. Most often this extended until midnight, but it might also continue until two o'clock in the morning.[160] As we already know, this "night-watch" is certainly not something new, but its regularity seems to date from the period of his fatherhood. The reason à Brakel gave for observing it

---

156. À Brakel, *De Trappen*, 175.
157. Ibid.
158. Ibid., 176.
159. Ibid.
160. Ibid., 178. See also 324 and 339.

is that, to his dissatisfaction, by going to bed earlier he was "often vexed with drowsiness and sleepiness"[161] and was "frequently estranged from the sweet and intimate communion with God and the Lord Jesus Christ and from his loving presence."[162] For him that was unbearable. He was always careful never to lose his God and Savior from his heart, but "always to have him present . . . day and night" and even to experience his "presence with him" when he slept.[163] "O, if I only might enjoy God at all times, without rest." He added with sorrow, "but my body is . . . a frail house of clay (Job 4:19) that needs its rest and refreshment."[164] But he knew how to limit that physical refreshment drastically.

He definitely connects his spiritual fatherhood with an intensification of his devotional exercises. Speaking as though he had not already begun this practice in his spiritual youth, namely his fourth time of reflection late in the evening, he offers the opinion that meditating at night is asking too much of "children and young people in Christ." But for fathers in Christ, however, he considered it an outstanding opportunity to glorify God.[165] That this could "well last until quite late," he did not regret in the least. To be sure, he was sometimes hindered by sleepiness, but on such occasions he paced back and forth "so as not to be overtaken with sleep."[166] The effect of his vigil was twofold. When he did lay down to rest after such a session, his soul was often "drawn into God" and he slept "as it were in him."[167] Above all, in the morning he could usually get up much earlier: "an hour of such sleep is frequently more satisfying . . . than if I had slept otherwise."[168] To be sure, it sometimes happened that he overslept, for the flesh is weak.[169] But his intention was to observe the fourfold pattern carefully. One gets the impression that he consistently met his intentions: he observed his "quiet time" at night, early in the morning, around noon and at dusk in the evening.[170] Daily family worship fell between his evening and nighttime spiritual exercises.[171]

In the part of his book dealing with spiritual fatherhood, à Brakel goes into the shape of his devotions extensively, particularly those at night.[172] He regularly begins by glorifying God. He does so "with meditation on heaven and by reading a little in God's Word, especially the Psalms."[173] He regards praising God as "the most important and exalted purpose of all his [i.e., God's] works."[174] Glorifying God is a more heavenly "work" than praying, he thinks. Whoever prays,

---

161. Ibid., 199.
162. Ibid., 178.
163. Ibid., 180.
164. Ibid., 187.
165. Ibid., 185-86.
166. Ibid., 196.
167. Ibid., 201.
168. Ibid., 205.
169. Ibid., 206-7.
170. Ibid., 222.
171. Ibid., 224.
172. Ibid., 225-93!
173. Ibid., 225.
174. Ibid., 226.

receives; he who glorifies, gives.[175] "To glorify my God makes me more heavenly minded and draws me ever closer to God in Christ." Through this activity he is more united in love than through prayer and lamentation.[176] Meditation on Christ's passion, which in his opinion one may never neglect, he reserves for the morning.[177] In former times he wanted to "awaken" his love by it and thereby rise to "higher grace." But at present he already experiences this higher grace consistently. In his fatherhood, therefore, the spiritual direction is reversed. Now he begins on an exalted level and thereafter descends into reflecting on the sufferings.[178] By higher grace Theodorus means the close union with God in which he "consistently" dwells with him and "constantly" lives in him,[179] even during his "severest temptations." However darkened grace can become to his way of thinking, the "inner union of love" remains present.[180] What he means by this paradox he explains a little later: although he may perceive God's love and grace to be receding from him, he still rests—heart and soul—by trusting in his love, and that positions him to love God. "What I cannot accomplish based on my feelings, I achieve by faith."[181]

What he did not achieve earlier was glorifying God because God himself wills this, apart from Theodorus' own salvation. At present that is different. À Brakel now even seems to be on the verge of resignation. But he does not cross that line. He writes this: "I would glorify him even if there were nothing in it for me, although at present I derive the greatest possible benefit from this; for everything that God is, he is to my benefit."[182] God is worthy of à Brakel's praise, therefore, because of all that he is in himself. But what he is in himself, he at the same time is for the sake of Theodorus. For him to praise God is not to adore some nameless being in himself, but to extol the God who has revealed himself for us (*ad nos*) in his works and his mercies.[183]

To the son's question of whether his father could offer him "a formula [model, paradigm] at present" for how glorifying God is to be conducted, the latter answers that this is really not possible. "For, it is more a matter of God working in the soul and of enjoying God in his all-sufficiency[184] than something that can be expressed in mere words." Nevertheless, an "account" then follows of the "sweet, shared union of love and the sweet communion enjoyed between God and the soul and her Bridegroom, Christ." What exactly is said in this dialogue, Theodorus is unable to put into words.[185] And especially the intense enjoyment

---

175. Ibid., 229.

176. Ibid., 227-28.

177. Ibid., 231.

178. Ibid., 231-32.

179. From the parallel use of "consistently" and "constantly," it appears that à Brakel in this instance intends "consistently" to be taken in the acceptable sense of his day as "continuously."

180. À Brakel, *De Trappen*, 234-35.

181. Ibid., 237.

182. Ibid., 246.

183. Ibid., 246-58.

184. With this notion of sufficiency, à Brakel wants to express clearly that in God one has enough, and perhaps also that in God one finds enjoyment.

185. Ibid., 253.

itself is "indescribable."[186] But he knows precisely how to describe how he conducts his nightly exercises and what experiences he derives from them. He always begins by glorifying God in words that "flow into" him from God's word.[187] Then he is often "highly enlightened for the purpose of contemplating God," is "drawn into him" and "tastes" his sweetness.[188] He reminisces in this vein for many pages about the joy and pleasure he has in God. "Why should I be discouraged, for my God, whose fellowship I enjoy, is never discouraged."[189] Also, whenever God happens to allow him to experience less of that sweetness, he satisfies himself "with God on the basis of faith" and does not swerve from the confidence that God still loves him.[190] For one is called to love God not only on quiet waters, but also when he leads us across "the dry desert of abandoned feelings."[191] The Heavenly Father sometimes withholds that higher, experiential grace from his children in order to have them yearn all the more intensely for "perfect satisfaction." What befalls them here on earth is merely "the first fruits of the Spirit." Just as the "spies" brought with them some of the fruit of Canaan in order to prove "what a beautifully fruitful land it was," so God lets us "sample now and then something of that great goodness that he has laid up for us."[192] For all the proleptic enjoyment that à Brakel *already* shares, he is also conscious of the *not yet.*

Theodorus customarily concludes his nighttime meditation by addressing the Trinity: "O Holy Trinity, Father, Son and Holy Spirit, in you I lay down to sleep, in your name, dear Lord Jesus Christ." Just as Luther's aim was to recall a biblical text before going to sleep—think of the monastic pattern of "to ruminate" (*ruminare*)[193] in this context—so Theodorus endeavored to occupy himself with God's love until sleep "overcame" him.[194] For him it is "unthinkable" that even as much as one moment might pass in which he could not glorify God. Such moments he regards as lost time, as though he really "had not lived them." Actually, he would have preferred to need no sleep at all, that he might glorify God his Savior without interruption.[195]

Only a few hours, if not less, separate his nighttime reflections from his morning meditation. This also begins by addressing God, but then develops into meditation on the passion. Clearly recognizable here is the middle section of the Reformed form for the Lord's supper, as he repeats the account of Jesus' sufferings. Here à Brakel ponders how the Savior was oppressed in order to deliver him from oppression, was imprisoned in order to set him free, was bound in order to loose him, was scourged in order to spare him from the stripes of the devil, was crowned with thorns, mocked and condemned in order to set him free,

---

186. Ibid.
187. Ibid., 254.
188. Ibid., 255.
189. Ibid., 260.
190. Ibid., 265.
191. Ibid., 273.
192. Ibid., 274.
193. De Reuver, "Een mystieke ader," 13.
194. À Brakel, *De Trappen*, 281-82.
195. Ibid., 283.

was crucified and forsaken by God in order to die an accursed death for him. He appropriates this all by faith. "Behold, O my God, it is for my life, atonement and ransom that you were pierced with a spear in your side, and that blood and water flowed from your heart; behold, by faith I wash myself in it, and in love I hide myself in your open side, am buried with you, and am raised again with you." In this manner, exactly as he had done in the phase of his spiritual youth, he retraces "the entire suffering of Christ to the end" and appropriates "all of it in faith, bit by bit," for his own comfort.[196] United with Christ, his "Brother," he rises from the grave and makes his way to heaven.[197]

Theodorus is briefer concerning the noon and early evening meditations. His account of them in principle includes quite a bit of repetition. This is not surprising, for it is his "trademark" to call on God day and night—"when rising or when going to bed"—and to find his delight in him. For him this is "the beginning of heaven."[198] Particularly in the later stages of spiritual fatherhood, he lives—thus confirming his earlier explanation—"in continuous peace and in very close and sweet union." Above all, God "now and then" fills him with "such clear illumination" and gives him "such spiritual vistas" of his majesty and love, that he dwells "as it were in him" and is "sometimes" led "into his bodega."[199] The latter is a motif in Song of Solomon that is worked out in an obviously mystical manner in *Het Geestelyke Leven*. There the soul is led into the Bridegroom's bodega and is feted with "finely spiced wine,"[200] "transported above herself," and intoxicated with the sight of God's appearance. There she is kissed with kiss of Jesus' lips and receives "the bridal garments and pledges of fidelity." By these confirming events yearning for the eschaton is portrayed. The bride longs "with a special longing that the day of her wedding feast might come . . . and that she might be completely united with her beloved Bridegroom, Jesus Christ." And so she drinks from the stream of living water, "as it were with great mouthfuls." But, however wonderful this may be, it involves merely "the foretaste of heavenly sweetness."[201]

From his autobiographical account it becomes obvious how much à Brakel spoke from his own experience in his first book. In *Trappen* he recalls diverse experiences from his own life, fifteen in all that reflect the "higher grace" that came to him in his spiritual fatherhood.[202] The first of these is the most intriguing. In it he reports that "at a certain time" he was so lifted up to God—it was the middle of the summer and a time "that the beginning of the day to its end

---

196. Ibid., 299-300. In *Het geestelyke Leven*, 151-56, à Brakel reflects the spirit of the Modern Devotion by designating for every day of the week some aspect of Christ's suffering and triumph on which a person can focus their meditation. See de Bruin, "De spiritualiteit," 120; de Kruijf, et al., *Een klooster ontsloten*, 33; and compare Ros, *Theodorus à Brakel*, 42-43.

197. Ibid., 301.

198. Ibid., 304.

199. Ibid., 305. Compare 163, where in the section on spiritual young manhood he recalls the same experience.

200. See Song of Solomon 8:2. In the biblical text, however, it is not the Bridegroom but the bride who is the subject of this activity! Compare Boot, *De allegorische uitlegging*, 171.

201. À Brakel, *Het geestelyke Leven*, 192-93.

202. À Brakel, *De Trappen*, 307-323.

lasted longest"—that he was, "like Moses," permitted to see God's face. How Christocentric Theodore's doctrine of God is becomes apparent from sentence constructions like these: "I long to see your face and your glory, Lord Jesus." His soul longed so intensely for Jesus that "it could not contain its desire." He grew weak as a result and he also said, "I want to die in this state." Thereupon the desired contemplation was immediately granted him. "I saw him so clearly and was drawn into communion with him like that of a friend with a friend."[203] He continued in this way "for some time, above the world," and he was permitted to see God and Christ's glory "from behind." This lasted until his body became so weak that he could no longer endure. Then he was forced to lie down so his body could regain its strength.[204]

What is so intriguing about this experience? To begin, the intimacy of the experience itself certainly is. But what interests me most is the question of whether this spiritual experience that is related to Paul's ecstasy[205] actually differs, content-wise, from the rapture that had already been his lot in his childhood and especially in his spiritual youth. Then he also experienced "being lifted up." Then he also "saw" God and was united with him. And then he also dwelt in heaven. That earlier mystical *excessus* unfolded no less contemplatively than that during his fatherhood, and its content was in essence the same. On this essential point the third phase of spiritual life seems to me to be, so to say, "on the same level" as both of the previous two.

Yet, one consideration remains that perhaps justifies the difference in levels claimed by à Brakel. I refer to his intense hunger for heavenly glory. This appears in the second illustration of his "special graces." There he reports that "at present" he cannot live without delighting in God. The light that he contemplates in his God and Savior is for him "a thought beyond thought, a sea without bottom." But he yearns for more, notably "to live the everlasting life eternally with God . . . and to fathom his all-sufficiency." For him it is almost "beyond endurance." The word spoken to Moses that no mortal can see God and live, he turns on its head: "My soul longs to die, so that I might see him always; for his servant longs to see his face."[206] To praise God and to see his glory: that for Theodorus is what it means, in the first place, to live!

On another occasion he was so preoccupied with heaven that he thought, "Nothing sustains me more than the thought of being transported from earth to heaven." À Brakel wanted to cross to the other side. "O, how sweet heaven will be."[207] For there is no more joyful satisfaction than that experienced in the "perfect enjoyment of God's face."[208] Perhaps it was this eschatological yearning, combined with his manifold experiences of anticipating heaven that constituted the basis for regarding his "contemplation of heaven" as on a "higher" plane than "during the first periods." By these preceding times he meant

---

203. This is a play on Exodus 33:11, where God as subject (!) speaks with Moses as a man speaks with his friend.

204. Ibid., 308-11.

205. 2 Corinthians 12, to which à Brakel himself appeals.

206. À Brakel, *De Trappen*, 312. Compare ibid., 320, on the same idea.

207. Ibid., 315.

208. Ibid., 316.

not just the phases of his childhood and spiritual youth, but definitely also the beginning of his spiritual fatherhood.[209]

The converse of à Brakel's anticipation of perfection is his pain over imperfection. The latter does not overwhelm him in the least. Although he repeatedly leaves the impression that he lives in permanent fellowship with God, he corrects that notion by honestly acknowledging that God "often substantially abandoned him" and seemed "estranged" from him.[210] Especially during the early years of his spiritual fatherhood this sense of abandonment recurred rather frequently.[211] But God repeatedly restored good experiences, generally during times of prayer. Then he held God to his Word and said, "My God, I find strength and hope in your Word and your promises; Lord, help me according to your Word."[212] Besides his petition on the basis of the promises, he also appealed to God's favor towards "holy men" in salvation history: "O, where can that grace of by-gone days be?"[213] Generally, this cry of faith by à Brakel was sufficient to restore the desired level of religious experience. Such faith was certainly determinative, but it was not his greatest aspiration. His actual longings were directed at the affective experience of communion with God. This stance is reminiscent of Bernard's expression, "I believe in order to experience" (*credo ut experiar*).[214] Concerning the matter of justification, "by faith alone" was sufficient and all-determinative for Theodorus; on the matter of religious experience, faith was certainly necessary, but it was not all-determinative. Thus, on the one hand he could be more or less in tension about his affective disposition, and he accorded faith the primary role of indicating that his spiritual experience remained at a less than desirable level. On the other hand, he could observe that faith is only a prelude to religious experience.

This somewhat paradoxical correlation between faith and emotions emerges clear as daylight in a passage with which I want to round off my discussion of *Trappen*. It deals with temptation. Those "spiritual conflicts" certainly did not last as long in à Brakel's spiritual fatherhood as they had earlier,[215] but their intensity appears to have increased greatly.[216] When he gives his son advice on the matter of how he should conduct himself in times of conflict, therefore, Theodorus knows exactly of what he speaks. He does not only know how intense it can be. He also knows of what the defense consists. He wishes to instruct his son concerning the latter. The passage begins with a subordinate clause of an unabashedly Brakelian nature: "In order to have intimate communion with God and to maintain the experience of his grace, we must. . . ." For him, that is the place to begin. But the rest of the sentence throws clear light on the vital role of faith. In order to maintain the experience of grace, we must "trust steadfastly in

209. Ibid., 322-23.
210. Ibid., 339.
211. Ibid., 343.
212. Ibid., 344.
213. Ibid., 347. This line comes from Datheen's versification of Psalm 89:19. See the facsimile of the 1566 Heidelberg edition, *The Psalms of David* (Houten, 1992).
214. See Schuck, *Das religiöse Erlebnis*, 95-96.
215. À Brakel, *De Trappen*, 382.
216. Ibid., 395-96 and 402-3, for example.

our God and Savior, no matter how we might be disposed toward this, or with what temptation we might be struggling, or how we might seem to have been abandoned by God." We need to give ourselves to him in faith, in the knowledge that our salvation depends solely on God's eternal and unchangeable love and not on ourselves or our disposition.

Also, when the feeling of fellowship with God grows dim, we should "nevertheless remain in fellowship with him and his love" and in him "be at rest in all our restlessness." "How often that faith in my God and Savior and in his Word and his love has upheld me, sustained me in that intimate fellowship with my God and Savior when I felt deeply forsaken and severely tested!" As soon as faith "grew quiet," that sense of fellowship weakened. Even then, the righteous shall live by faith . . . , not just "in the act of being justified, but in and under all circumstances." From "his own experience" Theodorus advised his son, therefore: "Heed no temptations, whatever they might be; do not answer them; let them pass, and continue to depend on God by faith whether you feel his love or whether you do not. And if it should seem that God is angry with you or has forsaken you, at such times always rise above your own self and remember that your salvation consists of God's eternal love and mercy. Flee to Christ, and remember that you are still justified in him." À Brakel would not be himself if he did not articulate this appeal to faith in the following call: "And by all means glorify God! Endeavor to be joyful in him, or you will diminish your confidence and joy in the Lord."[217] In this way, the circle is complete. Faith is the compelling basis of experience—nothing more, nothing less. For à Brakel, everything turned on faith. His objective was the experience of joy.

Evaluation

On the basis of the evaluative comments that I have gradually been making, I will summarize the most important results in this retrospective look. Here are three. The first is that à Brakel's *Trappen* devotes much more attention to the *form* of the spiritual life than to its *stages*, despite what the title suggests. To be sure, compositionally these degrees are deliberately divided and explained in three parts, but the actual point of interest is unmistakably the experience of God that Theodorus acquired in his spiritual childhood, youth and fatherhood.

By extension, in the second place, it is apparent that there is hardly any consideration of climbing from one level to another, at least content-wise. The frequency of à Brakel's mystical pleasures in the phase of his fatherhood may have increased, but in quality or intensity there is very little difference. Even if one considers that Theodorus wrote his *Trappen* in the mature phase of his spiritual fatherhood and that his memories of the previous phases were probably colored by that fact, one must still say that the three stages follow one another without actually adding anything to the previous ones. In any case, in content they are more repetitive than complementary. This seems to be the case, with two exceptions. The first is that in the account of fatherhood the yearning for heaven is more prominently present than before. While in both previous phases à

---

217. Ibid., 358-60.

Brakel's longing was directed toward "the foretaste of heaven,"[218] his present desires were more focused on eternal life itself.[219] The other exception concerns the role of faith. Faith's appeal to God's promises comes more prominently into play during the last phase than it does in the preceding phases.[220] On both these matters discussion should be limited to the increase and deepening of these realities. Much more in question, however, is whether à Brakel himself intended to focus on these dimensions when he described his later spiritual experiences as "another joy than I had at first." He leaves the impression that he was thinking of another sort of experience. But from the development of his account, that is precisely what cannot be documented.

The third matter that I want to discuss seems almost superfluous, but it is at the same time the most relevant. Theodorus is a full-blown devotee of mysticism. His attention to the *order* of salvation is marginal in *Trappen*, while that given to the *experience* of salvation is central. There is good reason for calling him one of the most mystical writers of the Further Reformation.[221] He stands in the tradition of those mystics who down through the ages have yearned for the most profound experience that they considered achievable in this life, namely the proleptic yet always broken and interrupted but nevertheless genuine experience of communion with God in Christ through the Holy Spirit. À Brakel's contemplative devotion reminds one at various times of that of Bernard. As appears from several citations, he knew his mystical sources, in any case sections of them. The glow and the intimacy of Theodorus' own work testifies of his affinity with the piety of the abbot of Clairvaux. This affinity is also telegraphed on various substantive points. The first concerns à Brakel's outspokenly Christocentric representation of God. Just as with Bernard, his meditation concentrates on Christ, both on his humanity and earthly humiliation as well as on his divinity and heavenly glory. The second is that one encounters in Theodorus a kind of contemplation typical of Bernard, one consisting of the anticipatory foretaste of heavenly glory. The third point of agreement is that also for à Brakel faith consistently appears to culminate in affectively experienced love. This compatibility does not suggest, however, that there are no differences. The most noteworthy is that Bernard's "exceptional hour" has become "numerous hours" for à Brakel. While Bernard's contemplative delights are exceptions, they seem to occur regularly for à Brakel. A difference in nuance that might be connected with this is that, in my estimation, humbling oneself assumes a less dominant place than it does with Bernard. While *humilitas* definitely is not

---

218. Ibid., 126 and 171.

219. Ibid., 312. Even so, a change in an absolute sense is not involved. In his young manhood he also longed for heaven. See 162.

220. Also concerning this point, one cannot speak of an absolute difference, given the fact that already in his childhood à Brakel appealed to what Christ promised in the Gospel of John. Ibid., 126.

221. As far as I am concerned, he is equaled only by Jodocus van Lodensteyn. See Trimp, *Jodocus van Lodensteyn*; de Reuver, "Een mystieke ader"; W. Snoeijer, *Wandelen voor Zijn aangezicht: Jodocus van Lodenstein, een mysticus uit de Reformatie* (Gent and Kampen, 2000). For the rest, at certain points Herman Witsius does not take a back seat to him either, as will become apparent shortly.

absent from à Brakel,[222] joyfulness (*hilaritas*) is much more dominant in him—certainly during the phase of his spiritual fatherhood. In spite of these modest divergences, the points of intersection are just as striking. Theodorus moves in the mystical tradition of Bernard.[223]

Again and again—and to this day—the critical question arises of whether this brand of mysticism strives for a kind of contemplation that minimizes the Word and faith. In à Brakel's case, he carries "a great deal of the Bible" in his head and his heart. Scripture is his foundation and at the same time defines the boundaries that he will not cross, although this last observation requires some qualification. I mean that Theodorus is definitely a representative of those Reformed devotional leaders whose spirituality—to put it as Van Ruler does—longs to penetrate via the spoken word to the "heart" of what that word mediates: through the verbal to the actual, that is, through the word of the gospel to the Father-heart of God.[224] À Brakel belongs to this class pre-eminently. He is not just someone who deals with God, he lives with God—to use the pointed language of H. H. Langelaar.[225] That explains his "joyfulness." Without hesitation one can call this joy the heartbeat of his piety.

Like all other mystics, Theodorus has the sense of explaining an experience of God that actually is incapable of being put into words. The paradox that one cannot keep quiet about what one regards as inexpressible is the warp and woof of the mystical tradition. One encounters this idea with regularity in Theodorus. What Luther writes in his *Magnificat*, namely that those that "mit gotlicher sussickeit und geyst durchgossen werden, mehr fuelen denn sie sagen kundenn,"[226] one finds continually confirmed in à Brakel's reflections.

That Theodorus' writings connect with his own social situation only sporadically has everything to do with the questionable but unmistakable fact that his material is literally disengaged narrative. Naturally, they were written during the hours of his day-to-day life as a minister. But they show no trace of the ordinary things of every-day life. Even if they were to provide extensive information on the nuts and bolts of his life, which they do not, his writings

---

222. See, for example, à Brakel, *De Trappen*, 144, 146, 148 (a passion meditation), and 229.

223. However, compare R. Bisschop, "De scheiding der geesten: grenzen en raakvlakken tussen piëtisme en mystiek: Th. à Brakel, Koelman en De Labadie," in *DNR* 14 (1990): 44-56. The author wants to compare Theodore's "mystically tinted experiences without further qualification . . . to the mysticism of someone like De Labadie." [trans.] "The mystical system" is absent from à Brakel. De Labadie stands in the tradition of the radical Reformation. À Brakel is in the tradition of "Calvinistic pietism's sanctification of life." [trans.] Ibid., 54-55. Bisschop's comparison with De Labadie is noteworthy. Based on Bernard's influence on à Brakel, however, it seems to me that his relation to mysticism is more complicated than Bisschop thinks. Insofar as I am able to determine, the influence of Bernard on De Labadie is less significant than A. Ritschl wants to make it. *Geschichte*, 1:254. Rather, De Labadie should be seen more in the line of Eckhart's identity mysticism. This is certainly not in the tradition of à Brakel. His is more in the footsteps of Bernard's bridal mysticism, which aspires to the highest personal fellowship but not to melting into the being of God. It involves a union in which the distinction between Creator and creature is honored. On how to nuance the idea of mysticism, see Oberman, *Die Reformation*, 38-39.

224. Van Ruler, *Theologische Werk*, 3:68-71.

225. Langelaar, "'Krank van liefde,'" 74.

226. *WA* 7, 550.

would still not—or would scarcely ever—be able to be brought into direct contact with these things. One can lament this, but one should not fault Theodorus for this. In order to meditate he retreated three or four times a day, when he sought heaven for hours at a time. He did this as though he lived in a cloister and not as though he served a congregation. He did so as though he had never married his wife and was alone in the world. He did so as though no Peace of Munster had been reached in 1648 and as though in the 1650s no war with England was underway. Whatever went on around him—witness his controversy with the Remonstrants and especially his obvious pain over the loss of his daughters—certainly did not simply pass him by, but he winged his way on high in the "holy solitude of fellowship with God."[227] At those times he left everything horizontal here below.[228] Then the vertical fellowship with God became the business at hand. Its context was not shaped by the changing climate of his times and circumstances, but by his timeless thirst for heaven and for being satiated with the Eternal One. That is what he wrote about, however well or however poorly it went.

À Brakel's works do not require academic analysis, but spiritual sensitivity and engagement. The extreme measures of his disciplined spiritual exercises are neither meant to be, nor capable of being imitated. Such rigorous devotional observance midway through the seventeenth century seems to have been exceptional already then—at least beyond the walls of the cloister. In the twenty-first century mimicking them is reaching much too high. However, what is certainly attainable and what Christian discipleship deserves—if I am permitted to make this observation—is a Christian retreat daily and at designated times from the busyness of life in order to return to the simplicity of intimacy with God. Such times of solitude are not in conflict with Christian solidarity, but promote it.[229] Not just those in monastic orders, but even someone as fully engaged as Calvin, make a case for everyone creating set times daily for spiritual devotions that give full attention to all the movements of the soul.[230] Theodorus'

---

227. "O holy, blessed solitude [*eenzaam*]! In communion with God [*gemeenzaam*]" is the nine-fold refrain from the well-known poem of Van Lodensteyn: "Eensaamheyd met Godt," included in *Uytspanningen* (4th ed.; Amsterdam, 1683), 396-98. While the first edition of this collection first appeared in 1676, some time after Theodorus' death the theme poem became a striking portrayal of his spiritual practice.

228. S. van der Linde, "De Godservaring bij W. Teellinck, D. G. à Brakel en A. Comrie," in S. van der Linde, *Opgang en voortgang der Reformatie: Een keuze uit lezingen en artikelen* (Amsterdam, 1976), 163. The author calls à Brakel's experience of God's presence "eigenlijk louter transcendent en metafysisch" [actually, clearly transcendent and metaphysical]. While van der Linde has a definite concept for it, de Boer speaks disapprovingly of a "geforceerde paranormale bewustzijnstoestanden" [instances of forced paranormal consciousness]. *De verzegeling*, 107.

229. Consider the title (and the content) of J. Beumer, *Intimiteit en solidariteit: Over het evenwicht tussen dogmatiek, mystiek en ethiek* (Baarn, 1993).

230. *Inst.* 3.20.50 (*OS*, 4:366): "Convenit ut sibi quisque nostrum exercitationis causa peculiares horas constituat quae non sine oratione effluant, et quae totos animi affectus in hoc penitus occupatos habent." Compare A. de Reuver, "Stellung und Funktion des Gebets in Calvins Theologie: Eine Skizze," in *Gebetsliteratur der Frühen Neuzeit als Hausfrömmigkeit: Funktionen und Formen in Deutschland und den Niederlanden*, ed. F. van Lingen and C. N. Moore (Wiesbaden, 2001), 288-89. On Luther's pietistic bent see J. Wallmann, "Zwischen

intention was no more and certainly no less—at least concerning the daily disciplines—when on his deathbed he charged his son Wilhelmus to publish his spiritual manuscripts. In the foreword of *Trappen* Wilhelmus observes that the author of this tract did not want "to prescribe a rule for anyone, to which everyone must submit and follow with precision, but to set an example for finding consolation and spiritual awakening." Wilhelmus' assessment seems to me to be both accurate and applicable.

Herzensgebet und Gebetsbuch; Zur protestanischen deutschen Gebetsliteratur im 17. Jahrhundert." in the same source, 13-46.

5

Guiljelmus Saldenus (1627-1694)

"A Skillful Healer"

Saldenus was held in high regard by his contemporaries and his spiritual successors. Notably, the praise accorded him was based on his book *De Droevigste Staet eens Christens, bestaende in de Doodigheydt ofte Ongevoeligheydt sijns Herten ontrent Geestelijke Dingen* [trans.: *The Extremely Sorry State of a Christian, Consisting of the Deadness or Unresponsiveness of His Heart concerning Spiritual Matters*]. It is a work in which the author's pastoral nature and great sensitivity are clearly seen in their best light. One of his best friends, Herman Witsius, extols him with a reference to *De Droevigste Staet*, as "a skillful healer of the wounds of Zion's daughters."[1] Saldenus' writings were also referred to gratefully by later, eighteenth-century pietists.[2] Worth noting in this connection is the testimony of Alexander Comrie in his *Verzameling van Leerredenen* (1749). When in the first sermon included in that collection he broaches the subject of spiritual deadness, which he does not want to develop in greater detail at that point, he advises his readers to delve more deeply into that doctrine by consulting Saldenus, for he has written on that subject with "unparalleled clarity."[3] At that point he also references "that tract that can never be too highly regarded," *De Droevigste Staet*.[4]

When further along in the same sermon Comrie summarizes just as many causes of "deadness" as there are letters in the Greek alphabet, then observes that "the number of letters in the Greek ABCs is insufficient," he invites his "attentive readers and listeners . . . to read" a number of "famous writers and men of good reputation in the church of the Netherlands." These men of good reputation are especially Van Lodensteyn, Fruytier, Witsius and also Saldenus. Comrie considers their works to be esteemed above "all the famous titles that he could give them." If he compares his own contributions to theirs, then his diminish to insignificance, "like the light of a candle compared with the light of the sun."[5] Until the beginning of the nineteenth century Saldenus was praised as one of "the old, practical theologians who possessed great ability in the care of the soul."[6] The twentieth was already far along when G. van den End first devoted a theological doctoral dissertation to this "skillful healer."

---

1. Herman Witsius, *Twist des Heeren met zynen Wyngaart* (6th edition; Utrecht, 1736), 414.

2. G. van den End, *Guiljelmus Saldenus (1627-1694): Een praktisch en irenisch theoloog uit de Nadere Reformatie* (Leiden, 1991), 117-18 and 260-62.

3. A. Comrie, *Verzameling van Leerredenen* (From the 3rd, unaltered edition, 1758; Utrecht, 1887), 26.

4. Ibid., 29.

5. Ibid., 58-59.

6. Van den End, *Guiljelmus Saldenus*, 117.

Biographical Sketch

Guiljelmus Saldenus was born in the month of May, 1627, in Utrecht.[7] This Latinized name dates from the period of his academic studies. At his birth his parents gave him the good Dutch name of Willem. He was the second child of Hendrick Willemszoon Salden and Elisabeth Jansdochter van der Son, who in 1623 moved to Utrecht from elsewhere. His father came from Sittard and his mother from Jutphaas. Father Salden had acquired a good position as a tailor. Of more importance for our account is the fact that Willem's parents were both godly people. The publication that I will consult as the most important source on his piety, namely *De Wech des Levens* [trans.: *The Road of Life*] (1657), is quite clear on this matter. In the "Acknowledgement" with which Saldenus prefaces his "little tract" by way of dedication, he explains that he can "present" what he calls "this paper child" to no one better than to his "loving father . . . who had carried [him] so often in his arms." But that is not his only memory. What most of all causes his thankfulness is that his father "sowed the first little seeds in his heart that have now produced these fruits [in this book]." At the same time, Guiljelmus memorializes his mother, who had meanwhile died. For Willem's religious upbringing, father Hendrick did not need to carry the load alone. For this he enjoyed "the wholehearted support of my godly mother." Guiljelmus is disposed to remember, "to this day, often with tears," her "exceptional concern" directed especially toward his spiritual welfare. He asks to what he owes it, "besides God himself," except to his parents "that I have been consecrated to the service of the church, and that I might proclaim the invaluable word with my unworthy mouth to the people of God."[8]

Young Willem received his education completely in Utrecht, not only that of his parental home, but also that of the school and of the academy. Apparently he attended the Hieronymus School from his seventh to his sixteenth years. This was an institute established in the fifteenth century and it originally bore the stamp of the Brothers of the Common Life.[9] This institution was reorganized in a Calvinistic direction after the Reformation, and it was the only school in Utrecht at the time where the ancient languages were taught. Students learned by memory entire passages from classical literature. As is apparent from his later works, this education stood Willem in good stead.

When he was sixteen, in 1643, Willem enrolled in the academy. His theological professors were Gisbertus Voetius, Carolus de Maets and Meinardus Scholtanus, who in 1644 was succeeded by Johannes Hoornbeeck. Voetius' adage that spirituality and science are intimately connected exercised a continuing influence on Saldenus' own approach to doing theology. A friendly relationship developed between him and his "highly esteemed teacher" Hoornbeeck.

---

7. The exact date is unknown. For the biographical details, except for the dedication in *De Wech des Levens* (Utrecht, 1657), I have relied on the article by D. Nauta, "Guiljelmus Saldenus," in *BLGNP* 3:317-20; and Van den End, *Guiljelmus Saldenus*.

8. Saldenus, *De Wech des Levens*, "Toe-eygening" [unpaginated].

9. Kuyper, *De Opleiding*, 564-65.

In 1649 Saldenus was installed as minister in Renswoude. During the three years that he labored there, he applied himself especially to the proper administration of the Lord's supper, to catechism instruction and to proper observance of the Lord's day. Concerning his ministry in Kockengen, where he spent the following three years, it is important to note that in 1655 he married Anna Twist. The same year he accepted a call to Enkhuizen, a prosperous city with a flourishing and rapidly growing church life. He would remain there for nine years. In the various writings that he published while there, he showed that he was a true proponent of the thought forms of the Further Reformation. He denounced several abuses in church and society.[10] It was also during these years that he developed a close friendship with Herman Witsius, who was born in Enkhuizen and who since 1657 had been connected with the nearby congregation of Westwoud. Saldenus suffered heavy blows during his stay in Enkhuizen. His wife, who was "the desire of my eyes," died in 1657, only a few months after their little son Justus had succumbed.[11] Moreover, Saldenus himself had to contend with poor health, about which he already complained during his years in Kockengen.

After Saldenus declined a call to Utrecht, where another close friend in the person of Jodocus van Lodensteyn lived, a call from Delft reached him early in 1664. The representatives from Delft, who visited the extended consistory of Enkhuizen at one of their meetings in order to add weight to their call, spoke of "an exceptional leading of God." Although Rev. Saldenus was unknown in their congregation, they "had been moved by good testimonies and the knowledge of his edifying books and tracts . . . concerning his worthiness."[12] Saldenus accepted the call. He was very aware of "how many unhappy and ailing souls" he left behind in Enkhuizen, but he left for Delft. In this city of princes he became intensely involved in the concerns of his rapidly growing congregation, concerns that in part once again involved sabbath observance and celebration of the Lord's supper. Church life in a wider context also received his attention. He was assigned to be a church visitor, and on three occasions he was delegated to the particular synod of South Holland. None of this inhibited him from advancing his work of publication.[13]

---

10. Dating from this period are, among others, his titles *De Wech des Levens* (1657), *Geestelijk Avontmael* (1660), *De Droevichste Staet Eens Christens* (1661) and *Een Christen vallende en opstaende* (1662).

11. Saldenus remarried in 1660. This marriage was also of short duration. His second wife died in 1663. A year later, he married for the third time. After his third wife also died, he married for the fourth time in 1681. *BLGNP* 3:317 erroneously indicates that Saldenus was married three times. See van den End, *Guiljelmus Saldenus*, 36.

12. *Kerke-boeck van Enkhuysen*, February 20, 1664. Cited in van den End, *Guiljelmus Saldenus*, 27.

13. Among other titles, there appeared, respectively, *Toetsteen van eens Christens Oordeel* (1665), *Leven uyt de Doodt* (1667), *d'Overtuyghde Dina, of Korte en nodige waerschouwingh tegen 't besien van de hedensdaeghsche Schouw-spelen* (1667) and a little catechism book bearing the title *Christelijke Kinder-School* (1668). On this last title, compare Verboom, *De catechese*, 299 and 309. For a complete bibliography, see van den End, *Guiljelmus Saldenus*, 285-89; van der Haar, *Schatkamer*, 319-20; and *BLGNP*, 3:319-20.

His final years, after 1677, Saldenus spent in The Hague. His complaints about physical ailments increased. Both his farewell service in Delft and his first service in The Hague he had to conduct "in a completely listless spirit and with a sick, feverish body." In spite of his weakened health, he also served in the wider ecclesiastical context during his final years in office.

In 1682 he was accorded a special honor. He was awarded an honorary doctorate by the theological faculty of Utrecht. His good friend Herman Witsius, who in the meantime had become a professor at Utrecht, was responsible for investing him with this honor. He explained with complete conviction that the sole reason for this honor was Saldenus' learning. The motivation for it was not contrived. Although the body of Saldenus' work is overwhelmingly edifying in character, he nevertheless emerges in it as a man of great erudition. His familiarity with the classical authors, the church fathers and medieval writers, the reformers, Puritans and continental pietists was not small. He was certainly not timid in his writing. In addition to his works written for edification, he wrote a handbook on homiletics, and during his ministry in The Hague he published a broadly conceived, two-volume bibliographic review of the classical, humanistic sources of his school days. His literary interests and gifts appear in a series of poems that one encounters in his various writings.[14] Obviously, the piety of this Further Reformation writer harmonized with his literary interests.

On January 26, 1694, he preached in the Nieuwe Kerk of The Hague. Remarkably enough, his text was Job 13:15, "Even if he slay me, will I not still hope?" The sermon was his second-to-the-last,[15] and is included as his final sermon in the posthumous collection *Geesteliken Hooning-Raat* [trans.: *Spiritual Counsel Sweet as Honey*].[16] Pre-eminently in this sermon, Saldenus issues a plea to rely on God's promise. However difficult and "improbable" our circumstances may be, we can place his promise over against them: "This I still believe, and in this I put my hope, for I have found his faithfulness toward me to be true on many occasions; it is his promise."[17] The sermon closes as follows: "And for that very reason he slays us, that we might yet hope in him—in everything that befalls us, whether in body or in soul—and look to him for our eternal and our temporal preservation. . . . Then it is appropriate and comforting for us to be still, if only the Lord alone receives the glory due his name in all things, just as he will receive, and just as we will receive the salvation of our souls. Amen."[18]

Twelve days later, during the night of February 8 to 9, Saldenus slipped away at the age of 67 and received "the salvation of his soul."

---

14. Van den End, *Guiljelmus Saldenus*, 236-38, provides an interesting analysis of this genre and its content.

15. His last sermon was based on the Lord's Day of the catechism that was next in line.

16. The collection was published in Rotterdam, 1695. The sermons were "collected" by "one of his members" and were reproduced as closely as possible as delivered, with the result that "they certainly contain for all practical purposes his own content, words and expressions." Saldenus usually did not write out his sermons. He preached on the basis of notes that he had written out beforehand—in Latin! See *BLGNP*, 3:318.

17. Guiljelmus Saldenus, *Geesteliken Hooning-Raat* (Published posthumously; Rotterdam, 1695. Reprinted; Rumpt, 1998), 582 [erroneously paginated as 382].

18. Ibid., 594.

The Road of Life

Before I turn to a review of Saldenus' piety, I think it would be beneficial to introduce the writing that serves as the most important source of information on this subject, namely *De Wech des Levens*. In light of the various reprints and several German translations that appeared already soon after it was published, its content obviously appealed to many people.[19] One of the first who read it was Claes Jacobszoon Wits, the father of Herman Witsius. In Enkhuizen he wore the mantles of elder and mayor. That he was not only committed to Reformed pietism, but that he must have been a person capable of loving deeply appears from the poem he wrote that is incorporated into one of Saldenus' publications. The fifth stanza is the most typical:

> A Christian soul who reads this poem,
> Truly humbled, he surely cries.
> Then the Spirit makes him his own,
> And draws the tears out of his eyes.

Wit's son Herman was also represented. Just as his father had, he contributed a poem to this edition of Saldenus' work, but then in Latin.

For us the most interesting feature of the book, however, is the unpaginated "Foreword" by Saldenus himself, because it consists of several givens that need to be weighed in reading the work. The first concerns the background of his literary effort. This is embedded, he tells us, in his sermons. To be sure, in *De Wech des Levens* the reader will not encounter word-for-word what he spoke from the pulpit, but certainly "its heart and soul." The second given concerns its stylistic form. Saldenus offers excuses for its "terrible style." On account of the overwhelming "distractions and impediments" that his official work brought, he had insufficient time at his disposal "to pay careful attention" to this matter. But that is not his only reason. He deliberately chose to use "the most child-friendly and most familiar way of speaking." He always wanted "to instruct the spiritually simple more effectively," and not so much "the learned, who know enough already." His trademark was "ordinary composition," and did not lay in a display of "high-flying incisiveness or polished prose."

The following is of more substantive weight content-wise. Here the reader should not think that "the road" indicated here is presented as "much too hard and narrow." In the "pure word of the Lord" this road is always precisely "prescribed as it is." It is not up to anyone "to make it one hair-breadth wider than our Lord and Master himself has walked it." What is remarkable is what Saldenus adds here: "O, if we could with only the least trouble help you out of this world and into heaven, it would not be denied us, but then we would also have to bear our own burden." The author would, therefore, see himself in a somewhat broader way than in the requisite scrupulousness—the precisionism (*praecisitas*) of the Further Reformation—imposed upon him.

---

19. Van den End, *Guiljelmus Saldenus*, 285; van der Haar, *Schatkamer*, 401-2.

Of interest from the perspective of the history of spirituality is the fourth point in his introduction. If the reader might have need of "further instruction," let him then seek counsel from "other edifying tracts" as well as "from this one." Saldenus points in this regard to the works of Puritans such as Daniel and Jeremiah Dijcke, W. Perkins, R. Bolton and G. Amesius.[20] But he also invokes Teellinck for his *Sleutel der Devotie* and his *Noordt-sterre*, Theodorus à Brakel for his *Geestelyke Leven*, "but especially Thomas à Kempis for his *Navolginghe Christi*, who can be very useful to the inexperienced Christian because of his simple spirituality."[21] His own "little works" Saldenus dare not "compare in the least" with all these writers and the body of their works. In this book he only wishes "to teach the ABCs, and the foregoing men will take you appreciably farther."

C. Graafland has researched which themes Saldenus makes use of from the *Imitation*. These are: "the true language of Canaan" that interprets "the mystery of salvation," the costliness of living by faith, the "pursuit of perfection," "heart-felt spirituality," striving "to become more spiritual," suffering according to God's will, intimacy with God, the "spiritual work" of self-denial, and the prevalence of obedience above the experience of sweet communion.[22] In the course of our study, opportunities will present themselves to explore several of these themes more fully. For the time being, I concur with the insight borrowed from Graafland that Saldenus is obviously dependent particularly on the practical, volitional aspects of Thomas' piety.[23]

According to his subtitle, the scope of Saldenus' tract is piety (*pietas*).[24] What he has in mind is an "explanation" of the nature and characteristics of the power of godliness.[25] His treatment bears not just a descriptive, but also a prescriptive character. He wants to instruct, but with the purpose of exposing those who are Christians only in appearance and of strengthening true Christians. He devotes the space needed to do so. Saldenus might call his work "a little tract," but in all its printings it always came to more than four hundred pages, although in a small format. So, he obviously has a lot on his heart. Concerning the format in which he wants to convey his message, he gave thoughtful attention. He composed his book so that in the first two chapters he describes the nature of godliness and in the remaining seventeen its features. The latter he

---

20. For Puritan influence on Saldenus, see *Het puritanisme*, ed. van 't Spijker, et al., 376.

21. See also the line-up of devotional authors with whom Saldenus is compared in the foreword of *Geesteliken Hoonig-Raat*, unpaginated. Also see van den End, *Guiljelmus Saldenus*, 86.

22. Graafland, "De invloed," 65-66. Respectively, the citations of Thomas can be found in Saldenus, *De Wech des Levens*, 32, 222, 279, 316, 322-23, 369-70, 374, 401, and 427-28.

23. Graafland, "De invloed," 67.

24. The subtitle is included in the bibliography and in translation is: *A Short and Simple Explanation of the Nature and Features of the True Power of Godliness. Presented in Order to Shame Merely External Saints and to Awaken and Strengthen Upright Christians.*

25. This formulation is reminiscent of Voetius' *Proeve van de Cracht der Godtsalicheyt* (1628), all the more because Saldenus also describes that "power" as a "proof" or test. See Saldenus, *De Wech des Levens*, 48.

divides into three rubrics: five chapters on "preparatory" features, six on "accompanying" features and six more on "consequent" features.[26]

Saldenus devotes far and away the most attention to the features, which serve simultaneously as tests for distinguishing apparent from true godliness. This distinguishing design appears clearly already in the first two chapters. The criterion that Saldenus discloses in them for separating true from false godliness is instructive. The norm consists of an "inner change" of heart.[27] External Christians have only the "mask" of Christianity. Saldenus wants to "tear off" that mask.[28] In this connection it becomes obvious that Saldenus' term "inner" is not synonymous with "inward." The contrast between external and internal Christians is identical for him with the contrast between "Christians in word" and "Christians in deed."[29] The inner-ness that he has in mind has a concrete external manifestation. But in this Christianity in deed, he is definitely concerned about a reality that is rooted in a renewed heart. To be sure, the inner "bursts out on the outside," but "the power, the core and the essence" of godliness nevertheless lie inside.[30] Saldenus is aware that he is not in a position to describe this "untraceable power" exactly. But that is not the issue. What is important is that the Lord cause "that we may increasingly feel this hidden work in our hearts that defies description."[31] Along these lines he illustrates his intention with a Latin quotation taken from the preface of Thomas' *Imitation* that in translation says, "I would rather experience the sorrow of repentance [*compunctionem*] than know how to define it."[32]

Saldenus explicitly states that in his writing he does not want to treat "the first implanting and infusion" of spiritual life, but "that moving and working of the spiritual life itself that always follows and flows from the first coming to life."[33] His subject, therefore, is not regeneration in the strict sense, but the practice of godliness that flows from it. The practice that he presents in this context is, as we saw, definitely not *purely* inner, yet it is certainly overwhelmingly inner and affective in character. This inner-ness determines its authenticity. "A soft, slightly tearful little stirring of this life is more precious than ten thousand merely external prayers." The tiniest little drop of "spiritual power" is immeasurably more pleasing to God than meeting all external obligations.[34]

For this reason one must pay careful attention to the "movements of the Spirit" that a person "feels" within "from time to time." Without referring to Teellinck, Saldenus here follows exactly the same line of thought that we saw in *Sleutel der Devotie*. In no case should a person "stand grumbling" against such

---

26. Saldenus, *De Wech des Levens*, 49, 193-94, 386-97.
27. Ibid., 6.
28. Ibid., 9. Compare 29.
29. Ibid.
30. Ibid., 32.
31. Ibid., 33.
32. *Imitatio*, 1.1, in *Opera*, 2:6.
33. Saldenus, *De Wech des Levens*, 35. On Saldenus' view of regeneration, see van den End, *Guiljelmus Saldenus*, 46-49.
34. Saldenus, *De Wech des Levens*, 41.

inner stirrings and "extinguish or deaden" them. Rather, one must affirm them. That Saldenus takes this position is because he does not regard them as the subject's emotions, but as active contacts by the Holy Spirit. "When you sometimes feel that you are being so inwardly compelled[35]—I cannot explain how—to pray, confess, shed tears, or something else, remember that such things happen from the Holy Ghost." At such times one is best served by hurrying "immediately to an out-of-the-way corner" in order to give expression to whatever the Spirit is laying on one's heart. If one does not, then the Spirit withdraws and allows such a person "simply to lie like a stone and a block." If one takes such a "first stirring" seriously, however, the Spirit "will bestow further power" to do what he motivates.[36]

Toward the end of the chapter in which Saldenus handles prayer,[37] he returns to these movements of the Spirit. There he explains that despite their "faulty prayers," believers still possess "enough evidence" to be assured of the Spirit of prayer. This assurance always rests not "in the external expression of words, but in the experience of the inner gripping and inspiring of the heart." The most impoverished prayer, even the feeblest sigh, is already enough. "Are you unable to pray? You can always sigh, can you not?[38] Well, that is also pleasing to God as long as it comes from his Spirit. . . . Yes, even if it takes sighing because you cannot sigh, that, too, God will not reject."[39] Saldenus wants to esteem even the least and smallest if only it is genuinely an inner expression, that is, if it comes from the Holy Spirit.

Two matters are clear to us. The first is that the godliness that Saldenus considers has deep roots in the inner life. The second is that this inner life does not constitute the source for creating godliness. It is nothing more and nothing less than the point of connection for the Holy Spirit, the point where he reaches and touches the human heart.

Before I turn to a discussion of a few select chapters from *De Wech des Levens*, one other matter deserves attention in this introductory material. I have in mind the question of how the working of the Holy Spirit is related to the Scriptural word. Because in Saldenus' tract this relationship is more implicit than explicit, I call attention to a passage in which he addresses it extensively by way of exception. It is a selection in which the knowledge of the duties of godliness is described. This knowledge is the fruit of word and Spirit. The Spirit is its "inner

---

35. That is to say, "enticed" or "drawn." See N. van Wijk, *Franck's etymologisch Woordenboek der Nederlandsche taal* (The Hague, 1912), entry on "*tokkelen*."

36. Saldenus, *De Wech des Levens*, 47-48.

37. Ibid., 161-93, "Van den Geest der Ghebeden." The chapter belongs to the section on qualities that precede the exercise of godliness. These constitute its presupposition. Saldenus includes among them holy despair, knowledge of duty, an inner principle, willingness to pray in the Spirit. To these he devotes chapters 3 through 7, respectively.

38. The personal pronouns "gij" [formal "you"] and "jij" [informal "you"], that in Saldenus' seventeenth century grammatical usage have the same emotional impact, are regularly used interchangeably, as they are here. On the relation of the two, see A. van Loey, *Schönfelds historische grammatica van het Nederlands: Klankleer, vormleer, woordvorming* (Zutphen, 1970), 137-38; C. G. N. de Vooys, *Nederlandse spraakkunst* (7th edition; Groningen, 1967), 78-79.

39. Saldenus, *De Wech des Levens*, 192-93.

cause" and the word its "external" cause. Precisely in this connection of word and Spirit Saldenus finds the normative characteristic for distinguishing true spiritual knowledge from "all spiritual fanaticism and willful conceitedness." If knowledge is not derived from God's word, it is useless.[40] Obviously, the Spirit draws from no other source than from the word. When this is absent, the result is fanaticism. The Spirit produces knowledge whose content is always shaped by the biblical word.

One must not ignore Saldenus' adjective "external." In this context the term is not to be taken disparagingly, by way of contrast with the context where he critically separates the inner fruit of godliness from a merely externalized form of godliness. Rather, in the external word tied to the Holy Spirit he sees the guarantee given by which the inner experience is protected from becoming subjective spiritualism. That this emphasis appears explicitly so infrequently is no basis for reproaching Saldenus. It is simply explainable in terms of his audience. The readership at which he is aiming does not consist of spiritual fanatics, but mostly of unspiritual external Christians. He had no need of instructing them on the correlation of word and Spirit. The message that he wants to direct to them is one in which all the emphasis falls on the inner working of the Spirit. The position that Saldenus takes here needs to be kept in mind in everything that follows.

In order to explain Saldenus' piety more fully, I select as points for our attention especially the chapters on the life of faith (chapter 8), intimacy with God (chapter 14), spiritual joy (chapter 15) and longing for heaven (chapter 19).

The Life of Faith

The chapter entitled "The Life of Faith" is the first of six that Saldenus devotes to the features of godliness.[41] In this material the boundaries between true faith and counterfeit faith are once again delineated. Some are Christians by profession, others by conviction. The first-named folk "believe that they believe." They give this impression "without having any inner working and influence of the Holy Spirit that would bind them to Christ, wherein the life of faith consists and which they have never felt or experienced." From this sentence it is immediately apparent that for Saldenus true faith "consists" of being closely tied to Christ, which comes about by the working of the Spirit. This is further emphasized when he writes that counterfeit Christians "are not rooted in him in the depths of their souls." In order to illustrate this, he appeals to an example drawn from the field of botany. "Just as a little sucker shoot superficially sprouts on a tree without being deeply joined to it and yet draws vital sap from it, so it is with a counterfeit Christian, who in being only superficially attached to Christ draws a little spiritual strength from him."[42] In such people faith is not a

---

40. Ibid., 83.

41. The "accompanying" features consist, in addition to the life of faith, of enjoyment, pursuit of perfection, spirituality of heart, steadfastness and the display of God's glory, and are found in chapters 8 through 13, respectively.

42. Saldenus, *De Wech des Levens*, 203-4.

"*hypostasis*," not a reality, but purely "window dressing." In true faith a person lives in Christ and "has become one with him in spirit."[43]

False faith knows nothing of this. It merely uses Christ when necessary. Saldenus compares it to "fire buckets" that people stow away as long "as things are fine," but run to get as soon as danger appears. That is the way they treat Christ. As long as a person is "fat and happy," he does not give the Savior a second thought. "But as soon as a person is laid up in bed and the soul wrestles with the prospect of death . . . , all Holland is in peril; then Christ has to come to the rescue." By contrast, true faith cannot bear to be without him for a moment, but is constantly fed and nourished by him.[44]

Whenever Saldenus thereafter writes further about the nature of true faith, he introduces a motif that is characteristic of his own experience of piety. Namely, the life of faith brings "Christ and heaven, which otherwise are so remote, close to you in your heart." That which seems to be reserved for the future "is displayed as being present," as proof of those things that cannot be seen. The eternal life that believers anticipate is therefore no other life than the life "that they already have, albeit only in part." Having it is still only partial, but that did not stop Saldenus from positing that through faith heaven is unlocked and the way is opened "to see the things that are behind the curtain." To this he adds the arresting question: "Are you not curious to know what the joy of the angels and the blessedness of the saints above are like?" He has a ready answer: "Only believe, and you will both see and feel them."[45] Although he emphatically announces that faith is confirmation of what we do not yet see, he at the same time explains that faith leads to a unique sort of affective contemplation.

Saldenus warns his readers emphatically to forsake unbelief, the "fountain of all other sins," and he arouses them to pursue the life of faith with all their strength.[46] He wants to be their guide in this regard. He gives them five mileposts. The first is healthy fear before God's judging law. "This is where your faith must begin." For the law "serves as that little crack in the door of grace that you see is open and that you take seriously as it is laid down for you." Numerous illustrations make this plain. No one "lives this life without pain." And nothing drives sailors to the harbor, says Saldenus using an image that would have spoken to the seafaring people of Enkhuizen, more than "the waves and winds of a storm." In the same way, God's accusations drive the soul to the arms of Christ.[47] The second marker is the conviction that a person is more apt to believe the needier she is. So, let no one think that she is too destitute. "Turn that just around and say to yourself, 'I must and I will [believe] precisely because I am so impoverished.'" A vessel that is completely empty is the one most disposed to receive oil. "If you have nothing at all, you have exactly the right currency for which Christ offers himself for sale."[48] The third is that a person must "impress"

---

43. Ibid., 204.
44. Ibid., 207-8. Compare 78, where Saldenus writes that the upright believer would rather feel "one little spark of Christ's love" than all the pleasures of the world.
45. Ibid., 211.
46. Ibid., 213.
47. Ibid., 214.
48. Ibid., 215-16.

on his heart "the completely unique" merits of Christ and "be refreshed" all day long with the thought of his gracious promises. These promises always constitute the "testament" of the Father, in which it is recorded that Christ is ours. "And when you see the promises of his grace recorded there, do not think that they apply to anyone else than specifically to you. And remember that he says directly to you Peter or Paul, Ann or Mary, 'Blessed are you, O poor of spirit.'" Matters are just as personal at the Lord's table. "Remember that Christ is speaking especially to you when he says, 'You who eat, you who drink, will I bless.'"[49] The fourth point is that one must keep the word of God without reservation, without letting oneself be diverted from it in any situation. His word is always infallibly true, and God would not be God if he did not bring to pass what he promised.[50] Finally, one must daily keep God's faithfulness in mind, for by it he shows us that he keeps his word.[51]

As one of the benchmarks by which believers have to evaluate themselves, Saldenus names the concern that they have for their faith. "An appropriately godly person would rather lose this world than his faith, for without the former he can still live spiritually but without faith he cannot."[52] In the margin he includes a citation from the *Imitation* that, in translation, reads, "The self-reflective person places spiritual concern for self above all other concerns."[53] The quotation suggests associations. Thomas' interest is not concern for faith, but it lays emphasis on one's own motives in interaction with others (*consideratio propria*). But the conclusion of Thomas' chapter heads in the direction of Saldenus' point: "God alone, the Eternal and Everlasting One who fulfills all things, is the soul's comfort and the heart's true joy."

Saldenus completes his discussion of the life of faith in a remarkable passage. He also finds this to be a mark of authentic faith, namely that it throws itself "entirely on Christ's favor" even when he hides grace behind wrath. It is a sign of true faith to regard him "as our greatest and only Friend" even then. "To be able to follow a wrathful Christ as well, that is grace!"[54] The key to this faith at all costs is that it clings only to the promises of God and in doing so remains assured of a good outcome without seeing or understanding what that might be.[55] Saldenus considers this to be essential for faith. "Do you have to see it right in front of your eyes? Then you do not need to believe it and you do not in fact believe it, for faith is the assurance of things not seen. Here you must not want to live by sight, but by faith." Faith is true to itself "when it merely trusts and works against all appearances." Should you, to the contrary, proceed on the basis of relying on God's promises only when the circumstances for doing so are favorable, "why would you even begin with the whole project of your salvation?" What other possibility is available for doing so than "the promise of

49. Ibid., 216-17.
50. Ibid., 217-18.
51. Ibid., 219.
52. Ibid., 222.
53. *Imitatio*, 2.5, in *Opera*, 2:67.
54. Saldenus, *De Wech des Levens*, 224.
55. Ibid., 226. Compare Saldenus, *Geesteliken Hooning-Raat*, 558 and 582.

God's gracious help?"[56] Saldenus' position is clear. Faith depends not on highly promising circumstances, but relies without reservation on the God of many promises.

This promise-based faith applies not only for personal salvation, but also for the further reformation of church and folk. In this regard Saldenus also points to a great deal of hesitant, minimal faith. "If anything is to be reformed in our land and in our church, it is certain that it will not succeed as long as men too often and too stubbornly think it cannot succeed."[57] His rejoinder is resolute: "If our forefathers had not allowed that wonderful and much needed branch of the Reformation to develop when they saw little prospect of it succeeding, as obviously was the case because seemingly the wrath and rage of the whole world was directed against it, where would we in our land and church be sitting today? But, no, they paid attention only to the will and the promises of God, truly lived by faith and paid attention not so much to the things they saw as to those that they could not see."[58]

Two features emerge in this part of the material. The first is the unambiguous emphasis that the essence of faith consists of being united with Christ. The second seems less straightforward. On the one hand Saldenus finds it to be a feature of faith that it is permitted a glimpse into heaven already in the present, and on the other hand he makes a powerful plea for faith at all costs that does not see but that relies purely on the promises of God. Apparently the one emphasis is in tension with the other. However, Saldenus gives no indication of being conscious of any contradiction here. I also think that the contradiction is only apparent and that his two-fold perspective is consistent. With his emphasis on the promise-based nature of salvation and the corresponding at-all-costs nature of faith, he articulates that faith has no other basis than the promise. This is the basis for the tight grip and the solid foundation of "blindly believing." As far as the "confirming" fruit that is inherent in faith is concerned, Saldenus does not hesitate to emphasize that God's promises contain so many indications of reality, that the eye of faith gives access to what is promised and kept in store. That this occurs in only a fragmentary way does not detract from the fact that it really happens.

Intimacy with God

After Saldenus has treated the features associated with the exercise of godliness, he begins to discuss "the glorious and reassuring sprouts of that scrupulous and godly life." Among them intimacy with God takes first place.[59] He describes it as "familiarity or sweet friendship with God and his Son Jesus Christ."[60] This definition provides immediate clarification of the at first glance mystifying fact

---

56. Ibid., 227.
57. Ibid., 226.
58. Ibid., 227-28.
59. The other features belonging to this category are: spiritual joy, love for the godly, hatred of the ungodly, contempt for the world and longing for heaven—respectively treated in chapters 15-19.
60. Saldenus, *De Wech des Levens*, 386.

that Saldenus positions the subject of intimacy with God here, after the subject of faith, and that he assigns it to those features that flow from the practice of godliness. The reason for this is not that he wants to deny the usual intertwining of fellowship with Christ and faith. We have already established that he regards union with Christ as the essence of faith. This implies that believing fellowship with Christ constitutes not the fruit but the root of godliness. But then, how can he nevertheless call intimacy a fruit of godliness? He can do so because by that intimacy he has something else in mind than the union of faith. What he wants to emphasize is that union with Christ brings about a profoundly moving expression of fellowship in which a person experiences what a person believes. This experience of "fellowship" has the features of friendship and intimacy that translate into totally familiar communion.[61] In this condition fellowship springs to life in godliness and is gradually deepened. From this perspective Saldenus adds precision to his explanation in order to posit that this intimacy, as the fruit of the Holy Spirit who effects union with Christ, unites us more and more with God through "the manifold exercise of godliness" and permits "an intimate communion with him" in which the heart "becomes inclined to all that is holy."[62]

Saldenus works out the motif of intimacy as follows. Between God and the believer, and especially between Christ and the believer, the Holy Spirit creates "a much more tightly knotted friendship and love than can be established or even contemplated than those between a bride and her bridegroom or between husband and wife."[63] In this "mutually sweet and familiar interaction," God and the soul become "like two loved ones and close friends who have been involved with each other for a very long time, an involvement proceeding from the aforementioned union."[64] Such familiar communion is not limited to exceptional times, but for the right-minded believer it is much rather an "ordinary and usual exchange," as when Moses conversed with God as "with his Friend."[65] Christ always lives in believers by means of faith. These "spiritual marriages" and

---

61. Although Saldenus' federal views are more Voetian than Coccejaan (see van den End, *Guiljelmus Saldenus*, 42), this motif of friendship is striking, since it is so typical of Coccejus. For Coccejus as well, this friendly relationship implied familiar communion (*commercium familiare*). See W. J. van Asselt, *Amicitia Dei: Een onderzoek naar de struktuur van de theologie van Johannes Coccejus (1603-1669)* (Ede, 1988), 135-36. Did Saldenus perhaps stand in the same Augustinian "friendship tradition" as Coccejus? Consider W. J. van Asselt, *Johannes Coccejus: Portret van een zeventiende-eeuwse theoloog op oude en nieuwe wegen* (Heerenveen, 1997), 254. On Saldenus' sympathy for Coccejus as a person, see van den End, *Guiljelmus Saldenus*, 221.

62. Saldenus, *De Wech des Levens*, 387.

63. Ibid., 388. Remarkably, Andrew Gray (1633-1656) employed the same image: "Faith is that golden and precious knot that doth eternally knit the hearts of these precious friends [!] together." *The Works of Andrew Gray* (Aberdeen, 1839), 19. Compare P. H. van Harten, *De prediking van Ebenezer en Ralph Erskine* (The Hague, 1986), 13.

64. Saldenus, *De Wech des Levens*, 388. In the middle Dutch, the word *"caer"* [appearing in this quotation] means "precious" or "beloved" from the Latin *carus*. J. Verdam, *Middelnederlandsch Handwoordenboek* (The Hague, 1981). Apparently this word was still in use during the seventeenth century.

65. Saldenus, *De Wech des Levens*, 388-89. In Exodus 33:11, to which Saldenus refers, it is not stated that Moses spoke as a friend with God, but that God did so with Moses. It is certainly in question whether Moses' experience was for him an "ordinary occurance."

"heavenly familiarity" Saldenus considered absolutely necessary for every Christian person. "We must always be married to Christ if we would be saved by him."[66] In a later connection we will note that Saldenus means to qualify this experience, at least in its affective dimensions. But in this context he complains first of all that "that inwardly sweet treatment of the heart regarding Christ, and of Christ regarding the heart, that we experience better than we can describe," is not to be found in most people. In his judgment all superficiality, which is a stranger to such intimacy, is of no benefit. "From now on you must walk with Christ in heaven, and while you are still here on earth you must already conduct all eating, speaking, embracing, kissing and taking meals with others as being the sweetest of exchanges between familiar friends."[67] At least here Saldenus is not talking about sporadic contemplation, but about continuous living in heaven that implies an intimate involvement with Christ.

Additionally, Saldenus with some emphasis warns against a communion that degenerates into ordinary amicability by becoming mere routine. Then "the sacred custom of spiritual exercises is shamefully misused and its objective is perverted." By contrast, these exercises ought to proceed as between "a well-married couple whose love is not diminished by ordinary communion but rather grows and increases." Saldenus attaches a little couplet, possibly of his own making:

> "For, friendship that contempt reveals
> Was never based on good appeals."[68]

In order to arouse his readers to that "sweet and pleasing communion," he injects the following exclamation: "O! To be able to wrap sweet Jesus in my arms, to be able to kiss him, to be enveloped in return by all the flames of his love, and to be addressed by him with names like 'my dearest,' 'my beloved,' 'my beauty,' 'my dove,' 'my sister who has stolen my heart' and to see his smile—who upon considering these things would not be inflamed at the thought of being able to enjoy these expressions of the Lord's love?"[69]

The blush of Bernard is obvious all over this language from Song of Solomon. Both its intimacy and its intensity are reminiscent, in an exceptional way, of Teellinck's mystical highlights that bear tints of Bernard. Just as is the case with Bernard and Teellinck, Saldenus considers intimacy with Jesus to be a miraculous strengthening of faith. In the same way as for the abbot of Clairvaux, for Saldenus the mystical experience is on the one hand the fruit of faith (*credo ut experiar!*) and is on the other hand an aide to faith, given in order to strengthen the assurance of faith. "How often do you not search your soul," Saldenus asks, "because you are not as fully assured of your salvation as you would like to be?" Saldenus assists such seekers out of their impasse: "Come;

---

66. Ibid., 391.
67. Ibid., 393.
68. Ibid., 395-96.
69. Ibid., 398. For a related passage—in a sermon, no less!—see Saldenus, *Geesteliken Hooning-Raat*, 69.

here is some advice for you." One receives certainty especially by being "familiar" with Christ. The person who has this Bridegroom as a friend shall undoubtedly come "to the wedding feast." And what can be more pleasing for someone than that "peaceful communion" that already here below is a prelude to the wedding feast?[70] In commending this communion Saldenus makes an unmistakable play on the words of one of Thomas' aphorisms without actually referencing the *Imitation* in this instance: "Just like living without him is nothing else than suffering the pain of hell, so will his fellowship here begin to provide you with the joy of heaven."[71]

In order to acquire the means for reaching the "bliss" of this spiritual fellowship, it is necessary in the first place to be busy "frequently" in "the work of the Lord." Saldenus understands that included in this are the "customs" of reading, listening, confessing[72] and praying. "Like Anna, do not neglect going to the temple, for often that place is well suited for meeting your Christ and he invites you to come there." By being "involved" with many others on a frequent basis, even "strangers" become "very close."[73] The second means is that whenever Jesus descends into our hearts, we give him a proper reception. Just as we would do for those whose friendship is dear to us, those "in every way regarded as beloved," we must work especially hard at our relationship with Christ. "You know what food tastes best to him, namely a humble and lowly heart." In accentuating this plea for humility, Saldenus included a short quote from the *Imitation* in the margin in which Thomas calls it a great gift to be able to commune (*conversari*) with Jesus. For this activity a person must be humble and content, devout and calm, (*humilis et pacificus, devotus et quietus*).[74] The pietist obviously resonates well with the Modern Devotion's spirituality.

The third means that Saldenus offers is a "very exact and precise" observance of the "sabbath." In this connection a person must not allow himself to be misled into disputes about the question "of whether this may be done or that may be done" on the day. Rather, in simple obedience he must observe the "expected exercises." For those duties we are given a whole day fifty-two times a year! "Judge for yourself: if you were involved with someone for an hour or an hour and a half each day, and then if you did nothing else for fifty-two entire days each year except speak and interact with him, would great familiarity between him and you not develop from all of this?"[75] From this illustration, can it be ascertained that Saldenus normally gave an average of an hour and a half to daily

---

70. Saldenus, *De Wech des Levens*, 398-99.

71. Ibid., 401. Compare *Imitatio*, 2.8, in *Opera*, 2:71. "Esse sine Iesu gravis est infernus: et esse cum Iesu dulcis paradisus." Further along Saldenus explicitly references this same chapter in the *Imitatio*.

72. The meaning of "confessing" here is not clear. Does it mean confessing one's guilt, or confessing God's name and worshiping? The reference to Anna argues for the latter.

73. Saldenus, *De Wech des Levens*, 401.

74. Ibid., 402. Compare *Imitatio*, 2.8, in *Opera*, 2:72. Bernard views the term "*caelestis conversatio*" as involving the very same "*unio mystica*" experience. See *DD*, 10:27, in *SW*, 1:120.

75. Saldenus, *De Wech des Levens*, 403.

meditations? Whatever that might be, he considered Sunday as a day on which a person did "nothing else" than concentrate "continuously on the Lord."[76]

As the fourth means, Saldenus advises to hold "conversations often" and alone with God. For this purpose we can best "retreat to a solitary place or, as Christ commands, to our inner chamber," there "to pour out" our hearts to the Father.[77] Whenever God "and the soul are so at one that they see things in completely the same way, then heart and tongue burst forth together and express without any restraint their full emotions and affections." This advice concerning the exercise of such soliloquies (*soliloquium*) is reinforced with quotations from Jerome and Bernard.[78]

What this chapter has yielded for us is, in the first place, the demonstration that for Saldenus union with Christ in faith constitutes the food supply for a piety that yields intimate and affectionate communion. The language of the Song of Solomon in which this exchange with Christ is cast is in tone and tenor here and there related to the bridal mysticism of Bernard. The second thing that strikes us is that Saldenus regards this intimacy as inherent in godliness as such. He does not restrict it to a special category or exceptional heights of religious experience. Bernard's "rare hour of short duration" is not to be found in this understanding of communion. The third thing that strikes us is the tint of Bernard's interplay between faith and communion found here. While on the one hand faith in Christ constitutes the source of communion, on the other hand faith is strengthened and assured through it. Fourthly, what is striking here is à Kempis' idea that Christ's entering and remaining in one's heart is promoted by humility.

Spiritual Joy

It cannot be accidental that the chapter on spiritual joy[79] immediately follows the section on intimacy with God. There Saldenus already characterized this intimacy as "a heavenly joy." To be sure, the word "joy" appears throughout Saldenus' tract. That the chapter on the life of faith is followed by the theme of the "enjoyment" of the godly life's spiritual exercises says a great deal.[80] Just as the life of faith is obviously and directly associated with enjoyment by Saldenus, he also connects intimacy with joy.

Saldenus regards joy as a fruit of the Holy Spirit. Its object is "fellowship with Christ."[81] This constitutes the difference from the enjoyment of which he spoke in the foregoing. Then it was about the joy found in spiritual exercises or devotions, but now he is dealing with the joy found in "God and his Son

---

76. Ibid., 403-4. Saldenus says that he does not want to work out his views on the sabbath more fully at this point. He refers to Hoornbeeck's *Des Heeren-Dags Heiliging* (1655).

77. Saldenus, *De Wech des Levens*, 405. Compare page 256, where Saldenus remarks, "Of necessity, we must also have our private devotions." See also page 235, where he appeals for the importance of a household to gather at least in the morning and in the evening for the purpose of reading, praying and singing "a Psalm or two."

78. Ibid.

79. Ibid., 410-34.

80. Ibid., 228-65.

81. Ibid., 411.

himself."[82] Saldenus describes the essence of this "spiritual joy" as "exaltation of the heart," a term strongly reminiscent of Bernard's "rapture" (*raptus*). The immediately following part of his description also seems to point in that direction. According to Saldenus, this is about "sublime and exalted matters," about which it is "inadequate" to offer the simple explanation of "those inner experiences that can be realized and felt by God's children."[83] Bernard addresses both their sublimity and their inexpressible nature.

Despite the great distance between the experience and its explanation, Saldenus still wants to say "something" about this joy. The first thing he says is that the experience of it consists of an overwhelming sense of God's favor. Then God allows us to see not only "his neck, but also his face," and he no longer reveals himself as the strict judge but also as the friendly father. The second is that it constitutes "such a possession and preoccupation of our hearts with heavenly feelings" that by comparison all earthly interests fall away. The soul reaches the point of being as filled with it as a container filled to the brim. This experience is nothing else than "to become drunken with the overflowing abundance of God's house (Psalm 36)."[84] The third way in which Saldenus approaches spiritual joy is with the explanation that it consists of contempt for everything that would otherwise be able to unsettle the soul, because "the strong rays of the light of God's grace cause all fogginess of this world to flee and disappear."[85]

Besides being related to Bernard's idea of *raptus*, as we have seen, the distance from it also comes to light in what follows. Saldenus stresses this in order to emphasize that this joy can be experienced "at all times and in all circumstances." It does not consist of a short-lived, "fleeting" emotion, but is "sustained, even eternally enduring" gladness.[86] Saldenus feels that some further explanation is desirable at this point. So, he hastens to clarify what he means. What he has in mind is that the "possession" of joy permanently belongs to the life of faith. Its "actuality" is something else again. As long as complete glorification is still unrealized, the "actual" feeling of joy "is certainly sometimes somewhat absent and diminished." But those admittedly sporadic, darker moments do not detract from the basic disposition. For even though believers sometimes "are overshadowed by a cloud of sadness," their joy remains their "governing attitude or *elementum praedominans*." Above all, the godly even find in their sadness "the substance and occasion" for their joy, "just as Paul very nicely harmonizes the two when he says, 'always afflicted, yet always [sic.] joyful.'" Saldenus finds his position supported by a quotation from Augustine: "Let the convert ever lament, but let him be joyful regarding his lamenting."[87]

The remarkable fact about this state of affairs is that joy triumphs. It certainly is not felt without interruption, but it is always available. Joy is not the

---

82. Ibid., 412.
83. Ibid.
84. Ibid., 413. Compare 431, where Saldenus writes that the child of God receives tangible and emotional impressions "in appetitu sensitivo."
85. Ibid.
86. Ibid., 414.
87. Ibid., 415-16. I cannot confirm the authenticity of this quote from Augustine.

exception, but the rule. Our preliminary conclusion, therefore, is that for Saldenus joy is not reserved for the pinnacle of mystical experience, but that it is bestowed with the life of faith. This comprises the significant difference with the *raptus* experience identified with Bernard and even some of Saldenus' own contemporaries. Even though the uninterrupted experience of joy is something still anticipated for Saldenus, he nonetheless believes that the godly "always can and must find their joy" in their fellowship with their Savior. They have good reason for so doing. For the King brings them into his inner chamber, where they report that they are delighted and overjoyed in his inexpressible love (Song of Solomon 1:4).[88] Spending time in the Bridegroom's inner chamber is not tied here by Saldenus to some special, mystical experience, but it represents the realities in which believers always share, whether they feel them or not. While Saldenus describes joy as "being uplifted" and considers it to be a fruit of the Spirit, he does not have in mind an episode that suddenly overwhelms believers as much as an underlying disposition or condition from which they can and must always benefit. They may "at one and the same time" be considered somber "as well as overwhelmed with heartfelt joy."[89]

Saldenus does not have a good word to say for Christians that "constantly go around hanging their heads and with sour and sad faces." These are people who always "endure their miserable existence with sighing and groaning almost without ever displaying a properly joyful expression." That this is a rather common occurrence among believers he considers a shameful and thankless "weakness." They neglect the joy "that nevertheless is their own right and inheritance, purchased by the blood of God himself."[90] They shortchange the "loving inner voice of their Savior and his Spirit." Saldenus calls this a "terrible disdain" of heavenly grace.[91] By behaving that way people give weight to the slander that "true religion," by which he means the Reformed faith, is beset with "difficulties and dreadful problems."[92] The positive alternative is that "joyful eyes" will entice our "closest neighbors" to serve God.[93] So, joy makes sense apologetically and possesses missionary powers.

That spiritual joy can be appreciated in a very emotionally restrained way, Saldenus does not doubt. This does not detract from the fact that he ascribes the lack to joy to a repression of the emotional life. The source of dismal, languishing Christianity he thinks lies in the misunderstanding that feelings of God's favor should be the basis of joy. However, "the presence of grace for you is not based on anything that you feel; O, no—for you can still certainly have grace, even if you cannot feel it." For that reason people need to ask themselves whether, despite the absence of feeling any grace, they can still "wish, sigh, and

---

88. Ibid., 416. The same text from Song of Solomon is cited on page 324 in order to characterize "the spirituality of the heart." By this Saldenus means that the godly are not satisfied with the external form (of Word and sacrament), but that they are looking for its "heart and core," which inheres in tasting God's love.

89. Ibid., 415.

90. The patripassionism coloring this formulation is remarkable.

91. Ibid., 421.

92. Ibid., 422.

93. Ibid., 426.

pray." If that is the case, they already have "big reasons" for being joyful in the Lord.[94] Saldenus considered this lack of feeling as the first means of strengthening spiritual joy. The second means is for people to submit in all things to the will of God. In the spirit of Thomas, whose *Imitation* he cited in the margin, Saldenus writes, "If God wills that things go so badly for you, will this for yourself. If he wills that things go well for you, will that as well, for this will make you joyful and content always."[95] The third means is for people to maintain as the "highest and only purpose and goal" of all their desires, fellowship with Christ. "Divided aims diminish the fruit of his presence."[96]

The fourth means that Saldenus identifies does not seem to harmonize entirely with the way in the previous context he extolled joy as a benefit that one could always possess. To be specific, here he writes that a person should not tie God "all too much" to a definite time for granting us joy. One must never want to experience it "per force." God does not tolerate that his creature "would prescribe such a thing" for him. One is better served by waiting on the Lord, as watchmen wait on the morning (Psalm 130:6) and as "the afflicted waiting for the angel to stir the waters of Bethesda" (John 5:3).[97] This passage sheds light on the definitely two-sided dimension of Saldenus' approach to joy. On the one side the joy kept in the heart is always available and the believer, by way of an imperative, is encouraged to make use of it. On the other side the feeling of joy is completely a gift of the Spirit, a gift simply to be awaited.

In concluding this chapter, Saldenus provides two criteria by which people can test whether joy is "properly spiritual." The first norm is particularly significant. He considers it to be a guarantee of authenticity when, in the complete absence of any "external reasons" for joy, they can "become aware" of joy "even at such times" when "everything seems to turn against them" and nothing else emerges than adversity in the form of "terrible mists and storms of sadness and dismay." While the external circumstances give every reason for discouragement, therefore, to be joyful in spite of them is the secret of true joy. However, believers themselves do not control this joy-in-spite-of-circumstances. Rather, it is the case that they "often feel uplifted—as it were beyond themselves—in holy joy, without knowing how or why but only that they see the love of Christ clearly depicted for them."[98] This involves a passive occurrence, therefore, whereby people understand in an unexplainable way that they have been lifted above themselves and their malaise. At the same time, however, the believer is completely absorbed in this experience in the sense that he fixes his attention on the love of Christ. While people do not control this joy-in-spite-of-circumstances and while it defies conceptual explanation, it is nonetheless dispensed during consciously pursued devotional activity. A gracious connection exists between joy and concentration on Christ. Whoever looks away from self

---

94. Ibid., 427.

95. Ibid., 427-28. Compare *Imitatio*, 3.15, in *Opera*, 2:173. "Tua voluntas mea sit; et mea voluntas tuam semper sequatur et optime ei concordet. Sit mihi unum velle et nolle tecum."

96. Saldenus, *De Wech des Levens*, 428-29.

97. Ibid., 429-30.

98. Ibid., 432-33.

and their situation and looks toward Christ alone, finds joy. This constitutes the guarantee of validity for Saldenus. To this he immediately appends his second criterion. When people are increasingly ready to serve the "Savior" because of joy, he considers this to be a "clear proof" of authenticity. "Joy and obedience must be partners here."[99] For Saldenus the mystical and the ethical components are bound together. The joy in which people rise above daily circumstances constitutes, simultaneously, the stimulus to humble themselves in daily discipleship. This twofold content has its unity in the love of and for the one and only Christ.

The yield that our analysis of Saldenus' chapter on joy produces consists first of all of the insight that he regards joy as inherent in the life of faith. Even the joyful experiences of "being uplifted" he does not regard, as does Bernard, as sporadic exceptions. Rather, for him they constitute experiences that are permanently available to all believers, at least in principle. While the language of the Song of Solomon with which Saldenus describes these experiences displays features of Bernard's writing and while he repeatedly cites Bernard in another connection, my observation is that he does not do so in the context of discussing "being uplifted." This is not accidental. The great joy that is awakened through fellowship with Christ is much more a part of "normal" Christian living for Saldenus than for Bernard. It is also significant, then, that for Saldenus admission to the inner chamber of the Bridegroom is not considered to be a special privilege, but rather the dwelling place of all true Christians.

The second matter that jumps out in Saldenus' exposé on joy is that he appeals to joy so convincingly. The somberness of his own situation to which he alludes he considers to be far less significant than life with Christ. The third matter is the striking manner in which he describes the nature of joy in-spite-of-circumstances. The fourth thing we note is the two-fold apologetic and evangelistic motivation for Saldenus' plea for joy.

Longing for Heaven

The last chapter of *De Wech des Levens* is devoted to "the longing for heaven."[100] Saldenus has it follow the chapter on forsaking the world. This last-named chapter, remarkably enough, contains no quotations from à Kempis, although it is certainly developed in his spirit. Especially its concluding passage sounds like à Kempis. In it Saldenus posits that believers should of course be disposed to serve God and their neighbors, but that at the same time they must see to it that they forsake "that wearisome busyness" of the world.[101] He embroiders on the last theme in his chapter on longing for heaven.[102] This longing is brought about by the Holy Spirit, but at the same time it is motivated by the imperfection of "the things of the world." Because the believer finds no

---

99. Ibid., 433-34.
100. Ibid., 505-31.
101. Ibid., 504.
102. On this material, K. Exalto's study is instructive: *De dood ontmaskerd* (Amsterdam, 1975), 169-77. In it he gives a presentation of Saldenus' book on dying, *Leven uyt de Doodt* (1667).

ultimate satisfaction in them, his heart pursues that which is better. "He longs for heaven because he cannot be satisfied with the earthly." For complete clarity Saldenus add that this longing is fixed on "the perfect possession" of that glory. A "small portion of this enjoyment" God bestows on his own children already here in the present life. The "full measure," however, is "stored up" for the time "of our deliverance and resurrection."[103] As far as perfection is concerned, Saldenus himself is obviously aware that he has to address both dimensions: the deliverance from earthly shackles at the time of death and the resurrection of the body upon the return of Christ. The specifics of heavenly blessedness he does not want "to investigate with precision." He only wants to say about it that it does not consist so much of the place where the blessed will find themselves as of the "indescribable sweetness" that they will enjoy. This is an "enjoyment" that flows out of "the loving contemplation of God's face and the full enjoyment of fellowship with Jesus Christ."[104]

The heart of the believer is "compelled" to yearn for this glory.[105] Through a painful awareness that he does not yet possess the highest good, this desire is awakened as "a powerful gasping and panting of the heart for that promised fruit." Saldenus compares it with a prisoner who longs for freedom and with a thirsty person who yearns to taste water.[106] For the person to whom this longing is a stranger, no salvation can be expected in Saldenus' opinion. He emphasizes this in the line of a poem:

> That one who for heaven never longs,
> To him heavenly fruit never belongs.[107]

He is emphatically concerned here with an attitude, not merely with an incidental impulse. "So, a flickering little sigh for salvation" is not the "appropriate longing." If it leaves "no enduring impression" on the heart, it might simply arise from "nature" and it is "certainly not to be regarded as an expression of special grace." The saving workings of God's Spirit are not "that superficial," but they "cleave" tightly "to the heart."[108]

Saldenus does not direct his attention only against a weak and fleeting longing for heaven, but also against a "fleshly" perversion of it. One thinks, in this instance, that one's worldly pleasures will continue in heaven. He calls this "taking an entirely wrong turn." In heaven pleasures will be spiritual, just as is the case with the pleasures that believers already have on earth. With joy it will be otherwise, but not a different joy: it will gradually increase, but remain materially the same. "The grace that we experience here on earth is an imperfect heaven, but heaven is nothing other than perfect grace," as he translates an anonymous quotation printed in the margin. That it originates with Bernard is

---

103. Saldenus, *De Wech des Levens*, 505-6. In *Geesteliken Hooning-Raat*, 478, Saldenus develops the same idea.
104. Saldenus, *De Wech des Levens*, 506-7.
105. Ibid., 507.
106. Ibid., 508.
107. Ibid., 511.
108. Ibid., 513.

plausible. In connection with the preceding citation—also in the margin—his name appears: "The reward of glory is that we see God, live with God, live out of God, are present with God and are in God, who will be all and in all."[109]

What Saldenus rejects in this connection is when people long for heaven, but at the same time harbor so much fear for death and the final judgment. To be sure, they want "to be with our dear Lord," but meanwhile "they sit trembling" as soon as "they hear about these two subjects." Apparently they do not understand that precisely these things comprise the way one is admitted to heaven. Otherwise, how could they get into such a panic at the thought "of the Man who comes to announce the time of their coronation?" Saldenus understands very well that by nature we shrink back from death. That happened "even with our Savior." But, where there is a longing for fellowship with Christ, there the fear of death is "bound and vanquished," so that "unavoidably dying" becomes "willingly dying." For that reason the "greatest saints" prayed to "the King of Terror" more than they feared him. They always knew that they "could satisfy their hunger and meet the cost of heaven in no other way than by him." A Christian would simply rather die a thousand deaths in order to be united with God, than live a thousand years without "his soul's Beloved." People, who in facing "this Heavenly Messenger would almost rather crawl into their shells," risk living with restricted longings for heaven, at least as long as they do not "try to fight against" their fears.[110] In connection with the coming judgment Saldenus thinks that "an unsettling reverence" is commanded, but that "an unbelieving fear" is misplaced.[111] One imagines that on the matter of the fear of death his readers would have wanted to hear something more. But while Saldenus generally is not sparing with his pastoral application, in this instance it fails to appear. The incidental reference to Jesus' fear in Gethsemane remains a formality, and apparently it does not afford him the opportunity to reach out with pastoral counsel.

Saldenus returns to his main theme, namely longing for heaven. In order to entice to such longing those believers who in this regard appear to be negligent, he introduces a powerful appeal. Christ has prepared eternal treasures, "if only you would desire them." If this inheritance can be had at such a small price, who would not make every attempt to kindle longings for it with a "holy intensity?"[112] The more we "contemplate" this heavenly blessedness, the more we "lose" ourselves in it and the less we "comprehend it or can say anything about it." But it is assured that all tears will "be wiped away" from our eyes and all sickness and pain will "be banished" for eternity.[113] All creation longs for this, "as it were, with a raised head." If even "creatures without souls look for heaven like this," what is more fitting than that we also direct our "sighs" heavenward?[114]

---

109. Ibid., 514-15.
110. Ibid., 515-16.
111. Ibid., 517.
112. Ibid., 517-18.
113. Ibid., 519.
114. Ibid., 521.

Merely the desire for heaven Saldenus already called "half a heaven," for it lets us "sample the sweet flavor" of it now. It is true that the absence of "the fullness of its fruit is a painful experience for the pious person," but for the godly that "hunger" for heaven is nevertheless also a source of joy. Purely the thought of it "often transports a person above herself and in this state of happiness causes extraordinary joy to spring to life."[115] This part of the text is intriguing. It seems to be just like his earlier case that in addition to a constant joy, a special joy exists. The ecstatic and unusual nature of the latter evokes an association with Bernard's idea of rapture (*raptus*). But the text also contains undeniable elements that point to the future. I have in mind, first of all, the adverb "often." Obviously Saldenus considers the joy of experiencing a foretaste of heaven as unusual, but not exceptional and infrequent. The qualification "unusual" does not connote time but intensity. What for Bernard constitutes an exceptional moment is a frequent event for Saldenus. This is the first difference. But there is more. While the foretaste of heaven has an unmistakably contemplative shape for Bernard, in Saldenus' text that is hardly recognizable, at least here. I say "hardly" for it is certainly not entirely absent. One could understand the exclamation with which he explains the sweet foretaste in a contemplative sense: "O! That glorious Jerusalem, that haven of rest that we see before our eyes and that grants God's children such holy pleasures."[116] This exclamation stands precisely in the context of longing. This renders it defensible that Saldenus intends by "we see before our eyes" not mystical contemplation but that he only means our expectation of heaven—always a hopeful prospect. Therefore, although the ecstatic and proleptic nature of Saldenus' experience shows points of contact with Bernard's *raptus*, the two are not identical. Saldenus' experience is neither sporadic nor contemplative. This is the difference.

Typical of Saldanus is that he develops his treatment of the subject by including a number of "aides" for increasingly "sharpening" this longing. To begin with, believers must endeavor to maintain a lively regard for their defects. "Here the 'Old Adam' is the heaviest burden that causes sighing for the relief of heaven," for they understand that there they no longer need "to drag along . . . the painful shackles of their depravity."[117] But it is especially the love for Jesus that intensifies this aching desire. "It cannot be otherwise than that the one you hold dear is the one for whose presence you increasingly long, for the soul longs more for loving than for living." Where one's treasure is, there one's heart is also. With a reference to Wessel Gansfort's *De Oratione*, Saldenus writes that whoever accepts Christ as his eternal "inheritance" never needs to doubt that his heart "will almost break with the desire that he be transported to heaven."[118] So, it is love for Jesus that awakens this longing. However, this does not unfold automatically. To maintain a living desire, one must "frequently" call to mind "the sweetness" that "now and then is already tasted in the piece-meal fellowship

---

115. Ibid., 521-22.
116. Ibid., 521.
117. Ibid., 522-23.
118. Ibid., 524.

with Christ."[119] Although the unusual joy, as we saw, is not a sporadic occurrence for Saldenus, he nevertheless also seems to know that it definitely is not common-place. Such experiences occur "now and then" and are engraved on the memory as proleptic delights that long for still more precisely because of their sporadic and partial nature. For this reason Saldenus adds, "It is impossible, if someone has ever seen a glimmering of God's glorious face, that he will not immediately long for its full sunshine."[120]

Remarkably enough, this quotation gives unambiguous evidence that certainly in this instance Saldenus has something like a contemplative event in mind. To be sure, he speaks carefully of a "glimmering," but one that nevertheless involves the face of God that is seen in glory. The contemplative interpretation is reinforced by what follows in Saldenus' text when he impresses the following on his readers' hearts: "Remember often, then, the excellent things that you already saw to be true at the gate of heaven." He also speaks carefully here about being just outside the gate, but this does not diminish its contemplative character. Whoever has tarried there and been caught up in a glimpse of heaven, will have a burning desire "to be permitted to contemplate all the beauties of the city of God itself." Whoever samples but "one drop of his living water," thirsts for more, "like a panting hart"[121] thirsts for flowing streams. The most striking thing is that Saldenus says that this proleptic experience is one in which a person "truly feels what it is to be united with Christ."[122]

The passage just cited provides the basis for repeating my initial conclusion. However, now it appears that the *enduring* nature of fellowship with Christ is not the only feature. In the eschatological context of longing for heaven, he introduces an experience of fellowship that overtakes the believer "already now," at least *sometimes*. This is an experience not only whose contemplative nature but also whose sporadic character is obvious. What comes to light here is that Saldenus' spirituality displays both divergence and important agreement with that of Bernard.

Initially he appears to have rejected that emphasis of Bernard in which the mystical union (*unio mystica*) is both sporadic and contemplative, but here he develops precisely that line. The question of how these two approaches are related to each other will not have escaped Saldenus, but for him the subject is not a matter for reflection let alone for clarification. Without any explanation he places the two lines of thought side-by-side. I need to return to this in my concluding evaluation.

In this connection, what Saldenus obviously gives greater attention is the assurance that proleptic contemplation preeminently heightens the notion of fragmentation. Because contemplation is only temporary and fragmentary, it

---

119. Ibid.

120. Ibid.

121. This verbal association undoubtedly plays on Datheen's versification of Psalm 42: "As the hart pants, O Lord, for refreshing waters, so my soul thirsts for you, my exalted God." Saldenus' preceding material is related to what follows these lines. Datheen's closing lines are: "Speak, then O Lord, to my complaint: When will the day arrive when I will be with you to praise you to your face?"

122. Saldenus, *De Wech des Levens*, 525.

feeds all the more the longing for uninterrupted fellowship with Christ. "You should pray that you might have him always."[123] The intensity of these desires in the eyes of "the children of this world" might be considered peculiar and exaggerated, but Saldenus sees things otherwise: "But it is a good omen when you are not like all Christians in that you are so fond of heaven and so in love with Christ that you can barely endure it when you are not in him and with him."[124]

In the concluding paragraphs of this chapter a note is sounded that is surprising and perhaps also significant for Saldenus' spirituality. We have already noted that the longing for heaven is advanced by sorrow and adversity. But that this longing can be advanced also by joy and prosperity is new. While Saldenus does not forget that God's children can also slide into a "shallow pit of slime" through prosperity, he is persuaded that generally their desire is "uplifted" to the extent that they are "more blessed." Whenever their ears hear a pretty melody here or there, they compare "that which is earthly with what is heavenly." For, if "the lesser" already produces so much enjoyment, what will it then be like "to be permitted to hear the eternal hallelujah?" When they enjoy "the pleasures" here below, they think, "To be sure, if what is lowly and temporal fills our hearts as wonderfully as this, what will it be like above where Christ will be all and in all and where these gratifying pleasures will be multiplied ten thousand times?" Natural enjoyment is obviously legitimate. That it is earthly and incomplete gives Saldenus no reason to disqualify it. Rather, he esteems it as positive. At the same time, he does not regard it as standing by itself. He regards it as pointing toward what is more valuable. The Christian's heart ascends up the "steps" of all "previous delights" to an "increased attraction and desire for that indescribable and imperishable inheritance" in heaven.[125] A Gnostic dualism that disparages this world is strange to Saldenus, therefore. Just as objectionable to him is a Renaissance worldview in which earthly enjoyment remains purely on a horizontal plane. Earthly beauty is significant in that it points, vertically, to perfection. The world denial for which he pleaded in the preceding chapter must also be taken comparatively, therefore, and not absolutely—"by comparison with the things of heaven!"[126] Denial is "only" the other side of expectation.

What remains for us to consider from this closing chapter of *De Wech des Levens* is, in the first place, that for Saldenus the longing for heaven is a constitutive feature of piety. It is not only felt in gusts, but accompanies Christian living for the duration.

The second thing that strikes us equally as much is the two dimensional nature of Saldenus' presentation of these matters. On the one hand this longing contains a proleptic joy that is experienced frequently, but on the other hand there is allowance for a longing that produces sporadic contemplation. Apparently this last mode is the exception that proves the rule. Given the fact

---

123. Ibid.
124. Ibid., 529-30.
125. Ibid., 530-31.
126. Ibid., 484.

that the one does not preclude the other, this twofold emphasis as such causes no tension. However, it certainly does so when Saldenus brings sporadic contemplation into conjunction with the experience of communion with Christ. While he initially always attached the adverbs "usually" and "often" to this experience of fellowship, and thereby digressed from Bernard's train of thought, he now seems just as disposed toward the experience of a mystical union (*unio mystica*) that is sporadic and contemplative in nature. This is an ambivalence of which he was probably aware but on which, in any case, he did not reflect. He himself devoted no attention to it.

The third thing that comes to mind is the large-hearted way in which Saldenus esteems earthly pleasure. Clearly, this positive assessment is a long way from a dualistic view of life. To my way of thinking, it is much rather an extension of Augustine's understanding of *uti* and *frui*. Just as the church father regarded earthly love as legitimate, even as it culminated in love for God, Saldenus also knew how to prize earthly pleasure, provided that it was related to the enjoyment of God. The "lesser" might be beautiful and good, but it points toward the "better," or rather, to him who is the Best.

Evaluation

Saldanus' piety has a mystical strain. That comes across clearly in the terminology related to bridal mysticism with which he portrays intimate fellowship with Christ. Not only the language, but often the form of his piety also has mystical features. This mystical dimension does not constitute some elite additive standing above the life of faith but is rather its inherent fruit—a fruit that in turn more deeply establishes faith's certainty of salvation.

The intimacy in which life with God is conducted is due to the work of the Spirit according to Saldenus. About that he leaves no doubt. We immediately recall, however, how tightly bound together he regards the word and the Spirit to be. The conclusion is justified, therefore, that in Saldenus' mind mystical experience never bypasses the word and faith, but that it is brought about by the Spirit precisely in the context of the living word itself. What the Spirit unveils is nothing other than the reality that lies hidden in the word. Saldenus' mysticism is a mysticism of the word that stirs a person all the way to the boundaries of one's faith. It rises high, but stops right at the border between faith and contemplation. To be sure, faith permits contemplation, but it is a contemplation that still belongs to *this* side and not yet to the *other* side. It is the believing contemplation of yearning. The complete contemplation of fulfillment is still beyond reach.

Although the soliloquy is defined as a personally appropriated means of reaching the inner experience of God, Saldenus does not develop the theme of meditation as a separate topic. He is content to remark in passing that a person should "intentionally put his mind to . . . snuffle through" God's word and to learn striking passages "by heart." One needs to reserve "definite times" for this activity.[127] Need for a definite approach to meditation seem to him to be obvious, therefore. Added to this is the way in which he conducts his sabbath observance,

---

127. Ibid., 103.

which has decidedly meditative features. To be sure, the whole mystically flavored experience that he describes evokes the atmosphere of a meditative lifestyle. It does not seem to me to be out of the question that Saldenus does not develop the theme of meditation precisely because he regards it as the presupposition on which the life of piety simply is conducted.

Mystically experienced fellowship with Christ implies for Saldenus deeply rooted joy. He designates this experience with the term "being uplifted." This is a designation that directly recalls Bernard's idea of *raptus*. Yet, the way in which Saldenus describes this event is not identical with Bernard's description. Saldenus' "being uplifted" is distinguished from his *raptus* by its continuous presence. While mystical union (*unio mystica*) consisted of a sporadic, short-lived and contemplative experience for the Abbot of Clairvaux, for Saldenus it is unusually profound, to be sure, but not unusually rare. At least this is the dominant emphasis. Alongside it, however, he develops an emphasis that certainly follows the trajectory of Bernard's approach. Saldenus likewise knows an experience of mystical union that, like Bernard's, appears sporadically and takes a contemplative form. One can only guess at the reason for this twofold emphasis. Perhaps Saldenus, who above all was a churchman and wanted to reach a broad public, realized that the contemplative experiences were the exceptions and displayed the pastoral sensitivity that, without denying them, yet in some sense relativized them by allowing them to hide behind the "normal" experience of joy. The unsatisfactory nature of this solution is that the question remains unanswered: why did not Saldenus make this relativizing explicit? Another explanation might be that he found both approaches legitimate and therefore presented them alongside one another without prejudice. Perhaps what I have identified as being in tension, Saldenus himself simply regarded as complimentary and saw in the sporadic experiences of communion purely an exceptional manifestation of the usual form it took.

That Saldenus worked out the motif of friendship so broadly in the framework of intimacy is salient. This might indicate the influence of Cocceijus. The sympathy Saldenus had for him makes this plausible. What can be established with certainty, however, is that Saldenus is indebted to Bernard and à Kempis. The eagerness with which he cites these medieval devotional figures leaves not the least doubt about this. Two things are striking in this connection. The first is that in a very calculated way Bernard does not emerge as an authoritative source in the mystical passages. The second is that Thomas is followed in his main lines, but is scarcely ever cited in the developing discussion. This distinguishes Saldenus from Teellinck, who is happy to connect with Bernard precisely with regard to mystical experiences and who incorporates the *Imitation* generously and literally into his own text. By contrast with Teellinck, Saldenus ignores book four of the *Imitation* entirely.

The final matter to which I give attention is the feature that Saldenus regards emotional experience as both desirable and common for all true believers, but that he still does not elevate it to the level of determining the authenticity of someone's state of grace. At any rate, he does not hesitate to reassure believers shored up by an overwhelmingly affective experiential piety, "It might well be that someone possessing true grace never realizes in his life a solidly established and constant walk or emotional state of assurance, but that he must continuously muddle his way toward heaven, sometimes falling and then standing back up, sometimes in a storm and then again in intervening periods of peace and sunshine."[128] Saldenus' piety is definitely characterized by deeply felt joy. He considered melancholy, especially when it was deliberately cultivated, as completely unacceptable. The person who does not feel joyful, however, might nevertheless be headed in the right direction. Whether one travels the road to heaven with light or heavy feet is not the determining thing. Saldenus would not be a pietist if he had not acknowledged that even in the latter instance sunlight was not entirely absent. Further, Saldenus would not have been Saldenus if he had not acknowledged that this light causes its own kind of joy. The "how" and the "why" of this "holy joy" the believer cannot explain. But one thing Saldenus certainly knew: "they depict the love of Christ for us."[129]

---

128. From *De Droevichste Staet eens Christens*, 117, as cited in van den End, *Guiljelmus Saldenus*, 124. This work was written only four years later than *De Wech des Levens*. The tone of the quotation is identical with what Saldenus writes there, 427.

129. Saldenus, *De Wech des Levens*, 433.

6

Wilhelmus à Brakel (1635-1711)

"Praying on the Road"

Wilhelmus à Brakel was a child of prayer. We have already learned how the milieu of his parental home was defined by communion with God. Abraham Hellenbroek in his book *Rouklagte* provides us with a few particulars from which it appears that the prayer life of Wilhemus' parents involved some ardent practices. Hellenbroek was well informed. He had heard these things from à Brakel himself, who had been his colleague in Rotterdam from 1695 and thereafter. Wilhelmus had recounted concerning his mother, Margaretha, how on various occasions she had confided to him "that she had wrestled in prayer so persistently and so long concerning him that she passed out." And concerning his father, Theodorus, Wilhelmus recalled "that when he went to school (the "Latin School") in Leeuwarden and came home on Saturday for the weekends, the custom was that on Monday morning his father would accompany him a set distance from Beers, where he was then the minister, and that he would then remain standing there praying to God on his son's behalf (one can only imagine what he did in his own prayer chamber) and watching him walk on until he could no longer see him. In his account to Hellenbroek, Wilhelmus had added "that he also often made his way praying on the road."[1] His mother's practices as well as those occurrences between Beers and Leeuwarden on his return trips were significant for the spiritual climate entrusted to Wilhelmus from the beginning of his life and perpetuated and reflected in his own, later work.

Biographical Sketch

Wilhelmus was born in Leeuwarden on January 2, 1635.[2] From tender youth, he gave evidence of the fear of the Lord. Later he often stated that he did not remember the time of his conversion, but that from his early youth he was affected by God's word and by Christ's love. The godliness of his parents, which permeated all of their family life, left its indelible impression on him.

---

1. Hellenbroek, *Algemeene Rouklagte*, 16. Included in *Redelijke Godsdienst* (new, second printing; Leiden, 1893), 3:357 and following.

2. For alternative dating, see Ros, *Theodorus à Brakel*, 27. For biographical information, use is made of Hellenbroek, *Algemeene Rouklagte*; Ritschl, *Geschichte des Pietismus*, 1:291-301; F. J. Los, *Wilhelmus à Brakel* (Leiden, 1892); J. van Genderen, "Wilhelmus à Brakel (1635-1711)," in *De Nadere Reformatie*, ed. Brienen, et al., 165-91; D. Nauta's article., "Wilhelmus à Brakel," in *BLGNP*, 4:48-51.

After his classical preparation in the Latin School of Leeuwarden, à Brakel signed the registry of the Franeker Academy in 1654 and commenced his theological studies there. He had his Franeker teachers Christiaan Schotanus and Johannes Valckenier to thank for the Cocceijan influence that remained with him throughout his life. In 1660 he continued his studies in Utrecht under professors G. Voetius and A. Essenius, who left an even more pronounced stamp on his theology. Two years later he returned to Friesland. There he served sequentially as minister of the congregations of Exmorra (1662), Stavoren (1665), Harlingen (1670) and Leeuwarden (1673), where among others, Herman Witsius was a fellow-officebearer.

His wife, Sara Nevius, to whom Wilhelmus was married in Utrecht in 1664, stimulated him not a little in the piety that he brought along from his parental home.[3] She published a posthumous little book of Wilhelmus' poems in a pietistic vein, entitled *Een aandactige Leerling van den Heere Jezus* [trans.: *An Attentive Student of the Lord Jesus*]. Four daughters and a son were born to the marriage of Sara and Wilhelmus; but only their daughter Sulamith outlived them. The other four children all died at a relatively young age.

À Brakel's ten-year ministry in Leeuwarden did not proceed entirely without friction. The civil authorities as well as some of his own colleagues were not endeared to him when he allowed—"by his own decision," as the official "Acts" put it—Jacobus Koelman[4] to preach to his Leeuwarden congregation, for the States General had deposed Koelman. À Brakel's argument that no political official had the authority to depose a preacher did not prevent his own suspension from the ministry for four weeks over the incident. But what earned him strong criticism above all, was the fact that he held religious conventicles without classical or consistorial permission. The final days of his Friesian ministry were equally blemished. Shortly after he had declined a call to Rotterdam, thereby indicating his intentions to remain in Leeuwarden, he nevertheless accepted the call when it was reissued. So in the fall of 1683, à Brakel, who by then was approaching 50, left by ship for prosperous Rotterdam, where he arrived much later than he had anticipated on account of life-threatening bad weather on the Zuiderzee.

The most well-known colleagues of à Brakel in Rotterdam were Wilhelmus Eversdijk, Abraham Hellenbroek and Jacobus Fruytier. The congregation had four churches distributed over ten preaching sites: the Grote or St. Laurenskerk, the Prinsenkerk, the Zuiderkerk and the Ooster- or Nieuwekerk. À Brakel served this huge congregation for twenty-eight years. He declined a call to Middelburg, just as he had done already when he was in Leeuwarden. He labored faithfully in the Rotterdam congregation until he died. The attachment was obviously mutual. According to Hellenbroek's *Rouklagte*, at least, à Brakel was then already known as "Father à Brakel."

Three matters are noteworthy about à Brakel's life. The first is his Friesian inflexibility when it came to defending the unique rights of the church. That was obvious when he contested the right of the authorities to block the approval of a

---

3. On Sara Nevius, see De Heer, "Sara Nevius."
4. A. F. Krull, *Jacobus Koelman: Een Kerkhistorische Studie* (Sneek, 1901).

minister lawfully called by the church. In this conflict he stood so resolutely for the independence of the church that he risked suspension and loss of his salary. To be sure, agreement was reached, but not without tensions.

The second matter that comes to mind is his loyalty to the church despite its decline and deficiencies. This loyalty appeared especially in connection with his opposition to Labadistic separatism. Initially, already in Stavoren, he was enchanted with this movement. In 1669 he paid De Labadie himself visits in Amsterdam for the purpose of becoming better acquainted. For some time he hesitated about whether he should join the Labadists. However, after fasting and praying from early morning until late at night secluded in his "courtyard" for the purpose of understanding God's will, the Lord "showed him clearly from his word" that he had to remain faithful to his "present charge" and that the Labadistic movement was "a deviation from the truth." Nevertheless, initially he was "favorably disposed" toward the movement. Because God repeatedly punished him when he persisted in this interest, however, he finally no longer dared to pray about joining. "But I resolved completely and joyfully to stay in the church and in my ministry, and I heartily thanked the Lord for this revelation of his will. And I still thank the Lord with all my heart that he protected me from taking that wrong turn."[5]

The third thing typical of à Brakel is his combination of dogmatic capability and a pastoral, experiential disposition. His *Redelyke Godsdienst* [trans.: *Reasonable Religion*] offers convincing proof of this.[6] His sermons also testify to it.[7]

During the last years of à Brakel's life, his health began to wane. Attacks of kidney stones sometimes paralyzed him with pain. On Sunday, August 30, 1711, the seventy-six-year-old minister completed his preaching assignment for the last

---

5. W. à Brakel, *Leere en Leydinge der Labadisten* (Rotterdam, 1685), 12-13. The congeniality of à Brakel's friend Jacob Koelman with this position is striking. See A. de Reuver "Koelman's anti-separatisme," *DNR* 20 (1996): 1-42.

6. *Logikè Latreia, dat is Redelyke Godtsdienst, in welke de Goddelyke Waerheden des Genadenverbondts worden verklaert, tegen partyen beschermt, en tot de practyke aengedrongen, als mede de Bedeelinge des Verbondts in het O.T. ende in het N.T. ende de Ontmoetingen der Kerke in het N.T. vertoont in een verklaringe der Openbaringe van Johannes*, 3 vols. in two (The Hague, 1700). Henceforth, abbreviated *RG*. Other works by à Brakel that he reworked and integrated into *RG* are: *Davids Hallelu-Jah, ofte Lof des Heeren, in den achtsten Psalm* (Leeuwarden, 1680), in subsequent, reworked reprints entitled *Hallelu-Jah, ofte Lof des Heeren, over het Genaden-verbondt, ende des selfs bedieninge in het O. en N. Testament. By occasie van de Verklaringe van den VIII. Psalm* (Rotterdam, 1687); *Trouwhertige Waerschouwinge . . . voor de Labadisten, ende haere dwalingen* (Leeuwarden, 1683); *Leere en Leydinge der Labadisten, Ontdeckt en Wederleyt in een Antwoort op P. Yvons Examens over onse Trouwhertige Waerschouwinge* (Rotterdam, 1685); *Waerschouwende Bestieringe tegen de Piëtisten, Quiëtisten en diergelyke, afdwalende tot een natuurlyken en geesteloosen Godtsdienst onder de gedaente van Geestelykheyt* ([n.p.], 1690); *De scrupuleuse ontrent de Communie des H. Avontmaals in een verdorvene Kerke onderrichtet* (Rotterdam, 1690). For the rest of à Brakel's writings, see the bibliographies in Los, *Wilhelmus à Brakel*, 294-302; and van der Haar, *Schatkamer*, 54-59; and *BLGNP*, 4:50-51.

7. *De waare Christen of opregte Gelovige, hebbende Deel aan God in Christus* (Amsterdam, 1712) appeared posthumously. This collection of sermons enjoyed various reprints. I possess the seventh reprint (Workum, 1777). It appeared in reprint twice even in the twentieth century.

time. A few days later he was bedridden. It would be his deathbed. The testimony he made from it is impressive. Hellenbroek has described it in almost hagiographic terms. During a night of oppressive discomfort, the sufferer asked that the congregation be told that he had preached to them the same truth that he himself had known and relished, and that sheltered in that truth, he could now die. He clung to the first question and answer of the Heidelberg Catechism, not because it was the basis of his faith, but because it agreed entirely with the word of God. From that faith, according to Hellenbroek, flowed a completely tender, glowing love for God and the Lord Jesus, a love that the dying man expressed in all sorts of "sweet exclamations." He repeated many times, just as his teacher Voetius had done on his deathbed, the lines from a Latin poem ascribed to Bernard: "O Jesu mi dulcissime, Spes suspirantis animae" ("O, my most sweet Jesus, Hope of a gasping soul."). When in his last hour he was asked how things stood with him, he answered, "Very well. I am at rest in my Jesus. I am one with him. I am simply waiting until he comes. I submit myself in complete peace." He entered his eternal rest as though falling asleep. It was October 30, 1711.

According to the Jews, says Hellenbroek, there are 903 kinds of death, but the sweetest death of all is that death in which God carries the soul away as with a kiss, just as Moses experienced. In the same way, Jesus carried off the soul of our "precious friend and soul-mate," wrote Hellenbroek in his *Rouklagte*.

Redelyke Godsdienst

In writing about à Brakel's view of piety, we have an overflowing source of material available in his three-volume work *Redelyke Godsdienst*.[8] It consists of some 2200 pages in quarto and constitutes his most extensive and most influential work. At first glance the table of contents of the first two volumes reminds one of a book in dogmatic theology. That impression is not entirely misguided. However, strictly speaking, it does not belong to the genre of systematic theology, certainly not in the academic sense of that term. *Redelyke Godsdienst* can be described, much rather, as a popular statement of doctrine with pastoral applications. Time and again the doctrinal treatment is interspersed with passages of a moral and edifying nature. For his readership à Brakel did not have in mind knowledgeable colleagues, but "God's church in the Netherlands,"[9] as the dedication states—especially, his present congregation in Rotterdam, the congregations he had served previously and the congregation in Middelburg that had called him twice. What he intended with his publication, he adds plainly: "Form little study groups with people you know well; have them read a relevant chapter or passage and let what was read be the basis for an edifying discussion."[10] It certainly would have made him happy if the content of his book would serve the purpose especially "of giving some guidance to students,

---

8. The first two volumes treat the exposition and study of the divine truths of the covenant of grace, and the third volume describes the various historical manifestations of the covenant of grace and concludes with an exposition of the book of Revelation. Use is made here of the twelfth printing (Rotterdam, 1733).

9. Compare this dedication with van Lieburg, *Profeten en hun vaderland*, 327.

10. *RG*, 1. The dedication is unpaginated.

thinking Christians and young ministers in rightly understanding divine truths." By giving it this more educational purpose, he shows his concern with "the building up of the church." À Brakel also notes in his dedication that he has reworked and included from his "earlier books" whatever "was applicable."

Apparently the demand for the book was substantial. In 1701, a year and a half after the first printing, the second appeared. Many more would follow.[11] With the third printing, in 1707, the content was expanded by three chapters. The first volume now concluded with a chapter entitled "On Living the Faith by Relying on the Promises," originally an extensive and specially published letter to a "God-fearing Merchant in the New Netherlands,"[12] and with another that had appeared even earlier, in 1690, and that arouses interest from the perspective of our theme and has a title with the allure of a tract: "Guidance, in Warning against the Pietists."[13] An explanation of the Lord's Prayer was added to volume two.[14] The commentary that à Brakel gives to this three-part expansion is too amusing to overlook: "If any are unhappy because the third edition has been expanded, let them be so only mildly and give their first or second edition to someone with fewer resources than they possess, for in so doing and by acquiring a copy of the third edition for themselves, they will be edified." Whoever can see his way clear to purchase the new edition, therefore, no longer need be embarrassed by having an outdated edition. Furthermore, the knife cuts two ways: edification would be broadened and the third edition would sell more widely.

Believing Fellowship with Christ

In considering à Brakel's spirituality, I begin with the theme that constitutes its main artery, namely believing fellowship with Christ. He devotes a brief but crucial chapter to it: "On the Believer's Fellowship with Christ and with One Another."[15] This is a chapter that assumes a significant position organizationally. À Brakel places it in the section in which he deals with the church, a section preceded by Christology and followed by pneumatology and the salvation order.[16] This implies that developing the theme of fellowship with Christ properly precedes that of the *ordo salutis*. Although by following the sequence of

---

11. See van der Haar, *Schatkamer*, 56-57.
12. *RG*, 1.42, 1048-80.
13. Ibid., 1.43, 1080-1134.
14. Ibid., 2.26, 392-480.
15. Ibid., 1.26, 617-33.
16. This structure deviates from that of Reformed theologians like Calvin (*The Institutes*, 1559), F. Turretin (*Institutio Theologicae Elencticae*, 1679-1685) and P. van Mastricht (*Theoretico-practica Theologia*, 1699), that following the doctrine of God employ the sequence of Christology, pneumatology, soteriology and ecclesiology. À Brakel follows another course: Christology, ecclesiology, pneumatology. C. Graafland, "De kerk in de Nadere Reformatie: Wilhelmus à Brakel," in *De Kerk: Wezen, weg en werk van de kerk naar reformatorische opvatting*, ed. W. van 't Spijker (Kampen, 1990), 165-66, suspects Coccejan influence at this point: "For à Brakel the church belongs to salvation itself, because it belongs to the covenant itself. The church is the embodiment of the covenant." On the structure of Coccejus' *Summa Doctrinae*, see van Asselt, *Amicitia Dei*, 22-27.

ecclesiology and pneumatology à Brakel diverges from Calvin's structure, an important agreement between them emerges in that for à Brakel as well as for Calvin partnership with Christ fulfills the function of being the source of appropriating salvation. According to the reformer as well, this is the mystery from which both justification and sanctification emerge.[17] For both of them this participation is a matter of faith. I admit that in connection with the order of salvation à Brakel devotes a separate chapter to faith after the chapter on fellowship with Christ, but this does not detract from the fact that faith in that sense is the means by which union with Christ occurs.[18]

This fellowship with Christ à Brakel approaches with words borrowed directly from the Song of Solomon: "My Beloved is mine and I am his" (2:16).[19] This well-known motif from the mystical tradition sets the tone. À Brakel also calls this fellowship a "covenant of marriage,"[20] in which both parties "become the possession of each other" by "mutually giving themselves to one another."[21] God and man give themselves into the possession of one another reciprocally, so that a "union" comes into existence. It is a union that can better be experienced than described. This does not mean, however, that à Brakel is silent on the subject thereafter. He first explains what it is not. It is not a union of being in the way that the divine persons are one, nor a union of persons in the way that the two natures of Christ are one, and even less a blending and changing as though the believer becomes Christ himself and is "deified or 'Christified.'" [22] At the same time, it is not a "mere relationship" and even less a kind of moral conformity to Christ such as manifests itself in sanctification. What is it, then? In answering that question à Brakel steps back and first explains how it comes about. He summarizes four aspects that apparently all have equal weight and that impact each other. The union occurs specifically through the in-dwelling of Christ's Spirit, through a spiritual marriage, through the unifying faith and love "whose nature it is not to be able to tolerate any division but to create a most

---

17. *Inst.*, 3.11.1, in *OS*, 4:182. See W. van 't Spijker, *Gemeenschap met Christus: Centraal gegeven van de gereformeerde theologie*, Apeldoornse Studies 32 (Kampen, 1995). Also see his "'Extra nos' en 'in nobis' bij Calvijn in pneumatologisch licht," in *Geest, Woord en Kerk*, 114-32.

18. *RG*, 1.26.3, 619. (The numbers refer to, respectively, the volume, chapter, paragraph and page.) See also 1.31.12, 748; 1.32.25, 779; 2.14.2, 212; 2.18.8, 261. While à Brakel chooses the sequence of regeneration and faith in his treatment of the order of salvation, he maintains with conviction that chronologically they are simultaneous, but that faith preceeds "in the natural order of things." The reason for this logical order is that the word is the seed of regeneration and that this word has no good effect "except through faith" (*RG*, 1.32.1, 762). One receives the "first principle of life" with the earliest "act of faith" (*RG*, 1.31.12, 748). Definitely in the same vein, he had already expressed himself on the subject in *Leere en Leydinge*, 48. See de Reuver, "*Bedelen bij de Bron,*" 113-15; K. Exalto "Genadeleer en heilsweg," in Brienen, et al., *De Nadere Reformatie*, 163-64.

19. *RG*, 1.26.2, 617.

20. Ibid., 618. Also in *RG* 1.16.7, 362, where à Brakel treats the covenant of grace, the term "covenant of marriage" appears and Song of Solomon 2:16 is quoted.

21. Ibid., 618.

22. Ibid., 1.26.3, 618. In the last disclaimer, à Brakel seems to distance himself from the terminology that Witsius applies in his *Twist des Heeren*.

intimate union." Consequently, the nature of this union "is to maintain[23] itself authentically, actually, truly, completely, unselfishly—unbroken throughout all eternity. It is spiritual; nothing physical comes into consideration concerning it."[24]

After à Brakel has described in this way the means and nature of this faith-union's coming into being, he describes its content. To begin with, he seizes on a number of expressions and images that he encountered in the Bible. Believers cloth themselves with Christ; they are baptized into him; they are rooted in him; they live in him and he lives in them. They are the bride of the Bridegroom, the body of Christ, the branches on the Vine.[25] Each one of them is a metaphor that indicates a most heartfelt union. From this established union, à Brakel sees a fully functioning fellowship flowing in a way comparable to the way that Saldenus distinguished union with Christ from fellowship with Christ. By fellowship à Brakel meant "the exercise and making use" of the union. Oneness with Christ, therefore, is not only a state of affairs, but a living reality. À Brakel expressly makes an appeal for this dynamic. The believer must "make work of the fact" that he is the possession of Christ. This says, in the first place, that one must concentrate on the person of Christ by maintaining faith, hope and love. "That will ensure that we mature in him."[26] Simultaneously, however, this personal union ensures fellowship with his benefits. Immediately, what is ours becomes his and what is his becomes ours. We share in his "Sonship" through adoption, and in him we have one and the same Father. We share in his satisfaction, and as a result we may approach God freely. We share in his holiness, and in him we are made perfect before God. We are included in his intercession, and we share in the inheritance of his glory. Christ's Spirit and power are ours. In short, all the fullness of Christ and all the treasures of the covenant of grace are lavished upon us in him. And à Brakel would not have been satisfied if he had not added to the benefits of this fellowship that we also share in his suffering. This dimension he also consistently calls, following Peter, "great glory."[27]

That this fellowship is a matter of experience for à Brakel comes clearly to light. He values it highly, using the language of mystical intimacy. "Is it not your greatest glory to be engaged in fellowship with Jesus as with your own [i.e., as with him who is yours]?" Both communion with the suffering of Christ as well as with his love receive the same designation: "glory." Wilhelmus entices his readers to communion with Jesus in the language of Song of Solomon. Nothing less is involved here than "drinking in every sweetness and pleasure." This is illustrated with quotations from the Song of Solomon: "He kisses me with the kiss[28] of his mouth. . . . He woos me in his bodega, and love is his banner

---

23. Here à Brakel does not acknowledge that in this connection an exception is Christ's divinity.
24. *RG*, 1.26.3, 618-19.
25. *RG*, 1.26.4-5, 619-20.
26. *RG*, 1.26.6, 620.
27. *RG*, 1.26.7, 620-21.
28. Just as had his father Theodorus, Wilhelmus also employs the singular at this point—along with Bernard and the Vulgate.

unfurled over me. À Brakel compares this with Moses' time "on the mountain" and calls it a "conversation with Christ" that causes the soul to glisten with holiness.[29] There is nothing to indicate that he limits this mystical experience to a special category. Rather, one gets the impression that it is inherent in fellowship with Christ that by definition all believers share in it. It also certainly seems that à Brakel here reckons with the temporary nature of this experience. Believers always love contemplating Christ's future appearance, because then they "will contemplate" their Bridegroom "close by for the first time and will be ushered into the New Jerusalem by him."[30]

When à Brakel gives an account of the exercise of this communion and begins it with "contemplation," it signals a strong similarity to his father Theodorus' *Trappen des Geestelyken Levens*. The object of this contemplation consists of the council of peace, Christ's incarnation, suffering, death, resurrection and ascension.[31] The soul "stops stock still" before all these aspects of the council of salvation and salvation history, "starry-eyed" with the anticipation of "a clearer and closer view" in order to be more greatly incited to love and to be awakened to praise. "For that reason, the believer gazes upon Jesus, and that gaze from her awakens in Jesus expressions of love toward her" (in reference to Song of Solomon 4:9). The second way this "exercise" is expressed consists of repeatedly showing "an outgoing love for Jesus." Also by this à Brakel obviously intends a form of contemplation. At least he notes that by such "gazing," love "increases still more" and the mutual "exchanges of love" are sustained. The third way is designated as "friendly and open" discussion.[32] This includes that the soul "acknowledges" all her love for Jesus—and her shortage of it!—implores him to fulfill all her desires and is attentive "to what Jesus speaks to her." By way of clarification, à Brakel adds that the soul directs itself to the word and recognizes this word as the voice of her Beloved, "especially when he impresses a scriptural passage on the heart with clarity, power and sweetness."[33] In the spirit of Bernard, he observes, "So, the soul loses and forgets itself, and it gives it pain if the discussion is terminated, or if the body becomes too weak to bear the weight of its heart's desires, loving kisses and impulses."[34] In describing the "manners" that follow, à Brakel's treatment is certainly less mystical, but not less intimate. The believer rests in Jesus' protection, is sheltered under his shadow, asks what pleases him and makes use of all that he has and provides. The soul may regard Christ's gifts so completely

---

29. *RG*, 1.26.8, 622.

30. *RG*, 1.26.9, 623.

31. This way of looking at the matter structured according to salvation history is typical of his father Theodorus, and Wilhelmus returns to it in *RG*, 2.36.5, 500.

32. Compare *RG*, 1.36.3, 915, where à Brakel within the framework of "spiritual peace" talks about a "friendly and open communion" in the display of mutual love.

33. *RG*, 1.26.10, 623-24. The citation is a striking illustration of the fact that in devotional language "the soul" is a synonym for the "the believer": *the soul* impresses a Scriptural passage on *the heart*! See W. à Brakel, *Davids Hallelu-Jah,*128, where "*the soul*" finds a heaven in "*the soul*."

34. Ibid., 1.26.10, 624.

as her own that this causes her to forget this world and allows her to live in heaven.[35]

On the question of how a person preserves continuity in exercising this fellowship—or, can remain "constantly" in it—à Brakel answers that one must guard oneself against sin and by faith must resolutely cling to the conviction that he is Christ's reconciled possession. In this connection he presents a remarkable vision of the relationship of faith and feelings. However emotional the nature of his piety might be, he does not hesitate to let faith predominate: "You may not see it, you may not feel it: belonging [that is, to belong to Christ] is not based on emotion." Fellowship with Christ never springs from emotions, but from faith. By "truly and actually" believing, one becomes the possession of Christ, the soul is ushered into fellowship and sustained in it. A person must hold God to his promise, depend on his word and wait in faith for the fulfillment of his promise. Just as surprising is à Brakel's motivation. As though he had not just spoken about "sweet" communion, he now decidedly takes the position that one must await the fulfillment of the promise in the awareness "that this sweetness is reserved for heaven and that the here-and-now is the time for strife." It is this understanding of faith that protects us from "being too far estranged" from God "until the Lord will shortly unite us with him in glory."[36] À Brakel gives the appearance of ambivalence right here in the same chapter. On the one hand, he testifies of emotional experiences and of kisses of love, and on the other hand he knows enough to qualify the affective to the extent that actual sweetness is still delayed. Above all, there apparently is still no talk about immediate union. That is always intended for the future glory. We nevertheless note, however, that this eschatological reserve seems to be in tension with statements that he makes elsewhere.

Summarizing, we note that union with Christ plays a key role in à Brakel's spirituality, originates and expands only through faith, is experienced emotionally, but is limited and provisional. Despite its contemplative tendencies, it belongs to the time of faith and not yet to the time of full sight. It is mediated by the word.

Love

À Brakel's piety exudes love. Both love for God and love for Jesus are themes of his, and he treats them in two separate chapters.[37] Love for God receives attention first. Wilhelmus regards its restoration as residing purely in God's love for us. Our love is a reflection, love returned. It is kindled by him who himself is "Love Eternal." À Brakel relies on the image of a mirror to help him here. "The sun cannot shine on a mirror without casting a reflection or on polished metal without heating it and causing it to cast off warmth in response." Then he asks whether anyone could resist the love of "the One who is the most beautiful and most loveable of all." "Shall God's love toward you who believe and who have

---

35. Ibid.
36. Ibid., 1.26.11, 624-25.
37. *RG* 2.14, 210-22 and 2.15, 222-34.

seen and felt just a small ray of that love not inflame your heart with that same love?"[38] The object of love is also its source. It flows from God and streams back to him.[39]

The appearance can even be that this display of reciprocal love occurs without any mediation. But this is not the case. That was the way it once was, according to à Brakel. Prior to the fall into sin, Adam knew and loved God "without mediation." However, following the break with God, enmity became a factor and the exchange of love could only be restored through "the intervention of the Mediator." He replaced estrangement from God with fellowship. Between enmity and friendship lies atonement. This is what à Brakel means when he denies that the ties of love with God are not unmediated. They are mediated by the Mediator. To this he attaches the important conclusion that love for God comes about only through faith. He writes, "This friendship is exercised through the faith by which the regenerate person appropriates the merits of Christ as the ransom and finds peace with God." It is through faith in the Mediator that a person enjoys showing love for God, and through the same faith love for God is awakened.[40] For à Brakel this is precisely what constitutes the difference between true and false love. All love for God that "is separated from faith" he considers to be a mere imitation. "Naturally," people are able to speak and write nicely about love, but that is "blind man's work." With their minds they can certainly "give the appearance of understanding it, but their hearts are cold and devoid of love."[41] Love for God is only made possible where his love for us is *believed*. In the chapter dealing with becoming like children, "Father à Brakel" writes that the mystery of God's love is so immense that a person would not be able to believe it "unless God himself had not said it." But, in John 3:16 God so assures us of his love "that now we want to believe, recognize . . . and be so ignited by his love, that we love him in return."[42]

In the definition that à Brakel provides for this reciprocal love, he describes it as "a sweet movement of the emotions toward God" worked by the Holy Spirit. In it the believer, "through union with him" and through the contemplation of God's perfections, takes delight in him and embraces his will entirely.[43] Without following à Brakel's development of this explanation step for step, I give attention to a detail of special importance for understanding his spirituality. I refer to the passage in which he goes into the relation between love and union with God. In his explanation, union with God functions as the source of love. He does not retract this perspective. But he certainly amplifies it when he adds that love can only be satisfied with "the most intimate and the most complete union." Because all enjoyment in this life is only partial, however, and because "complete and unmediated union with God" is reserved for life in heaven, "one who loves God" yearns to be set free and to be with Christ "in order to be

---

38. *RG*, 2.14.9, 219.
39. *RG*, 2.14.1, 210.
40. Ibid.
41. *RG* 2.14.1, 211.
42. *RG*, 1.35.5, 899. À Brakel is referring to 1 John 4:19.
43. *RG*, 2.14.2, 211.

perfectly satisfied in his love."[44] Just as was the case for his father Theodorus, love was intensified for Wilhelmus by longing for its perfection and its unmediated expression.

When he discusses love for Jesus, à Brakel's vocabulary is marked by increased fervency. True believers receive him. According to à Brakel this implies that they do not merely "become infatuated" with his gifts, but that they dedicate themselves to their "Source" himself. They desire to be united with him and to remain united with him "emotionally." The desire for atonement and peace drive them to him continually. "And above all else, is love; love draws them there more than anything."[45] Christ is so amiable for them, and for them to enjoy him is so "sweet and lovely that for them everything else disappears." When they enjoy him, they know what a priceless treasure they have found. "They take great care that they do not lose him."[46] Their hearts remain fixed on Jesus, and they "are not pleased" until they "actually" enjoy fellowship with God in Christ. When he is far off, they long to be near him "and become weak with longing and grow dull." À Brakel illustrates this longing by once again quoting Song of Solomon 1:2: "He kisses me with the kisses of his mouth."[47]

In the second volume of *Redelyke Godsdienst* the author even devotes a separate chapter to love for Jesus, as already noted. How this love is related to love towards God is not a point of discussion for à Brakel. In any case, they are not identical. Christ is simply "Immanuel, God and man in one person . . . and in that role or position he is the object of our love."[48] In the fourth paragraph he develops the obviously Bernardian understanding of the fervency and uniqueness of the mystical experience. There Wilhelmus explains that the believer's "sweetness" emerges from receiving "signs of Jesus' love when he kisses her soul with the kisses of his mouth, while he puts his left hand under her head and embraces her with his right hand."[49] Further along he calls it "sitting in the shade of Jesus' love." Then the love of the soul is directed toward its Beloved and it experiences a heavenly joy, "then it is well pleased for the first time and it hopes that that love will never be diminished."[50] À Brakel, with Bernard—who remains unmentioned by name—regards this as "a rare experience that quickly passes."[51] Even if the meaning of Bernard's characterization is relativized, this does not detract from its mystical tone.

---

44. Ibid., 2.14.3, 215.

45. *RG*, 1.33.32, 815.

46. *RG*, 1.33.33, 816.

47. *RG*, 1.33.35, 818-19. It is noteworthy that in this instance à Brakel uses the plural "kisses." This citation agrees with *Davids Hallelu-Jah*, 240. The most substantial part of this chapter on characteristics is, in fact, borrowed from this earlier work.

48. *RG*, 1.15.1, 222. À Brakel's understanding of the person of Christ can be found in *RG*, 1.15.18, 400-421.

49. *RG*, 1.15.4, 226. There is no trace in à Brakel of the separate significance that Bernard sees between Jesus' left and right hands. See *SC*, 51:8, in *SW*, 6:190.

50. *RG*, 1.15.7, 231. To what extent this "sitting in the shade" anticipates the eschaton becomes obvious in *RG*, 1.61.14, 769, where à Brakel uses the same expression, but now to characterize the glory of heaven.

51. *RG*, 1.15.4, 226.

Nevertheless, this reference appears in a critical context. "Father à Brakel" wants his readers to be sure of the fact that love does not depend on affective experience. Even though one is not always "involved in an emotional outpouring of the heart," and even though one does not live "in the embrace of sweet conversation," love for Jesus can still certainly "live in the heart authentically and spread out in deeds of love." He finds that two things must be distinguished here, namely the "existence" (or "truth") of love and its "passion." To illustrate his views he draws a comparison with the love of a mother for her child. Even though not a word is said about a "sweet, emotional attachment," a mother loves her child "truly and from the word 'go.'" Does she only love that child when she sometimes puts it on her lap and coddles it, or only as long as she "has pleasure from contemplating the beauty of her child?" Everyone knows that the heart of a true mother "maintains a loving disposition toward her child" even when she is caught up in other obligations. As soon as her child needs her, however, love springs into action. And that is the way it is with love for Jesus, according to à Brakel. While there are those occasional moments of fervent intimacy, "a constant love exists in the heart and occasionally comes to expression and shows itself by our actions."[52] By using these three verbs, he gives expression to the fact that besides his distinction between existence and "passion" he recognizes a third mode of love, namely the expression of talk and walk. Thus, the mystical experience of love for Jesus as an "occasional" occurrence lies between the existence of love in the heart and the ethical display of that love in action.

Reflection

The short chapter bearing the title "Concerning Spiritual Reflection"[53] is preceded and prepared for by an even briefer chapter on "solitude."[54] A person cannot force communion with God via meditation, but one can certainly prepare for it. By that solitude à Brakel understands "a separation from all human contacts for a time in order to devote oneself more earnestly and freely to spiritual exercises in seeking God."[55] The place one chooses for this activity is incidental. One can look for a "lonely field" and sit there, or if one has a farm or garden, one can retreat to it—it makes no difference.[56] What it comes down to first of all is a "solitary disposition of the heart," an attitude toward life not dictated by what the world has to offer, but which understands that here we are on a pilgrimage as strangers whose life's purpose is entirely directed toward God.[57] À Brakel called this "the enduringly solitary disposition" of believers. With this somewhat remarkable designation, therefore, he focuses on an introspective attitude and inner distance. However, it is a stance that demands

---

52. Ibid.
53. *RG*, 2.36, 498-502.
54. *RG*, 2.35, 493-98.
55. *RG*, 2.35.1, 493.
56. Ibid., 494.
57. *RG*, 2.35.2, 495.

attentiveness and discipline. This occurs first of all in the form of "ordinary exercises," by which he obviously means the regular, daily times of prayer.[58]

For the "increase in godliness" it is useful above all for a person to set aside "special time" now and then to isolate oneself entirely for several hours "or several days!" As à Brakel understood, one's social position must then be such as allows for this to happen. Above all, "spiritual condition" is a matter of importance. For example, a person who is subject to "special temptations" should not begin this. A conflicted soul needs to avoid solitude, finds à Brakel.[59] However, if the circumstances are propitious, he thinks that such a retreat is definitely beneficial.[60] Just as his father had done, Wilhelmus points to the example of Jesus himself, who regularly sought solitude.[61] This isolation creates another opportunity to draw close to God. Then he approaches us with so much love that we "are overwhelmed by it." Then he leads the soul into his inner chamber and shows it the eternal intentions of his love, the covenant of salvation,[62] the miracle of the incarnation, the power of Christ's atoning death, the glory of his resurrection and ascension and the comfort of his intercession. "Thus, he woos her in his bodega and unfurls his banner over her so that they become drunk with love."[63] This is the way that à Brakel lays the groundwork for the chapter "On Spiritual Reflection."

He begins this chapter on meditation with a definition. He describes reflection as a religious exercise in which the believer, with a heart that turns away from the world and is lifted toward heaven, contemplates God and the things of God. Its purpose is to be led deeper into the knowledge of God's mysteries, to be ignited in love and to be comforted and awakened to a lively engagement.[64] He indicates immediately that a person must not confuse this exercise with "being emptied." During meditation a person is not "passive" and purely "receptive," like a mirror reflecting the sun. No, this is about an "activity" in which "the soul is busy contemplating."[65] Apparently in conflict with this active approach is Wilhelmus' explanation that spiritual reflection is the work of God's Spirit. "The believer is not qualified for this in and of himself, as we know

---

58. Compare *RG*, 2.25.23, where in the chapter on prayer, à Brakel pleads for maintaining a pattern of praying three times a day: in the morning, at noon, and in the evening. He calls this conducive "to bringing and keeping us in continuous fellowship with God."

59. For the same thought in Luther, see P. Bühler, *Die Anfechtung bei Martin Luther* (Zurich, 1942), 134.

60. *RG*, 2.35.3, 495.

61. *RG*, 2.35.6, 496.

62. In *RG*, 1.7.20, 214, à Brakel gives an extensive definition: "To be an object of that eternal, mutual pleasure shared by the Father and Christ in saving you—that is bliss; that is a miracle! Love moves the Father; love moves the Lord Jesus. It is a covenant of love that arises from their love of one another, not from the loveableness of the object. Oh how blessed is the one who is included in this covenant and who being surrounded by this everlasting love becomes so radiant and warmed as to love in response."

63. *RG*, 2.35.6, 497.

64. *RG*, 2.36.1, 498.

65. *RG*, 2.36.2, 498.

both from our own experience and from Scripture."[66] However, the contradiction is only apparent. What à Brakel intends is that meditation is due entirely to the Spirit of God, but that he truly activates the spirit of the person meditating. Thus, illumined and led by the Spirit, the "empty" soul seeks to be filled and nourished: "it presents itself, opens itself, looks outward, waits and works."[67] The activity intended here consists of activity, therefore, that at the deepest level is dependent and receptive.

The object of reflection consists of God and divine things. This definition gives à Brakel the freedom to focus meditation on "the way" in which salvation was appropriated as "the Lord led us from the time of our childhood onward." But at the same time he is above all interested in the way in which God himself framed and accomplished salvation through election and atonement. In the spirit of his father, Theodorus, he makes a case for pondering in the heart the dimensions of the council of salvation and the actual achievement of salvation in chronological sequence. "We ought to spend some time on each point if it stirs some response in us; hastily moving from one to the other removes the benefit."[68] "Generally speaking," the design of this approach is to "develop and grow in spiritual life" and especially to exercise fellowship with God and to find pleasure in him, with the result that we are "aroused in our love for God, in trusting and feeling God's love, and in being moved once again in sweet love for God." Furthermore, its purpose is to be reassured in times of "heavy-heartedness" and to be spurred on to "sanctification."[69] À Brakel concludes this chapter with the following challenge: "Learn this secret and little-practiced art." Apparently he does not give much thought to the level at which the meditative life operates. He is more interested in the joy that it produces. This amounts "to tasting the beginning of heaven." A person must concentrate on it, he advises. "If it is initially demanding and difficult work, later it will certainly become easier."[70]

Although this chapter in *Redelyke Godsdienst* embraces important material for understanding à Brakel's views on meditation, his exposition here nevertheless remains basically formal. The question of how meditation is expressed practically receives only secondary attention. That the structure and progression of spiritual reflection reveal strong ties to the method that his father, Theodorus, maintains is quite apparent. The question arises whether the two are materially analogous and whether that can be demonstrated. Considering the recommendation with which Wilhelmus introduced and published *Trappen des*

---

66. *RG*, 2.36.6, 500. Compare W. à Brakel, *Davids Hallelu-Jah*, 130, where the Spirit of Christ is seen as the author of this event. The contemplation of Jesus would have "no place in such an evil and misguided subject as man is, unless the power of Jesus is poured out and the Spirit of Christ flows into him through that special, intimate union into which the Lord brings the soul."

67. *RG*, 2.36.3, 499. In the chapter on prayer, à Brakel calls the person "simply an empty vessel" that needs to look beyond itself for being filled" *RG*, 2.25.8, 365.

68. *RG*, 2.36.5, 500.

69. *RG*, 2.36.7, 501.

70. *RG*, 2.36.8, 501-2.

Geestelyken Levens, we would expect nothing less.[71] By contrast with the legacy of Wilhelmus' father, the genre of *Redelyke Godsdienst* is not explicitly, and certainly not exclusively, devotional. At the same time, this does not prevent him from incorporating passages that have an unmistakably devotional character. Curiously enough, these are to be found not in the chapter that develops the idea of reflection, but they are spread elsewhere throughout his magnum opus. I call attention to three examples.

The first example concerns a portion of the chapter on Christ's humiliation.[72] After à Brakel has concentrated in a doctrinal sense on the separate aspects of Christ's suffering, he comes to his concluding application. He begins this with the explanation that knowing the truths just handled is necessary but that the believing contemplation of them is at least as "profitable and soul-stirring." From this perspective he points to "holy meditation" that is so continuously focused that it produces "a habitual disposition of the heart." Then meditation is internalized as a sort of second nature. À Brakel laments that this "exercise" is "hidden" for many, even for many believers. If one only had "more faith" in holding the sufferings of Christ before him or her, and if one could only stay busy with "quiet, sweet reflecting," then a person would "regard more highly" the weight of that suffering and would understand more deeply the terrible nature of sin and the purity of God's righteousness. One would celebrate Christ's sufferings more intensely and "hold" him "dearer." "You are certainly well advised then: stay much busier with such meditation."[73]

To give his appeal added weight, à Brakel calls to mind the example of the bride in the Song of Solomon: "My Beloved is to me a sachet of myrrh that rests between my breasts" (Song of Solomon 1:13). In the footsteps of his father, Theodorus, who unlike Wilhelmus refers to Bernard,[74] he relates this sachet to the sufferings of Christ. "What was that little sachet of myrrhe [sic] except the bitter, redemptive sufferings of Christ that guard against ruin, quicken the heart, strengthen us and show us his love?" The bride not only carried it "daily on her chest" like a "fragrant bouquet," but it even lay "on her heart each night." She went "to sleep with these reflections; and when she awakened, she was still engaged in them." According to Wilhelmus, the prophets and also Paul were of the same mind. "And how many of God's blessed people were preoccupied with these thoughts not only in the early days of the New Testament but also since the Reformation, is testified to by their writings." À Brakel is certain that for all of them this meditative style of life was a "sweetness" that "became sweeter and dearer over time." For "us" this must also be a stimulus "to devote ourselves to those exercises whose sweetness one does not taste without effort." The joy in

---

71. In the chapter "Waerschouwende Bestieringe" [trans.: "Cautionary Guidance"] (*RG*, 1.43, 1130), he advises people to read as "an example of holy meditation" the *Trappen* of his father. At the same time, he also gives the advice there to consult the meditations ("on a lower level"!) of his wife, Sara Nevius.

72. *RG*, 1.22, 471-514.

73. *RG*, 1.22.32, 505.

74. À Brakel, *Het geestelyke Leven*, 56. Compare *SC*, 43:3, in *SW*, 6:98; and Boot, *De allegorische uitlegging*, 205. On the possible influence of G. Udemans and of the notes in the *Statenvertaling*, see Verduin, *Canticum Canticorum*, 598-602 and 641.

reflection comes to a person, therefore, through a process of mental discovery. By the hearing and reading of "history," the understanding and the memory are nourished; but "people never experience spiritual warmth except by meditating and by applying to themselves that on which they meditate."[75]

In this connection à Brakel achieves a model of passion meditation that reveals the content he would give this activity. Two features are noteworthy. In the first place, the content begins with an "introduction" of the person of Christ and in the second place attention is given to the atoning nature of Christ's suffering in its entirety and to its saving significance for us personally. God's children do not consider the suffering Jesus as some anonymous martyr, but as their personal "Surety" who paid for their sins by taking their place. The person who suffers is God, "the Lord of Glory," who empties himself to the point of assuming our human mortality. This "greatest of all miracles," the incarnation, that overshadows even the creation of heaven and earth, deserves to be contemplated continually. What a person needs to ponder no less thoroughly, is that the subject of our meditation is none other than him who is always calling us to conversion, sought us when we were dead in sin and gave us new life.   In this way à Brakel places reflection on obtaining salvation in the perspective of appropriating salvation. This pneumatological viewpoint gives the Christological events profound significance for meditation. To be sure, in his estimation the meditator reaches across the ages to a distant past, but in so doing does not in the least focus on One who remains distant or strange. On the contrary, "He is certainly the very One who once revealed himself to you, who once kissed you with the kisses of his mouth and caused you to feel his love." This Bridegroom is the one whose atoning love is the object of meditation. To express it in the manner and the language of father Theodorus: "Stay here, stay awhile; allow your love to flow forth from you in recognition of his love for you; hear the voice of your Beloved when he says to you, 'My dear friend, I truly love you. . . . When I bled so profusely from my head to foot, I suffered willingly.' That 'such an exalted person' has come so close to us causes our hearts to dissolve into tears of love and 'gives power and emphasis to reflecting on the sufferings of Christ.'"[76]

According to à Brakel, meditation needs to occur with this awareness of intensely personal involvement and amazement. "In this manner, make your way from the crib to the cross and contemplate every part of his suffering by itself." Not for nothing are they recorded in such detail in the gospels. "Something exceptional lies locked up in every little detail." Careful contemplation teaches us to see that it was our sins that caused the sufferings of Christ. "O, how sweet it is to feel deeply ashamed over our sins . . . and to say, 'My dear Jesus, deeply it pains me;' and on the other hand, however, 'I am overjoyed in heart that you stood in my place.'"[77]

The monastic tradition recognized two focal points in meditation on the passion, namely the *affectus* and the *effectus*. Respectively, they refer to the

---

75. *RG*, 1.22.32, 505-6.
76. *RG*, 1.22.24, 507-508.
77. *RG*, 1.22.36, 509.

emotions and to their expression. By the first is meant living into the suffering that Christ experienced, and by the second is meant the practical effect that this produced by way of concrete discipleship.[78] A man like Luther identified with this tradition formally, although he preferred the Augustinian concepts of *sacramentum* and *exemplum*, and for him the affective involvement had a totally *pro me* character.[79] To what extent à Brakel was familiar with the monastic tradition is unclear. In any case, he followed Luther's line of thought. Also, for à Brakel the *affectus* dimension of meditation on the passion was not expressed as emotional compassion but fostered personal knowledge of sin and salvation. The classical two-fold division appropriated by Luther one finds in à Brakel as well. After praising meditation as good medicine for dealing with a sense of guilt and temptation,[80] he arouses his readers to regard the suffering of Christ "as part of discipleship." The implication of that attention is that they then conduct themselves in their own suffering just as Jesus did in his suffering.

The way that à Brakel makes this discipleship concrete is striking. Just as Christ lamented about "feeling oppressed from within and without," we are also permitted to complain about our needs to God and others. "Stones [groans, sighs] in response to pain is neither impatience nor sin!" Just as Christ persevered in the faith and exercised that faith even "in his greatest darkness and forsakenness, and even then still said, 'My Father, my God,'" so we should never lose candor in our faith. Just as Christ consoled himself with the promised outcome and its glory, so we should also look to "the promises that are yea and amen."[81] First of all, the effect of his example has a positive dimension. However, it also has a negative one in the sense that Jesus' example requires not only a "yes" but also a "no." This is the "no" spoken against sin. Because sin has been crucified in Christ, we must consider that sin as "given up." By being united with the Crucified One through faith, we shall receive his power to put to death the power of sin. "Likewise, regard yourself as being dead to sin but alive to God in Christ Jesus our Lord (Rom. 6:11)."[82]

To this point it has become apparent to us that the filling up that à Brakel connects with spiritual reflection—at least with meditating on the passion—has two parts. On the one hand it consists of an attentive, applicable consideration of Christ's person and saving work, and on the other hand it constitutes the basis for discipleship. The first example of a model for meditation in *Redelyke Godsdienst* has yielded this insight for us. But now I want to discuss two others. The second is found in the chapter on the love of Jesus that is already familiar to us. Toward the end of it, à Brakel makes an appeal in a manner true to his style that invites his readers to consider Jesus "in all his loveliness." Once again he recalls the bride in the Song of Solomon, who describes her Bridegroom "from head to toe" and concludes that "everything about him is completely lovely (5:16)."[83] As soon

---

78. Nicol, *Meditation bei Luther*, 120.
79. Ibid., 127-32.
80. *RG*, 1.22.38-39, 510-12.
81. *RG*, 1.22.40, 512.
82. Ibid., 513.
83. *RG*, 2.15.7, 230.

as a person contemplates this King in his beauty, a love for him is created that begins to pour out. For, à Brakel understands that "love begets love." He is apparently convinced that meditation is preeminently the time when this begetting of love occurs. He consistently urges his readers to reflect on the manifestations of Jesus' love. At the same time, he leads the way by reviewing the dimensions of that display of love—in the same way that we encountered earlier. At this point he also sounds the appeal: "Go to the crib, and follow him to the cross." Father à Brakel then becomes very direct: "Consider him in his utter fear and sense of oppression, and think about the fact that he appeals to you as he does in his deepest pain: 'Look at me, my chosen one, my beloved; my love for you has brought me to this state of affairs; yet, my love for you is so great that I would rather suffer a thousand times more than I am rather than allow you to be lost.'" Then à Brakel adds this assurance: "He lays you on his heart; he thinks constantly about you; he prays for you." Following this he makes a transition to the experience of his readers on the road of conversion and in serving Jesus; and he once again invites them to reflect. This time, however, reflection is not focused on the objective but on the subjective side of salvation. "Reflect on how lovingly he has drawn you to himself. . . . How often has he not spoken to your heart and how often has he not given you the kiss of his love?"[84]

Could a person conclude from this that by Jesus' kiss of love à Brakel means Christ speaking to our hearts? He does not say exactly what he intends with this expression. One would want to know especially how he sees the relation between meditation and the reading of Scripture. Remarkably, he pays no attention to this point. Does he proceed from the position that spiritual reflection happens before an open Bible? Or, does he mean that Scripture is stored in the memory as though in a reservoir from which the Spirit simply draws? One thing is certainly clear, namely that the intimate experience of love that one encounters in meditating is nurtured by the gospel of the cross. Jesus' love as interpreted for us in the gospel is the object of meditation as well as the source of its power. Apart from faith in the gospel, meditating is fruitless. Not insignificantly, à Brakel closes this passage with the admonition: "Reflect on this, believe this."[85]

This second model sharpens still further the picture we get of à Brakel's perspective on the content of meditation. Meditating is directed toward Christ both in the affective-applicatory and in the effective-exemplary senses, and it is nurtured by a believing consideration of the gospel. Here the models considered to this point valued especially meditation on the passion. The third example that can be labeled a model of meditating involves Christ's ascension. According to à Brakel, reflecting on it has more value in a way than meditating on the passion. This does not mean that a person can ignore reflection on Christ's sufferings, but that one should not isolate his suffering from his glory. For, then one impedes spiritual "growth." He therefore makes an appeal "for adding" reflection on Christ's ascension.[86] Thus, one should not consider the Crucified One without realizing that he is also risen and glorified. Just as humiliation must be seen in

---

84. Ibid., 230-31.
85. Ibid., 231.
86. *RG*, 1.23.38, 540.

the perspective of exaltation, so too, meditating on the passion must be done in the context of reflecting on Christ's glorification. À Brakel calls this kind of reflection "the beginning of heaven." He inspires it with the thought that the contemplation of Christ's glorification defines life in heaven according to John 17:24, but that Christ discloses this only to those who love him already here on earth so that they "may already be involved in this work [i.e., in contemplation] here below." We are dealing here with a preliminary expression of life in heaven, a preparation stimulated by Christ's self-disclosure. A definite interplay exists between his self-disclosure and this reflection. Wherever Christ reveals himself, love that contemplates him is aroused. To it, Christ in turn responds by revealing himself "in clearer and clearer" ways. "So, the one causes the other."[87]

Reflection on Christ in heaven and on life in heaven is associated by à Brakel with two aspects of faith in particular: joy and anticipation. Characteristic of his piety is that joy receives such a prominent place in it, just as it does for Teellinck and Saldenus and especially for his father, Theodorus. He devotes a separate chapter to the subject.[88] This joy issues from justification by faith, while it is intensified by the promised glory. À Brakel arouses his readers to treasure "the excellence of these promised benefits" and to rejoice in their "claim to this inheritance." Although the definitive glory is not yet enjoyed, a person may be gladdened by the "certainty possessing it in the future." Does anyone "yearn for heaven?" Let him yearn for joy. For what else will people have to do in heaven? "There nothing exists except being joyful." For à Brakel heaven is simply "joy in the Lord."[89]

Whoever endeavors to understand how the glorified Christ is extolled in heaven, will be "inflamed" with joy and will "discover their heart-of-hearts and join the singing multitude."[90] But life here and now involves only a foretaste of complete joy, as à Brakel emphasizes in the chapter on everlasting glory.[91] Then one will be present with the Lord continuously. In the present, however, believers discover that their foretaste of joy is disrupted by the realization that they still live so "far from the Lord." This causes them "many tears," for all their longings and "yearnings" are directed toward the glory of heaven, where their fellowship with God will be "unmediated and everlasting." "O, how sweet it will be to sit under the shadow of the almighty, the good, the loving, the all-sufficient, the friendly God." There Jesus will be seen "with the eyes of the flesh," to our "complete joy and love." Then one will discern in him "the rays of divine glory."[92] At present the believing soul sees only "a little glimmer and that [still] as it were only a reflection" of this brightness.[93] To be sure, this gladdens

---

87. Ibid.

88. *RG*, 1.37, 927-37.

89. Ibid., 934-35.

90. *RG*, 1.23.41, 542. À Brakel also devotes a separate, short chapter to the subject of singing: *RG*, 2.37, 503-8.

91. *RG*, 2.61, 762-74.

92. *RG*, 2.61.14, 769. À Brakel distinguishes in this connection a seeing with the eyes of the body and a seeing with the "eyes of the mind." The object of the first is Jesus, of the second is God.

93. Ibid. Compare Exodus 33:23.

her "wondrously," but—à Brakel notes once again in the famous words of Bernard—it is still only "a rare occurrence of short duration." Such euphoria recedes quickly and leaves behind only a powerful, painful longing.[94] But, the time is coming when everything temporary will be in the past and the soul will "lose itself completely in God." That will "be without end and will be for all eternity."[95]

The result of our survey is that in à Brakel's piety meditation assumes an indispensable place. While it tends toward eschatological contemplation and even proleptically achieves this, it is conducted within the boundaries of faith.[96] It is directed at Christ and contemplates him in the inseparable unity of his humiliation and his exaltation. The life of meditation constitutes the source of joy and anticipation. To this one must add one word, however, namely sanctification. As became apparent from à Brakel's not only affective but also effective approach to meditation, he maintains a harmonious relationship between mysticism and ethics. It is not by chance that just before he concludes his section on contemplation of the ascended Christ, he remarks: "Behold, in this way one contemplating Jesus in his glory becomes inflamed with love that is the fountain of the soul and the proper form of sanctification."[97]

Contemplation

In the foregoing it repeatedly became obvious that à Brakel was not unfamiliar with the contemplative features that typified his father's meditative practice. The question that I now want to scrutinize explicitly is precisely what content Wilhelmus gave these moments.

Even less than his father, Wilhelmus shies away from the synonymous terms "observation" and "contemplation." He is convinced that already in this life believers are favored with "a view" of the eschaton by way of foretaste. Despite the anticipatory feature characteristic of contemplation, it still actually belongs to the realm of faith. Being caught up to the third heaven, as overwhelmed Paul, à Brakel obviously regards as a unique and unrepeatable, apostolic privilege. At least, he writes—differently than his father[98]—that this is not permitted "for us" in this age. But what we certainly "may and must" experience is nevertheless practiced but little. For us it is permitted and commanded, namely, "to see by faith Jesus crowned with glory and honor." For although faith is proof of things not seen, that faith in no way stops with an account of the historical events in

---

94. *RG*, 2.61.15, 769. It is noteworthy that Bernard puts the same idea into words: that the Bridegroom frequently alternates his brief visit (*visitatio*) with his disappearance is cause for pain (*molestat*). See *SC*, 32:2, in *SW*, 5:502. This involves a motif that is always current in the mystical tradition.

95. *RG*, 2.61.18-19, 770-71.

96. A. de Reuver, "Wilhelmus à Brakel en het piëtisme," *DNR* 22 (1998), 88-89.

97. *RG*, 1.23.44, 545.

98. T. à Brakel, *De Trappen*, 309-10, tells of an experience during which he was caught up so high into God's presence, that "like Paul" he could not describe it. He heard "unutterable words that a human being is not considered capable of speaking (II Corinthians 12:4)." Apparently, in this regard Wilhelmus could not imitate his father.

Christ's life but is committed to penetrating "to an observation of those events themselves."[99] Faith, therefore, consists of a special way of seeing by which it contemplates what is incapable of being seen with the naked eye.

If one asks how this contemplative experience is produced in à Brakel's opinion, he appears—consistent with his view of meditation—to think first of all of a fully involved human activity. He urgently calls his readers: "Consider the exalted Jesus as God." Thereupon, however, he emphasizes that this is an experience that one cannot achieve by oneself. At least he immediately shifts to a passive construction, noting that it is an experience "to which the soul is admitted." The place where the contemplating soul is admitted is nothing less than heaven. He does not state this explicitly, to be sure, but it is clear by implication from what follows this sentence. Namely, he says that the believer is admitted in order to see Jesus in all of his glorious perfections.[100] When à Brakel turns to a description of the content of this heavenly experience, one detects a certain hesitation. On the one hand he plainly admits that "the limited understanding of the creature" does not have the power to see "eternity," let alone to comprehend it. On the other hand, however, he believes that the soul "becomes aware" of something of it. This awareness is completed not only "through mental conjecture and second-hand accounts," but as an "experiential sighting" in which the strength and sweetness of the experience is felt and tasted. "Then, then," writes à Brakel with double emphasis, "the soul loses itself" and is in a position to praise Christ willingly in all his glory.[101] Although in his chapter on eternal glory à Brakel reserves being lost in God for the eschaton,[102] it appears here that beholding the heavenly Christ is an experience that is enjoyed already now.

Up to this point à Brakel has given the impression that the contemplative moment in communion with God is certainly rare and short in duration, but that all true believers share in it. While the event itself is exceptional, the class of believers that experience it is not. This last insight seems to be in tension with the way matters encountered elsewhere in *Redelyke Godsdienst* are represented—particularly in Wilhelmus' subsequently appended chapter entitled "Waerschouwende Bestieringe tegen de Piëtisten."[103] Before I address this issue, I want to consider the curious fact that à Brakel represents himself the way that he does in this polemic against the pietists, since he as a writer may without any hesitation be regarded as a representative of pietism when he is measured by contemporary standards.[104] The content that the term "pietism" had for him was

---

99. *RG*, 1.23.38, 540.

100. What the difference is between this permissible experience and the being caught up allowed only for Paul, is not made clear by à Brakel.

101. *RG*, 1.23.39, 541.

102. *RG*, 2.61.18, 770.

103. *RG*, 1.43, 1080-1134. [In translation: "Cautionary Advice against the Pietists."]

104. De Reuver, "Wilhelmus à Brakel," 83-90.

different from what it carries today.[105] This becomes clear when one considers the ideas that he opposes.

It should be noted that his primary objection to these "mystical" representatives, among whom he includes the Labadists, comes down to the fact that their piety gives the pretension of spirituality but rests entirely on the natural mind and is developed through fantasy and imagination. While they might represent themselves as being filled with the Spirit, à Brakel makes no excuse for labeling them as lacking the Spirit entirely. This pneumatological deficiency manifests itself, in his opinion, in two ways. The first concerns the position of Christ. The explanation that à Brakel provides here is surprising. True believers live by faith and not by contemplation! For that very reason they approach the Father only through Christ, who is their righteousness, and they "are accustomed" in so doing "to contemplate God in the face of Jesus Christ." However, this mediatorship of Christ is disregarded by these "mystics."[106] In this connection à Brakel is definitely concerned about the knowledge of Christ's atoning work. "All the beautiful language" of the "pietists" whom he opposes "is only about the Lord Jesus as King or as the patron of discipleship." But what is really essential is that people know him as High Priest, "so that they seek peace with God in his perfect atonement and do so through a continuous and frequently repeated offering of faith." À Brakel calls this "the heart and core of true Christianity."[107]

This Christocentric standard obviously determines the authenticity of contemplation. À Brakel introduces an unmistakable nuance by appealing to the Pauline contrast between faith and contemplation. This contrast is valid only as long as the way of contemplation is pursued apart from the mediation of justifying faith in Christ; it does not obtain when contemplation is pursued indirectly, that is on the basis of justification. We now understand how in one and the same breath à Brakel can say that the godly live by faith and not by contemplation, and at the same time that they are accustomed to contemplating God in the face of Christ.

The second point of criticism lies in the extension of the first. À Brakel reproaches the "pietists" for proceeding apart from and even against the written word of God.[108] They maintain that people "must rise above the word in a higher form of contemplation."[109] In so doing they betray authentic communion with God, which à Brakel regards as illicit. His criticism is addressed, therefore, toward so-called godly people who have dispensed with meditation on Christ and

---

105. By "pietism," à Brakel means "fanaticism," which he associates with quietists, Quakers and followers of David Joris, and which is reflected in figures like Böhme, De Molinos, Fénelon and also De Labadie. *RG*, 1.43, 1082-83 and 1109.

106. *RG*, 1.43, 1083. Because this chapter is subdivided into six propositions, each of whose paragraph numbers always begin with "1," I limit the notes simply to the page numbers.

107. Ibid., 1121.

108. Ibid., 1083. On the same criticism, see W. à Brakel, *Leere en Leydinge*, 64-66.

109. Ibid., 1098. Compare 1109 and 1114, where it is stated that they regard the word as a "dead letter."

the Bible. He explains with emphasis that his polemic "does not have in mind" the truly godly. "Truly, truly I say unto you!"[110]

It is exciting when à Brakel explains his own ideas about contemplation. As we already know, he regards contemplation as completely legitimate. However, he wants to distinguish sharply between natural and spiritual contemplation. The first is directed toward God as he "discloses himself in nature," that is to say, God in himself aside from reconciliation in Christ. The second, by contrast, contemplates God-for-us as he makes himself known in Christ as a reconciling Father. About this God in Christ à Brakel says that he once in awhile reveals himself "without mediation" with so much light and sweetness that it defies description. Sometimes that is accompanied with the divine assurance that he loves us with an eternal love.[111] Although in natural contemplation union with God is nothing more than "a union with one's own fantasy," true union happens "only through faith." From a comparable qualification it seems that the "unmediated" means of revelation does not exclude the instrumentality of faith, but includes it. In this way, that is, by believing, a person is united with "one and the same" God through spiritual contemplation. What this intimacy entails à Brakel explains: while natural contemplation leaves man as he is naturally, spiritual contemplation lets him share increasingly in the divine nature.[112]

In order to be protected from what à Brakel calls "that particular fanaticism," one must bear in mind that the Holy Spirit, who convicts one of sin and re-creates from death to life, is "a Spirit of faith." This implies that the Spirit always directs people to Christ as their "ransom and righteousness," and that he "leads" the believer "in everything according to the word."[113] Such definite statements make all the more weighty the question of what à Brakel exactly means by "unmediated." Is he still not suggesting by this a kind of contemplation that rises above the word? In order to answer this question, we must first investigate what he understands by the term "unmediated."

His doctrine of the Lord's supper includes a passage that can put us on track to answer this. He writes that during the Lord's supper people exercise a communion with Christ that signifies that he assures believers of their partnership in him. This occurs in a twofold way. The first is *mediated* in nature and comes by means of the "practical syllogism." Its three elements are as

110. Ibid., 1083.

111. Ibid., 1113. Here an analogy is presented with the way à Brakel describes the (immediate) anointing with the Holy Spirit in *RG* 2.52.6, 645. See W. van 't Spijker, *De verzegeling met de Heilige Geest* (Kampen, 1991), 112-13 and de Reuver, "Een mystieke ader," 38.

112. *RG*, 1.43, 1113.

113. Ibid., 1115. À Brakel was much more critical towards the term "fanaticism" than was Jodocus van Lodensteyn (1620-1677). While the latter was well aware of its dangers, according to him Reformed Christians "had to be outstanding fanatics, driven in everything by the Spirit of the Lord." See his *Beschouwinge van Zion* (4th ed.; Amsterdam, 1718), 38. The standard that he established is that this "mystical theology" had to be in complete agreement with the "H. Gereform. Waarheyd" [trans.: "sacred Reformed truth"] (*Beschouwinge*, 43). For the way in which this perspective took shape in Van Lodensteyn's preaching, see his sermon on Song of Solomon 1:4 in *Geestelyke Opwekker* (3rd edition; Amsterdam, 1732), 251-287. Compare de Reuver, "Een mystieke ader," 24.

follows. First, the Holy Ghost "discloses" the biblical marks characteristic of true faith. Then he turns attention to the inner "graces" in which the believer participates. Finally, he leads the believer who perceives that he bears these marks "to conclude based on the word" that the promised communion with Christ applies to him as well. À Brakel follows his explanation with a second method of assurance. This one is *unmediated* in nature. Here believers do not observe, reflectively, that they possess the marks described, but they direct their attention entirely toward the signs of the supper "as seals and confirmations" that they belong to Christ. "Here the Holy Spirit works without intermediaries . . . and impresses so powerfully on her heart by means of the word and the seal the conviction that the Lord Jesus loves her," that she experiences "intimate fellowship" with him.[114] This passage is so informative because it makes it obvious that the term "unmediated" poses no inconsistency for à Brakel with the means of the word and the sign, but that it is simply a way of contrasting this approach with that outlined in the "practical syllogism." The unmediated work of the Holy Spirit does not exclude the word, but includes it.

I think that the circuitous route that we took can show us the direction for interpreting à Brakel's exposé of unmediated revelation. The framework within which this revelation is considered is contemplation. Here he draws the distinction between the activity of the individual soul and that of God.[115] À Brakel is of the opinion that the soul's possibilities are limited. Although the believer is certainly in a position to engage in reflection, through it he will never be capable of rising to "the sight of God." The person meditating can never progress further than increasingly to long "to understand what he can know about God through the word, through faith and through understanding." God's capabilities extend much farther. He is able to satisfy those longings. He surely "satisfies one engaged in spiritual reflection with extraordinary and further unmediated revelations of himself, according to his promises in John 14:21 and 23, and he allows her to see God more closely and to experience who God is and what he is to her in Jesus Christ."[116] Further along Wilhelmus adds that during this contemplation the believer "always remains close to Christ" and that "in that context" always contemplates God's goodness and greatness. It is a setting that he describes with precision as "an intimate conversation conducted trustingly, contemplatively and with love overflowing."[117] That this summary gives priority of place to faith is not accidental.

On the basis of this formulation, I think I may conclude that the unmediated experience that à Brakel has in mind implies no denial of being mediated through faith and the word. In a similar manner as when he described the unmediated experience of communion in the Lord's supper, here he wants to articulate that direct contemplation is not the result of one's own activity and effort, but of divine illumination. It is entirely the Spirit who imparts this "insight." But the Spirit does not work apart from Christ or from faith in the word.

---

114. *RG*, 1.41.9, 1027.
115. Ibid., 1.43, 1122.
116. Ibid., 1123.
117. Ibid., 1130.

That à Brakel here once again notes that this experience is all about "a rare occurrence of short duration," does not surprise us anymore. But what is surprising is his explanation that it is bestowed "not on all, but only on some." The question arises, therefore, of whether in his opinion a difference exists between the mystical rapture that he considered to be a possibility for all believers and this contemplative experience that apparently he sees as reserved only for some. Wilhelmus does not explicitly go into this matter. He is content simply with an attempt to describe this "revelation." He designates it as "being enraptured—the *raptus*[118]—with a love for the holy God," one that a person "in one sense might call contemplation and a foretaste of eternity, when one will no longer live by faith but by contemplation."[119] With the relative word "in one sense" à Brakel admits, it seems to me, that the contemplation experienced here on earth is not identical with that in heaven. The former is only a prelude, a preparation, for the latter, and precisely on account of its provisional character belongs to the stage of faith. One once again notes the paradox: the contemplation that à Brakel describes occurs during the phase in which one does not yet live by contemplation but by faith. This is the basis upon which I conclude that here contemplation does not negate faith, but rather presupposes it.

Meanwhile, it remains an open question as to the way this experience is to be distinguished from those mystically defined times that in principle are available to all believers. Although à Brakel does not answer this question explicitly, implicitly his discussion provides adequate clarification. To the extent that I understand it, the mystical experience in which *all* believers are able to share always involves the contemplation of Jesus, particularly Jesus in his glorification. The contemplation that he reserves exclusively for *some* involves God, not Jesus. À Brakel would certainly have added with emphasis that this contemplation of God does not occur apart from Christ. His problem with the "pietists" is precisely that they forget this. The mediation of Christ as a "ransom" is non-negotiable. True contemplation occurs exclusively "in Christ." But, in that bond of faith a person nevertheless sees God himself. Obviously, the oneness of God had sufficient trinitarian breadth[120] to permit the distinction between the divine persons also in the sense that contemplation of Christ was tied to contemplation of the Father, but still was not identical with it. The contemplation involving Christ constitutes the prerequisite for the contemplation of God. This is a contemplation that is not "preoccupied" with God's works—in either nature or grace—"but it concentrates directly on God," in adoration of his person and his virtues. By this direct engagement à Brakel does not want to by-pass Christ, but God's works. He is concerned here not with contemplating what God *does*, but with marveling at who he *is* for us. À Brakel calls it "a foretaste of our contemplation in heaven."[121] This level of contemplation he apparently considers to be so exalted that in the present age it is reserved for only a very few people.

---

118. *RG* 2.61.19, 771, is another place where he talks about "being uplifted," which he identifies as experiencing "oneness and communion with God."

119. *RG* 1.43, 1123. Compare Boot, *De allegorische uitlegging*, 208.

120. On à Brakel's doctrine of the Trinity, see *RG* 1.4., 109-53.

121. *RG* 1.43, 1129.

When we summarize in this chapter the vision that "Father à Brakel" develops concerning contemplation, then the two features just reviewed jump out at us, namely immediacy and unusualness. What I suspect in this regard is that he emphasizes both these aspects because he considers them to be important in his debate with the "pietists." With the note of immediacy, he demonstrates that Reformed contemplation is not inferior to theirs. He immediately adds, however, the critical note that any form of immediacy that intends to circumvent the word and faith is merely fantasy. He judges that it is not only a form of baseless anticipation, but he regards it as a fiction. Although he himself discusses a form of unmediated contemplation in which one aspires to glory, he at the same time wants to strictly honor the boundary of the "not yet." His reproof of the "pietists" is that they ignore this.

À Brakel's observation that extraordinary revelation occurs only in rare instances also seems to me to have a critical purpose. I must acknowledge that this hunch is not directly substantiated by the text. My interpretation is hypothetical and rests on indications derived from the course of his argument. What he posits is that the circle of true observers is limited to those who have come to know Christ through faith as their "Surety," and that not even all of them receive extraordinary revelation. Within the circle of true observers are found, therefore, a narrower, concentric circle of those who receive a special grace. To this point à Brakel's argument is explicit. What I propose is that he implicitly implies by this that the "pietists" make the circle much too large. They reckon neither with the condition of justifying faith, nor with the exceptional nature of the category. Their circle is too wide to suit à Brakel. While they assert that proleptic contemplation is common to all who engage in spiritual contemplation, he ascribes that to only an exceptional circle of believers.

By way of conclusion we note that à Brakel introduces a two-fold certainty in connection with the subject of contemplation. The first involves contemplation of the glorified Christ. Only those who reflect on him as their righteousness share in it. The second involves the "unmediated" contemplation of God. It is reserved exclusively for some who belong to this first group. À Brakel skirts the obvious question of what the motive for this exceptional treatment might be. Nothing surfaces to suggest to him that the special character of their piety accounts for this. What is obvious is that he leaves the explanation completely within the realm of God's freedom. His intention is merely to distinguish the legitimate, faith-based form of contemplation from its spiritualistic perversion that he observed in the "pietists."

Evaluation

In the review just completed, à Brakel has emerged as an author who connects his systematic interests with both pastoral and mystical attitudes. His *Redelyke Godtsdienst* is an example of the proposition that Reformed orthodoxy should not be contrasted with Reformed piety, but that the two can coexist harmoniously.[122] On numerous occasions à Brakel provides examples of doctrinally described accounts of the life of faith which includes a very personal, loving communion with God. While, seen logically, faith receives priority, in practice he knows from experience that faith and love are interwoven. He gives close scrutiny to this experience. This appears from the applicatory passages that he consistently inserts, and especially from his frequent encouragement to "reflect" on the locus he is treating. In these spiritual subsections the inner working of the Holy Spirit is unusually prominent. Nevertheless, my observation is that the pneumatological dimension does not emerge at the expense of the Christological, and the *extra nos* of salvation history is not overshadowed by the *in nobis* of the dimensions of the salvation applied. Rather, what the Spirit applies is anchored in the atoning work of Christ.

In à Brakel's spirituality, believing fellowship with Christ assumes a key position. This grounding in Christ quite simply functions as the source of the experience of salvation. Like Theodorus, Wilhelmus wants to represent this experience as true to life. While he provides no account of his personal communion with God, as his father had done, the body of his work provides unmistakable confirmation that he no less than Theodorus spoke from personal experience. The approval with which he published his father's manuscripts was genuine. The spirituality that Wilhelmus depicts testifies to a deep spiritual kinship between father and son. On two points a difference does exist. The first is formal. The extremely quantified nature of Theodorus' own meditative practices is not encountered in Wilhelmus. The second difference is related to content. While the contemplation that Wilhelmus describes often achieves the point of great ecstasy associated with mystical *raptus*, he never dared to consider this comparable to Paul's experience of rapture. Obviously, for the son this was a boundary at which he stopped. His father crossed it.

When one compares à Brakel's devotion with Teellinck's, the results are ambivalent. On the one hand, Teellinck's depiction of devotion appears to be more intense than à Brakel's. Especially Teellinck's yearning for heaven exceeds à Brakel's heart's desire. On the other hand, where anticipation of eschatological fulfillment is involved, he is less restrained than Teellinck. Throughout, this never exceeds the level of expressed longings. Yet, one must not posit an absolute contrast on this point. Teellinck also knew moments when longings were fulfilled provisionally. And for à Brakel, also, the proleptic experiences of communion were brief and only occasional.

While à Brakel does not acknowledge the name of Bernard,[123] he quotes his—at least in translation—famous expression repeatedly: *"rara hora, parva mora."* This indicates not simply a formal analogy. In my opinion one can speak of a substantive congeniality with Bernard's mystical spirituality. This appears

---

122. See R. A. Muller, "Covenant and Conscience in English Reformed Theology: Three Variations on a 17th Century Theme," *Westminster Theological Journal* 42 (1979): 308-34. The opening sentence reads, "Reformed theology in the late sixteenth and the seventeenth century was not so rigidly scholastic that it failed to related doctrine to piety." This proposition strikes me as applicable also to seventeenth-century Dutch Reformed theology.

123. Boot, *De allegorische uitlegging*, 209.

especially in those brief references that Wilhelmus makes when he describes sporadic "occasions of being lifted up." That he had direct knowledge of the corpus of Bernard's work is not obvious to me. It is possible that his thought-world, as well as that of his father, Theodorus, was conveyed to him by his teacher Voetius and his spiritual kinsman Witsius. However that may be, à Brakel also makes mention of a heavenly delight in which the love of God is tasted. That this experience is sporadic, temporary and partial does not detract from its reality.

The distinction that à Brakel introduces concerning contemplation is noteworthy, namely contemplation of the glorified Christ that is stored up for all believers and the contemplation of God that is permitted only to some and is linked with unmediated revelation. The position that the latter form of contemplation assumes is certainly marginal within the totality of his writings, but nevertheless too striking to be regarded as beyond grasp. Obviously, he assigns contemplation a special position in which the consideration of Christ as God is followed by a consideration of God. While à Brakel is motivated, albeit implicitly, by trinitarian considerations in making this distinction, he does not invoke it here to clarify its pastoral relevance, in my estimation. The point is simply that God as the "object" of consideration can never be anything except God in Christ, according to à Brakel. All contemplation of God apart from Christ he considers to be fictitious and forbidden. But precisely this point underlines the urgency of the question of what actually constitutes the "extra" that distinguishes this consideration of God in Christ from the consideration of Christ as God. À Brakel probably wanted to show by this that the Father lets himself be seen in the Son as the unique source of creation and redemption who is totally worthy of our worship. This preserves unimpeded Wilhelmus' explanation that it is precisely in this connection that valid contemplation "always occurs in Christ."

"Father à Brakel's" spirituality is one that is rooted in Christ through the word believed, even in its most intimate and mystical moments. This foundation protects his mysticism from spiritualism. It is this same foundation that he is convinced protects people who are assaulted by despair. For, believers are certainly tossed back and forth, but they cling tightly to Jesus; "and not seeing, they still believe that God is also their God and will remain so by virtue of the eternal redemption that he has brought to pass." Like a ship outfitted with strong ropes and anchors has sure "mooring" and "during a storm is certainly tossed around by the breakers but nevertheless remains securely in place; in the same way the Lord Jesus is their anchor through every tempest, and they ride out the storms in the steadfastness of faith until their darkness dissipates and they are revived again by a sweet calm."[124]

When life comes to this, à Brakel finds security in the "nevertheless" of faith, which stands in sharp contrast to all feeling and subjective experience. In this regard he demonstrates that he is a true son of his father. Above all, however, their kinship is obvious from the perspective of the sweet refreshment that beckons them both.

---

124. *RG* 1.43, 1108.

HERMANNUS WITSIUS S.S. LITTERARUM IN ECCLESIA ET ACADEMIA ULTRAIECTINA DOCTOR ET PROFESSOR ÆTAT. XLIV A. MDCLXXXI.

7

Herman Witsius (1636-1708)

"Unusually Learned and Gifted"[1]

That Witsius returned to pay an old debt when in 1680 he accepted the office of professor in Utrecht is perhaps saying too much. But that he owed much to the cathedral city—"if not everything, then almost everything"—he did not conceal. With a slight sigh tinged with pathos not unusual for his day and citing Psalm 137, he explained that his right hand could better have lost track of itself and his tongue could better cleave to the roof of his mouth that that he should forget the blessings that were accorded him there by church and academy.[2] Witsius was deeply honored by his Utrecht appointment. That he had accepted it could not have made the trustees any less satisfied than he. When in the fall of 1679 it came to filling the vacancy caused by the death of Franciscus Burmannus, the gentlemen had considered various accomplished theologians, but they found the most gifted to be Witsius. He had established his reputation during the five years that he had spent at the Academy of Franeker and already had several publications to his name. The corporation endorsed this opinion. It unanimously judged, "He is unusually learned and gifted, possessing those qualities required in a professor of theology."[3] The corporate fathers had good reason to be satisfied. Witsius was an erudite person, and above all, they had accomplished what Groningen was unable to achieve.

The new professor committed himself to Utrecht in the conviction that he had major obligations there to both the church and the academy. For that reason he took great satisfaction in the fact that he was not only named as a professor, but also as a minister. Four days after his installation as minister, the obligatory inauguration occurred. It took place on April 25, 1680. Two academic officials flanked him on the way to the city hall, and two trustees en route to events in the senate hall. He delivered his address—naturally, in Latin—in the large auditorium. It was entitled, "Oratio inauguralis Trajectina de praestantia veritatis evangelicae" ("A Utrecht Inaugural Address on the Excellence of Gospel Truth.").[4] Its content is too interesting for us merely to pass over it. So, to begin, it becomes clear from it what exactly it was for which Witsius thanked Utrecht. He expressly named two things: here the word of God became a blessing to him, and here he enjoyed exceptional academic instruction. Regarding the first, he

---

1. In shortened form, this chapter on Witsius appeared earlier in *Vier eeuwen theologie in Utrecht: Bijdragen tot de geschiedenis van de theologische faculteit aan de Universiteit Utrecht*, ed. A. de Groot and O. J. de Jong, (Zoetermeer, 2001).

2. Herman Witsius, *Miscelleanorum Sacrorum*, 4 vols. (Utrecht, 1692), 2:681-82.

3. Corporate Resolutions, February 23 and March 1, 1680, as cited in J. van Genderen, *Herman Witsius* (The Hague, 1953), 65.

4. Found in Witsius, *Miscelleanorum*, 2:680-705.

would have especially thought of the preaching and pastoral leadership of Justus van den Bogaard, and regarding the second, especially of Voetius' colleagues.[5] Now that Witsius himself was connected with Utrecht, he longed for nothing less than to repay the obligations that he had incurred there.

But the address is interesting primarily because it provides insight for us into the basis of Witsius' spirituality. Knowledge of the truth of the gospel provides enjoyment, he maintains in his address. Whoever reflects on the mysteries of salvation is embraced by the love of God and experiences an inner joy. No one needs to fear that such abundant happiness should be undeserved, for it is God himself who invites people to this sacred, mystical transport. Finally, Witsius' address—more precisely, the prayer with which it closes—includes a passage that may be considered typical of his thinking. In his petitions for the church and the students, he asks, "May we preserve unity in that which is essential; freedom in that which is not; and in both, wisdom and love, and in all things, a clear conscience until the day of the Lord."[6] In a somewhat shortened form these words constitute the motto of Witsius' life, which is characterized by his irenic bearing.[7]

In the opinion of J. van Genderen, both the address and the prayer are typical of Witsius.[8] One can dispute this appreciation to the extent that this peaceable quality is truer of the later than of the earlier Witsius. His well-known *Twist des Heeren met syn wijngaert*, 1669 (with several reprints[9]), was a polemical work with sharp criticism of all sorts of abuses in church life and was accompanied by "blunt judgements" about Cartesian and Cocceijan "innovations."[10] It is not apparent that as to content he later regretted this critique. What is noteworthy is that throughout his career he came to prefer a thetic rather than a combative approach, a disposition that he had in common with his irenic, bosom friend, Guiljelmus Saldenus.[11]

This facet of his oration is not so much what interests me in this chapter, however, as the emphasis that Witsius lays on the mystical component—or better, the mystical dimension—of the life of faith. I want to concentrate on it in what follows. I make this choice in the awareness that in so doing the important theological-historical aspect of Witsius' synthetic position in federal theology remains outside the picture.[12] However, I am at the same time convinced that it is

---

5. I will return to his time of study at Utrecht.

6. Witsius, *Miscelleanorum*, 2:703. "In necessariis unitatem custodiant, in non necessariis libertatem, in utrisque prudentiam et charitatem, in omnibus conscientiam inoffensam in diem Domini." On the broader application and the variants of this sentence, see van Genderen, *Herman Witsius*, 67-68.

7. J. van Sluis, "Herman Witsius," *BLGNP*, 4:456.

8. Van Genderen, *Herman Witsius*, 67.

9. Van der Haar, *Schatkamer*, 565-66.

10. Van Sluis, "Witsius," 456.

11. Van den End, *Guiljelmus Saldenus*.

12. On this matter see van Genderen, *Herman Witsius*, 213-20; van Asselt, *Amicitia Dei*, 141-42; B. Loonstra, *Verkiezing, verzoening, verbond: Beschrijving en beoordeling van de leer van her pactum salutis in de gereformeerde theologie* (The Hague, 1990), 115-16; C. Graafland, "Structuurverschillen tussen voetiaanse en coccejannse geloofsleer," in F. G. M. Broeyer and E. G. E. van der Wall, ed., *Een richtingenstrijd in de Gereformeerde Kerk: Voetianen en coccejanen*

both legitimate and within the spirit of the author to direct special attention to the spirituality he advocated. Although I dare not argue that this yields a complete picture of it, I do think that a very remarkable feature of Witsius as an academic comes to light in this way. On purpose, I say as an academic. For it is definitely not the case that he reserved his mystical piety for ethical publications, although in the academic setting he certainly would have struck "a more scientific" tone. The sources that I consulted for this research are with only one exception (the *Twist des Heeren*) the records of his academic lectures.

Biographical Sketch

Witsius' biography need not be written up extensively at this point.[13] At the same time, the highlights of his life should not be ignored, the more so because they shed light on his spirituality.

Herman was born in February, 1636, and was raised in a devout, Enkhuizen family characterized by their pietism. According to the testimony of his friend Johannes à March,[14] who wrote Witsius' eulogy, his parents were godly people.[15] Already before Herman had been born, they had dedicated him—their first-born—to the service of the Lord. Raised in that atmosphere, and after leaving the Latin school, he began his theological studies in Utrecht at the age of fifteen. There he sat under the influence of Voetius and his spiritual compatriots. The study of languages suited him better than philosophy. It was to his advantage that shortly before his arrival at Utrecht, Johannes Leusden had been named as extraordinary professor in the oriental languages, in which the young student could prepare himself under this scholar's tutelage. His theological formation occurred pre-eminently under Voetius and Hoornbeek. The Voetian ideal consisting of a synthesis of *pietas* and *scientia*[16] left an indelible stamp on him. While Witsius resisted an all-too scholastic approach to doctrine and never became a thorough-going Voetian,[17] one does find in him a fully Voetian commitment to *praxis pietatis*.

After a one-year interim in Groningen, which extended from the fall of 1654 to the fall of 1655, Witsius continued his studies in Utrecht. It was during this

---

1650-1750 (Zoetermeer, 1994), 32-33; N. T. Bakker, *Miskende gratie: Van Calvijn tot Witsius, Een vergelijkende lezing, balans van 150 jaar gereformeerde orthodoxie* (Kampen, 1991), 170-71.

13. See van Genderen, *Herman Witsius*, 5-107 (and its extensive bibliography, 243-59); J. van Genderen, "Herman Witsius (1636-1708)," in *De Nadere Reformatie. Beschrijving*, ed. Brienen, et al., 193-218. Also see the sketch by van Sluis, "Herman Witsius," 456-58 (also with extensive bibliography).

14. On à Marck, see Nauta, "Johannes à Marck," 259-61.

15. Johannes à Marck, *Oratio funebris in obitum Hermanni Witsii* (Lugdunum Batavorum, 1708). See van Genderen, *Herman Witsius*, 2.

16. See Gisbertus Voetius, *Inaugurele rede over Godzaligheid te verbinden met de wetenschap, gehouden aan de Illustre School te Utrecht op de 21ste augustus 1634*, trans. and ed. A. de Groot (Latin text newly published with a Dutch translation, introduction and comments; Kampen, 1978).

17. Van Sluis, "Witsius," 457. Van Sluis notes, indeed correctly, that Witsius was even less of a Cocceian.

second phase of his work in Utrecht that he came into contact with the preacher Justus van den Bogaard, a man of unusual devoutness. This bosom friend of Jodocus van Lodensteyn perhaps was more significant for Witsius' own spiritual formation than any one of his theological professors.[18] The sermons Witsius heard him preach and the extended pastoral conversations that he had with him led him into the mysteries of the kingdom of God and of mystical Christianity. Van den Bogaard made transparent for him the distinction between objective theological knowledge that one appropriates through study and the heavenly wisdom that is received through meditation, prayer and the cultivation of communion with God. For the first time this last sort of knowledge produced the experience and discovery of spiritual realities for Witsius. While to that point Witsius had lived only in the outer court, thanks to van den Bogaard he was now admitted to the inner court of the sanctuary. It was especially this deeply incisive experience that he recalled in his own oration. In the fellowship of the Utrecht church he received the life-giving word, he disclosed. It was there that he received mystical nourishment and where he found the freedom to approach the Lord's table.[19]

When in 1657 the young Witsius was called to Westwoud, located between Hoorn and Enkhuizen, and was ordained there on July 8, the congregation received in him a preacher whose methods were not fully Voetian but who in any case gave flesh and blood to the Voetian agenda: scientific discernment coupled with the experiential fruit of godliness. In Westwoud Witsius produced his first publication, *'t Bedroefde Nederland* [trans.: *The Sad State of the Netherlands*], in 1659. It is a book in which his undiluted ideals of the Further Reformation came to expression.

Witsius, who meanwhile had gotten married, moved with his family to Wormer, where he ministered from 1661 to 1666. There *Practycke des Christendoms* [trans.: *The Practice of Christianity*] saw the light of day in 1665. It is a catechetical tract in which he developes practical themes like faith, sanctification and prayer. In a second volume of this work he develops a consideration of the spiritual life: *Geestelijke Prenten, van een Onwedergeboorne op syn beste, en een Wedergeboorne of syn slechtste* [trans.: *Spiritual Portraits: Of an Unregenerate Person at His Best and Of a Regenerate Person at His Worst*].

Goes followed Wormer. The brief years that Witsius spent there he regarded as the most peaceful and most pleasant of his life. "With contentment and satisfaction I took on the work of the Lord in the flourishing congregation of Goes, which afforded me a lovely refuge after the many storms I endured elsewhere. There, by God's blessing and with the service of my faithful helpmeet, I saw all sorts of devotional practices in full bloom, growth in the power of salvation, harmony of mind, and God's elect making their way hand in

---

18. Van Genderen, *Herman Witsius*, 17. He calls attention to the fact that no fewer than seven ministers of the same type were connected with the Reformed congregation of Utrecht during these years, 1651-1655. Among them were Jodocus van Lodensteyn, Justus van den Bogaard and Johannes Teellinck.

19. Witsius, *Miscelleanorum*, 2:681. According to van Genderen, *Herman Witsius*, 18.

hand on their journey toward heaven."[20] But within two years he was called to leave his "refuge" in Zeeland. The congregation of Leeuwarden extended a call to him and Witsius accepted it. Peace gave way to discord. In addition to lack of harmony between the consistory and classis, Witsius was caught up in a conflict that involved him personally. He occasioned it. Under the title *Twist des Heren met syn Wyngaart* [trans.: *The Lord's Quarrel with His Vineyard*], 1669, he published a book without waiting for the usual ecclesiastical approval; it was a further development of his first publication. Here and there the book occasioned a commotion, not just because it developed a very critical view of church and society, but especially because it satirized Cartesian and Cocceijan positions as damaging new ideas. These frictions played out against the background of the community's needs resulting from the flood of 1672. Generally speaking, Witsius enjoyed a positive relationship with his colleagues Wilhelmus à Brakel and Johannes vander Waeijen. He was an especially close friend of the latter, at least before vander Waeijen changed directions and left the Voetian for the Cocceijan camp.[21]

In the beginning of 1675 Witsius was appointed as preacher and professor at the Academy of Franeker. After he was promoted to the position of doctor of theology in March, he was inaugurated in April. On this occasion Witsius gave an address entitled *"De vero theologo"* [trans.: "Concerning True Theology"]. Here he developed a theme that was completely typical of his theological work and of his spirituality. A true theologian is a student of Scripture and of the Holy Spirit. He needs to be not only an academic theologian, but a theological expert (*expertus theologus*) who can recite what he himself has heard, seen, experienced and tasted, and who by his holy way of life is an example for others.[22] The spiritual Witsius developed his agenda.

Witsius enjoyed good relations with his academic colleagues Nicolaus Arnoldi and Johannes à Marck, who in 1676 at the tender age of twenty was appointed as professor. Together the three of them protested—to little avail—the appointment of vander Waeijen, who meanwhile had switched from a Voetian to a Cocceijan position. Witsius' most important work appeared in 1677, while he was at Franeker: *De Oeconomia Foederum Dei cum Hominibus Libri quator*. It was dedicated to *stadhouder* King Willem III, who bore the honorary title of "Defender of the Faith" (*Defensor fidei*).[23]

We have already indicated that in 1680 Witsius was appointed to the Utrecht Academy. He labored there for eighteen years, also there in the combined position of professor and preacher. Among his best known colleagues were Petrus van Mastricht and Melchior Leydekker. Witsius' academic tenure at Utrecht produced a respectable stream of publications. Among them, of most importance are *Exercitationes Sacrae in Symbolum quod Apostolorum dicitur*

---

20. Witsius, *Twist des Heeren*, "Dedication," 3.

21. J. van Sluis, "Het omzwaaien van Johannes vander Waeijen," in *Een richtingenstrijd*, ed. Broeyer and van der Wall, 95-103.

22. Witsius, *Miscelleanorum*, 2:673-78. According to van Genderen, *Herman Witsius*, 52.

23. The work was translated by Martinus van Harlingen, preacher at Hoorn, under the title of *VierBoecken van de Verscheyden Bedeelinge der Verbonden Gods met de Menschen* (Utrecht, 1686). It is hereafter abbreviated as *Verbonden*.

(Franeker, 1681),[24] in which his debates—generally held in Franeker—are reworked, and *Miscelleanorum Sacrorum libri IV* (Utrecht, 1692). *Theologia practica* was published posthumously by his colleagues,[25] and from it becomes evident once again that during his lectures Witsius treated topics like holy amazement concerning God's virtues, spiritual marriage, self-denial and meditation. While he only gave three public lectures a week, Witsius followed the practice of extending his instruction in private lessons. The demand was heavy, not only by students but also by various ministers. Worth noting is that additionally he gave catechism instruction during the summer for confessing members, and he called them "lectures" or "exercises."

Witsius spent the last years of his life in Leiden. In 1698 he was appointed professor there. His inaugural address was on *"De Theologo modesto"* ("Concerning Modesty in Doing Theology"). In Leiden he worked with the Cocceijan Simon van Til, and once again with his spiritual brother Johannes à Marck. In the last book that Witsius published[26] he gave an account of his life's work: "I am at liberty to say that in my work I have above all kept in mind God's honor and the purity of the gospel, the promotion of godliness, without which all scientific fame is idolatry, and the harmony of the brethren."[27]

Witsius fulfilled his calling until a year before his death. Physical weakness compelled him to request retirement. After a brief, severe illness he died on October 22, 1708. He was buried in the Buurkerk of Utrecht. Johannes à Merck, who along with Guiljelmus Saldenus belonged to the circle of his closest friends and who had known him for more than thirty years, gave the memorial address. In it the learned and modest Witsius was characterized as a man who maintained his daily times of prayer and who was able to retreat from the companionship of his friends in order to exercise sweet communion with God.[28]

Witsius' Mysticism

Witsius makes ample use of the term "mysticism" in his writings, and that certainly in a positive sense.[29] His spirituality shows, therefore, an unmistakable continuity with the medieval mystical tradition in a way that is particularly

---

24. The second edition was expanded under the title *In Orationem Dominicam* (Franeker, 1689). The entire work was translated by Johannes Costerus, minister in Delft, under the title *Oeffeningen over de Grondstukken van het Algemeyne Christelijke Geloove, en het Gebed des Heeren. Tot ophelderinge der Waarheit, en aandrang ter Godzaligheid* (with two sermons, a lament, and an expansion of Song of Solomon 5 in poetic form; Delft, 1700). It is hereafter abbreviated as *Grondstukken*.

25. *Schediasma Theologicae Practicae* (Groningen, 1729). In 1731 it was translated by the minister of Nieuwkerk, H. C. Bijler, under the title *Practicale Godgeleerdheid of algemeene Pligten der Christenen ten opzigte van Godt, van Christus, van zich zelven en zyn naasten* (Delft, 1731). It is hereafter abbreviated as *Godgeleerdheid*.

26. Herman Witsius, *Meletemata Leidensia* (Leiden, 1703).

27. See van Genderen, *Herman Witsius*, 96.

28. Ibid., 102.

29. Ibid., 173.

reminiscent of the Augustinian-Bernardian tradition.[30] Various researchers have demonstrated a definite relationship with the bridal mysticism of Bernard of Clairvaux.[31] A. Ritschl draws the following conclusion: "Von allen Niederländern jener Zeit hat keiner die Bernhardinische Frömmigkeit zu so genauen Ausdruck gebracht, wie dieser akademische Theologe."[32] I. Boot does not hesitate to speak of "an influence."[33] It is an influence that is above all, but definitely not exclusively, recognizable in Witsius' *Schediasma* or improvisations, the distillation of a series of lectures on practical theology, or the practice of godliness, that he gave in Utrecht[34] sometime around 1696 and that were published in Dutch translation under the title of *Practicale Godgeleerdheid* in 1731.[35]

Whether this fascination with Bernard was stimulated by a direct knowledge of the body of Bernard's work, I have been unable to document. Possibly the writings of Francis Rous (1579-1659) played a mediating role in this regard. Rous was an English politician of a Presbyterian-Puritan stripe, an erudite person, whose mystical spirituality radiated an undeniably Bernardian spirit.[36] Ritschl already pointed to a striking congeniality between Rous' thought-world and Witsius' writings.[37] Van Genderen and Boot follow him in this regard,[38] in my own opinion accurately. As will appear in what follows, Witsius at noteworthy moments connects with mystically driven Puritans both in terminology and in content. Their admiration for Bernard is obvious. The quotations of Bernard that this body of literature contains—everywhere enveloped in a range of other pre-Reformation devotional literature—establish

---

30. On the various forms taken by medieval mysticism, see Oberman, *Die Reformation*, 49-51, and Raitt, ed., *Christian Spirituality*.

31. Ritschl, *Geschichte des Pietismus*, 1:276-83; van Genderen, *Herman Witsius*, 174-76; Boot, *De allegorische uitlegging*, 192-202. Also compare op 't Hof, "Rooms-katholieke doorwerking," 73-120.

32. Ritschl, *Geschichte des Pietismus*, 1:282.

33. Boot, *De allegorische uitlegging*, 203.

34. Ritschl, *Geschichte des Pietismus*, 1:277-78; van Genderen, *Herman Witsius*, 174-75; Boot, *De allegorische uitlegging*, 192.

35. See Van Sluis "Herman Witsius," 457.

36. Rous's tracts *Mysticum Matrimonium Christi cum Ecclesia* and *Academia coelestis* were originally published with *Grande Oraculum* as *Interiora Regni Dei* (London, 1655). They were translated into Dutch from the English versions entitled *The Mystical Marriage* (1635) and *The Heavenly Academy* (1638) by a certain "P.H." and J. Koelman, respectively, and were published by Koelman under the title *Het binnenste van Gods Koninkrijk, of de Hemelsche Academie* (Amsterdam, 1678), in which edition *Het Verborgen Houwelyk* was included. See C. J. Meeuse, "Jacobus Koelman (1631-1695): leven en werken," in *Figuren en thema's*, ed. Brienen, et al., 75. I have made use of the eighteenth-century edition *Het binnenste van Godts Koninkryk, Vertoont in twee Tractaten: Genaemt het Verborgen Houwelyk, en de Hemelsche Academie* (Rotterdam, 1731). On Rous, see Ritschl, *Geschichte des Pietismus*, 1:128-29 and 281; Wakefield, *Puritan Devotion*, 103-106; F. E. Stoeffler, *The Rise of Evangelical Pietism* (Leiden, 1971), 85-87; J. van den Berg, "De Engelse Puritein Francis Rous (1579-1659) en de vertaling van enkele van zijn geschriften in het Nederlands," in *De Zeventiende Eeuw* 2 (1985) 2:48-66; van den Berg, "Die Frömmigkeitsbestrebungen," 59, 77, 94 and 99.

37. Ritschl, *Geschichte des Pietismus*, 1:282. "Witsius hat sich zunächst nach dem Muster von Francis Rous gerichtet."

38. Van Genderen, *Herman Witsius*, 175-76; Boot, *De allegorische uitlegging*, 203.

overwhelming testimony to this fact. It is not impossible that Witsius came under Bernard's influence through Rous. It occurs to me that it is more likely, however, that the studious and spiritual Witsius had become acquainted already earlier with the widely disseminated work of the renowned *doctor mellifluus*, and that Rous only reinforced and deepened the affinity that Witsius already perceived.

However this may be, there can be no doubt about Witsius' spiritual kinship with Bernard and Rous. When one factors into this the deep impression that the mystical experientialism of Justus van den Bogaard had on the student Herman, the mystical glow characteristic of Witsius' writing is not surprising. What definitely arouses one's curiosity, however, is the question of how this Reformed theologian integrates or transposes elements of this pre-Reformation spirituality with his definitely Reformed conceptions.[39] When one defines this position briefly and with the well-known term "*sola fide*," the question intensifies of whether Witsius adequately protected the well-delineated boundaries. This way of posing the question assumes important proportions, whether implicitly or explicitly, in light of my reconnaissance of his actual spirituality.

Taste and Contemplation

Already in the first chapter of his *Practicale Godgeleerdheid*, Witsius remarks that the knowledge of God resides in a holy activity of the enlightened understanding by which God in Christ is contemplated in a spiritually fruitful way.[40] What he understands by this kind of contemplation is unambiguous. The intellectualistic and speculative connotation that the contemporary understanding of "contemplation" has, is precisely what he does not have in mind. Much rather, it is its opposite. The knowledge of God turns precisely on the fact that we "are not satisfied with external instruction from books"—by which books he meant the triad of nature, conscience and biblical revelation—but rather strive for the inner formation that happens "in a spirit of submissiveness." Otherwise, a person will only "remain focused on the peelings and not penetrate to the core."[41] Witsius urges his readers, therefore, to devote themselves to trying "to be admitted at all times to the most inner precincts of the heavenly academy, where we shall be instructed not by hearing, by precise reasoning or even by believing, but by seeing and tasting in drawing near to God."[42] Divine matters contain "secret manna," he adds with an image cherished in mystical literature.[43] The

---

39. See Witsius, *Verbonden*, 3.6.6, 342. Here Witsius resolutely distances himself from the idea that a person "can claim a few acts of love that are apparently involved in the exercise of one's faith as the basis for one's justification."

40. Witsius, *Godgeleerdheid*, 2.

41. Ibid., 12. The expression "the peelings of truth" originated with Bernard. It was also used by Van Lodensteyn in, among other places, the "Nareden" of his second "Zamenspraak" in *Beschouwinge*, 47. "You merely take the peelings of the truth just confessed as the truth itself. But, poor man, you err terribly. That Being is the Truth who shines from above in the rational soul." Compare Trimp, *Jodocus van Lodensteyn*, 181-82; and de Boer, *De verzegeling*, 144-45.

42. Witsius, *Godgeleerdheid*, 12-13.

43. See Revelation 2:17. Bernard also uses this image. See *SC*, 3:1, in *SW*, 5:76, where this manna is identified with the spiritual kiss of Christ: "Spirituale osculum . . . , est quippe manna absconditum."

purport of this passage seems to have been lifted right from Rous's *Hemelsche Academie*. Rous consistently finds that spiritual matters are only seen and appreciated when God instructs us in this advanced academy.[44] Here is an education that results in an "excellent, engaging knowledge that grows out of experience and a developed taste."[45] With an appeal to Basil, Cyprian, Dionysius and Gerson—among others—Rous makes an appeal for knowledge through such acquired taste. His insight is that the Bible uses such earthly images with the intent that we "might rise above them by employing them, and that we would even climb to these heavenly things themselves, in order that we may know them truly by actually tasting them." In this way the visible manna during Israel's sojourn in the desert became a sign of this hidden manna.[46]

How, then, is Witsius' distinction between faith and sight to be interpreted? Is faith transcended through contemplation, and is the latter reserved for a category that stands above the level of faith? In order to answer this question it is useful to consult his book *Grondstukken*.[47] Characteristic of the affective nature of Witsius' piety is a passage—likewise inspired by Rous—such as the following: "A genuine disciple of Christ does not only know and does not only believe, but also sometimes tastes and feels what the forgiveness of sins is, what the privilege of adoption as children is, what the familiar interchange with God is, what the grace of the Spirit who dwells within is, what the love of God poured into the heart is, what the hidden manna is, what the sweetest kisses of Jesus are, and finally what the pledge and even the ultimate surety of perfect bliss are."[48] The school into which the most congenial Teacher leads his students is "like the location of a special meal" where he extends the following invitation: "Friends, eat and drink; become intoxicated, O Most Beloved." And thus, lavishly replenished by the spiritual wine of the Savior, "they receive much clearer vision with which to contemplate heavenly matters, just as long ago Jonathan had after he had tasted from the honeycomb."[49]

The "spiritual exercise" just reviewed touched on the name of Christ, and following it Witsius developed a chapter entitled "On the Name 'Christian.'" This name emphasizes participation in Christ's anointing and in his threefold office. Christians, therefore, also participate in the office of prophet. According to Witsius, this means that believers by means of outward service to others are profoundly instructed by "the inner and unmediated illumination of the Spirit." This instruction applies to all Christians in common.[50] However, Witsius immediately introduces an exception. With this "common discovery" of the

---

44. Rous, *Het binnenste [Academie]*, 176. Compare 181 and 237.

45. Ibid., 183.

46. Ibid., 183-85.

47. Also here he frequently employs mystical terms like "sweetness," "preciousness," "taste" (*dulcedo, suavitas, gustus*). Significant in this regard is Witsius, *Grondstukken*, 5.6, 69.

48. Ibid., 10.46, 177. The related passage in Rous, *Het binnenste [Academie]*, 180, consists of the following citation: ". . . communion with God, a spiritual childhood, an indwelling of the Spirit, a guarantee of eternal inheritance . . . , the mystical manna, the foretaste of blessedness, the kisses of Christ Jesus."

49. Ibid.

50. Witsius, *Grondstukken*, 11.23, 191.

things a Christian has to believe, there arises "sometimes a more special and familiar revelation of the Lord Jesus to the soul," and especially when he holds her by the hand and leads her into his inner chamber (Song of Solomon 1:4), lifts the curtain and pushes to the side the draperies of heaven in order to permit her a glimpse of "the pleasures of heaven itself and of the joys of the life to come in order that she might consider them with her mind and receive a foretaste of them in her soul." What Witsius adds at this point is noteworthy: "This is what he promised to those who love him (John 14:21)."[51] One may assume that by this he had all God's children in mind. This assumption is confirmed by a reference in his *Verbonden* which offers a summary of "the most prominent things that the Spirit of Adoption works in God's children without any distinction." This Spirit not only works in them "a taste of God's love" and kindles a response of love in their hearts, but he also discloses the promised inheritance so that the soul might enjoy it by way of anticipation ("in hope, beforehand"): "Yes, he sometimes raises her up to the heights so that he may push aside the curtains and lift up the draperies in order to afford her a look at those benefits that await her in her heavenly home." In this way that which is yet to come is enjoyed proleptically.[52]

From various perspectives—that of the prophetic offices as well as that of sonship—Witsius describes the same mystical experience. It is an experience that is sporadic (occurs "sometimes," he says), but is one that all believers who love God have. Elsewhere, he appears to introduce a nuance on this point. He does so in his *Practicale Godgeleerdheid*. There he discusses this identical—in my opinion—experience, this time in yet another connection and one that is less proleptic in tone, at least less explicitly so. In the context of "holy amazement at the divine perfections," he regards admittance to the inner chambers of the heavenly Bridegroom (once again referencing Song of Solomon 1:4) as reserved for "his most familiar friends."[53] At the very least Witsius suggests here that the contemplative experience that he has in mind not only occurs sporadically, but that it belongs to a special category. The King of Glory allows only his closest friends to have the experience. Is there a sort of duplicity operating in Witsius' presentation of the matter here, by on the one hand according the experience in question to everyone but on the other hand only to an elite group?

What is striking is that in Witsius' *Verbonden* we encounter a consistent ambivalence. That is certainly the case in the same context in which we just heard him posit that all believers indiscriminately are permitted to have a look behind the curtain.[54] A little further along, he again describes how God "sometimes, as it were, bears up" his elect "into the heights," gives them a glimpse of his face and kisses them with a kiss on the mouth. It is an experience

---

51. Ibid., 11.24, 191-92.

52. Witsius, *Verbonden*, 3.11.5-7, 427-28. Proleptic contemplation as a foretaste of glory is, as is well-known, a favorite theme in the mystical tradition. Especially in Witsius, *Grondstukken*, 11.25, 192, Witsius' formulations employed in interpreting this prolepsis push the boundaries. He talks there about "very clear representations of heavenly matters," so that one contemplates them "as though they are present" to the eye, "almost like the prophets of old saw them." For this theme in Bernard, see *SC*, 41:3 and 52:1, in *SW*, 6:74 and 196, respectively.

53. Witsius, *Godgeleerdheid*, 48.

54. Witsius, *Verbonden*, 3.11.7, 428.

that "believers perhaps see and taste, but which no pen based on a merely formal education can truly or fully describe." Then he concludes the sentence with the remarkable observation that "these things not all God's children experience, neither always nor often."[55] In my opinion this apparent inconsistency can be explained as follows: in principle every believer can have this experience, but in actual practice that seems to be the case for only a group of God's most faithful children, and then only "sometimes."

Now, one might get the impression that this sporadic experience transcends Scripture and faith. But I suspect that this would misrepresent Witsius' intentions. Worked out in his explanation entitled "Wat het zy te Gelooven" [trans.: "What It Means To Believe"], he discusses at length the joy that experiences "by tasting divine sweetness."[56] It seems to me, then, that for Witsius there is no thought of by-passing faith, but that the experience is the affective climax of faith itself. That this interpretation could be in conflict with his manifest assurance that an upstanding Christian not only knows and believes the things of God but also tastes and feels them, is only apparent. What he wants to emphasize by this is that believing has a cognitive dimension, to be sure, but that it is not limited to this. Rather, faith is only complete when the cognitive dimension is qualified by the experiential dimension. Those mystical experiences discussed by Witsius do not ignore faith, but constitute the very point of the life of faith. While this mountain-top experience is certainly not an every-day one, it definitely belongs to the life of faith. The appeal that Witsius explicitly makes in this connection to 1 Peter 1:8, where the apostle makes mention of the joy of faith, says a great deal.[57] Exactly as Witsius had already done in his Utrecht address, he notes in this connection that no one need be afraid that he "would sin by experiencing too much of such joy." I think that on this point he engages the unarticulated question of whether in this way the boundary of Scripture and faith has not been transgressed. "No," he says on the matter, for this elation of the soul in which the Holy Spirit "carries us away" (the *raptus*) is nothing else than the precious joy "of the Christian faith" that arises from joy in the Lord, since this God is our God.[58]

Faith and Love

Whoever would suggest at this point that Witsius would rather treat the theme of love than that of faith, ought to recall that he incorporates love into faith. In his handling of faith he recognizes three elements: knowledge, assent and love. Faith is kindled in love of God's "amicable qualities;" it especially delights in Christ, who is precious to the believer. Faith and love are "so intimately bound up with one another that we cannot fully express our faith without some accompanying acts of love."[59] Witsius calls this love "a spiritual passion in which the soul is

---

55. Ibid., 3.11.34, 436.
56. Witsius, *Grondstukken*, 5.13, 68. Further on, in 5.18, 70, this experience is called "spiritual drunkenness."
57. Ibid., 5.13, 68.
58. Ibid., 5.18, 70.
59. Witsius, *Verbonden*, 3.7.17, 348. Witsius, *Godgeleerdheid*, 23, sounds the same note.

entirely directed toward God."[60] With a "graceful" quotation from Bernard, whose name he explicitly invokes, he explains why we are doubly obligated to love God: because we are not only created by him, but are also re-created by him—emphasizing the latter ("for in this regard I am not as easily re-created as created!").[61] Playing on Bernard's words, Witsius admits that our love for God is definitely not equal to the love with which he loves us, but that this does not diminish the fact that the soul is united with God, intoxicated with love for him.[62]

This faith qualified by love results in a godly walk of life. It is the "holy ambition of the loving soul to try to exalt God in her life." Witsius reinforces this insight by once again appealing to Bernard's words: "For to will the same [as he wills], and not to show self-will, that is the first principle of true love."[63] While the natural knowledge of God at its best causes some "semblance of piety and conversion,"[64] Christian faith is the mother of true sanctification. It elevates the soul to the contemplation of the Holy One. Just as Moses' countenance glistened with a lustrous shine after his stay on Mount Sinai, so goes it in a spiritual sense for those "who contemplate God frequently and diligently in the light of faith." The rays of the heavenly Spirit that are received through faith penetrate to the innermost parts of the soul. The more that divine holiness is considered, the more clearly it is understood. The more clearly it is understood, the more fervently it is loved.[65] And the more fervently it is loved, the more a person dedicates himself to be conformed to it. "For love reaches out to be conformed to the beloved."[66] By means of such love a person will dedicate himself to more precise holiness.[67] In this way the mystical and the ethical embrace one another for Witsius. They constitute an indissoluble two-in-oneness that arises from faith.

Meditation

Witsius considered meditation to be of essential importance. Both in his academic instruction and in his preaching he recommended it. On the occasion of

---

60. Witsius, *Godgeleerdheid*, 69.

61. Ibid., 71-72. The quote from Bernard can be found in *DD*, 5:15, in *SW*, 1:100, where the central idea is: "Nec enim tam facile refectus, quam factus." Apparently Witsius liked this idea, for he also quoted it in *Grondstukken*, 5.24, 73, and included it earlier in *Twist des Heeren*, 172.

62. Witsius, *Godgeleerdheid*, 74-76. Also see Bernard, *DD*, 10:27, in *SW*, 1:120, and Rous, *Het binnenste [Houwelyk]*, 151. In the same context (76-77), Witsius quotes Bernard yet again: "In his book, Bernard graciously says that he loves God, noting that retribution comes to those who do not love God, although he is certainly loved without any consideration of retribution; genuine love is content with itself alone; it does make a reckoning, but that is only about whether one loves." See *DD*, 7:17, in *SW*, 1:102-3: "Non enim sine praemio diligitur Deus, etsi absque praemii sit intuitu diligendus. . . . Verus amor seipso contentus est. Habet praemium, sed id quod amatur."

63. Witsius, *Godgeleerdheid*, 72. See Bernard, *SC*, 83:3 in *SW*, 6:612.

64. Witsius, *Grondstukken*, 5.19, 70.

65. Ibid., 5.21, 71. See Rous, *Het binnenste [Academie]*, 187: "The more we know these things [i.e., the things of God], the more we shall love him."

66. Witsius, *Grondstukken*, 5.21, 71. See Rous, *Het binnenste [Houwelyk]*, 150, where the longing of the soul is compared to God's measureless love, "to be like it in the same way that a poor and specific or limited creature can be compared with the unbounded and limitless God."

67. Witsius, *Grondstukken*, 5.22, 72.

his farewell from Leeuwarden in 1675 he admonished his congregation: "Give yourselves to devotional meditation; sit in silence, and let your thoughts roam through the endless expanse of all God's attributes . . . . Through spiritual exercises awaken your faith, in which the soul is poured out to the Lord Jesus."[68] Witsius knew that the whole of spiritual life was borne and nourished by it. When in his *Verbonden* he summarized the requirements for "daily increasing the intimacy of divine friendship," he identified as the first in importance "a daily awakening of love for God through thoughtful reflection." This first requirement was made concrete in the second: "a frequent interaction with God, in which for a little while the cares of the world are shut out and a quiet solitude is sought through the regularly repeated practices of reading, pondering, and praying—so that in this way with a humble candor you penetrate to familiarity with God." In this connection, "however," he relays the advice of Jerome: "Always protect the secret places of your bedroom, so that the Bridegroom can always engage you within. If you pray, you speak to the Bridegroom. If you read, he speaks to you."[69]

Prayer and reflection correlate. One is called to do both. According to *Oeffeningen over 't Gebed des Heeren*[70] [trans.: *Spiritual Practices Involving the Lord's Prayer*], one is always dependent on "the Spirit of prayer." This dependence may never lead to passivity, however. Just as Teellinck's "movements of God's Spirit" set the human spirit in greater motion, so was the case for Witsius. As soon as the Spirit "engages the heart," thereby awakening one to pray, one should immediately set aside all encumbrances and follow the Spirit's leading. "As soon as the Headwind of Heaven starts blowing, we must without hesitation hoist the sails of our desires" and take great care that we not, either through slowness or "distraction," allow the favorable tide "to slip away." Precisely because "those all-too-precious stirrings of the Spirit" are beyond our power and overtake us by grace, we must "attend them with an attentiveness that is always prepared."[71] At the same time Witsius strongly rejects the idea that a person should only pray when the Spirit moves one to do so. The influence of the Spirit may certainly be "expected" trustingly, but the norm for prayer is that it is God's command.[72]

In connection with the name of Jesus, Witsius devotes a section of his *Grondstukken* to meditative fellowship with God. It maintains that in the sacredness of godly prayer and reflection one might contemplate him "with uncovered eyes." Witsius calls this "the enjoyment of God himself." This consists of the fact "that with the greatest pleasure the soul lies down on him as on her Beloved . . . , satisfied with his fullness." Yet, this still involves only "the first fruits" of perfect enjoyment. But he nevertheless calls this experience being

---

68. *Affscheyd van Leeuwardern*, 26 (included in Witsius, *Grondstukken*). Witsius, *Twist des Heeren*, 185-93, already makes a strong appeal for spiritual reflection.

69. Witsius, *Verbonden*, 3.9.20, 405.

70. Appended to Witsius, *Grondstukken*.

71. Witsius, *Grondstukken* [*Gebed des Heeren*], 78-79.

72. Ibid., 82-83.

filled with God's sufficiency.[73] When Jesus assures someone of his fellowship, that person "will melt in love for Jesus and in a very holy way become thoroughly distraught if he should suffer being torn out of his embraces (Song of Solomon 8:6-7)." This and similar "stirrings of the believing and loving soul with regard to Jesus," Witsius points out Bernard detailed in a beautiful song that is worth learning by heart: "O Jesu, Mi Dulcissimi."[74] How substantial the place of spiritual reflection is in Witsius' *Grondstukken* appears from the fact that his treatment of the various lines from the Christological, central section of the Apostles' Creed repeatedly conclude with an admonition to "practical application." In this connection the passages on Christ's suffering, his death on the cross and his descent into hell are especially impressive. Both their soteriological and their exemplary dimensions were painted on the canvass of medieval meditation on suffering[75]—a genre that Luther also reflected in his day.[76] *Practicale Godgeleerdheid* also shows how much the contemplation of the person of Christ was at the center of meditation. It involves this: "not just that we only engage some scriptural testimonies concerning Christ, but that we engage Christ himself in the light of Holy Scripture and the Holy Spirit's presence, and that we contemplate him enthusiastically and completely, and that we stand still in amazement before all these miraculous events."[77] During the act of meditation it becomes clear that the bridge is crossed between past and present, between heaven and earth, and that one becomes contemporary and one with Christ.

Moreover, Witsius understands that this Christocentric spirituality is not only practiced through private meditation but also through preaching. In his academic teaching he called ministers of the word friends of the Bridegroom. They stand in the service of God, who is searching for a bride for his Son. He gives them the mandate to recommend the benefits of this heavenly marriage. With an eye toward this, he "has given them a painting that they might show to everyone as faithfully portraying life." Witsius illustrates this with an extensive recitation

---

73. Witsius, *Grondstukken*, 9.26, 149. Compare Witsius, *Godgeleerdheid*, 52, where he develops the idea of reflecting on God's being and works in the following ample sentence: "These things are powerful, able to carry the soul beyond itself in ecstasy, so that it forgets itself and everything that is outside itself and is engulfed in the abyss of the divine." Undoubtedly, this is reminiscent of Bernard, *DD*, 10.27, in *SW*, 1:120: "Ut animus, oblitus sui . . . , totus pergat in Deum."

74. Witsius, *Grondstukken*, 9.39, 154. Witsius incorporates the integral text of the hymn ascribed to Bernard, along with the translation by Adrianus Pars. It enjoyed great popularity in pietistic circles. What are perhaps the most loved lines were quoted by Voetius on his deathbed: "O Jesu, mi dulcissime, spes suspirantis animae." See Duker, *Gisbertus Voetius*, 3:345. W. à Brakel did the same. See Los, *Wilhelmus à Brakel*, 99. Others who quoted these lines are F. Costerus, *De Geestelyke Mensch* (Amsterdam, 1721), 768, and A. Comrie, *Het A.B.C. des Geloofs* (8th edition; Leiden, 1761), 26.

75. See especially Witsius, *Grondstukken*, 16.65-75, 297-302, on Christ's death on the cross; and 18.42-45, 330-34, on the descent into hell. Toward the end of the "devotional" on Christ's death on the cross (16.74, 301-2), Witsius places a "moving" appeal in the mouth of Christ, directed toward those who in their reflection "are present on Golgotha." It is an appeal that in tone and tenor reminds one of the devotional writings of Thomas à Kempis.

76. Compare Nicol, *Meditation bei Luther*, 117-50. See Luther's "Sermon von der Betrachtung des heiligen Leidens Christi" (1519), *WA* 2:126-42.

77. Witsius, *Godgeleerdheid*, 124.

based on Song of Solomon 5, a passage in which the beauty of the Bridegroom is considered in detail and praised lyrically, and the conclusion of which explains that everything related to him is completely desirable.[78] When one recalls that Witsius had sitting before him students who revered the office of minister of the word, one need not guess as to the purpose of this little sample of homiletical instruction. He obviously wanted to impress on their hearts that the meditative element had to be integrated with preaching in a way that stimulated private reflection.

Union with Christ

Witsius' *Grondstukken* attains a spiritual high point when he writes about the mystical union (*unio mystica*) in connection with the Holy Spirit and "spiritual exercises." He is Christ's Spirit who draws our spirits to Christ, Witsius proposes, in order that we might cling to him and embrace him. Through the announcement of his grace Christ comes down to us. "In these highly pleasurable meetings in mutual love, that mysterious and spiritual union occurs, and if it is permitted to say so, so does a blending, so that the believing soul slips away, as it were, and melts into the Lord Jesus and becomes one Spirit with his (1 Corinthians 6:17)."[79] The *unio* is described here as a "melting," not without some hesitation but yet candidly, in order to express by means of this metaphor—in the spirit of Bernard, it would seem—that the two "become one Spirit."[80] Witsius sees in this union a heightened comparison with the union of the bride and the Bridegroom in the Song of Solomon. How fervently the bride once exclaimed, "I am my Beloved's and my Beloved is mine," expressed the bond that the Spirit of the new order forged and that expressed something of that more excellent age: not just a *union*, but a *unity*. This is a unity that unites one so closely to Christ that in it, as it were, we have a true "and unique representation of the already perfect unity of the three persons of the godhead." Witsius illumines this with an appeal to John 17:21: "So that they all may be one, just as you, Father, are in me and I am in you, may they be one in us." What comes to expression in this "working of the Holy Spirit" he identifies as a miraculous work of divine love.[81]

That fellowship with Christ is completely mediated by the Holy Spirit—and therefore at the same time by the promises of the gospel, as we shall see shortly—is what is intriguing about this representation of matters. So is the fact that this establishes a unity that in a sense is a reflection of the Trinity itself. How ought this perspective to be understood? In no sense is it to be regarded as a

---

78. Ibid., 128-29.

79. Witsius, *Grondstukken*, 23.37, 444.

80. Compare Bernard, *DD*, 10.28, in *SW*, 1:122: Just as air is transformed by sunlight into the same clarity, in a similar way in the lives of his saints, humanity's preoccupation with self must flow out and give way entirely to God's will ("a semetipsa liquescere atque in Dei penitus transfundi voluntatem"). Instructive on this passage is Gilson, *La théologie mystique*, 149-52. Also noteworthy is that Rous, *Het binnenste* [*Houwelyk*], 5, is able to approach the idea "to become one Spirit" from another angle: "And if you should be united with him and married to him, his Spirit flows into your spirit and the divine life pours itself out into your soul."

81. Witsius, *Grondstukken*, 23.37, 444.

merging with God's being, in the sense of the mysticism of identity. With the metaphor of "mixing" or "melting" Witsius does not have in mind a unity of being, but a unity of faith and love. This becomes apparent from his foregoing explanation that the Holy Spirit awakens living faith in the gospel and a strong love for God in Christ. In *this* way "a new realm of grace is brought into being in humanity."[82] Following this accolade Witsius discusses union with Christ, which exists under the signs of faith and love. In the meanwhile, this fellowship with Christ progresses beyond a relationship of ownership based on conversion and expressed in possessive terms. It consists of being spiritual grafted into Christ and is a unity that can be experienced better than it can be explained. In his effort to put this mystery into words Witsius compares this unity with that of the three persons of the godhead. With considerable emphasis, he speaks of the miracle of God's love. The union with Christ based on faith is a unity of substance, therefore, but has an ethical character. It is a unity in love.[83] In this way Witsius wants to do justice to the Johannine insight that believers are one in the Father and the Son. He does so one-sidedly—the scope of John 17:21 strikes me as somewhat different—but not without shedding light on an important dimension of the truth, namely that the unity of believers is a unity *in God*. On this scriptural basis he immediately provides a glimpse into his insight that fellowship with Christ is not to be isolated from participation in the Father through the Spirit.

Witsius follows his treatment of unity with the person of Christ with his treatment of fellowship with Christ's benefits. Christ took on himself that which was rightfully ours—sin and misery. And through his Spirit he made ours what was his—the riches of his grace.[84] Thereupon, he sets forth how the Spirit fills the office of Comforter. It seems to me that at this point Witsius implicitly gets into the question of *how* the Spirit brings about fellowship with Christ and his benefits. If this hunch is well-founded, it is imperative for the interpretation of the foregoing to pay close attention to what follows. The Spirit offers comfort in four ways, Witsius explains. The first way that he develops is that the Spirit seals the promises of the gospel in the heart. This seems to me to be an important point. The Spirit works through the word, and this way has primacy, generally speaking. In the second place, he offers the first fruit and foretaste of the full harvest as a down payment and pledge. Thirdly, by means of the "external speech" of the apostles and prophets, "even of the Lord Jesus himself," he issues the "inner call" by which the word falls on good soil. If he did not do this, he would be called "a simply Miserable Comforter!" Fourth, the Spirit leads the believer into the inner chamber and to "the kiss of the King," where the soul is refreshed with the sweetness of "heavenly pleasures."[85] That this last comes only in good time and then intermittently is not communicated here. It occurs to me,

---

82. Ibid., 23.36, 444.
83. See *Affscheyd van Leeuwarden*, 26 (included in Witsius, *Grondstukken*), where he awakens the congregation to approach Jesus in faith and to express their love toward him so that the soul "is totally and completely transformed by love, just as God is Love."
84. Witsius, *Grondstukken*, 23.38, 444-45.
85. Ibid., 23.39, 445-46.

however, that by this fourth way of expressing the Comforter's work Witsius has nothing else in mind than the fellowship with Christ about which he has already written and works out here in more detail.[86] Then the conclusion is certainly justified that the mystical union with Christ is an experience that is enjoyed through faith in the promises of the word as these are sealed to one's heart.

Starlight and Sunlight

While we have covered the most salient points in Witsius' mysticism, it makes good sense to me to have a glance yet at an interesting passage for our theme that comes from his pre-academic *Twist des Heeren*.[87] This is all the more interesting since in it he uses expressions that seem to reach further than the ones we have already considered. To begin with, he poses here the idea that genuinely godly people receive an enlightened understanding by which they are admitted to the inner chamber of "God's mysteries in Jesus." This is "in principle" the same as the perfect knowledge of the eschaton. The godly man knows about God and Christ not only by studying or from "a second-hand source," but by the anointing of God himself. He has heard about these matters not just with his ears, but he has contemplated these mysteries with his own eyes and tested them in his own soul. And what he accepts as totally true, he sees not merely "by the dim twilight of nature, as also do the heathen in their blindness; or only by the star-light of Scripture, as do the Jews and the external Christians; but in the full sunlight of the Holy Ghost streaming into his soul."[88] The tone of the material under consideration here suggests a measure of depreciation of Scripture. But that only appears to be the case, I think.

Word and Spirit do not stand in opposition to one another here, but alongside one another.[89] What Witsius wants to emphasize is that Scripture by itself is inadequate. It is the Spirit who renders the scriptural word adequate so that it occasions a heart-to-heart meeting and causes the transformation of a person so that he is conformed to God. At least it is in this sense that I think his explanation must be understood: "So, then, the holy understanding of a Christian is not empty; it does not merely hover over his mind; it does not push these divine truths aside into some obscure corner of his memory, where they abandon the natural man to mould and rust; but it is lively and active, and it keeps the soul engaged in reflecting the image of God so that it increasingly transforms him

---

86. In the following "exercise" (Ibid., 24.1, 450-51) on the communion of the saints, he returns to this. He begins by asking for renewed attention to union with Christ, which he here explicitly compares with a marriage in which "the sweetest exchange of mutual love" takes place.

87. It involves chapter 17: "Evidences that We Have not Produced the Fruits of Spiritual Blessedness that We Should Have," 165-85.

88. Witsius, *Twist des Heeren*, 166-67. Rous, *Het binnenste* [*Academie*], 181, comes to a similar division: "While outwardly he calls us by his external word, he instructs us internally with his effectual word." In fact, it is a distinction that was not strange to Calvin. For example, see *OS* 3:303; *Inst.* 2.5.5: "Bifariam Deus in electis suis operatur: intus per Spiritum, extra per verbum" ("God works in two ways in his elect: internally by the Spirit, externally by the word.")

89. Compare Witsius, *Twist des Heeren*, 434, where he mentions an instruction that takes place "immediately out of God's word and by his Spirit."

into his likeness."[90] Also here Witsius is concerned with the simultaneously mystical and ethical nature of the knowledge of God, which is based on the word as applied by the Spirit.

In the unmistakable spirit of Bernard it follows, then, that "the illumined understanding of the godly man" is the kind of contemplation that "renders a person divine and Christ-like," at least "insofar as that can happen to a person."[91] At first appearance it might seem as though we are dealing here with pantheistic divinization. But that is certainly not Witsius' intention.[92] This is obvious from the comparative word "as," and particularly from the qualifying expression "insofar as." These restrictions are not empty phrases, but they carry weight. In using them Witsius wants to indicate that the humanity of the person does not disappear into God's divinity. What he definitely means is that the human *will* is united with God's holiness to such an extent that the soul has no rest unless it participates in it "to the measure and after the fashion" that it is able.[93] In this participation the will is not eliminated by God but maintains its own identity fully intact. But, this is an identity that does not seek itself, but finds its joy in God and will never be content "with half-way measures." Such a person desires nothing more than to exalt God, not his own interests, but simply to praise him "century in and century out with the beautiful harmony of endless hallelujahs." For, the godly person maintains this "as an inviolable rule," that to do good is the objective of love. And this "good" is a person, namely God in Christ. He wants to glorify Him with songs of praise, a life of service and submissiveness.[94] When will the time ever come, sighs Witsius in words borrowed from Thomas à Kempis, "that I find myself fully in you, so that on account of your love I no longer feel myself but you alone, beyond all feeling and without measure and in a way unknown to all others?"[95] This yearning for undivided submission is the other side of Witsius' idea that presently God is never ascribed the worth owed to him. Citing Bernard, he writes, "What shall I repay God for him? For if I could compensate him a thousand times over with my own self, what am I to God?"[96]

Already in this early work we look deep into the heart of Witsius the mystic. It becomes obvious that he did not only articulate his spiritual ideas from the chancel and the professorial chair, but that he also propagated them in his important publications aimed at more thorough reformation.

---

90. Ibid., 167.

91. Ibid., 168. The term deification (*deificatio*) is sounded also by Bernard, albeit sporadically. See *DD*, 10.28, in *SW*, 1:122. It involves no melting down of one's being, but fellowship of the will, as is also apparent from *SC*, 71:10 in *SW*, 6:456. On the term *deificatio* see R. Williams' essay in Wakefield, *A Dictionary*.

92. Compare Boot, *De allegorische uitlegging*, 202.

93. Witsius, *Twist des Heeren*, 168.

94. Ibid., 169-70.

95. Ibid., 171. The quotation is taken from Thomas, *Imitatio*, 3.21 (in the margin, Witsius mistakenly gives "3.32"). See à Kempis, *Opera*, 2:183. The passage from Thomas is definitely tied to Bernard, *DD*, 10.27, in *SW*, 1:120.

96. Witsius, *Twist des Heeren*, 172. The quote involves one from the previously cited *DD*, 5.15, in *SW*, 1:100.

Evaluation

In the review of Witsius offered here he emerges for us as a mystically inspired theologian. The warmth of his spirituality does not take a back seat to that of the pre-Reformation devotional writers like Bernard and à Kempis. In line with that of Francis Rous, Witsius' spirituality is explicitly Bernardian in language and tone. This is not to say that he appropriates in any integral way the concepts of Bernard's mysticism. The Abbot of Clairvaux was not as much a model whom he followed as he was a source of inspiration, as he also was for countless other pietistic writers. What distinguished Witsius from the "sweet flowing teacher" is that he was too deeply convinced of the reformational emphasis on *sola fide* to support Bernard's inclination to regard love as a higher level of faith.[97] In my judgment the spiritual expression of love constituted for Witsius not a higher level *than* faith, but the highest level *of* faith, and was therefore an expression of faith itself. This does not detract from the fact that the affective fullness of the faith experience in general and the motif of a foretaste of heaven specifically linked him with the medieval mysticism of Bernard. This was an affinity, as we see it, that he had in common with several spiritual compatriots of the Further Reformation movement. That mystical yearning within his spirituality received partial satisfaction already now by way of anticipation is an indication of his congeniality with pietists we have mentioned, especially with a figure like Jodocus van Lodensteyn.[98] Furthermore, just as was the case with them, the intertwining of the mystical and the ethical cannot be dismissed from Witsius' works. The same applies to his frequent emphasis on joy.

Whenever Witsius introduces mystical delights with the adverb "sometimes," it is not his intention, I think, to restrict them to the mystical elite. He does not have such a class in mind, but sees them as a unique favor that all believers can in principle experience, although they are not part of the warp and woof of religious experience. In fact, in practice they appear to be an exception permitted only to those whose faith-life displays a high level of intimacy. My total impression is that the mystical dimension of the life of faith does not constitute some elitist "add-on" for Witsius, but is much rather distinctive of faith itself. This implies that for him genuine faith simply develops as emotional and experiential, in contrast with being "argumentative" and rationalistic. For this reason he regards faith and love as interwoven. Whether he would have endorsed Rous, his favorite source, when he said, "The most important quality of a believer is that they [sic] believe even if they [sic] cannot feel,"[99] still needs to be documented. For me, at any rate, this "nevertheless trait" of faith is not conspicuous in Witsius' body of writings.

---

97. Compare Boot, *De allegorische uitlegging*, 78-83.

98. On van Lodensteyn, see de Reuver, "Een mystieke ader," 23-38.

99. Rous, *Het binnenste* [*Houwelyk*], 140. It is striking that this idea is not strange to Bernard, as appears in *SC*, 28:9, in *SW*, 5:444: "Fides nescia falli, fides invisibilia comprehendens, sensus penuriam non sentit; denique transgreditur fines etiam rationis humanae, naturae usum, experientiae terminos." ("Faith knows no error; faith comprehends invisible things; it does not feel the deficiencies of sense perception; finally, it overrides the limitations of human reason as well as the usual course of nature and the limitations of experience.")

In the use of mystical language Witsius goes further, insofar as I see it, than his Further Reformation brothers. That he does not restrict his mystical approach to the chancel or to catechism instruction, but carries it explicitly into his academic lectures, proves how normative he considers this specific style of piety to be for doing theology.

The short paragraph in the *Verbonden* with which he concludes his extremely mystical exposition on the "Geest der Aenneminge tot Kinderen," [trans.: "The Spirit of Our Adoption as Children,"] is striking for its intensity—I could almost say, "passion": "And these things we have brought forward, albeit in a very stammering fashion, concerning those spiritual matters that are the marrow of fervent Christianity [*medulla interioris Christianismi*]: praying with fervent desire that the Holy Spirit himself will make these teachings internal for his Nazarines, and that he will cause us to hear them, see them and taste them. May it be so, Lord Jesus. Amen."[100]

---

100. Witsius, *Verbonden*, 3.11.41, 439.

Conclusion

In this abbreviated look back on what we have covered, it is not intended to repeat the assessments made along the way. What I have in mind even less is to present a critical evaluation based on biblical-theological criteria. I am only interested in two things, namely a short characterization of Further Reformation spirituality and a positioning of this movement in the history of spirituality. With that in mind, I proceed on the basis of the five authors consulted as being representative of this movement in spirituality.

As far as the first matter is concerned, the conclusion seems warranted, based on the material investigated, that in the five authors treated the secondary differences in emphasis do not thwart the spiritual basis that all of them have in common. Without exception they all promote a spirituality in which the heart experiences communion with God created by the word and Spirit. This is an experience in which the characteristics of fervency and mysticism are pronounced. To my way of thinking, the piety so qualified is not merely to be regarded as one of the components characterizing this movement, it is constitutionally its main feature.[1]

The second matter involves the unique position that the Further Reformation's piety takes on the entire historical spectrum of medieval and reformational spirituality. What this piety has in common with Bernard's mysticism is the strong emphasis on emotional love in the experience of communion with God. The question that arises in this connection is whether the decisive nature of faith is sufficiently honored in this way and whether continuity with the reformational principle of *sola fide* is safeguarded. For, although reformers like Luther and Calvin do not shun affective terminology in the least, and while they advocate an unmistakably existential experience of faith,[2] one can only assert with great difficulty that according to them love should have a higher value than faith. Bernard is certainly ambivalent on this point, but more than once he appears inclined to this emphasis. It looks as though the representatives of the Further Reformation considered here move in this direction, although generally more implicitly than explicitly. The faith dimension of the "not yet" then seems to be superceded by the "already" of love. As the highlight of sweet communion with God, mention is always made of the brief and rare "exaltation" which amounts to a temporary and fragmentary contemplation of what the believers await in heaven. The form of this contemplation and—not to be forgotten—the language of the Song of Solomon in which it is articulated, is

---

1. Compare the remarks of W. J. op 't Hof in "Gereformeerde mystiek," *Praktische theologie: Nederlands tijdschrift voor pastorale wetenschappen*, 22 (1995): 329.

2. de Reuver, "Een mystieke ader," 12-18.

more reminiscent of Bernard than of the Reformation.[3] The same certainly holds true for the effusiveness and the emphasis with which mystical experience is described. Luther and especially Calvin are noticeably more restrained in this regard.

At the same time it is not suggested, and still less is the conclusion advocated, that Further Reformation spirituality amounted to a regression into Roman Catholic spirituality in which the inheritance of the Reformation was bartered away. This viewpoint is unfounded for two reasons. In the first place, it must be remembered that our five pietists received their articulate attention to the inner working of the Holy Spirit from no stranger. No one less than Calvin preceded them in this regard. In the second place, it seems to me to be undeniable that the three "*solas*" of the Reformation formed the framework within which pietistic mysticism flourished. However lively emotional love might be within it and however much faith might sometimes seem to be overshadowed by this love, with thoughtful investigation it appears that we are dealing with a love that must be considered as an expression of faith. It involves an experience that is nurtured by the biblical word, that is carried by grace and that is enjoyed in faith. I close with the vision of C. Graafland, who is of the opinion that the all-controlling center of pietistic spirituality lies in the Reformation's confession. This confession defines the vein of this mysticism. On the basis of careful research Graafland posits the proposition that Puritan piety is and remains "faith piety."[4] In my opinion this qualification is equally applicable to the piety of the Further Reformation. For mysticism that by-passes faith, one must go to the "dissident reformers,"[5] not to the men of the Further Reformation.

What ties the last-named figures closely to Thomas à Kempis is a meditative devotional attitude. Although this is with none of them as dominant as with Theodorus à Brakel, whose almost monastic practice of contemplation dominated his entire lifestyle, the meditative life assumed a cardinal place also with the other authors about whom we have spoken. At the same time, theirs was certainly not an attitude that was only the legacy of medieval spirituality. Also the reformers, above all Luther, valued meditation highly. Meanwhile, it remains a striking phenomenon that the devotion of Thomas, even on a material level,

---

3. Concerning the use of Song of Solomon in Bernard's mysticism, it is noteworthy that this influence is not reflected in the notes of the *Statenvertaling* (1637). The conclusion of Verduin, *Canticum Canticorum*, 700, is namely "that we nowhere meet in the notes the mysticism so typical of Bernard." Compare pages 517 and especially 565, where the author remarks that Udemans (the primary source of these notes) does not adopt Bernard's mystical line of thought. Boot, *De allegorische uitlegging*, 134-35, agrees. What needs to be added, naturally, is that the earliest representatives of the Second Reformation did not have these notes available to them, even though Udemans' commentary on the Song of Solomon dates from 1616 and laid the groundwork for them. Thus, this commentary apparently carried greater weight for the translators of the *Statenvertaling* than for the pietists of the Further Reformation.

4. Graafland, "De invloed," 15. Compare de Vries, *Die mij heeft liefgehad*, 132-33.

5. See C. B. Hylkema, *Reformateurs: Geschiedkundige studiën over de godsdienstige bewegingen uit de nadagen onzer Gouden Eeuw* (Amsterdam, 1938). Compare J. Lindeboom, *Stiefkinderen van het Christendom* (Arnhem, 1973, originally published in 1929); C. W. Roldanus, *Zeventiende-eeuwse geestesbloei* (Amsterdam, 1938); and van den Berg, "Die Frömmigkeitsbestrebungen," 99-107.

worked its way powerfully into the literature of several in the Further Reformation. Apparently they perceived in their own spiritual experience a deep connection with the spirituality of this leader of the Modern Devotion.

Perhaps the complex question of the relation of the Further Reformation to the Middle Ages and the Reformation can be formulated like this: the piety of the Further Reformation constitutes a moment in the spiritual tradition that through the ages has lived by the pneumatological mystery that a Christian is permitted to know God heart-to-heart. The leaders of the Further Reformation were in that sense catholic spirits. They not only drew from the piety of the Reformation, but they also freely availed themselves of that spirituality from the pre-Reformation tradition, be it eclectically and not uncritically, in which they knew how to interpret the recognizably sweet communion with the God of the word. Their mysticism is one with that which is drenched in the scriptural word that by means of the secret operation of the Holy Spirit brings about a gracious and highly real faith-encounter and a loving fellowship with God in Christ—both marked by hope. That the Spirit here is a down-payment and a foretaste of glory is the heartbeat of this mysticism. It is not higher *than* faith, but it is the high point *of* faith.

Bibliography

Primary Sources (arranged chronologically)

Bernardus Claraevallensis. *Bernhard von Clairvaux: Sämtliche Werke*, vols. 1, 5, 6 and 7, ed. G. B. Winkler. Innsbruck, 1990-1996.

Thomae Hemerken à Kempis, *Opera Omnia*, 7 vols., ed. M. I. Pohl. Freiburg, 1920-1922.

Martin Luther. *Werke: Kritische Gesamtausgabe*. Weimar, 1883 and following.

John Calvin. *Ioannis Calvini Opera quae supersunt omnia*, 59 vols., ed. G. Baum, E. Cunitz, E. Reuss. In *Corpus Reformatorum*, vols. 29-87. Braunschweig, 1863-1900.

_____. *Opera Selecta*, 5 vols., ed. P. Barth, G. Niesel and D. Scheuner. Munich, 1926-1962.

Willem Teellinck. *Nieuwe Historie van den Ouden Mensche. Daer in verhandelt wert het leven ende sterven van den ouden mensche ende hoe dat uyt de doot des ouden mensches, de nieuwe mensche op-staet ende voort-comt; ende welcke dat de gelegentheyt zy des nieuwenmensche, die daer blijft levende in der eeuwicheyt.* Amsterdam, 1623.

_____. *Soliloquium ofte Betrachtinghen eens sondaers die hy gehadt heeft inden angst zijner Weder-gheboorte. Dienstich om te voorderen de Bekeeringe van de doodelijcke wercken tot den levendighen God; ende tot een hartsterckinghe tegen alle weereltsche droeffenisse.* Reprinted from the 1628 Middelburg edition; introduction by E. Stronks. Rumpt, 1999. (A new edition of this work was done by H. Vekeman. Erftstadt, 1984.)

_____. *Noodtwendigh Vertoogh, Aengaende den tegenwoordighen bedroefden Staet van Gods volck. Waer-inne Ghetrouwelijck aenghewesen wordt, in wat swaricheyt ende vervallinghe wy hekomen zijn, in wat perijckel wy noch staen, met de noodighe remedien om ons verderf te erhoeden. Hier is by ghevoeght een korte Verclaringhe van des Autheurs ghevoelen over het stuck vanden Sabbath.* Rotterdam, 1647.

_____. *Huys-boeck, ofte Eenvoudighe Verklaringhe ende toe-eygheninghe vande voor-naemsteVraeg-stukken des Nederlandtschen Christelijcken Catechismi.* Final edition; Middelburg, 1650.

_____. *De worstelinghe eenes bekeerden Sondaers, Ofte Grondige Verklaringe van den rechten zin des VII. Capittels tot den Romeynen.* Vlissingen, 1650.

_____. *'t Nieuwe Jerusalem Vertoont in een t'samensprekinge, tusschen Christum en Mariam, sittende aen sijn voeten.* Utrecht, 1652.

_____. *Sleutel Der Devotie Ons openende De Deure des Hemels.* Utrecht, 1655/1656.

_____. *De Toetsteen des geloofs. Waer in De gelegentheyt des waren saligmakende Geloofs nader ontdeckt wordt soo dat een yder sich selven daer aen kan Toetsen of hy oock het ware Salighmakende Geloove heeft.* Amsterdam, 1662.

Francis Rous. *Het binnenste van Gods Koninkryk, Vertoont in twee Tractaten: Genaemt het Verborgen Houwelyk, en de Hemelsche Academie* (translations of *The Mystical Marriage* (1635) and *The Heavenly Academy* (1638) by "P. H." and J. Koelman, respectively). Rotterdam, 1731.

Gisbertus Voetius, *Proeve van de Cracht der Godtsalicheyt alsmede Meditatie van de ware Praktijk der Godzaligheid.* Reprinted from the 1628 Amsterdam edition, with an introduction by A. de Reuver. Rumpt, 1998.

    _____. *Inaugurele rede over Godzaligheid te verbinden met de wetenschap, gehouden aan de Illustre School te Utrecht op de 21ste augustus 1634.* Latin text newly published with a Dutch translation, introduction and comments by A. de Groot. Kampen, 1978.

    _____. *De praktijk der godzaligheid (Ta Asketika sive Exercitia pietatis.* Trans. of the 1664 edition, with an introduction and commentary by C. A. de Niet, 2 vols. Utrecht, 1996.

Anna Marie van Schurman. *Eucleria, of Uitverkiezing van Het Beste Deel.* Facsimile of the 1684 Amsterdam edition; Leeuwarden, 1978.

Theodorus à Brakel. *Het Geestelyke Leven, ende De Standt eens gelovigen Mensches hier op Aarden; uit Godes Heilig Woordt vergadert en by een gesteldt. Nog zyn hier achter by gevoegt eenige Kenteekenen, waar uit men hem kan verzekeren dat men van Godt is bemindt. Als mede eenige Christelyke Meditatien, Gebeden en Dankzeggingen.* 8th edition; recently reviewed, expanded and improved by the author during his lifetime. Amsterdam, [n.d.].

    _____. *De Trappen des Geestelyken Levens.* According to his directive, published after his death by W. à Brakel. 7th edition; Groningen, 1739.

Jodocus van Lodensteyn. *Beschouwinge van Zion, ofte Aandagten en Opmerkingen over den tegenwoordigen toestand van 't Gereformeerde Christen Volk. Gestelt in eenige t' Samen- spraken.* 4th ed.; Amsterdam, 1718.

    _____. *Geestelyke Opwekker, voor het Onverloochende, Doode en Geesteloose Christendom. Voorgestelt in X. Predicatien.* 3rd edition; Amsterdam, 1732.

Guiljelmus Saldenus. *De Wech des Levens, ofte Korte en Eenvoudige Onderwysinge van de Natuer ende Eygenschappen van de ware Kracht der Godsalicheyt. Den Schijn-heyligen tot bechaminge, ende alle oprechte Christenen tot noodige Opweckinge ende Versterckinge voor- gestelt.* Utrecht, 1657.

    _____. *Geesteliken Hooning-Raat van eenen gesturve zijnde. Een versameling van eenigen stichtelike Predicatien over verscheyde stoffe. Waar by gevoegt is De Vaste Hoope van een Geloovige staande op zijn vertrek na zijn Eeuwig huis.* Published posthumously; reprinted from the 1695 Rotterdam edition. Rumpt, 1998.

Florentius Costerus. *De Geestelyke Mensch.* 4th edition; Amsterdam, 1721.

Andrew Gray. *The Works of the Reverend and Pious Andrew Gray.* Aberdeen, 1839.

Wilhelmus à Brakel. "De Laaste Uiren van den Autheur," in Theodorus à Brakel, *De Trappen des Geestelyken Levens.* 7th edition; Groningen, 1739.

    _____. *Leere en Leydinge der Labadisten, Ontdeckt en Wederleyt in een Antwoort op P. Yvons Examens over onse Trouwhertige Waerschouwinge.* Rotterdam, 1685.

    _____. *Hallelu-Jah, ofte Lof des Heeren, over het Genaden-Verbondt, ende des selfs bedieninge in het O. en N. Testament. By occasie van de Verklaringe van den VIII. Psalm.* Rotterdam, 1687.

    _____. *Logikè Latreia, dat is Redelyke Godtsdienst, in welke de Goddelyke Waerheden des Genaden-Verbondts worden verklaert, tegen partyen beschermt, en tot de practyke aengedrongen. Als mede de Bedeelinge des Verbondts in het O.T. ende in het N.T. Ende de Ontmoetingen der Kerke in het N.T. vertoont in een verklaringe der Openbaringe van Johannes.* 3 vols. in two. 12th edition; Rotterdam, 1733.

    _____. *De waare Christen of oprechte Gelovige, hebbende Deel aan God in Christus.* Amsterdam, 1712.

Herman Witsius, *Twist des Heeren met zynen Wyngaart, Dezelve overtuigende van misbruik zyner Weldaden, Onvruchtbaerheid in 't goede En al te dertele Weeldrigheid. In schandelyke nieuwigheden van Opinien, En schandelyke Oudheid van quade zeeden. Met bedreyginge van zyn uyterste ongenade.* 6th edition; Utrecht, 1736.

_____. *De Oeconomia Foederum Dei cum Hominibus Libri quator.* Leeuwarden, 1677.

_____. *VierBoecken van de Verscheyden Bedeelinge der Verbonden Gods met de Menschen,* trans. Martinus van Harlingen from *De Oeconomia.* Utrecht, 1686.

_____. *Exercitationes Sacrae in Symbolum quod Apostolorum dicitur.* Franeker, 1681. (The second edition was expanded to include *In Orationem Dominicam*; Franeker, 1689.)

_____. *Oeffeningen over de Grondstukken van het Algemeyne Christelijke Geloove, en het Gebed des Heeren. Tot ophelderinge der Waarheit, en aandrang ter Godzaligheid,* trans. Johannes Costerus. Published with two sermons, a lament, and an expansion of Song of Solomon 5 in poetic form; Delft, 1700.

_____. *Schediasma Theologicae Practicae.* Published posthumously; Groningen, 1729.

_____. *Practikale Godgeleerdheid of algemeene Pligten der Christenen ten opzigte van Godt, van Christus, van zichzelven en zyn naasten,* trans. H. C. Bijler. Published posthumously; Delft, 1731.

Abraham Hellenbroek. *Algemeene Rouklagte in de straten van Rotterdam, over den Zeer Eerwaarden, Godvrugtigen en Geleerden Heere Wilhelmus à Brakel, voorgestelt uit het laatste gedeelte van Prediker XII:5.* 7th edition; Amsterdam, 1737.

Wilhelmus Schortinghuis. *Het innige Christendom.* Republished from the 1740 edition; Nijkerk, 1858.

Alexander Comrie. *Het A.B.C. des Geloofs, of Verhandeling van de benamingen des Saligmakenden Geloofs volgens de letteren van het alphabet.* 8th edition; Leiden, 1761.

Secondary Sources (arranged alphabetically)

Aalders, C. *Spiritualiteit: Geestelijk leven vroeger en nu.* The Hague, 1969.

Aalders, W. J. *Mystiek: Haar vormen, wezen en waarde.* Groningen and The Hague, 1928.

À Kempis, Thomas. *De navolging van Christus,* translated with an introduction by B. Wielenga (fourth edition; Delft, [n.d.]).

_____. *De navolging van Christus, naar de Brusselse Autograaf,* trans. G. Wijdeveld, with an introduction and commentary by B. Spaapen and A. Ampe. 2nd edition; Antwerp and Kampen, 1985.

Adam, A. *Lehrbuch der Dogmengeschichte,* vol. 2. Gütersloh, 1968.

Albert, K. *Einführung in die philosophische Mystik.* Darmstadt, 1996.

Angenendt, A. "Die Zisterzienser im religiösen Umbruch," in *Bernhard von Clairvaux und der Beginn der Moderne,* ed. D. R. Bauer and G. Fuchs. Innsbruck and Vienna, 1996, 54-69.

Acquoy, J. G. R. *Het klooster te Windesheim en zijn invloed,* 3 vols. Utrecht, 1875-1880.

Augustine, *Regel voor de gemeenschap,* trans with a commentary by F. J. van Bavel. Averbode and Kampen, 1982.

_____. *Selbstgespräch: Von der Unsterblichkeit der Seele,* text in both Latin and German. Munich and Zurich, 1986.

_____. *De stad van God*, trans. with introduction by Gerard Wijdeveld. Amsterdam, 1984.

_____. *Über Schau und Gegenwart des unsichtbaren Gottes*, trans. with introduction by Erich Naab (Stuttgart and Bad Cannstatt, 1988).

Axters, S. *Geschiedenis van de vroomheid in de Nederlanden*, 4 vols. Antwerp, 1950-1960.

Bakker, N. T. *Miskende gratie: Van Calvijn tot Witsius, Een vergelijkende lezing, balans van 150 jaar gereformeerde orthodoxie*. Kampen, 1991.

Bange, P., C. Graafland, A. J. Jelsma and A. G. Weiler, eds. *De doorwerking van de Moderne Devotie, Windesheim 1387-1987*. Hilversum, 1988.

Bauer, D. R. and G. Fuchs, eds. *Bernhard von Clairvaux und der Beginn der Moderne*, Innsbruck and Vienna, 1996.

Bauer, J. B. "Bernards Bibeltext," in *Bernhard von Clairvaux: Sämtliche Werke*, vol. 5, ed. G. B. Winkler. Innsbruck, 1994.

Beeke, J. R. *Personal Assurance of Faith: English Puritanism and the Dutch "Nadere Reformatie," from Westminster to Alexander Comrie (1640-1760)*. Ann Arbor, 1988.

Bélier, A. *La pensée économique et sociale de Calvin*. Geneva, 1961.

Bell, T. *Bernhardus dixit: Bernardus van Clairvaux in Martin Luthers werken*. Delft, 1989.

Benedict, *De Regel van Sint-Benedictus*, trans. V. Hunink. Amsterdam, 2000.

Beumer, J. *Intimiteit en solidariteit: Over het evenwicht tussen dogmatiek, mystiek en ethiek*. Baarn, 1993.

_____, ed. *Als de hemel de aarde raakt: Spiritualiteit en mystiek—ervaringen*. Kampen, 1989.

Bisschop, R. "De scheiding der geesten: grenzen en raakvlakken tussen piëtisme en mystiek: Th. à Brakel, Koelman en De Labadie," *DNR* 14 (1990), 44-56.

Blommenstijn, H. H., and F. A. Maas. *Kruispunten in de mystieke traditie: Tekst en context van Meester Eckhardt, Jan van Ruusbroec, Teresa van Avila en Johannes van het Kruis*. The Hague, 1990.

Bohatec, J. *Calvin's Lehre von Staat und Kirche mit besonderer Berücksichtigung des Organismusgedankens*. Reprinted from the 1937 edition; Aalen, 1968.

Böhner, P. and E. Gilson, *Christliche Philosophie: Von ihren Anfängen bis Nikolaus von Cues*. Paderborn, 1954.

Bohren, R. *In der Tiefe der Zisterne: Erfahrungen mit der Schwermut*. Munster, 1990.

Bonaventure. *Itinerarium*, ed. J. C. M. van Winden. Assen, 1996.

Boot, I. *De allegorische uitlegging van het Hooglied voornamelijk in Nederland: Een onderzoek naar de verhouding tussen Bernard van Clairvaux en de Nadere Reformatie*. Woerden, 1971.

Böttger, P. C. *Calvins Institutio als Erbauungsbuch: Versuch einer literarischen Analyse*. Neukirchen, 1990.

Bouter, P. F. *Athanasius van Alexandrië en zijn uitleg van de Psalmen: Een onderzoek naar de hermeneutiek en theologie van een psalmverklaring uit de vroege kerk*. Zoetermeer, 2001.

Bouwman, H. *Willem Teellinck en de practijk der godzaligheid*. Kampen, 1928.

Bredero, A. H. *Bernardus van Clairvaux (1091-1153): Tussen cultus en historie*. Kampen and Kapellen, 1993.

Brienen, T. "Abraham Hellenbroek (1658-1731)," in *De Nadere Reformatie en het Gereformeerd piëtisme*, ed. T. Brienen et al. The Hague, 1989. 181-201.

_____. "Theodorus à Brakel (1608-1669)," in *De Nadere Reformatie en het Gereformeerd piëtisme*, ed. T. Brienen et al. The Hague, 1989, 123-48.

_____, et al., eds. *Figuren en thema's van de Nadere Reformatie*. 2 vols. Goudriaan and Kampen, 1990.

_____, et al., eds. *De Nadere Reformatie en het Gereformeerd piëtisme*. The Hague, 1989.

_____, et al., eds. *De Nadere Reformatie: Beschrijving van haar voornaamste vertegenwoordigers*. The Hague, 1986.

_____, et al., eds. *Theologische aspecten van de Nadere Reformatie*. Zoetermeer, 1993.

Broeyer, F. G. M., and E. G. E. van der Wall, eds. *Een richtingenstrijd in de Gereformeerde Kerk: Voetianen en coccejanen 1650-1750*. Zoetermeer, 1994.

Brouette, É. "Devotio moderna (I)," *TRE*, 8:605.

Brümmer, V. *Liefde van God en mens*. Kampen and Kapellen, 1993.

Brunner, E. *Die Mystik und das Wort*. Tübingen, 1924.

Bühler, P. *Die Anfechtung bei Martin Luther*. Zurich, 1942.

Burgess, S. M. *The Holy Spirit: Medieval Roman Catholic and Reformation Traditions*. Peabody, 1997.

Bush, S., Jr. *The Writings of Thomas Hooker: Spiritual Adventure in Two Worlds*. Madison and London, 1980.

Carlson, C. P., Jr. *Justification in Earlier Medieval Theology*. The Hague, 1975.

Davies, O. "Ruysbroeck, à Kempis and the Theologia Deutsch," in *The Study of Spirituality*, ed. C. Jones, G. Wainwright and E. Yarnold. London, 1992, 321-24.

De Boer, J. *De verzegeling met de Heilige Geest volgens de opvatting van de Nadere Reformatie* Rotterdam, 1968.

De Bruin, C. C. "De spiritualiteit der Moderne Devotie," in *Geert Grote en de Moderne Devotie*, ed. C. C. de Bruin, E. Persoons and A. G. Weiler. Zutphen, 1984, 102-44.

_____. *De Statenbijbel en zijn voorgangers: Nederlandse bijbelvertalingen vanaf de Reformatie tot 1637*, ed. and adapted by F. G. M. Broeyer. Haarlem and Brussels, 1993.

_____. "Thomas a Kempis: *De Imitatio Christi*," in *Kerkelijke Klassieken*, ed. J. Haantjes and A. van der Hoeven. Wageningen, 1949, 77-114.

De Greef, W. *"De Ware Uitleg": Hervormers en hun verklaring van de Bijbel*. Leiden, 1995.

De Groot, A., and O. J. de Jong, eds., *Vier eeuwen theologie in Utrecht: Bijdragen tot de geschiedenis van de theologische faculteit aan de Universiteit Utrecht*. Zoetermeer, 2001.

De Heer, J. M. D. "Sara Nevius (1632-1703) and Personal Piety," a lecture in the 2000-2001 winter series of the SSNR, published by the Stichting Studie Nadere Reformatie in 2001.

De Knijff, H. W. *Sleutel en slot: Beknopte geschiedenis van de bijbelse hermeneutiek*. Kampen, 1980.

De Kroon, M. "Gerard Groote," in *Gestalten der Kirchengeschichte*, vol. 4: *Mittelalter II*, ed. Greschat. Stuttgart, Berlin, Cologne and Mainz, 1983.

De Kruijf, U., J. Kummer and F. Pereboom. *Een klooster ontsloten: De kroniek van Sint- Agnietenberg bij Zwolle, door Thomas van Kempen*. Kampen, 2000.

De Lubac, H. *Medieval Exegesis*, vol. 1, *The Four Senses of Scripture*, trans. Mark Sebanc. Edinburgh, 1998.

De Reuver, A. *"Bedelen bij de Bron": Kohlbrugge's geloofsopvatting vergeleken met Reformatie en Nadere Reformatie*. Zoetermeer, 1992.

_____. "Dank en vreugde in de gereformeerde traditie," *DNR* 24 (2000), 82-87.

_____. "Inleiding," in G. Voetius, *Proeve van de Cracht der Godtsalicheyt*. Reprinted from the 1628 Amsterdam edition. Rumpt, 1998, 3-23.

_____. "Koelman's anti-separatisme," *DNR* 20 (1996), 1-42.

_____. "Een mystieke ader in de Nadere Reformatie," *DNR* 21 (1997), 1-54.

_____. "Stellung und Funktion des Gebets in Calvins Theologie: Eine Skizze," in *Gebetsliteratur der Frühen Neuzeit als Hausfrömmigkeit: Funktionen und Formen in Deutschland und den Niederlanden*, ed. F. van Lingen and C. N. Moore. Wiesbaden, 2001, 259-90.

_____. "Wat is het eigene van de Nadere Reformatie?" *DNR* 18 (1994), 145-54.

_____. "Wilhelmus à Brakel en het piëtisme," *DNR* 22 (1998), 83-90.

_____. "Zo'n trotse titel voor een zo geringe zaak," *TR* 37 (1994), 265-89.

De Rijk, L. M. *Middeleeuwse wijsbegeerte: Traditie en vernieuwing*. Assen, 1981.

De Vooys, C. G. N. *Nederlandse spraakkunst*. 7th edition; Groningen, 1967.

De Vries, P. *Die mij heeft liefgehad: De betekenis van de gemeenschap met Christus in de theologie van John Owen (1616-1683)*. Heerenveen, 1999.

Duker, A. C. *Gisbertus Voetius*, 3 vols. with index. Leiden, 1897-1915, 3:344-45.

Dinzelbacher, P. "Die 'Bernhardinische Epoche' als Achsenzeit der europäischen Geschichte," in *Bernhard von Clairvaux und der Beginn der Moderne*, ed. D. R. Bauer and G. Fuchs. Innsbruck and Vienna, 1996, 9-53.

_____. "Bernhards Mystik: Eine Skizze," in *Bernhard von Clairvaux und der Beginn der Moderne*, ed. D. R. Bauer and G. Fuchs. Innsbruck and Vienna, 1996, 180-93.

Elm, K., ed. *Bernhard von Clairvaux: Rezeption und Wirkung im Mittelalter und in der Neuzeit*. Wiesbaden, 1994.

Engelberts, W. J. M. *Willem Teellinck*. Amsterdam, 1898.

Ernst, W., K. Feiereis and F. Hoffmann, eds. *Dienst der Vermittlung* (Festschrift Priesterseminar Erfurt). Leipzig, 1977.

Evans, G. R. *Bernard of Clairvaux*. New York and Oxford, 2000.

_____. *The Mind of St. Bernard of Clairvaux*. Oxford, 1983.

Exalto, K. *De dood ontmaskerd: De voorbereiding op de dood in de late middeleeuwen, in de reformatie en in de gereformeerde theologie in de 17de en begin 18de eeuw*. Amsterdam, 1975.

_____. "Genadeleer en heilsweg," in *Theologische aspecten van de Nadere Reformatie*, ed. Brienen, et al. Zoetermeer, 1993, 151-207.

_____. "De Nadere Reformatie in de polemiek met Rome," in *DNR* 15 (1991), 121-31.

_____. "Willem Teellinck (1579-1629)," in *De Nadere Reformatie: Beschrijving van haar* voornaamste vertegenwoordigers, ed. Brienen, et al. The Hague, 1986, 17-47.

Fischer, R. "Kloster/Klosteranlage," in *TRE*, 19:275-81.

Frank, K. S. "Nachfolge Jesu, II," in *TRE*, 23:686-91.

Gilson, E. *La théologie mystique de Saint Bernard*. Paris, 1934.

Goeters, W. *Die Vorbereitung des Pietismus in der Reformierten Kirche der Niederlande bis zur labadistischen Krisis 1670*. Rreprinted from the 1911 Leipzig edition; Amsterdam, 1974.

Golverdingen, M. *Avonden met Teellinck: Actuele thema's uit zijn werk*. Houten, 1993.

Goossens, L. A. M. *De meditatie in de eerste tijd van de Moderne Devotie*. Haarlem and Antwerp, 1952.

Graafland, C. *Van Calvijn tot Barth: Oorsprong en ontwikkeling van de leer der verkiezing in het Gereformeerd Protestantisme*. The Hague, 1987.

_____. *Gereformeerden op zoek naar God: Godsverduistering in het licht van de gereformeerde spiritualiteit*. Kampen, 1993.

_____. "De invloed van de Moderne Devotie in de Nadere Reformatie, ca 1650-c 1750," in *De doorwerking van de Moderne Devotie, Windesheim 1387-1987*, ed. P. C. Bange, C. Graafland, A. J. Jelsma and A. G. Weiler. Hilversum, 1988, 47-69.

_____. "De invloed van het Puritanisme op het ontstaan van het Gereformeerd piëtsime in Nederland," *DNR* 7 (1983), 1-19.

_____. "De kerk in de Nadere Reformatie: Wilhelmus à Brakel," in *De Kerk: Wezen, weg en werk van de kerk naar reformatorische opvatting*, ed. W. van 't Spijker. Kampen, 1990, 163-86.

_____. "Kernen en contouren van de Nadere Reformatie," in *De Nadere Reformatie: Beschrijving van haar voornaamste vertegenwoordigers*, ed. T. Brienen et al. The Hague, 1986, 349-67.

_____. "Schriftleer en Schriftverstaan in de Nadere Reformatie," in *Theologische aspecten van de Nadere Reformatie*, ed. T. Brienen, et al. Zoetermeer, 1993, 29-97.

_____. "Structuurverschillen tussen voetiaanse en coccejannse geloofsleer," in *Een richtingenstrijd in de Gereformeerde Kerk: Voetianen en coccejaanse 1650-1750*, ed. F. G. M. Broeyer and E. G. E. van der Wall. Zoetermeer, 1994, 28-53.

_____. *De zekerheid van het geloof: Een onderzoek naar de geloofsbeschouwing van enige vertegenwoordigers van reformatie en nadere reformatie*. Wageningen, 1961.

_____, W. J. op 't Hof and F. A. van Lieburg. "Nadere Reformatie: Opnieuw een poging tot begripsbepaling," *DNR* 19 (1995), 105-184.

Greschat, M., ed. *Gestalten der Kirchengeschichte*, vol. 3: *Mittelalter I*. Stuttgart, Berlin, Cologne and Mainz, 1983.

Groenendijk, L. F. "Opdat de mensche Gods volmaekt zy. Lectuur voor de religieuze vorming der gereformeerden tijdens de zeventiende eeuw," *Pedagogische Verhandelingen: Tijdschrift voor wijsgerige en historische pedagogiek*, 9 (1986), 17-54.

Haas, A. M. *Nim din selbes war: Studien zur Lehre von der Selbsterkenntnis bei Meister Eckhart, Johannes Tauler und Heinrich Seuse*. Freiburg, 1971.

_____. "Zur Einführung," in *Johannes Tauler Predigten*, 2 vols., trans. and ed. Georg Hofmann. Einsiedeln, 1987.

_____, ed. *"Der Franckforter:" Theologia Deutsch*. Einsiedeln, 1993.

Habel, E., and F. Gröbel. *Mittellateinisches Glossar*. Paderborn and Zurich, 1989.

Hambrick-Stowe, C. E. *The Practice of Piety: Puritan Devotional Disciplines in Seventeenth- Century New England*. Chapel Hill, 1982.

Hamm, B. *Frömmigkeitstheologie am Anfang des 16. Jahrhunderts: Studien zu Johannes von Paltz und seinem Umkreis*. Tübingen, 1982.

_____. *Promissio, Pactum, Ordinatio: Freiheit und Selbstbindung Gottes in der scholastischen Gnadenlehre*. Tübingen, 1977.

Hellmann, J. A. W. "The Spirituality of the Franciscans," in *Christian Spirituality: High Middle Ages and Reformation*, ed. Jill Raitt. London, 1989.

Hensen, R., et al., "Mystiek in de westerse cultuur," in *Rondom het Woord: Theologische Etherleergang vande NCRV* 2 (1973), 1-146.

Heppe, H. *Geschichte des Pietismus und der Mystik in der Reformirten Kirche, namentlich der Niederlande*. Leiden, 1879.

Hollebender-Schmitter, B. "Willem Teellinck: *Soliloquium*, mystisches Gebet im Zeitalter des Barock: Eine Analyse." An unpublished manuscript, Cologne, 1989.

Huizinga, J. *Herfsttij der Middeleeuwen*, vol. 3 in *Verzamelde Werken*, 9 vols. Haarlem, 1948-1953.

Hylkema, C. B. *Reformateurs: Geschiedkundige studiën over de godsdienstige bewegingen uit de nadagen onzer Gouden Eeuw*. Amsterdam, 1938.

Hyma, A. *The Christian Renaissance: A History of the "Devotio Moderna."* New York and London, 1924.

Illmer, D. "Artes Liberales," in *TRE*, 4:156-71.

Jelsma, A. J. "Doorwerking van de Moderne Devotie," in *De doorwerking van de Moderne Devotie, Windesheim 1387-1987*, ed. P. Bange, C. Graafland, A. J. Jelsma and A. G. Weiler. Hilversum, 1988.

Jones, C., G. Wainwright and E. Yarnold, eds. *The Study of Spirituality*. London, 1992.

Kahl, H. D. "Bernhard von Fontaine, Abt von Clairvaux," in *Gestalten der Kirchengeschichte*, vol. 3, *Mittelalter I*, ed. M. Greschat. Stuttgart, Berlin, Cologne and Mainz, 1983, 173-91.

Keller, C. A. *Calvin mystique: Au cœur de la pensée du Réformateur*. Geneva, 2001.

Kleineidam, E. "Ursprung und Gegenstand der Theologie bei Bernhard von Clairvaux und Martin Luther," in *Dienst der Vermittlung* (Festschrift Priesterseminar Erfurt), ed. W. Ernst, K. Feiereis and F. Hoffmann. Leipzig, 1977.

Köpf, U. "Einleitung," *Bernhard von Clairvaux: Sämtliche Werke*, vol. 5, ed. G. B. Winkler. Innsbruck, 1994, 27-47.

————. "Monastische und scholastische Theologie," in *Bernhard von Clairvaux und der Beginn der Moderne*, ed. D. R. Bauer and G. Fuchs. Innsbruck and Vienna, 1996, 96-135.

————. "Die Rezeptions- und Wirkungsgeschichte Bernhards von Clairvaux: Forschungsstand und Forschungsaufgaben," in *Bernhard von Clairvaux: Rezeption und Wirkung im Mittelalter und in der Neuzeit*, ed. K. Elm. Wiesbaden, 1994, 5-65.

————. "Schriftauslegung als Ort der Kreuzestheologie Bernhards von Clairvaux," in *Bernhard von Clairvaux und der Beginn der Moderne*, ed. D. R. Bauer and G. Fuchs. Innsbruck and Vienna, 1996, 194-213.

Krull, A. F. *Jacobus Koelman: Een Kerkhistorische Studie*. Sneek, 1901.

Kuyper, H. H. *De Opleiding tot den Dienst des Woords bij de Gereformeerden*. The Hague, 1891.

Lambert, B. M. "Ruminatio," in *Praktisches Lexikon der Spiritualität*, ed. C. Schütz. Freiburg, Basel and Vienna, 1992, 1072-73.

Lane, A. N. S. "Calvin's Use of Bernard of Clairvaux," in *Bernhard von Clairvaux: Rezeption und Wirkung im Mittelalter und in der Neuzeit*, ed. K. Elm. Wiesbaden, 1994, 303-32.

————. *John Calvin: Student of the Church Fathers*. Edinburgh, 1999.

Langelaar, H. H. "'Krank van liefde,' De gelukzalige ongezondheid van Theodorus à Brakel," *DNR* 21 (1997), 67-76.

Langer, O. "Affekt und Ratio in der Mystik Bernhards," in *Bernard von Clairvaux und der Beginn der Moderne*, ed. D. R. Bauer and G. Fuchs. Innsbruck and Vienna, 1990, 136-50.

Leclercq, J. "Bernhard von Clairvaux," in *TRE*, 5:644-51.

————. *Bernhard von Clairvaux: Ein Mann prägt seine Zeit*. Munich, Zurich and Vienna, 1997.

Le Goff, J. *De cultuur van middeleeuws Europa*, trans. Roland Fagel and Luuk Knippenberg. Amsterdam, 1987.

Leurdijk, G. H. "Theodorus à Brakel," in *Figuren and thema's van de Nadere Reformatie*, ed. T. Brienen et al. Kampen, 1987.

Lindeboom, J. *Stiefkinderen van het Christendom*. First edition, 1929; Arnhem, 1973.

Lohse, B. "Luther und Bernhard von Clairvaux," in *Bernhard von Clairvaux: Rezeption und Wirkung im Mittelalter und in der Neuzeit*, ed. K. Elm. Wiesbaden, 1994, 271-301.

Loofs, F. *Leitfaden zum Studium der Dogmengeschichte*, vol. 2. 7th edition; Gütersloh, 1968.

Loonstra, B. *Verkiezing, verzoening, verbond: Beschrijving en beoordeling van de leer van her pactum salutis in de gereformeerde theologie*. The Hague, 1990.

Los, F. J. *Wilhelmus à Brakel*. Reprinted with an introduction by W. van 't Spijker from the original, 1892 edition; Leiden, 1991.

Lourdaux, W. "Zur Devotio Moderna," in *Studien zur Devotio Moderna*, ed. K. Egger, W. Lourdaux and A. van Biezen. Bonn, 1988, 3-25.

Louth, A. "Mystik, II," *TRE*, 23:547-80.

Loyola, Ignatius of. *Geistliche Übungen*, trans. Knauer, S. J. Würzburg, 1998.

Maas, F. *Van God houden als van niemand: Preken van Meester Eckhart*. Kampen and Averbode, 1997.

Maron, G. *Ignatius von Loyola: Mystik—Theologie—Kirche*. Göttingen, 2001.

McGinn, B. *Die Mystik im Abendland*, vol. 1, *Ursprünge*, trans. Clemens Maaß. Freiburg, Basel and Vienna, 1994.

_____. *Mystik im Abendland*, vol. 2, *Entfaltung*, trans. Wolfgang Scheuermann. Freiburg, Basel and Vienna, 1996.

McGrath, A. E. *Christian Spirituality: An Introduction*. Oxford and Malden, 1999.

_____. *The Intellectual Origins of the European Reformation*. Oxford and Cambridge, MA, 1987.

_____. *Iustitia Dei: A History of the Christian Doctrine of Justification*, vol. 1, *The Beginnings to the Reformation*. First edition, 1986; Cambridge, 1994.

_____. *Reformation Thought: An Introduction*. Oxford, 1988.

Meertens, P. J. *Letterkundig leven in Zeeland in de zestiende en de eerste helft der zeventiende eeuw*. Amsterdam, 1943.

_____. "Willem Teellinck," *BLGNP*, 1:373-75.

Meeuse, C. J. "Jacobus Koelman (1631-1695): leven en werken," in *Figuren and thema's van de Nadere Reformatie*, ed. Brienen et al. 2 vols. Goudriaan and Kampen, 1990, 63-93.

Meijering, E. P. *Calvin wider die Neugierde: Ein Beitrag zum Vergleich zwischen reformatorischem und patristischem Denken*. Nieuwkoop, 1980.

Mikkers, P. E. "Sint Bernardus en de Moderne Devotie," in *Cîteaux in de Nederlanden: Mededelingen over het Cisterciënzer leven van de 12de tot en met de 18de eeuw*, vol. 4. Abdij Westmalle, 1953, 149-86.

Miskotte, K. H. *Als een die dient: volledige uitgave van het "Gemeenteblaadje Cortgene."* Baarn, 1976.

_____. *In de gecroonde allemansgading: Keur uit het verspreide werk van prof. dr. K. H. Miskotte*. Nijkerk, 1946.

Mokrosch, R. "*Devotio moderna, II*," in *TRE*, 8:609-16.

Mooi, R. J. *Het kerk- en dogmahistorisch element in de werken van Johannes Calvijn*. Wageningen, 1965.

Muller, R. A. *Christ and the Decree: Christology and Predestination in Reformed Theology from Calvin to Perkins*. Grand Rapids, 1986.

_____. "Covenant and Conscience in English Reformed Theology: Three Variations on a 17th Century Theme," *Westminster Theological Journal* 42 (1979), 308-34.

_____. *Dictionary of Latin and Greek Theological Terms, Drawn Principally from Protestant Scholastic Theology*. Grand Rapids, 1985.

_____. *Post-Reformation Reformed Dogmatics*, vol. 1, *Prolegomena to Theology*. Grand Rapids, 1987.

_____. *Post-Reformation Reformed Dogmatics*, vol. 2, *Holy Scripture: The Cognitive Foundation of Theology*. Grand Rapids, 1993.

_____. *The Unaccommodated Calvin: Studies in the Foundation of a Theological Tradition*. New York and Oxford, 2000.

Nauta, D. "Guiljelmus Saldenus," in *BLGNP*, 3:317-20.

_____. "Wilhelmus à Brakel," in *BLGNP*, 4:48-51.

Nicol, M. *Meditation bei Luther*. Göttingen, 1991.

Noordegraaf, A. *Leesbril of toverstaf: Over het verstaan en vertolken van de Bijbel*. Kampen, 1991.

Nuttall, G. F. *The Holy Spirit in Puritan Faith and Experience*. Chicago and London, 1992.

Oberman, H. A. *Die Reformation: Von Wittenberg nach Genf*. Göttingen, 1986.

————. "Fourteenth-Century Religious Thought: a Premature Profile," *Speculum* 53 (1978), 80-93.

————. *Spätscholastik und Reformation*, vol. 1, *Der Herbst der mittelalterlischen Theologie*, trans. Martin Rumscheid and Henning Kampen. Zurich, 1965.

————. *Werden und Wertung der Reformation: Von Wegestreit zum Glaubenskampf*. Tübingen, 1989.

Opitz, P. *Calvijns theologische Hermeneutik*. Neukirchen, 1994.

Op 't Hof, W. J. *Bibliografische lijst van de geschriften van Willem Teellinck*. Rotterdam, 1993.

————. "Eenen tweeden Thomas à Kempis (doch ghereformeerden)," in *De doorwerking van de Moderne Devotie, Windesheim 1387-1987*, ed. P. Bange, C. Graafland, A. J. Jelsma and A. G. Weiler. Hilversum, 1988, 151-65.

————. *Engelse piëtistische geschriften in het Nederlands, 1598-1622*, Monografieën Gereformeerd piëtisme, vol. 1. Rotterdam, 1987, 583-625.

————. "Gereformeerde mystiek," *Praktische theologie: Nederlands tijdschrift voor pastorale wetenschappen*, 22 (1995), 322-41.

————. "Gisbertus Voetius en de gebroeders Teellinck," in *De onbekende Voetius: Voordrachten wetenschappelijk symposium Utrecht 3 maart 1989*, ed. J. Van Oort et al. Kampen, 1989.

————. *"Een onbekende zoon van Willem Teellinck,"* DNR 25 (2001), 84-89.

————. "Rooms-katholieke doorwerking binnen de Nadere Reformatie: Een eerste algemene verkenning," *DNR* 15 (1991), 73-120.

————. "Studie der Nadere Reformatie: verleden en toekomst," *DNR* 18 (1994), 1-50.

————. "Thomas à Kempis bij Willem Teellinck," 3 parts, *DNR* 13 (1989), 42-68; 14 (1990), 88-112; 15 (1991), 1-13.

————. *Voorbereiding en bestrijding: De oudste gereformeerde piëtistische voorbereidingspreken tot het Avondmaal en de eerste bestrijding van de Nadere Reformatie in druk*. Kampen, 1991.

————. *"Willem Teellinck in het licht zijner geschriften."* A series in *DNR*, vols. 1-25.

Otto, R. *Het Heilige: Een verhandeling over het irrationele in de idee van het goddelijke en de verhouding ervan tot het rationele*, trans. J. W. Dippel and O. Noordenbos. Hilversum, 1963.

Quint, J., ed. *Meister Eckehart: Deutsche Predigten und Traktate*. Munich, 1985.

Quispel G., et al., *Mystiek en bevinding*. Kampen, 1976.

Persoons, E. "De verspreiding van de Moderne Devotie," in *Geert Grote en de Moderne Devotie*, ed. C. C. de Bruin, E. Persoons and A. G. Weiler. Zutphen, 1984, 57-100.

Peters, G. *Soliloquium ignitum cum Deo*, trans. A. Bellemans. Bussum, 1947.

Post, R. R. *The Modern Devotion: Confrontation with Reformation and Humanism*. Leiden, 1968.

Prenter, R. *Spiritus creator: Studien zu Luthers Theologie*. Munich, 1954.

Puckett, D. L. *John Calvin's Exegesis of the Old Testament*. Louisville, 1995.

Raitt, Jill, ed. *Christian Spirituality: High Middle Ages and Reformation*. London, 1989.

Rapp, F. "Gottesfreunde," in *TRE*, 14:98-100.

Richard, L. J. *The Spirituality of John Calvin*. Atlanta, 1974.

Ritschl, A. *Geschichte des Pietismus*, 3 vols. Bonn, 1880-86.

Ritter, J. and K. Gründer, eds. *Historisches Wörterbuch der Philosophie*. Darmstadt, 1992.

Roldanus, C. W. *Zeventiende-eeuwse geestesbloei*. Amsterdam, 1938.

Ros, A. *Theodorus à Brakel, 1608-1669: "Een voorbeeld van allertederste Gods vrucht."* Barneveld, 2000.

Ruh, K. *Geschichte der abendländischen Mystik*, vol. 1, *Die Grundlegung durch die Kirchenväter und die Mönchstheologie des 12. Jahrhunderts*. Munich, 1990.

_____. *Geschichte der abendländischen Mystik*, vol. 2, *Frauenmystik und Franziskanische Mystik der Frühzeit*. Munich, 1993.

_____. *Geschichte der abendländischen Mystik*, vol. 3, *Die Mystik des deutschen Predigersordens und ihre Grundlegung durch die Hochscholastik*. Munich, 1996.

_____. *Geschichte der abendländischen Mystik*, vol. 4, *Die niederländische Mystik des 14. bis 16. Jahrhunderts*. Munich, 1999.

_____. *Meister Eckhart: Theologe, Prediger, Mystiker*. Munich, 1989.

Schaab, R. "Bibeltext und Schriftstudium in St. Gallen," in *Das Kloster St. Gallen im Mittelalter*, ed. P. Ochsenbein. Darmstadt, 1999, 119-36.

Schenkl, M. A. "Bernhard und die Entdeckung der Liebe," in *Bernhard von Clairvaux und der Beginn der Moderne*, ed. D. R. Bauer and G. Fuchs. Innsbruck and Vienna, 151-79.

Schuck, J. *Das religiöse Erlebnis beim hl. Bernhard von Clairvaux*. Würzburg, 1922.

Schültz, C., ed. *Praktisches Lexicon der Spiritualität*. Freiburg, 1992.

Sheldrake, P. *Spirituality and History: Questions of Interpretation and Method*. London, 1991.

Snoeijer, W. *Wandelen voor Zijn aangezicht: Jodocus van Lodenstein, een mysticus uit de Reformatie*. Gent and Kampen, 2000.

Steenbeek, B. W. "Theodorus à Brakel," in *BLGNP*, 1:55-56.

Steinmetz, D. C. *Calvin in Context*. New York and Oxford, 1995.

_____. "The Judaizing Calvin," in *Die Patristik in der Bibelexegese des 16. Jahrhunderts*, ed. D. C. Steinmetz. Wiesbaden, 1999, 135-145.

_____. *Luther in Context*. Grand Rapids, 1995.

_____. "The Scholastic Calvin," in Carl R. Trueman and R. Scott Clark, eds. *Protestant Scholasticism: Essays in Reassessment*. Carlisle, 1999, 16-30.

Stoeffler, F. E. *The Rise of Evangelical Pietism*. Leiden, 1971.

Stolt, B. *Martin Luthers Rhetorik des Herzens*. Tübingen, 2000.

Tamburello, D. E. "Bernard of Clairvaux," in *Historical Handbook of Major Biblical Interpreters*, ed. Donald K. McKim. Downers Grove and Leicester, 1998, 91-95.

_____. *Union with Christ: John Calvin and the Mysticism of St. Bernard*. Louisville, 1994.

Tauler, J. *Johannes Tauler: Predigten*, 2 vols, ed. G. Hofmann and A. M. Haas. Einsiedeln, 1987.

Thiselton, A. C. *New Horizons in Hermeneutics*. London, 1992.

Tinsley, E. J. "Thomas à Kempis," in *A Dictionary of Christian Spirituality*, ed. G. S. Wakefield. London, 1983, 378-79.

Torrance, T. F. *The Hermeneutics of John Calvin*. Edinburgh, 1988.

Trimp, J. C. *Jodocus van Lodensteyn: Predikant en dichter*. Kampen, 1987.

Trueman, Carl R., and R. Scott Clark, eds. *Protestant Scholasticism: Essays in Reassessment*. Carlisle, 1999.

Turner, D. *Eros and Allegory: Medieval Exegesis of the Song of Salomon*. Kalamazoo, 1995.

Vacandard, E. *Vie de Saint Bernard.* Paris, 1895.

Van Asselt, W. J. *Amicitia Dei: Een onderzoek naar de structuur van de theologie van Johannes Coccejus (1603-1669).* Ede, 1988.

_____. *Johannes Coccejus: Portret van een zeventiende-eeuwse theoloog op oude en nieuwe wegen.* Heerenveen, 1997.

_____. *Inleiding in de gereformeerde scholastiek.* Zoetermeer, 1998.

_____ and E. Dekker, ed. *Reformation and Scholasticism: An Ecumenical Enterprise.* Grand Rapids, 2001.

Van Bavel, T. J. *Als je hart bidt . . . Augustinus' leer over het gebed.* Leuven, 1996.

Van Biezen, A. "Zur Spiritualität von Windesheim," in *Studien zur Devotio Moderna,* ed. K. Egger, W. Lourdaux and A. van Biezen. Bonn, 1988, 26-42.

Van de Beek, A. *Jezus Kurios: Christologie als hart van de theologie.* Kampen, 1998.

Van de Ketterij, C. *De weg in woorden: Een systematische beschrijving van het piëtistische woordgebruik na 1900.* Assen, 1972.

Van den Berg, J. "De Engelse Puritein Francis Rous (1579-1659) en de vertaling van enkele van zijn geschriften in het Nederlands," *De Zeventiende Eeuw* 2 (1985), 48-66.

_____. "Die Frömmigkeitsbestrebungen in den Niederlanden," in *Geschichte des Pietismus,* vol. 1, *Der Pietismus vom siebzehnten bis zum frühen achtzehnten Jahrhundert,* ed. M. Brecht. Göttingen, 1993.

Van den Brink, G. *Oriëntatie in de filosofie,* vol. 1. Zoetermeer, 1994.

Van den End, G. *Guiljelmus Saldenus (1627-1694): Een praktisch en irenisch theoloog uit de Nadere Reformatie.* Leiden, 1991.

Van den Goorberg, E., and T. Zweerman. *Was getekend, Franciscus van Assisi: Aspecten van zijn schrijverschap en brandpunten van zijn spiritualiteit.* Assen, 1998.

Van der Haar, J. *Internationale ökumenische Beziehungen im 17. und 18. Jahrhundert.* Ederveen, 1997.

_____. *Schatkamer van de gereformeerde theologie in Nederland, c. 1600-c. 1800: Bibliografisch onderzoek.* Veenendaal, 1987.

Van der Linde, S. *Opgang en voortgang der Reformatie: Een keuze uit lezingen en artikelen.* Amsterdam, 1976.

Van der Pol, F. "Spiritualiteit in de Middeleeuwen," in van 't Spijker et al., eds., *Spiritualiteit.* Kampen, 1993, 99-148.

Van Deursen, A. T. *Mensen van klein vermogen: Het kopergeld van de Gouden Eeuw* Amsterdam, 1992.

Van Dijk, I. *Gezamenlijke Geschriften,* vol. 4. Groningen, [n.d.].

Van Geest, P. *Thomas a Kempis, 1379/80-1471: Een studie van zijn mens- en godsbeeld.* Kampen, 1996.

Van Genderen, J. *Herman Witsius.* The Hague, 1953.

_____. "Herman Witsius (1636-1708)," in *De Nadere Reformatie: Beschrijving van haar voornaamste vertegenwoordigers.* The Hague, 1986, 193-218.

_____. "Wilhelmus à Brakel (1635-1711)," in *De Nadere Reformatie: Beschrijving van haar voornaamste vertegenwoordigers,* ed. T. Brienen et al. The Hague, 1986, 165-191.

Van Harten, P. H. *De prediking van Ebenezer en Ralph Erskine.* The Hague, 1986.

Van Hecke, L. *Bernardus van Clairvaux en de religieuze ervaring.* Kapellen and Kampen, 1990.

Van Lieburg, F. A. *Profeten en hun vaderland: De geografische herkomst van de gereformeerde predikanten in Nederland van 1572 tot 1816.* Zoetermeer, 1996.

Van Loey, A. *Schönfelds historische grammatica van het Nederlands: Klankleer, vormleer, woordvorming.* Zutphen, 1970.

Van Oort, J. "Augustinus, Voetius und die Anfänge der Utrechter Universität," in *Signum pietatis*, ed. A. Zumkeller. Festgabe für C. P. Mayer OSA zum 60. Geburtstag; Würzburg, 1989, 566.

_____. *Jeruzalem en Babylon: Een onderzoek van Augustinus' De stad van God en de bronnen van zijn leer der twee steden (rijken)*. The Hague, 1986.

_____, ed. *De kerkvaders in Reformatie en Nadere Reformatie*. Zoetermeer, 1997.

Van Ruler, A. A. *Theologisch Werk*, vol. 3. Nijkerk, 1971.

Van Ruusbroec, J. *Werken, naar het standaardhandschrift van Groenendaal*, 4 vols. Mechelen and Antwerp, 1932-1934.

Van Sluis, J. "Herman Witsius," in *BLGNP*, 4:456.

_____. "Het omzwaaien van Johannes vander Waeijen," in *Een richtingenstrijd in de Gereformeerde Kerk: Voetianen en coccejanen 1650-1750*, ed. F. G. M. Broeyer and E. G. E. van der Wall. Zoetermeer, 1994, 95-104.

Van 't Spijker, W. "Bronnen van de Nadere Reformatie," in *De Nadere Reformatie en het Gereformeerd piëtisme*, ed. T. Brienen et al. The Hague, 1989, 5-51.

_____. *Calvin: Biographie und Theologie*, in the series *Die Kirche in ihrer Geschichte: Ein Handbuch*, vol. 3, ed. B. Moeller Lieferung J 2; Göttingen, 2001, 101-236.

_____. "Experientia in reformatorisch licht," *TR* 19 (1976), 236-55.

_____. *Geest, Woord en Kerk: Opstellen over de geschiedenis van het gereformeerd protestantisme*. Kampen, 1991.

_____. *Gemeenschap met Christus: Centraal gegeven van de gereformeerde theologie*. Apeldoornse Studies 32. Kampen, 1995.

_____. "De Nadere Reformatie," in *De Nadere Reformatie: Beschrijving van haar voornaamste vertegenwoordigers*, ed. T. Brienen et al. The Hague, 1986, 5-16.

_____. "Reformatie tussen patristiek en scholastiek: Bucer's theologische positie," in *De kerkvaders in Reformatie en Nadere Reformatie*, ed. J. van Oort. Zoetermeer, 1997, 45-66.

_____. "Teellincks opvatting van de menselijke wil—Voornamelijk in verband met de uiteenzettingen van W. J. M. Engelberts en W. Goeters," *TR* 7 (1964), 125-42.

_____. *De verzegeling met de Heilige Geest: Over verzegeling en zekerheid van het geloof.* Kampen, 1991.

_____, R. Bisschop and W. J. op 't Hof. *Het puritanisme: Geschiedenis, theologie en invloed.* Zoetermeer, 2001.

_____, et al., eds. *Spiritualiteit*. Kampen, 1993.

Van Wijk, N. *Franck's etymologisch Woordenboek der Nederlandsche taal*. The Hague, 1912.

Vekeman, H. "Inleiding," to *Soliloquium, ofte alleensprake eens zondaers, in den angst zijner wedergeboorte*, by Willem Teellinck, published with an explanation by H. Vekeman in the series Veröffentlichungen des Instituts für Niederländische Philologie der Universität zu Köln. Erfstadt, 1984, v-xlix.

Veldhuis, H. "Onrustig is ons hart: Over onrust en verlangen naar God," in *Onrustig is ons hart. . . . Mens-zijn in christelijk perspectief*, ed. H. Veldhuis. Zoetermeer, 1994, 11-27.

Velema, W. H. *Nieuw zicht op gereformeerde spiritualiteit*. Kampen, 1990.

Verboom, W. *De catechese van de Reformatie en de Nadere Reformatie*. Amsterdam, 1986.

Verdam, J. *Middelnederlandsch Handwoordenboek*. The Hague, 1981.

Verduin M. *Canticum Canticorum: Het Lied der liederen, Een onderzoek naar de betekenis, de functie en de invloed van de bronnen van de Kanttekeningen bij het Hooglied in de Statenbijbel van 1637*. Utrecht, 1992.

Vogelzang, E. "Die Unio mystica bei Luther," *Archiv für Reformations-Geschichte,* 35 (1938), 63-80.

Von Loewenich, W. *Luther als Ausleger der Synoptiker.* Munich, 1954.

Vosicky, B. "Bernhards Leben mit der Eucharistie," in *Bernhard von Clairvaux und der Beginn der Moderne,* ed. D. R. Bauer and G. Fuchs. Innsbruck and Vienna, 1996, 214-28.

Waaijman, K. *Spiritualiteit: Vormen, grondslagen, methoden.* Gent and Kampen, 2000.

Wakefield, G. S. *Puritan Devotion: Its Place in the Development of Christian Piety.* London, 1957.

_____, ed. *A Dictionary of Christian Spirituality.* London, 1983.

Wallmann, J. "Bernhard von Clairvaux und der deutsche Pietismus," in *Bernhard von Clairvaux:Rezeption und Wirkung im Mittelalter und in der Neuzeit,* ed. K. Elm. Wiesbaden, 1994, 353-74.

Wallmann, J. "Zwischen Herzensgebet und Gebetsbuch: Zur protestanischen deutschen Gebetsliteratur im 17. Jahrhundert," in *Gebetsliteratur der Frühen Neuzeit als Hausfrömmigkeit: Funktionen und Formen in Deutschland und den Niederlanden,* ed. F. van Lingen and C. N. Moore. Wiesbaden, 2001, 13-46.

Weijnen, A. *Zeventiende-eeuwse Taal.* Zutphen, 1956.

Weiler, A. G. "Leven en werken van Geert Grote," in *Geert Grote en de Moderne Devotie,* ed. C. C. de Bruin, E. Persoons and A. G. Weiler. Zutphen, 1984, 9-55.

Winkler, G. B. "Einleitung," in *Bernhard von Clairvaux: Sämtliche Werke,* vol. 1, ed. G. B. Winkler. Innsbruck, 1990, 15-37.

Zumkeller, A. *Johannes von Staupitz und seine christliche Heilslehre.* Wurzburg, 1994.

_____, ed. *Signum pietatis: Festgabe für C. P. Mayer OSA zum 60. Geburtstag.* Würzburg, 1989.

Zur Mühlen, K. H. *Nos extra nos: Luthers Theologie zwischen Mystik und Scholastik.* Tübingen, 1972.

_____. *Reformatorisches Profil: Studien zum Weg Martin Luthers und der Reformation.* Göttingen, 1995.

Index of Personal Names

Aalders, C., 20, 22
Aalders, W. J., 21-22
À Brakel, Margaretha Homma, 166, 231
À Brakel, Sulamith, 232
À Brakel, T., 20, 58, 163-197, 206, 231, 237-238, 241, 244-246, 249-250, 257-258, 282
À Brakel, W., 20, 75, 99, 163-164, 166-170, 183, 199, 231-258, 265, 274
Abelard, 30
Acquoy, J. G. R., 63, 71, 76
Adam, A., 75
À Kempis, T., 17-18, 20, 63-102, 105-106, 112-114, 116-118, 121, 125-130, 133, 143-144, 147-150, 154-156, 159-160, 180, 206-207, 211, 216, 219-220, 227, 274, 279, 282-283
Albert, K., 21
À Marck, J., 263, 265-266
Ambrose, 48, 98
Ames, W., 105, 206
Angenendt, A., 30
Arminius, J., 108
Arnoldi, N., 265
Athanasius, 88
Augustine, 27, 37, 40, 48, 50, 53, 56, 57, 67-68, 71, 75-76, 78, 80, 84, 86, 88-89, 94, 96, 114, 119, 126-127, 133, 157, 172, 217, 226
Axters, S., 63, 65, 69, 71

Bakker, N. T., 263
Basil, 269
Bauer, J. B., 42
Beeke, J. R., 139
Bélier, A., 101
Bell, T., 35
Bellemans, A., 94
Bernard, 17-18, 20, 27-60, 67, 69, 71-72, 75-76, 78, 80, 84, 91-92, 94, 97, 105, 114, 117, 122, 126, 128, 131-132, 142, 145, 154-155, 158-160, 165, 174, 181-183, 185, 194, 196-197, 214-217, 218, 220-221, 223-224, 226, 227-228, 234, 237, 241, 245, 250, 257-258, 267-268, 270, 272, 274-275, 278-279, 281-282
Beumer, J., 20, 198
Beza, T., 60

Bisschop, R., 108, 197, 206
Blommenstijn, H. H., 21
Bohatec, J., 101
Böhme, J., 252
Böhner, P., 29, 50, 96, 170
Bohren, R., 69
Bolton, R., 206
Bonaventure, 23, 174
Boot, I., 19, 45-47, 50-52, 56, 113, 117, 128, 132, 163, 165, 181, 192, 245, 255, 257, 267, 278-279, 282
Böttger, P. C., 80
Bouter, P. F., 88
Bouwman, H., 106, 140
Brandt, G., 115
Bredero, A. H., 30
Brederode, G., 115
Brienen, T., 163-164
Brinckerinck, J., 70, 73
Brouette, É., 67
Brümmer, V., 96
Brunner, E., 23
Bucer, M., 18, 22
Bühler, P., 243
Burgess, S. M., 34, 48
Burmannus, F., 261
Bush, S., 35

Calvin, J., 18, 22, 35, 42, 56, 60, 80, 85, 89, 99-101, 119, 137, 139-141, 147, 157, 159, 198, 235-236, 277, 281-282
Carlson, C. P., 98
Chrysostom, 80
Clark, R. S., 18,
Clement of Alexandria, 21,
Cocceius, J., 213, 227, 235
Comrie, A., 201, 274
Costerus, F., 274
Costerus, J., 266
Cyprian, 268

Datheen, P., 194, 224
Davies, O., 71
De Boer, J., 23, 127, 164, 198, 268
De Bruin, C. C., 66-69, 70-71, 74-75, 192
De Greef, W., 60
De Groot, A., 42, 261, 263
De Heer, J. M. D., 167, 232
De Jong, O. J., 261

Dekker, E., 17
De Knijff, H. W., 43
De Kroon, M., 63, 67
De Kruijf, U., 73, 168, 192
De Labadie, J., 197, 233, 252
De Lubac, H., 43
De Maets, C., 202
De Molinos, M., 252
De Niet, C. A., 75, 101, 165, 167, 169
De Reuver, A., 17, 21, 50, 53, 59, 89, 106,
    135, 137, 139, 141, 159, 187, 183,
    187, 191, 196, 198, 233, 236, 250-
    251, 253, 279, 281
De Rijk, L. M., 29, 32
De Vooys, C. G. N., 208
De Vries, P., 35, 282
Dinzelbacher, P., 27, 31, 33, 36, 38-39,
    42, 46-48, 52-55
Dionysius the Areopagite, 169-179, 269
Duker, A. C., 40, 274
Dyke, D., 206
Dyke, J., 206

Eckhart, 154, 197
Engelberts, W. J. M., 106, 110-111, 139-
    140
Essenius, A., 232
Eugenius III, 30, 34
Evans, G. R., 28, 30-32, 34, 37, 54
Eversdijk, W., 232
Exalto, K., 106, 113, 220, 236

Faukelius, H., 109
Fénelon, F. de Salignac de la Mothe, 252
Fischer, R., 31
Frank, K. S., 76
Frederick Hendrik, 110
Fruytier, J., 201, 232

Gansfort, W., 223
Gerard Zerbolt of Zutphen, 70, 117
Gerson, J., 71, 269
Gilson, E., 29, 45, 47-52, 54-55, 58, 96,
    170, 275
Goeters, W., 164, 166
Golverdingen, M., 106
Gomarus, F., 108-109
Goossens, L. A. M., 31, 69
Gottfried of Auxerre, 33
Graafland, C., 16, 20, 75, 89, 102, 106,
    113, 135, 139, 164, 206, 235, 262,
    282
Gray, A., 213
Greendon, M. A., 108
Gregory the Great, 27, 47, 88
Gröbel, F., 41

Groenendijk, L. F., 112
Groote, G., 63, 65, 67-73, 91-93
Gründer, K., 17

Haas, A. M., 80-81, 126, 154
Habel, E., 41
Hambrick-Stowe, C. E., 35
Hamm, B., 59, 77-78, 98, 114
Heer, F., 31
Hellenbroek, A., 163, 166, 231-234
Hellmann, J. A. W., 69
Hemerken, Johan, 71
Hemerken, Johannes, 71-72
Hensen, R., 21
Heppe, H., 164
Hippolytus of Rome, 48
Hofmann, G., 154
Hollebenders-Schmitter, B., 113
Hondius, J., 165
Hooft, P. C., 115
Hoornbeeck, J., 16, 202, 216, 263
Huizinga, J., 66
Hunink, V., 84
Huygens, C., 115
Hylkema, C. B., 282
Hyma, A., 63, 71

Ignatius of Loyola, 74
Ipes, H., 167

Jelsma, A. J., 67, 75
Jenni, E., 15
Jerome, 88, 216, 273
Jones, C., 54, 170
Joris, D., 252
Junius, F., 111

Kahl, H. D., 33
Keller, C. A., 22
Kleineidam, E., 48
Knauer, P., 75
Koelman, J., 16, 232-233, 267
Kohlbrugge, H. F., 183
Köpf, U., 31-32, 34, 38-40, 43-44, 48, 72
Krull, A. F., 232
Kummer, J., 73, 168
Kuyper, H. H., 108, 166, 202

Lambert, B. M., 31
Lane, A. N. S., 34-35
Langelaar, H. H., 164-165, 167, 197
Langer, O., 32, 51
Le Goff, J., 27, 65
Leclercq, J., 29-36, 39
Leurdijk, G. H., 164
Leusden, J., 263

Leydekker, M., 265
Lindeboom, J., 282
Lohse, B., 35
Loofs, F., 98
Loonstra, B., 262
Los, F. J., 163, 231, 233, 274
Lourdaux, W., 65, 67
Luther, M., 18, 22, 32, 35, 58, 60, 89, 99-
    101, 130, 141, 159, 172, 185, 191,
    198, 243, 247, 274, 281-282

Maas, F. A., 21, 154
Maron, G., 75
Marshall, I. H., 43
McGinn, B., 27-39, 44-46, 48-56, 58, 155
McGrath, A. E., 20, 43, 77, 98
Meertens, P. J., 106-107
Meeuse, C. J., 267
Meijering, E. P., 88
Meusevoet, V., 60
Mikkers, P. E., 34, 72, 76, 84, 91
Miskotte, K. H., 15
Moerkerken, A., 21
Mokrosch, R., 101
Mooi, R. J., 35
Muller, R. A., 17-18, 33, 43-44, 54, 77,
    98, 257

Naab, E., 56
Nauta, D., 202, 231, 263
Nevius, S., 167, 232, 245
Nicol, M., 32, 69, 101, 247, 274
Noordegraaf, A., 43
Nuttall, G. F., 35, 122

Oberman, H. A., 17-18, 21-22, 66, 68, 77-
    78, 97-98, 132, 154, 197, 267
Oomius, S., 20, 75
Opitz, P., 59
Op 't Hof, W. J., 16, 19-20, 35, 74-75,
    94, 101, 105-109, 111-113, 164, 206,
    267, 281
Origen, 21
Otto, R., 21

Pars, A., 274
Pereboom, F., 73, 168
Perkins, W., 105, 139, 206
Persoons, E., 63, 67
Peters, G., 94
Pohl, M. I., 71, 73, 76, 113
Pomerius, H., 67
Post, R. R., 63, 67-72, 74-75
Prenter, R., 59
Puckett, D. L., 59

Quint, J., 154
Quispel, G., 21

Radewijns, F., 63, 69, 71, 73
Raitt, J., 267
Rapp, F., 67
Richard, L. J., 67, 75-76, 80, 101, 114
Richard of St. Victor, 75
Ridderus, F., 110, 232
Ritschl, A., 23, 164, 197, 231, 267
Ritter, J., 17
Rochais, H., 35
Roldanus, C. W., 282
Ros, A., 163-169, 192, 231
Rous, F., 267-269, 272, 275, 277-279
Ruh, K., 33, 35-36, 44-46, 48-50, 52-55,
    75-76, 80-81, 117, 154, 170

Salden, H. W., 202
Saldenus, G., 20, 75, 201-228, 237, 249,
    262, 266
Saldenus, J., 203
Schaab, R., 73
Schenkl, M. A., 31, 36-38, 46-48, 54
Schortinghuis, W., 81, 183
Schotanus, C., 232
Schotanus, M., 166, 202
Schuck, J., 51-52, 194
Scotus Eriugena, 54
Seneca, 71
Sheldrake, P., 36
Sibbes, R., 122
Sixtus, R., 166
Snoeijer, W., 195
Steenbeek, B. W., 164
Steggink, O., 21
Steinmetz, D. C., 17-18, 32
Stoeffler, F. E., 267
Stolt, B., 32
Stronks, E., 111
Sudbrack, J., 167

Talbot, C. H., 35
Tamburello, D. E., 33-35
Tauler, J., 80-81, 99, 105, 154
Teellinck, E., 106-107
Teellinck, Johannes, 108, 110, 264
Teellinck, Joost, 108
Teellinck, Justus, 108
Teellinck, M., 105, 108
Teellinck, T., 108, 110
Teellinck, W., 16, 20, 74-75, 89, 94, 105-
    160, 164, 180, 206-207, 214, 228,
    249, 257, 273
Thiselton, A. C., 44, 59
Thomas Aquinas, 22

Tilenus, D., 139
Tinsley, E. J., 71
Torrance, T. F., 98
Trelcatius, L., 108
Trimp, J. C., 97, 196, 268
Troeltsch, E., 101
Trueman, C. R., 18
Turner, D., 47, 50
Turretin, F., 235
Twist, A., 203

Udemans, G., 108, 164, 245, 282

Vacandard, E., 33
Valckenier, J., 232
Van Asselt, W. J., 17, 30, 32, 213, 235, 262
Van Bavel, T. J., 50, 80, 84, 119, 126
Van Biezen, A., 68
Van Bijler, H. C., 266
Van de Beek, A., 39
Van de Ketterij, C., 15, 53
Van den Berg, J., 23, 106, 164, 267, 282
Van den Bogaard, J., 262, 264, 268
Van den Brink, G., 29
Van den End, G., 201-207, 213, 228, 262
Van den Goorberg, E., 69
Van den Vondel, J., 115
Van der Haar, J., 106, 166, 169, 203, 205, 233, 235, 262
Van der Linde, S., 21, 23, 198
Van der Meer, F., 97
Van der Pol, F., 21-22, 74, 100
Van der Son, E. J., 202
Vander Waeijen, J., 265
Van Deursen, A. T., 109
Van Dijk, I., 99
Van Fécamp, J., 52-53, 155
Van Geest, P., 63, 65-66, 68, 71-74, 91-93
Van Genderen, J., 231, 261-267
Van Ginneken, J., 71
Van Harlingen, M., 265
Van Harten, P. H., 213
Van Hecke, L., 51
Van Laren, D., 165
Van Laren, J., 165
Van Lieburg, F. A., 16, 106, 164, 234
Van Lodensteyn, J., 20, 75, 195, 198, 201, 203, 253, 264, 268, 279
Van Loey, A., 208
Van Mastricht, P., 235, 265
Van Oort, J., 40, 96, 126

Van Ruler, A. A., 23, 197
Van Ruusbroec, J., 72
Van Schurman, A. M., 167
Van Schurman, J. G., 167
Van Sluis, J., 262-263, 265, 267
Van Til, S., 266
Van 't Spijker, W., 20, 22, 54, 101, 106, 108, 114, 134, 136-137, 140, 159-160, 163, 206, 235-236, 253
Van Wijk, N., 208
Van Winden, J. C. M., 174
Vekeman, H., 111, 113, 126, 133, 142, 155, 158, 179
Veldhuis, H., 133
Velema, W. H., 20, 167
Verboom, W., 166, 203
Verdam, J., 213
Verduin, M., 46-48, 60, 245, 282
Voetius, G., 16, 20, 40-42, 75, 105-106, 108, 110, 139, 164-165, 167, 169, 201-203, 206, 232, 234, 258, 262-264, 274
Vogelsang, E., 154
Von Loewenich, W., 59
Vos van Heusden, J., 67
Vosicky, B., 51

Waaijman, K., 20-21, 63, 114
Wainwright, G., 54
Wakefield, G. S., 35, 267, 277
Walaeus, A., 109
Wallmannn, J., 35, 198
Weber, M., 101
Weijnen, A., 115
Weiler, A. G., 63, 67-68
Westermann, C., 15
Wielenga, B., 74-75
Wijdeveld, G., 74, 76, 88, 157
Willem III, 265
William of St. Thierry, 33, 75
Williams, R., 54, 278
Winkler, G. B., 29, 33, 35, 53
Wits, C. J., 205
Witsius, H., 20, 75, 183, 196, 201-205, 232, 236, 258, 261-280

Yarhold, E., 54

Zumkeller, A., 98
Zur Mühlen, K. H., 22-23
Zweerman, T., 69

Board of the Dutch Reformed Translation Society